AVENGERS ASSEMBLE!

AVENGERS ASSEMBLE!

CRITICAL PERSPECTIVES ON THE MARVEL CINEMATIC UNIVERSE

TERENCE McSWEENEY

WALLFLOWER PRESS
LONDON & NEW YORK

A Wallflower Book
Published by
Columbia University Press
Publishers Since 1893
New York • Chichester, West Sussex
cup.columbia.edu

Wallflower Press® is a registered trademark of Columbia University Press

Cataloging-in-Publication Data is available from the Library of Congress

ISBN 978-0-231-18624-7 (cloth)
ISBN 978-0-231-18625-4 (pbk.)
ISBN 978-0-231-85122-0 (e-book)

Cover image:
The Avengers (2012) © Walt Disney Studios Motion Pictures

CONTENTS

Acknowledgements   vii

Prologue: The Heroes We Need Right Now?:
Explaining 'The Age of the Superhero'   1

Introduction: Superheroes in the New Millennium
and 'The Example of America'   14

PHASE ONE

1   'That's how Dad did it, that's how America does it ... and
     it's worked out pretty well so far': The Stark Doctrine in
     Iron Man and *Iron Man 2*   41

2   Allegorical Narratives of Gods and Monsters: *Thor* and
     The Incredible Hulk   72

3   State Fantasy and the Superhero: (Mis)Remembering
     World War II in *Captain America: The First Avenger*   97

4   'Seeing ... still working on believing!': The Ethics and Aesthetics
     of Destruction in *The Avengers*   109

PHASE TWO

5   'Nothing's been the same since New York': Ideological
     Continuity and Change in *Iron Man 3* and *Thor: The Dark World* 129

6   'The world has changed and none of us can go back':
     The Illusory Moral Ambiguities of the Post-9/11 Superhero
     in *Captain America: The Winter Soldier*   150

7   Blurring the Boundaries of Genre and Gender in *Guardians
     of the Galaxy* and *Ant-Man*   167

8   'Isn't that why we fight? So we can end the fight and go home?':
     The Enduring American Monomyth in *Avengers: Age of Ultron*   186

THE MARVEL CINEMATIC UNIVERSE ON TELEVISION

9   'What does S.H.I.E.L.D. stand for?': The MCU on the Small Screen
    in *Marvel's Agents of S.H.I.E.L.D.* and *Marvel's Agent Carter*   207

10 The Necessary Vigilantism of the Defenders: *Daredevil*
    Jessica Jones, Luke Cage and *Iron Fist*   223

    Conclusion: 'Whose side are you on?': Superheroes Through
    the Prism of the 'War on Terror' in *Captain America: Civil War*   237

    Epilogue: The Superhero as Transnational Icon   262

    Filmography   269
    Bibliography   273
    Index   302

ACKNOWLEDGEMENTS

Every project presents its own unique set of challenges and this one has been no different. The words on the page are mine, but they would not have found their way there without the help and support of too many people to mention here.

I would like to thank the wonderful staff and students at my own institution, Southampton Solent University, especially Donna Peberdy and Darren Kerr, for their continued support, and Stuart Joy who has always been a source of wise counsel. Also, the staff of two remarkable libraries: the Vere Harmsworth Library at the University of Oxford's Rothermere American Institute where some of the writing of this manuscript was done during my tenure as Visiting Research Fellow in 2015–16, and those at the Queen Mary University of London where I was fortunate enough to have a similar position in 2016–17.

Special thanks are always reserved for my family, not just my loving wife, Olga, but my two beloved sons. Harrison: your love of writing, even from such a young age (*I Hate Shark!*), has always moved me and I look forward to seeing the writer you will become in the future. Wyatt: your unconditional love of superheroes has been inspirational and I hope one day you might read this book and remember the golden years during which it was written. I wish they could have lasted forever.

Dedicated to Lewis, Billy, Jimmy,
Harrison, Wyatt and Nancy Lou

The only real superheroes

The Heroes We Need Right Now?: Explaining 'The Age of the Superhero'

Due to the fact that superheroes have been perpetually subject to revisionism, they become symptomatic signifiers of contemporary consciousness and thus can serve as embodiments of specific needs in a given time.

– Johannes Schlegel and Frank Habermann (2011: 33–4)

People need dramatic examples to shake them out of apathy and I can't do that as Bruce Wayne. As a man, I'm flesh and blood, I can be ignored, I can be destroyed; but as a symbol … as a symbol I can be incorruptible … I can be everlasting…

– Bruce Wayne, *Batman Begins* (2005)

We are living in the age of the superhero and we cannot deny it. The subject of this book, the Marvel Cinematic Universe (MCU), is the most financially successful film series ever produced, with earnings of more $12 billion at the international box office since 2008, comfortably surpassing rivals like the James Bond (1962–) and *Star Wars* (1977–) franchises, even though they have both existed for decades longer.[1] The image of the superhero is now one of the most pervasive in contemporary global popular culture: whether we like it or not, it is they that serve as examples for our children, who play with their likenesses and aspire to be them, it is their imposing personages we use as a barometer to measure our real-world figures and even ourselves by, and it is films about them which fill multiplexes all over the world, topping the box office from Argentina to Zimbabwe. It does not matter whether we call this phenomenon a 'resurgence' (Chermak *et al.* 2003: 11) or a 'renaissance' (Greene and Roddy 2015: 2) or describe their return as leading to a superhero decade (see Gray and Kaklamanidou 2011: 1) or a 'cultural catastrophe', as renowned graphic novelist Alan Moore suggested (qtd. in Flood 2014) – it is here.

Since around the year 2000 there have been hundreds of superhero films and television shows produced all around the globe, but it is undoubtedly their American incarnation that has emerged as the most prominent, the most successful and the most influential example of the form. Selecting almost any summer at random in the last ten years allows us to see the substantial impact the genre has had on the marketplace: 2008, the date of the first MCU films, *Iron Man* and *The Incredible Hulk*, also saw the release of *The Dark Knight*, *Hancock*, *Hellboy II: The Golden Army*, *Punisher: War Zone* and *Wanted*, to name just a few. Three of them, *The Dark Knight*, *Iron Man* and *Hancock*, were in the top ten grossing films of the year. Eight years later in 2016 the genre showed no sign of losing its popularity, despite many predicting that market saturation would have an impact on its appeal (see McMillan 2014; Khatchatourian 2015), and four of the highest grossing films worldwide were from the superhero genre: *Captain America: Civil War*, *Deadpool*, *Batman v Superman: Dawn of Justice* and *Suicide Squad*, with *Doctor Strange* and *X-Men: Apocalypse* appearing just outside the top ten. The combined international gross of just these six American superhero films alone totalled almost $5 billion dollars.[2]

It was certainly not always like this. While superheroes have been on the cultural landscape since Superman (who made his debut in June 1938), Batman (May 1939) and Captain America (March 1941) first graced the pages of their respective comic books, and had periodically reached the television and cinema screens in the subsequent decades, the three Salkind-era Superman films (1978–1983) and the Burton/Schumacher-era incarnation of Batman (1989–1992; 1995–1997), culturally and commercially impactful on their release though they were, did not inspire the veritable wave of additions to the genre the likes of which we are currently experiencing. Throughout the 1980s until the phenomenal success of *Batman* (1989) only one other superhero film made it into the top ten US domestic box office, *Superman II* (1981), and in the whole of the 1990s a superhero film only appeared in the top ten three times and never in the top five: *Teenage Mutant Ninja Turtles* (1990), *Batman Returns* (1992) and *Batman Forever* (1995). Yet the first decades of the new millennium have seen a proliferation of superhero films and television shows like never before.

Why then has the superhero genre, which, it should be noted, is one of the only truly American film genres, alongside the gangster film and the western, re-emerged so emphatically in recent years? The answer to this question is a complicated one which requires an interrogation of technological, industrial, economic and ideological perspectives. In short, as the title to this prologue suggests, the superhero film returned because *it was needed*. It was needed by the American film industry, which saw declining ticket sales throughout this period in spite of record-breaking grosses and it seemed to be needed by audiences who turned to superheroes in two of the most turbulent decades in living memory (see Cowden 2015). Might Brian Kaller have been right then when he asserted in his article entitled 'Why We Need Superheroes' (2016) that 'In troubled times, Americans turn to the heroic ideal'? Joss Whedon, the director of *The Avengers* (2012) and *Avengers: Age of Ultron* (2015), which each made more than a billion dollars at the box office, was only joking when he stated in his director's commentary accompanying the Blu-ray release of *The Avengers*, that 'We saved movies', but his remark does have an element of truth to it. In an age where people have stopped going to the cinema as frequently as they used to, they returned to it in droves for the superhero film. There is a straightforward reason for this financial success, but it is one which does not entirely explain *why* the genre re-emerged and has been unequivocally embraced by audiences in recent years.

Simply put, recent additions to the superhero genre have been able to transcend *en masse* the demographic audience usually associated with films of this type. So, although it is convenient to say, as many do, that it is an infantile genre which only appeals to children and teenagers, as David Cronenberg did, stating that it is 'adolescent in its core. That has always been its appeal, and I think people who are saying, you know, [*The*] *Dark Knight Rises* [2012] is supreme cinema art, I don't think they know what the fuck they're talking about' (qtd. in Zakarin 2012b) or Susan Faludi who, in her indispensable volume *The Terror Dream: Fear and Fantasy in the Post-9/11 Era*, argued that the superhero only appeals to 'someone, typically a prepubescent teenage boy, who feels weak in the world and insufficient to the demands of the day and who needs a Walter Mitty bellows to pump up his self-worth' (2007: 51), significant evidence points to the contrary. A film like *The Avengers* does not make $623 million at the US box office, plus $896 million at the global box office, then a quarter of a billion on DVD and Blu-ray sales in the US alone by selling tickets *only* to juveniles. In fact, as Nikki Finke (2012) at *Deadline* reported, the demographic for Joss Whedon's film was extremely diverse, with its audience divided exactly in half: fifty percent under twenty-five years old and fifty percent over. It skewed towards males, as one might expect, with sixty percent of its audience being male, but forty percent of those who bought tickets were female. Chief of Distribution at Disney, Dave Hollis, was quite right to say, 'We were clearly an option for everyone' (qtd. in Stewart 2012). Disney executives had every reason to be ecstatic at the box office success of *The Avengers* having purchased Marvel Entertainment just three years before in 2009 for $4 billion dollars. Like their equally high-profile acquisitions of Pixar ($7.4 billion; 2006) and Lucasfilm ($4 billion; 2012), these transactions consolidated Disney's position as the world's leading entertainment brand and in 2016 the MCU films were central in enabling Disney to break the $7 billion global box office record, which had never been achieved by a single studio before (see Sweney 2016).

If the levels of revenue stopped there for a film like *The Avengers* the statistics would be remarkable enough, but the figures mentioned above do not take into account global digital rentals and purchases, television rights and, even more importantly, subsidiary revenue streams like video games, comic books and other merchandising products connected to the film and its characters, about whom Jan Füchtjohann wrote, 'with their iconic costumes [they] function exactly like Coca-Cola – as easily identifiable, sold everywhere and hence valuable brands' (2011). The business of movie-making in the last twenty years has transformed from a state in which the film itself functioned as the primary revenue-generating product in the industry to it being just one part of an extensive multi-media tapestry, the metaphorical steel ball in the pinball machine that Thomas Elsaesser described in his article, 'The Blockbuster: Everything Connects, But Not Everything Goes'; writing in 2001 Elsaesser could not have anticipated the MCU, but he did see how the American film industry had begun to be increasingly defined by the interconnection of diverse markets to an extent it had never been before:

> The principle behind it would be something like this: you launch with great force the little steel ball, shoot it to the top, and then you watch it bounce off the different contacts, pass through the different gates, and whenever it touches a contact, your winning figures go up. The media entertainment business is such a pinball machine: the challenge is to 'own' not only the steel ball but also as many of the contacts as possible because the same 'ball' gets you ever higher scores, that is, profits. The contact points are the cinema screens and video stores, theme parks and toy shops, restaurant chains and video arcades, bookstores and CD record shops. (2001: 18)

The result of this is, in financial terms concerning the Marvel Cinematic Universe alone, a multi-billion-dollar industry which sometimes earns in the region of $2 billion per year at the box office, but also billions more in merchandising on top of that (see Graser 2015), because, unlike what David Cronenberg and Susan Faludi would have us believe, in actual fact, the appeal of the superhero 'transcends age, gender and ethnicity' (Robin Korman, qtd. in Palmeri 2012).

There are other more technological and industrial reasons for the rise of the superhero film to prominence as the genre came to both embody and define a range of contemporary film production, distribution and exhibition practices. The genre has ridden the crest of a wave of technological developments, both benefitted from *and* driven advances in computer-generated imagery (CGI), a symbiotic relationship Yvonne Tasker described as one in which 'the reinvigoration of superhero action depends on and has in turn facilitated significant advances in digital imagery' (2015: 181). So while in 1978 Richard Donner's *Superman* was advertised with the tagline 'You'll believe a man can fly' and the film was at the vanguard of special effects for its time, advances in CGI now allow filmmakers, for the first time ever, to put superheroes onscreen the way they were originally envisioned in their comic books: whether it is the dynamically realised exotic environments of Asgard (*Thor*), Wakanda (*Black Panther*) and Sakaar (*Thor: Ragnarok*), spectacular battles in cities (real and imagined) like New York (*The Avengers*), Xandar (*Guardians of the Galaxy*) and Sokovia (*Avengers: Age of Ultron*), the creation of entirely computer-generated characters with supramimetic precision that are able to seamlessly interact with the physical presence of live actors on set, as in the cases of the Hulk, Ultron, Rocket and Groot (full grown, baby and teen), or where CGI is now able to replace characters without the audience even being aware of it to have them accomplish physically impossible action sequences like those performed by Stephen Strange and Karl Mordo in *Doctor Strange*, or Spider-Man and Iron Man in *Spider-Man: Homecoming*. CGI is now also used to convincingly de-age performers, enabling actors to play themselves in flashbacks to the past, something which allowed the then fifty-year-old Robert Downey Jr. to portray his twenty-something self in *Captain America: Civil War*, the sixty-five-year-old Kurt Russell to play himself at the turn of his thirties, around the time of his iconic roles in *Escape From New York* (1981) and *The Thing* (1982), in *Guardians of the Galaxy: Vol. 2*, or the seventy-something Michael Douglas to play the character of Hank Pym in 1989 in *Ant-Man*, recreating exactly how he looked two years after *Wall Street* (1987) and *Fatal Attraction* (1987). Douglas joked about this technology being able to give him the opportunity to star not in a sequel to *Romancing the Stone* (1984) and *Jewel of the Nile* (1985), but a *prequel*, and it is perhaps reasonable to speculate that this will become more common in the future given the high-profile use of CGI to bring deceased performers back to life in films like *Furious 7* (2015) and *Rogue One: A Star Wars Story* (2016) (see Stolworthy 2015). These practices have defined the tendency of modern blockbusters to prioritise image, action and spectacle over narrative which has been described by some as a return to the 'cinema of attractions', Tom Gunning's categorisation of trends in the early decades of cinema history to directly solicit 'spectator attention, inciting visual curiosity, and supplying pleasure through an exciting spectacle – a unique event' (1990: 58), a description which, without a doubt, could just as well be applied to the contemporary blockbuster.[3]

The global market for these American films has also changed in ways which have benefitted the proliferation of the superhero genre and others which primarily rely on spectacle. The sequel paradigm which defined Hollywood film production from the 1980s to the early 2000s is now seen as progressively outdated for larger brands in an age where the 'universe' model is considered a more compatible long-term business strategy. One could argue that this idea of a shared universe in which separate films exist in the same diegetic world can be seen as early as the original Universal monster cycle (1931–48), but in the wake of the success of the MCU many studios began to experiment with the form: like the expansion of the cinematic *Star Wars* universe from the main series, *Star Wars: The Force Awakens* (2015), to include the so called 'Anthology Series' titles set in the same world like *Rogue One: A Star Wars Story* and *Solo: A Star Wars Story* (2018), and Universal's 'Dark Universe' franchise that began with *The Mummy* (2017) and was planned to be the start of an intertwined six-film series before disastrous reviews and disappointing box office figures for the first instalment threw the whole project into disarray. This process has even necessitated the emergence of new terminology to delineate its intricacies: an evolution from simple terms like remake, sequel and prequel, to the more complicated lexicon of reboot, re-imagining, sidequel, midquel, interquel and stealth sequel (see Jolin 2012).[4] These complexities led Peter Vignold in his *Das Marvel Cinematic Universe Anatomie einer Hyperserie* to argue that the MCU

> can no longer be fully understood as a linear film series, rather it forms a hierarchical structure of encircling hyperseries and series within series that are interconnected. The result is a potentially endless franchise that so far has successfully escaped the almost inevitable narrative exhaustion encountered by almost every other linear series, and with it has established itself in a comparatively short time as an economically dominant model. (2017: 10)

A large amount of this increasing revenue is due to the expanding influence of global markets which have grown exponentially since 2008, the largest and most important being China, but the list of countries impacting on growing box office receipts for American films is diverse: from India to Venezuela, Nigeria to Peru, five countries which were described in *Variety* in 2016 by Eric Schwartzel as 'the five fastest-growing markets' in the world. Only $15 million of *Iron Man*'s gross came from China, but by the time of *Iron Man 3* this had increased to $121 million. This extraordinary success was certainly not a one off; *The Avengers* made

$86.3 million of its $1.5 billion there and *Avengers: Age of Ultron* would go on to make $240 million of its $1.4 billion in China also. However, even these huge numbers were overshadowed by the success of *The Fate of the Furious* (2017), the eighth film in the *Fast and Furious* franchise (2001–), which made nearly $400 million in China, almost twice as much as it earned in the United States. These figures clearly indicate the growing importance of the Chinese market for American films which has resulted in a range of Chinese-American co-productions like *The Great Wall* (2016) and *Kong: Skull Island* (2017), films having scenes specifically shot in China (see *Transformers: Age of Extinction* [2014] and *Iron Man 3*), or having their narratives altered to appeal to Chinese audiences (see *World War Z* [2014]).[5]

So, the American film industry might have *needed* and even came to be defined by the superhero film in this era, but what might it have been about these films in particular which led them to resonate so powerfully with audiences, not just in the United States, but all over the world? Might their principal appeal be the escapist, wish-fulfilment fantasies of their narratives? Could American audiences (and those around the globe) have been seeking solace from the tempestuous realities of their day-to-day lives in the decades impacted upon by the 'War on Terror' and the global financial crisis? Or might it be the case, as Peter Coogan argues in *Superhero: The Secret Origin of a Genre*, that 'Superheroes are the closest our modern culture has to myths'? (2006: 124) Undoubtedly, it is possible to discern a great deal about a society from its heroic mythology, those exemplary figures it selects to be a manifestation of its highest values. While the ancient Greeks had tales of Hercules, Achilles and Odysseus, and late-nineteenth century America turned to mythologised portraits of Wyatt Earp, Davy Crockett and Jesse James, through the mid-twentieth century and into twenty-first, contemporary Western culture found its heroic ideals embodied in superheroes like Superman, Batman and Captain America. Danny Fingeroth, in *Superman on the Couch*, goes back even further to seek antecedents for these characters who have always endorsed prevailing cultural values, to the likes of the Ancient Mesopotamian Gilgamesh, the king of Uruk (writings on whom were found on Babylonian stone tablets dated as early as 18th century BC) and Biblical heroes like Samson and David, which he calls the 'precursors of superheroes' (2004: 16). Jerry Siegel, the co-creator of Superman, envisioned his most famous character as a modern-day demi-god, stating 'I conceived a character like Samson, Hercules, and all the strong men I have ever heard of rolled into one' (qtd. in Reynolds 1992: 9). Thus, the original incarnations of Superman and Captain America, as Chris Rojek suggested, 'present idealized representations of American heroism and the defence of justice' (2001: 25) on the eve of America's entry into World War Two, and characters like the Fantastic Four (November 1961), the

Fig. 1: The heroes we need right now? The superhero as an articulation of contemporary mythology in *Batman v Superman: Dawn of Justice* (2016)

Incredible Hulk (May 1962), Iron Man (March 1963), Spider-Man (August 1963) and the X-Men (September 1963) were, according to Matthew Costello, 'born under the mushroom cloud of potential nuclear war that was a corner-stone of the four-decade bipolar division of the world between the United States and the USSR' (2009: 1). The narratives of the new millennial American super-heroes explored in this monograph similarly provide a cultural battleground on which a war of representation is waged. Their backdrop, one which forms them, nourishes and sustains them, is the post-9/11 period, as the discourse of what became referred to as the 'War on Terror' era emerged quite clearly, and not coin-cidentally, as the dominant themes of the revivified superhero genre. American superhero films very rarely explicitly mention the events of 11 September 2001 and the 'War on Terror', but they self-consciously evoke them almost obsessively, both as thematic motifs and also visually in their detailed recreations of its *mise-en-scène*. The 'War in Terror' and 9/11 are embedded within the frames of films like Christopher Nolan's *Batman* trilogy (2005–2012), the *X-Men* series (1999–), the DC Extended Universe (DCEU) (2013–) and the Marvel Cinematic Universe, where they are restaged and refought in allegory by very American heroes like Batman, Wolverine, Iron Man, Captain America, Superman and Wonder Woman, projected through the prism of the superhero genre in reassuringly pal-liative narratives which John Shelton Lawrence and Robert Jewett have called a 'mythic massage' (1977: xiii) and Charmaine Fernandez refers to as 'therapeutic intervention' (2013: 1).

In this way, one should regard the superhero film as the descendent of that other truly American genre, the western, which, for a number of decades, was one of the most popular genres during the Classical Hollywood era. It has large-ly retreated from our cinema and television screens today, with some notable exceptions; nevertheless the western and its evocative frontier mythology still remain a culturally resonant motif in debates about American ideology and identity. The genre's themes and that which they portray as normative behaviour are not too far removed from those promulgated by the superhero film: in both, 'real men' are those who are strong, self-reliant, courageous and resolute, simplistically drawn bad guys are there to be vanquished, women are to be saved and adored, the law is inherently unreliable, and the only answer to a problem, regardless of what it might be, is righteous and redemptive violence. Just as importantly, both genres are primarily about the experiences of the same group, as what Jane Tompkins wrote of the western is equally true of the superhero film, that its lead characters are primarily 'male, and almost all of the other characters are men' (1992: 38).

Part of the former appeal of the western and the current popularity of the superhero film is undoubtedly their malleability. They are able to mould themselves into a variety of sub-genres and moods, and they both, as Barry Keith Grant observed, take 'social debates and tensions and cast them into formulaic narratives, condensing them into dramatic conflicts between individual characters, heroes and villains, providing familiar stories that help us "narrativize" and so make sense of the large abstract forces that effect our lives' (2012: 4). In its long history, the western has been able to subsume diverse variations into its central narrative and visual parameters: from gritty and realistic tales, to comedic and even musical variations of the genre, both in film and on television. In the same way, superhero texts of the new millennium have also had a considerable range: from light-hearted and fantastical (*Fantastic Four* [2005] and *Sky High* [2005]), more grounded and quasi-realistic (*Special* [2006] and *Defendor* [2009]), quirky and offbeat (*Hellboy* [2004] and *Deadpool* [2016]), period-set (*Wonder Woman* [2017] and *Captain America: The First Avenger* [2010]), adult-oriented (*Watchmen* [2009] and *Logan* [2017]), animated (*The Incredibles* [2004] and *The LEGO Batman Movie* [2017]) to parodic and comedic (*Kick Ass* [2010] and *The Green Hornet* [2010]), even an entry into the Found Footage cycle (*Chronicle* [2012]).

After 9/11, several commentators used the western as shorthand for assertions about what American brands of justice might resemble in response. Dianne Amrie Amann wrote that President George W. Bush had 'swaggered onto the foreign-policy scene like a latter-day Matt Dillon [from the TV series *Gunsmoke*, CBS, 1955–75] aiming to shoot down the supposed menace of international entanglement' (qtd. in Lawrence and Jewett 2003: 12). Bush seemed to embrace this idea about himself and even channelled the iconic figures of John Wayne and Clint Eastwood with his repeated evocations of the Old West: only one week after 9/11 he demanded that Osama Bin Laden be taken 'dead or alive' (see Harnden

2001) and he also said that the best way to find terrorists was to 'smoke them out' (qtd. in Knowlton 2001). In 2002 he suggested that, 'Contrary to my image as a Texan with two guns at my side, I'm more comfortable with a posse' (qtd. in Bumiller). However, it was the superhero that many seemed to turn to more and more frequently as a frame of reference as the decade progressed. Peggy Noonan wrote that after seeing Bush at Ground Zero in New York she expected him to 'tear open his shirt and reveal the big 'S' on his chest' (2003) and some of Bush's rhetoric did seem reminiscent of the genre: his quest to 'rid the world of the evil-doers [in] a monumental struggle of good versus evil' (2002) or a pledge to 'wage a war to save civilization itself' with a cause that is 'just and victory is ultimately assured' (2001e). President Obama was frequently envisioned as a superhero during his election campaign (see Gopolam 2008), but almost as often as a supervillain by his political opponents, including, most memorably, the image of him as Batman's nemesis, the Joker, by Firas Alkhateeb (see Borrelli 2009). In similar ways, the larger than life figure of Donald Trump became a malleable icon for those on both sides of the political spectrum and his election victory in 2016 was even directly blamed, by more than one person, on the superhero film itself (see Hagley 2016; Melamid 2017). In an episode of *Real Time with Bill Maher* (HBO, 2003–) broadcast on 19 May 2017, host Bill Maher stated that Hollywood's obsession with superhero films was responsible for the rise in popularity of Trump in language more colourful than that used by John Shelton Lawrence and Robert Jewett in *The American Monomyth* (1977), but expressing very similar sentiments:

> If you're asking, what's the problem? The problem is that superhero movies imprint this mindset that we are not masters of our own destiny, and the best we can do is sit back and wait for Star-Lord and a fucking raccoon to sweep in and save our sorry asses. … Forget hard work, government institutions, diplomacy, investment. We just need a hero to rise, and so we put out the Bat Signal for one man who could step in and solve all of our problems very quickly. And that's how we got our latest superhero: Orange Sphincter.

This monograph maintains that the superhero has largely replaced the western hero in the cultural imaginary and performs a very similar cultural function as it once did. Instead of being raised on western serials screened almost perpetually on television and playing 'Cowboys and Indians' in the backyard, today's generations are raised on superhero narratives, and children now play with (and as) Iron Man, Superman, Batman, Captain America and Spider-Man.[6] Despite the retreat of the western genre from the forefront of popular culture, its mythology and the frontier narrative remains a vital part of the American experience,

Fig. 2: The superhero film as the descendent of the western. Here in *Logan* (2017), one of its most explicit articulations, an aging Wolverine (Hugh Jackman) holds up an X-Men comic book while *Shane* (1953) plays in the background

as Geoff King commented: 'The traditional generic western may be in a state of near terminal decline, but many aspects of the mythic or ideological narrative that animated it remain alive and well in Hollywood' (2000: 2). The western has become subsumed into the superhero genre and can be seen quite clearly in many of its films, whether explicitly in *Logan*, which draws extensively and artfully from *Shane* (1953) and *Unforgiven* (1992), or implicitly in films like *Iron Man*, *Avengers: Age of Ultron* and the rest of the MCU. [7]

This idea of what might have been *needed* by American culture in the post-9/11 era is particularly relevant for the superhero film above all genres as it emerges as one of its central motifs to an extent it had never been before. In *Spider-Man* (2002), one of the first films in this superhero renaissance and a film very much marked by 9/11 in terms of its themes and iconography, but one which *never* mentions the event by name, thereby establishing a paradigm that will be followed, for the most part, by superhero films throughout the decade, Peter Parker's Aunt May suggests: 'We *need* a hero, courageous, sacrificing people, setting examples for all of us. Everybody loves a hero, people line up for 'em, cheer for them, scream their names.' Raimi's film provided audiences with the single most influential line of dialogue in the genre in the two decades after, one which has been linked by many not just to fictional superheroes, but to America as a whole: 'With great power comes great responsibility' (see Peltonen 2013). In Bryan Singer's *Superman Returns* (2006) Lois Lane wins a Pulitzer Prize for her article, 'Why the World Doesn't Need Superman' and she later asks the iconic hero, 'How could you leave us like that? I moved on. So did the rest of us. That's why I wrote it. The world doesn't *need* a saviour. And neither do I...' In *The Avengers*, after more than sixty years frozen in the ice, a newly revived

Captain America is reluctant to put on his old red, white and blue uniform as he has seen how much the world has changed since 1945. He asks Agent Coulson, 'Aren't the Stars and Stripes a little old-fashioned?', to which Coulson responds, 'With everything that is happening and things coming to light people just might *need* a little old-fashioned'. It is Christopher Nolan's genre-redefining Batman trilogy which offers the most sustained meditation on this theme. In *Batman Begins* Rachel Dawes tells Bruce Wayne, 'Maybe someday, when Gotham no longer *needs* Batman, I'll see him [Bruce Wayne] again'; and in the sequel, *The Dark Knight*, the Joker lectures Batman about the capricious nature of the residents of Gotham City by telling him, 'They *need* you right now, but when they don't, they'll cast you out, like a leper!' But it is from Lieutenant James Gordon that the title of this prologue is derived, as at the climax of *The Dark Knight* Batman accepts being framed for the murder of Harvey Dent in order to allow the residents of Gotham City to continue believing in Dent's integrity, even though it is a lie. Gordon suggests it is the appropriate course of action 'because he's the hero Gotham deserves, but not the one it *needs* right now'. It is my contention that the return of the superhero in the first decades of the new millennium can be explained, to a significant extent, by the fact that it was the superhero that the United States *needed* in the fractious post-9/11 period. Outside the frames of the screen in the aftermath of 9/11, Jack Valenti, the then Head of Motion Picture Association of America, certainly felt that America needed the movies then more than ever before. He stated, 'Here in Hollywood we must continue making our movies and our TV programmes. ... The country *needs* what we create' (2001; emphasis added). An interrogation of what the Marvel Cinematic Universe offered audiences in this era and what they might have to say about the times in which they were made is the subject of this monograph.

Notes

1 The MCU has also earned considerably more than other franchises which began in the first decade of the twenty-first century like the *Harry Potter* series (2001–), *The Fast and Furious* series (2001–), *The Lord of the Rings* (2001–2014) and the *Transformers* (2007–) series.

2 In fact, 2017 was one of the biggest years for the superhero genre with *Wonder Woman*, *Logan*, *Spider-Man: Homecoming*, *Guardians of the Galaxy Vol.2*, *The LEGO Batman Movie*, *Thor: Ragnarok* and *Justice League* topping the box office all over the world on their release.

3 Despite the seemingly contemporary nature of these assertions, they have been around for decades. As early as 1986 Tom Gunning wrote, 'Clearly in some sense recent spectacle cinema has reaffirmed its roots in stimulus and carnival rides, in what

might be called the Spielberg-Lucas-Coppola cinema of effects' (1990: 70). See also Wanda Strauven's *The Cinema of Attractions Reloaded* (2006).

4   A sidequel is a sequel that takes place at the same time as a previous film i.e. *The Bourne Legacy* (2012); a midquel or an interquel is a sequel which is set during a gap in a previously completed film series i.e. *Rogue One: A Star Wars Story*; and a stealth sequel is a film which is not marketed as a sequel but is revealed to be one during the course of its narrative, as in *Split* (2017). The universe model can be very lucrative, but can also collapse after one poorly received film, as ambitious plans for franchises to follow *Ghostbusters* (2016) and *King Arthur: Legend of the Sword* (2017) disappeared.

5   This marked growth in earnings around the globe can be tracked in country after country. In Venezuela and India, two of the markets mentioned in Schwartzel's article (2016), *Iron Man* made $1.9 million and $2 million respectively; just a few years later *Iron Man 3* made $12.4 million and $12.2 million in the same locations.

6   Intriguingly, this transition is commented on directly in *Spider-Man: Homecoming* by Adrian Toomes (Michael Keaton) who goes on to become the charismatic villain the Vulture. In the film's prologue, set in the aftermath of the Battle of New York that was the climax of *The Avengers*, the Toomes Salvage Company are shown to be contracted to clean up the city. When he sees a picture of the Avengers drawn by a child he remarks: 'Things are never gonna be the same now. ... You got aliens, you got big green guys tearing down buildings. When I was a kid I used to draw cowboys and indians.'

7   The director of *Logan*, James Mangold, introduced a special screening of *Shane* at the Academy of Motion Picture Arts and Sciences' Samuel Goldwyn Theater on 7 October 2013, with the following comment, 'The best western films (and this is an example of the very best) are not centered on nostalgia, are not historical in nature (the moment in history when these films took place is largely a manufacture of imagination). The best of these films create a landscape that has evolved into an American mythology, one as resonant and evocative as religious parables, Japanese Samurai tales and the Greek Gods of Olympus' (qtd. in Coleman 2017).

Superheroes in the New Millennium and 'The Example of America'

To overcome extremism, we must also be vigilant in upholding the values our troops defend, because there is no force in the world more powerful than the example of America.

– President Barack Obama (2009)

We of the twenty-first century, although unable to believe in the literal reality of such heroes, nevertheless still dream our myths onward, clothing them in modern dress. ... We dream them onward, give them colorful costumes, and pseudoscientific origins, but we no longer consider them real. Or do we?

– Don LoCicero (2007: 229)

This book is a critical exploration of the range of films and television shows which are commonly referred to as the Marvel Cinematic Universe. Starting with the release of *Iron Man* in May 2008, Marvel Studios endeavoured to create a cohesive narrative in which the characters and events portrayed reside within the same diegetic world. While this had been commonplace in comic books for decades, in the film industry, at the time, it was largely unprecedented. As a body of work the MCU emerges as a remarkable range of case studies, representative both of the changes that swept through the film and television industries during the period and of how profoundly immersed in the tumultuous political climate of the era new millennial American cinema became.

Although popular film and television shows are often dismissed as shallow frivolities with the assertion that 'popular culture, or at least the part of it transmitted by the mass media, tends to "go in one eye and out the other"' (Gans 1999: xiii), a considerable amount of critical writing has argued that media texts have a much more complicated relationship with the cultures that produce them and, in actual fact, can be regarded as striking encapsulations of the shifting ideological coordinates of their eras. John Shelton Lawrence and Robert Jewett in their ground-breaking volume *The American Monomyth* called this lingering belief in the superficiality of popular culture the 'bubblegum fallacy' (see 1977: 1–22), and even though it is something that has been comprehensively refuted in the decades since, it remains pervasive. Many have contended that, on the contrary, popular films (and other visual media) are able to bear witness to, record and even engage with the ideological currencies of their times (see Kracauer 1947 and Kaes 2011 on Weimar-era German cinema; Starck 2010 on Cold War American science fiction). For example, writers like Robin Wood, Peter Lev, Michael Ryan and Douglas Kellner argue that the volatile political climate of 1970s America became viscerally materialised within the frames of films from a wide variety of genres like *Dirty Harry* (1971), *Chinatown* (1974), *The Texas Chainsaw Massacre* (1974), *Three Days of the Condor* (1975), *Taxi Driver* (1976), *Star Wars: A New Hope* (1977), *Invasion of the Body Snatchers* (1978), *Apocalypse Now* (1979) and many others. These films do much more than reflect the prevailing cultural discourse; in fact, they contribute to it in a range of palpable and compelling ways. Notable monographs like Robin Wood's *Hollywood from Vietnam to Reagan* (1986), Michael Ryan and Douglas Kellner's *Camera Politica: The Politics and Ideology of Contemporary Hollywood Film* (1990) and Peter Lev's *American Films of the 1970s: Conflicting Visions* (2000) postulate that it is naïve to regard something as culturally impactful as popular film *only* as disposable entertainment. Not only can we discern that 'the ideology of the contemporary Hollywood film is therefore inseparable from the social history of the era' (Ryan and Kellner 1990: 7), but also that the richly textured and dynamic tapestry of these films should be understood as 'key moments of a debate on what America is and what America should be' (Lev 2000: 185).

In a very similar way to this, this volume asserts that the films produced by the American film industry in the first decades of the twenty-first century provide a vivid testimony to an era David Holloway argued was defined by a 'national security crisis, an imperial crisis, a crisis in capitalist democracy and governance, a crisis in the relationship between the US and Europe, multiple crises in the frameworks and institutions of international law and order (notably the UN and NATO), as well as a series of military and humanitarian crises' (2008: 6). Of course, American films which explicitly depict aspects of the 'War on Terror' like *United 93* (2006), *Zero Dark Thirty* (2012) and *American Sniper* (2014), the global financial crisis like *Up in the Air* (2009), *Margin Call* (2011) and *The Big Short* (2016), or issues of race relations like *12 Years a Slave* (2013), *Fruitvale Station* (2013) and *O.J.: Made in America* (2016), are those most often connected by commentators and audiences to the discourse of the era. However, one must also consider popular films like those from the science fiction, horror and action genres, which, while often critically marginalised, frequently emerge as potent cultural artefacts. As Anton Kaes maintains, this is a complicated process which means 'repositioning films within the cultural production of a time and a place, but also appreciating them as complex appropriations of the world and unique interpretations (not reflections) of historical experience' (2011: 6).

In this way I maintain that the superhero genre should be considered as an articulation and manifestation of contemporary cultural mythologies.[1] Here we must understand the term mythology in the Barthesian sense as a participatory cultural discourse which Richard Slotkin called 'a complex of narratives that dramatizes the world vision and historical sense of a people or culture, reducing centuries of experience into a constellation of compelling metaphors... [which] provides a scenario or prescription for action, defining and limiting the possibilities for human response to the universe' (1973: 6). If it is self-evident that concepts of national identity are a product of a narrativisation process, as Benedict Anderson described in his book *Imagined Communities: Reflections on the Origins and Spread of Nationalism* (1983), what better approximation of this is there than popular cinematic narratives embraced by the public at large?[2] I argue then that national cinemas are to be understood as the product of an Institutional State Apparatus (ISA) in the Althusserian sense and even superficially simplistic seeming popular films emerge as powerful examples of what Frederic Jameson called highly 'socially symbolic acts' (1981: 20).

It is within these parameters, given their considerable financial success, intense levels of popularity and acute cultural impact that this monograph situates the films and television shows of the Marvel Cinematic Universe. The MCU provides us with a range of affective texts which function as an embodiment of their era in a range of ways, viewing the turbulent political and social climate of the new millennial decades through the prism of the superhero genre, and in so doing present us with a materialisation of ideological discourse intrinsic to the period. This book considers how the mythopoetic narratives of the MCU legitimise enduring fantasies of American exceptionalism in the post-9/11 era by frequently returning to the moral binarisms that defined World War II and the Cold War in the cultural imaginary; in doing so they participate in the perpetuation and consolidation of configurations of American identity not just within the US but, given their international impact, all around the globe.

While this monograph intends to argue that the MCU is incontrovertibly a product of the era in which it was made, it is imperative to be wary of simplistic connections which writers like Geoff King (2016) have warned of. Elsewhere, I have called this process '9/11 apophenia' (McSweeney 2014: 23), using the term to illustrate the desire to see direct causality between the events of the 'War on Terror' and cinematic texts produced in the ensuing years, which, in fact, might not be there. In this respect, one might regard that Tom Pollard reaches too far in his volume *Hollywood 9/11 Superheroes, Supervillains and Superdisasters*, when he insists there is a 'subtle yet distinct post 9/11 message' (2011: 44) in Robert Zemeckis's *Beowulf* (2007), which apparently equates the three monsters Beowulf defeats with Bush's 'Axis of Evil': Iraq, North Korea and Iran. Even Francis Pheasant-Kelly, in her excellent *Fantasy Film Post 9/11* (2013), which persuasively situates the Marvel Cinematic Universe in the 'War on Terror' era, might be considered as reading a little too much into one of the several Afghanistan-set scenes in *Iron Man*. Before he becomes the eponymous hero of the film's title, Tony Stark (Robert Downey Jr.) visits the Kunar Province in Afghanistan which was then regarded by some as 'the deadliest place on earth to be an American' (Maxwell 2013: iv) and a location firmly associated with what Jason Burke (2011) called 'the 9/11 Wars' in his book of the same name. The year of the release of *Iron Man* and the one preceding it saw a wave of Iraq- and Afghanistan-set combat films including (but not limited to) *In the Valley of Elah* (2007), *Redacted* (2007), *Stop-Loss* (2008) and *The Hurt Locker* (2008), the vast majority of which had underperformed so substantially at the box office that to set one's film in Iraq or Afghanistan was widely regarded as 'box office poison' (Everhart 2009). As Stark demonstrates his new range of weapons of mass destruction, suggestively titled the 'Freedom Line', to the grateful American military for whom he is the primary supplier (a role which sees him hailed as both 'visionary, genius, American patriot' and the 'merchant of death' in a sense embodying some of the central paradoxes of the film), Pheasant-Kelly suggests that 'the camera then cuts to the onlooking military personnel, whose caps are swept off by the blast's shockwave (the resultant dust clouds reminding viewers of media footage at the Twin Towers collapse)' (2013: 148). *Iron Man* (and Iron Man himself) is a product of the 'War on Terror', both literally and figuratively, but the connections here are too explicitly drawn. Instead, I will argue that *Iron Man*, featuring a character described by Bradford Wright as 'the most political of Marvel's superheroes' (2003: 222), and the MCU films as a whole, function as a manifestation of some of the prevailing fears *and* fantasies which defined the era. Thus, just as comic book icons like Superman, Batman, Captain America, the Hulk, Thor (first appearance August

1962) and Iron Man are intrinsically connected to the times in which they were first created, the new millennial incarnations of these characters are immersed in the geopolitical climate of the post-9/11 decades. This is evident not only in the Afghanistan-set opening of *Iron Man*, the first film of what Marvel Studios called Phase One (2008–12), but in the film's subsequent representation of the military industrial complex and in Iron Man's virtuous extra-judicial incursions into Afghanistan ('I had my eyes opened ... I saw young Americans killed by the very weapons I created to defend and protect them. And I saw that I had become part of a system that is comfortable with zero accountability'). This process continues in the representation of the Hulk in *The Incredible Hulk*, once an icon of the Cold War, but in the MCU updated to configure distinctly new millennial articulations of American military power, surveillance and influence ('That man's body is the property of the US Army!'). It can also be seen in the allegorical narrative of *Thor*, ('A wise King never seeks out war. But he must always be ready for it...') in which many saw the Bush administration reflected (see Arnold 2011; Mills 2013). This cultural battleground is also evident in the MCU's nostalgic portrayal of World War II in *Captain America: The First Avenger* ('General Patton has said that wars are fought with weapons but are won by men. We are going to win this war because we have the best men!'), which despite being fantastical, depicts the conflict in a very similar way to the likes of *Sands of Iwo Jima* (1949), *Saving Private Ryan* (1998) and *Fury* (2014), films that have actively participated in the erasure of the complicated and troubling realities of the war in favour of a reification of the 'greatest generation' rhetoric which has come to define how it has been remembered ever since.

Phase One of the MCU culminated in *The Avengers* in which the characters from the five previous individual films, often referred to as the Avengers Prime, were united in something more than a sequel, rather in a cinematic 'mega event' (Kevin Feige qtd. in Surrell 2012: 13) to prevent the Asgardian God Loki and his invading army of Chitauri from taking over the world in what becomes known throughout the diegetic universe of the MCU as the Battle of New York.[3] If even one of the previous stand-alone adventures had been a financial failure, it would have thrown the entire MCU experiment into jeopardy; yet *The Avengers* had the biggest opening weekend in the history of American film at the time with over $200 million dollars at the US box office alone, almost its entire budget recouped in one weekend.[4] Philip French was dismissive of the film in *The Observer* where he wrote, 'Karl Marx could have been anticipating 9/11 and this movie when he said that history repeats itself first as tragedy, then as farce' (2012), but he was one of several cultural commentators who drew sustained connections between the film and the events of 11 September 2001 (see Brody 2012; Hoberman 2012). *The Avengers* is one of many science fiction films of the new millennium which have filled their screens with barely coded images and situations self-consciously designed to evoke 9/11 and the 'War on Terror', a fact that was commented on in the United States and abroad. Kyle Buchanan, writing for the *The Vulture*, felt obliged to ask, 'Is It Possible to Make a Hollywood Blockbuster Without Evoking 9/11?' (2013) and Thomas Sotinel, writing in *Le Monde*, observed that *The Avengers* was one of many films to embed itself within 'the images of that day [which] have now become motifs of American popular cinema' (2012).[5]

The Battle of New York is deliberately constructed as a 9/11-style event within *The Avengers*, but also in terms of its aftermath in both the films and the television shows which followed. Marvel's Phase Two (2013–15) began with *Iron Man 3* which saw Tony Stark suffering from symptoms of post-traumatic stress disorder (PTSD) as the direct result of his experiences in New York and the emergence of the Bin Laden-esque terrorist called The Mandarin ('Some people call me a terrorist … I consider myself a teacher. America, ready for another lesson?'), which was followed by *Captain America: The Winter Soldier* as the titular character is forced to come to terms with the moral vagaries of the twenty-first century, confronting intrusive governmental policies in a narrative which for many was explicitly connected to cultural discourse surrounding America's domestic and international security and surveillance policies in the era (see Eddy 2014; Edelstein 2014).

This volume argues that MCU provides audiences with wish-fulfilment fantasies that operate on both personal and national levels. It offers us powerful individual fantasies about who we *could be*: stronger, faster, more virile and more attractive (which are literalised within the diegesis in the cases of Steve Rogers, Bruce Banner and Peter Quill), but also fantasies of empowerment on the global stage. This is not a new assertion with regard to the relationship between cinema and national identity: witness how the James Bond franchise (1962–) has frequently been read as an illusory allohistorical fantasy of continued preeminence in the international sphere which ignores Britain's readily apparent declining geopolitical status (see Chapman 2007; Baron 2009); or how the paramnesiac romances of Hindi commercial cinema elide and obfuscate real-life political and social instabilities (see Kaur and Sinha 2005; Dayal 2014). In this respect, popular films are to be understood as heterotopic narratives, that is, physical representations (whether conscious or unconscious) of what society considers its idealised dimensions, which, in the case of the superhero film, reimagine a crisis-filled era through the comforting and nostalgic prism of a largely reactionary genre. They alleviate and assuage real-world anxieties in a process defined by Lawrence and Jewett as a 'mythic massage [that] soothes and satisfies. It imparts the relaxing feeling that society can actually be redeemed by anti-democratic means' (1977: xiii). This is why a great many superheroes are explicitly, and accurately, connected to the ideologies of the countries which produce them, resulting in them emerging as what Jason Dittmer describes as nationalist superheroes in his book *Captain America and the Nationalist Superhero: Metaphors, Narratives, and Geopolitics* (2012).

Superhero films, then, should be understood as performing a cultural function for audiences, whether they are intended to by their creators or not, in a very similar way to how American cinema has played a prominent role in the way many conflicts have become remembered in the cultural imaginary, whether we consider World War II (1939–45), as previously mentioned, or the Vietnam War (1955–75), which was comprehensively remodelled and reshaped by Hollywood to fit more readily into American concepts of itself, its global role and its place in the history of the twentieth century. Therefore, while the public at large considered films like *Platoon* (1986), *Full Metal Jacket* (1987), *The Deer Hunter* (1978) and *Apocalypse Now* to be critical of the Vietnam War, their primary ideological function was actually to 'address and alleviate this trauma in order to restore American self-belief and credibility' (Westwell 2014: 57) as they rewrite the conflict as a noble failure fought for honourable reasons. These films do what popular American cinema has done since its inception and, as André Bazin suggested, manage 'in an extraordinarily competent way, to show American society just as it wanted to see itself' (2014: 143).

It should be noted that, at the time of writing, the MCU has spanned the administrations of three American presidents. *Iron Man* and *The Incredible Hulk* were released in the final months of the George W. Bush administration (2001–2009), and the third film, *Iron Man 2* (2010), until the fourteenth, *Doctor Strange* (2016), were produced during Barack Obama's presidency (2009–2017). Ben Walters saw Obama reflected in the MCU as early as *Iron Man 2* and called Stark's struggles with what it might mean to be a superhero in the new millennium as 'the first superhero film of the Obama era' (2010). While *Push, Watchmen, X-Men Origins: Wolverine* and *Defendor* (all 2009) are chronologically the first superhero films released during the Obama administration, Walters is perhaps partially right to offer a distinction between some of the Bush-era superhero films which were quite often 'about the use and abuse of power' and those of the Obama era which 'suggests a country anxious and uncertain about what lies at its core and beyond its reach, and with a taste for the comforts of nostalgia' (ibid.). At one point in *Iron Man 2* Stark picks up an image of Iron Man designed in the style of Shepard Fairey's iconic 'Hope' poster which Peter Schjeldahl called 'the most efficacious American political illustration since "Uncle Sam wants you"' (2009) and turns to Pepper Potts telling her he is 'tired of the liberal agenda'. The comment is ambiguously presented, but might be seen as referring to the growing sense of 'disconnect between the expectations created by Obama's campaign rhetoric and the reality of how he governed' (Savage 2015: 108) which was already evident by the time of the film's release. Two years later *The Avengers* was one of many Hollywood films released in 2012, rightly or wrongly, to be called an example of 'Obama Cinema' alongside *Lincoln, Django Unchained, The Hunger Games, Beasts of the Southern Wild* and many others (see, also, Izo 2014).[6] These interpretations of *The Avengers* were not restricted to the United States and were indeed global, with the likes of Oliver Delcroix in *Le Figero*, titling his review of the film '*The Avengers*: le film étendard des années Obama' (2012) and Luis Martínez, writing in *El Mundo*, 'Obama, contado por Hollywood' (2013).[7] A.O. Scott and Manohla Dargis suggested Joss Whedon's film

> might have been called 'Team of Rivals' — the title of the book, by Doris Kearns Goodwin, that was one of the sources for *Lincoln*. And Joss Whedon's Marvel costume party is, like Mr. Spielberg's historical costume drama, largely about an urgent response to a political crisis. It is also about community organizing, as Fury mobilizes a fractious group of individuals whom he must persuade to pursue a set of common interests. As such, *The Avengers* may be the exemplary Obama Era superhero movie, replacing the figure of the solitary, shadowy paladin with a motley assortment of oddballs and, despite the title, focusing less on vengeance than on interplanetary peacekeeping. (2012)

In May 2017 *Guardians of the Galaxy: Vol. 2* (2017) became the first MCU film of the Trump presidency, but even by then several films released during the first hundred days of Trump's administration like *Logan, Get Out, Kong: Skull Island* and *The Boss Baby* (all 2017), had already been connected by some to the discourse of the incipient Trump era.[8] By April 2017 Trump himself had become subsumed into the Marvel Cinematic Universe with fairly explicit allusions to him and his administration in *Marvel's Agents of S.H.I.E.L.D.* In the episode 'Identity and Change' (4.17) broadcast on 11 April 2017, inside the alternate computer reality known as the Framework, Leopold Fitz, in that world a high-ranking member of HYDRA, states, 'Believe me, we will defeat these terrorists and we will make our society great again!', and later in 'All the Madam's Men' (4.19), broadcast on 25 April 2017, Coulson refers to HYDRA's lies as 'alternative facts', just three months after Counselor to the President, Kelly Conway, infamously coined the neologism in an episode of *Meet the Press* (NBC, 1947–) on 22 January 2017.

So, while *Iron Man*, the film which started the MCU, *is* just a superhero film, it is also a product of the ideological system in which it was produced and, as Tanner Mirrlees convincingly argues, reinforces three separate but interconnected aspects of American power: 'US economic power (as a Hollywood blockbuster and synergistic franchise), US Military power (as a DOD-Hollywood co-produced militainment) and cultural power (as a national and global relay for US imperial ideologies)' (2014: 5). Like many American films (and much, although not all, of the MCU), *Iron Man* received both privileged access and extensive material in exchange for its favourable representation of the US military, the cultural implications of which are investigated in detail in works like David L. Robb's *Operation Hollywood: How the Pentagon Shapes and Censors the Movies* (2004), Tricia Jenkins' *The CIA in Hollywood: How the Agency Shapes Film and Television* (2012) and Matthew Alford and Tom Secker's *National Security Cinema: The Shocking New Evidence of Government Control in Hollywood* (2017). These authors explore how texts like *Pearl Harbor* (2001), *Black Hawk Down* (2001), *The Kingdom* (2007), *Act of Valour* (2012), *Lone Survivor* (2013), *Zero Dark Thirty*, and *24* (Fox, 2001–10) are provided with substantial governmental support which then has a demonstrable impact on how the military or agencies like the FBI or the CIA are portrayed onscreen.[9] Perhaps the most pertinent example of this relationship is the 1980s Bruckheimer/Simpson production and Cold War power fantasy *Top Gun* (1986) which, according to a variety of sources, had a substantial impact on Navy recruitment figures after May 1986 due to its glamourisation of the subject matter (see Suid 2002: 500). About the film, Douglas Kellner has written, '*Top Gun* positions the audience in ways to induce spectators to identify or sympathize with its politics; while many of us may resist these positions and may not buy into their ideologies, we must actively resist the text itself' (1995: 80). For many, *Top Gun* might seem to be 'just a movie', but it is quite clear to see how it is a product of the ideological system in which it was made at a very particular time in American history; furthermore, it functions not just as a reflection of these times, but an active participant in them in a way that this volume will suggest is true for the Marvel Cinematic Universe. It was no coincidence that nearly twenty years later in 2003 it was *Top Gun* that Karl Rove, Senior Advisor and Deputy Chief of Staff during the George W. Bush administration, seemed to be evoking when he orchestrated Bush's landing on the deck of the USS Abraham Lincoln which was followed by the now infamous 'Mission Accomplished' speech. In a similar way, the films of the MCU bind audiences to their own ideological perspectives, which also have real-world ramifications. If it is true, as Neal Curtis wrote in his volume *Sovereignty and Superheroes*, that 'rather than simply being read as allegorical representations of real-world issues, the comics themselves make a direct contribution to the culture from which they arise, and that in a very important way make their own contribution' (2016: 5), what might we conclude then about the power of popular film, with its affective cinematic mechanisms, its privileged status and its truly global impact? Almost a year before the release of *Iron Man*, after the production shot scenes at the historic Edwards Airforce Base in California, Captain Christian Hodge, the Defense

Department's project officer for the film, stated that 'the Air Force is going to come off looking like rock stars' and Master Sergeant Larry Belen, superintendent of technical support for the air pilot school, directly evoked the iconic 1986 Tom Cruise film when he suggested, 'I want people to walk away from this movie with a really good impression of the Air Force, like they got about seeing the Navy in *Top Gun*' (qtd. in Miles 2007).[10]

On a broader level, the MCU has produced narratives which reify notions of American exceptionalism in the wake of the 'monstrous dose of reality' (Sontag 2001) that was 9/11. They are a body of films which articulate, as Godfrey Hodgeson suggests, 'the idea that the United States is not just the richest and most powerful of the world's more than two hundred states but also the most politically and morally exceptional' (2009: 10). This book asserts that the trauma of 9/11 and the ensuing 'War on Terror' posed such powerful challenges to some of the essential tenets on which American identity is based, that these events had to be rewritten, reframed and replayed in ways more conducive to how America sees itself. This master narrative which emerged in the aftermath of 9/11 was one promulgated by the Bush administration but was readily embraced by the media and it was one which centralised some potent and formative myths about American identity in its reconfiguration of America as a reluctant superpower, the continuation of the enduring underdog/world's number one paradox, the legitimisation of the use of American military force for good around the globe, the belief in World War II as an unambiguous 'good war', the marked certainty of America's moral superiority (and lack of moral equivalency) and the nobility of America's divinely ordained mission abroad.[11] While these ideas are not unique to the new millennium, they can be seen as a reaffirmation of an America that is still 'the exemplar of freedom and a beacon of hope for those who do not now have freedom' (Ronald Reagan, 1981), on 'the right side of history' (Barack Obama, 2015),[12] as 'the indispensable nation [which is able to] see further into the future' (Madeline Albright, on an episode of *The Today Show* [NBC, 1952–], 19 February 1998) and 'the world's best hope for peace and freedom' (George W. Bush, 2001b) at a time of national crisis.[13] These very motifs find themselves strikingly replicated in the MCU and even function as some of the undergirding tropes of its entire narrative framework. Yet this understanding of American identity is quite profoundly disconnected from the real world and is a manifestation of what Donald Pease calls 'The United States of Fantasy' in his book *The New American Exceptionalism* (2009: 1) and is described as 'the imperial logic of the American Dream' by Jim Cullen in *Democratic Empire: The United States Since 1945* (2016: xiii). However, they are foundational identificatory mechanisms embraced by Americans and perpetuated in cultural texts and discourse in a range of ways.

The films of the MCU emerge as embodiments of national fantasies and consolidate a range of decidedly American views on the world to the extent that a more comprehensive literalisation of American exceptionalism would be hard to find. In the films of the MCU the United States is at the centre of the world, both its global leader and also the world's primary victim of acts of violence (see Grieder 2009). It is for this reason, as well as the obvious nature of cultural relevance, that the vast majority of the superheroes within the MCU are American, most obviously so in the case of Steve Rogers/Captain America, who Matthew Costello memorably described as 'an avatar of American ideology' (2009: 13), but also Tony Stark/Iron Man who Bryn Upton suggested '*is* America after 9/11' (2014: 33; emphasis added). Even the Norse God of Thunder, Thor, who in spite of being from Asgard (one of the nine worlds of Norse mythology), emerges as distinctly American in the way he is constructed, both in the Americanisation of his values and Asgard's depiction as a proto-American Empire. Kenneth Branagh's *Thor* opens with Odin's characterisation of Asgard as being a 'beacon of hope shining across the stars', heavily reminiscent of remarks made by many about America over the decades. For George H. W. Bush, America was 'the last beacon of hope and strength around the world' (1992), Barack Obama called America 'the engine of the global economy and a beacon of hope around the world' (2010) and George W. Bush stated in his address to the nation on the day after 9/11 that 'America was targeted for attack because we're the brightest beacon for freedom and opportunity in the world. And no one will keep that light from shining' (2001c). These allusions and a narrative which follows an impetuous and vain young man on a journey to maturity led to many reviews with pun-laden titles like 'The Summer's New Hero: Thor-Ge W. Bush' (Singer 2011) and 'Blockbuster: Bush v. Thor' (Stewart 2011). *Thor*, like the majority of MCU texts, functions as a powerful wish-fulfilment fantasy which represents how many Americans chose to view the world after 9/11. However, as Susan Faludi asserted, 'No doubt, the fantasy consoled many. But rather than make us any safer, it misled us into danger, damaging the very security the myth was supposed to bolster. There are consequences to living in a dream' (2007: 289).

These new millennial superheroes embody values and traits explicitly coded as American, just as many heroic figures in Hollywood cinematic history have themselves been seen as representations of American values: from the fictional construct that is 'John Wayne' (see Wills 1999; Noonan 2001) to Sylvester Stallone's John Rambo (see Tasker 1993; Jeffords 1994) in the culturally impactful Rambo franchise (1982–). These synechdocal icons are to be read as embodying perceived national characteristics and their bodies as a symbolic battleground for competing visions of America. J. Bowyer Bell even regarded these two particular figures as being the most symptomatic cinematic creations in

Fig. 3: *Avengers: Age of Ultron* (2015) as legitimisation of enduring fantasies of American exceptionalism in the turbulent new millennial decades

American film history, stating, 'Rambo is a Hollywood artefact and John Wayne was a Hollywood actor but each reflects haltingly actual American hopes and fears' (1999: 245). Susan Jeffords wrote that the hard-bodied icons of masculinity which dominated the cinema screens in the 1980s, actors like Stallone, Arnold Schwarzenegger and Chuck Norris, 'came to stand not only for a type of national character – heroic, aggressive, and determined – but for the nation itself' (1994: 25). In a similar way, superhero films emerge as a barometer for attitudes towards national identity but also endorse what a culture regards as its norms of gender, sexuality and race. In the wake of 9/11 writers like Peggy Noonan called for a remasculinisation of both the individual and the nation in her demand that America return to a more traditional brand of masculinity which she saw embodied in the figure of John Wayne in an article called 'Welcome Back, Duke: From the ashes of Sept. 11 arise the manly virtues' (2001). Noonan called for a reappearance of the kind of men who

> push things and pull things and haul things and build things, men who charge up the stairs in a hundred pounds of gear and tell everyone else where to go to be safe. Men who are welders, who do construction, men who are cops and firemen. They are all of them, one way or another, the men who put the fire out, the men who are digging the rubble out, and the men who will build whatever takes its place. (Ibid.)

Might the emergence of the superhero genre itself be a manifestation of this return? It is the bodies of a culture's heroic figures and the way they are constructed on film, as Lisa Purse suggested, that become of primary importance in the way they are perceived by audiences. She wrote, 'This body is a physically empowered one, strong, agile and resilient, asserting itself in the field of action and risk, and thus acts out fantasies of empowerment that are inherently literalised and physicalised, rather than abstracted' (2011: 3). In the same way, the bodies of Tony Stark, Bruce Banner, Thor, Peter Quill and Captain America are richly symbolic significatory systems pregnant with meaning and association just as Wayne's and Stallone's were to the discourse of their own respective eras. However, as we will see, the MCU heroes can be seen to display a more unstable and variegated depiction of masculinity, although no less hegemonic, which Yann Roublou defined as the 'complex masculinities' of the post-9/11 era (2012: 76).

Noonan's use of Wayne is both relevant and ironic in the case of Captain America, given John Wayne's now central role in American cultural memory of World War II (despite the ambiguity of his war record) and the fact that Captain America would have been his (albeit imaginary) contemporary. Yet Noonan's understanding of 'John Wayne' is just as fictional as the character of Captain America and the other MCU superheroes who are explored in the pages of this book, each of which offers insights into, among other things, changing articulations of what cultures define as masculine values.[14] In the MCU these changes are seen most clearly in the effectively drawn contrast between Tony Stark's new millennial cynicism and Cap's 'old-fashioned' ideals when they are first paired onscreen in *The Avengers* and come to a head in *Captain America: Civil War*. Both men, even with their differences, can be read as a concerted attempt to reclaim American national identity in the wake of 9/11 in very specific ways and primarily through the regenerative powers of violence which Richard Slotkin classified as the definitive 'structuring metaphor of the American experience' (1973: 5). In fact, as one might expect, not a single film across the MCU explicitly challenges the idea that righteous violence is the path to redemption.[15] In *Iron Man 3* Tony Stark's PTSD seems to disappear only after he overcomes his nemesis Aldrich Killian; the only way Bruce Banner can come to terms with his dissociative disorder seems to be through confronting and beating Abomination in *The Incredible Hulk*; and Thor's rites of passage narrative in *Thor* is only completed when he commits a heroic act of self-sacrifice in battle and vanquishes his enemies. In *Captain America: Civil War*, a film which challenges some of the central tenets of the genre, Black Widow asks Captain America, 'Do you really want to punch your way out of this?', ostensibly suggesting that diplomacy might be worth pursuing, only to reveal that violence seems to be, once again, the only answer to his dilemmas in the way that both the genre, and the culture which produced it, demands.

Even those superheroes who are not American are portrayed as having been Americanised or convinced by the superiority of what we might call the 'American experience': Black Widow aka Natasha Romanoff, the Russian secret agent, identifies leaving Russia and the KGB and joining S.H.I.E.L.D. as 'going straight' (*Captain America: The Winter Soldier*) and the Sokovian twins Quicksilver and Scarlett Witch, aka Pietro and Wanda Maximoff, begin *Avengers: Age of Ultron* seeking revenge on Tony Stark for his role in the death of their parents, only to end it joining the Avengers and by extension embracing the United States of America. This transformation occurs after seeing American beneficence and altruism first-hand in the form of the virtuous Captain America and the Avengers' intervention in Sokovia, a fictional Eastern European country coded as being reminiscent of Kosovo circa 1991–2001, even though their decision will later result in the death of one of them and the persecution and internment of the other. *Avengers: Age of Ultron* and the MCU as a whole, embodies the fantasy of how America sees itself on the global stage and one which empowers American and international audiences to do the same. Just as large parts of John Wayne's body of work (see in particular *The Searchers* [1956] and *The Man Who Shot Liberty Valence* [1962]) and Stallone's *Rocky IV* (1985) and *Rambo: First Blood Part II* (1985) literalised American fantasies by reconsolidating essential myths about its supposed values and national character, the MCU functions in exactly the same way, although as a response to very particular crises of national identity which emerged in the wake of the trauma of 9/11.

The morally unambiguous mission to save Sokovia from an event directly caused by Tony Stark mentioned above is just one of many examples throughout the MCU of extra-judicial interventions in foreign countries which, until *Captain America: Civil War*, were almost always portrayed as entirely moral, necessary *and* effective: from Tony Stark's altruistic sojourn to Afghanistan, through the liberation of Europe in World War II-set *Captain America: The First Avenger*, to the rescue of civilians in modern-day Germany in *Avengers Assemble* and Greenwich, London in *Thor: The Dark World*. In their *International Politics and Film: Space, Vision and Power* (2014), Sean Carter and Klaus Dodds correctly assert that this unsanctioned behaviour is portrayed as entirely necessary: 'in order to secure justice or otherwise, the superhero is required because s/he is able to operate beyond the law and this is made possible, in part, because they are tolerated, even encouraged, by grateful city authorities and/or national governments' (2014: 55–6). This becomes most effectively articulated in the exculpatory globe-hopping storylines featured in *Marvel's Agents of S.H.I.E.L.D.* (ABC, 2013–), where the titular parastatal agency is firmly presented as an international organisation, but it is resolutely American in its construction, values and how it chooses to exercise its considerable power in which the heroes prevent disasters and save lives in countries all over the world, week after week, year after year. One is tempted to refer to this as a variation of what has been called 'trauma tourism' (see Tumarkin 2005; Rothe 2011), but what I will refer to as 'virtual terror tourism'. The practice of setting scenes in exotic locations which have frequently experienced real-life trauma and inviting spectators to revel in spectacularly orchestrated violence only for the benefit of portraying their American heroes in a positive light is evidence of the pronounced symbolic hierarchy of American popular film and, just as dubiously, masks a lack of moral equivalency for the actions of the heroic figures which populate these narratives. Thus in Gulmira in 2008 Stark is an unproblematic American hero saving women and children in an Afghanistan which is portrayed in a similar way to many of the combat films which emerged from the 'War on Terror' era, as 'a space of threat to America, a space that must be contained and controlled with military might' (Mirrlees 2014: 8) and a new millennial frontier for American men to prove both their masculinity and their altruism, in a land populated only by victims to be saved and savages to be killed. The ramifications of these extended extra-judicial incursions and the often catastrophic damage they result in were rarely addressed in the films throughout Phases One and Two (although sometimes mentioned in the television branch of the MCU) until the beginning of Phase Three and *Captain America: Civil War*, which seemingly confronted several previously unspoken taboos from the superhero genre at the same time: their endorsement of vigilantism ('while a great many people see you as heroes … there are some who would prefer the word vigilantes'), the America-centric nature of the heroes, and the collateral damage their activities frequently caused ('What would you call a group of US-based enhanced individuals who routinely ignore sovereign borders and inflict their will wherever they choose and who frankly seem unconcerned about what they leave behind?'). *Captain America: Civil War*, the thirteenth film in the MCU, offers a rare critique of the actions of these heroes which proves to be not so easily disregarded. Criticisms are present in other films in the MCU prior to this, but the fact that they most often come from the villains themselves means they have little resonance and are easily ignored by audiences, like those of Ivan Vanko (Mickey Rourke) in *Iron Man 2* who tells Tony Stark, 'You come from a family of thieves and butchers', or Adrian Toomes (Michael Keaton) in *Spider-Man: Homecoming* who asks Peter Parker, 'How do you think your buddy Stark paid for that tower or any of his little toys? Those people Pete, those people up there, the rich and the powerful, they do whatever they want. They don't care about us. We build their roads and fight all their wars…'; or the Red Skull in *Captain America: The First Avenger*, who suggests, 'Arrogance may not be a uniquely American trait, but I must say, you do it better than anyone!' (see also Aldrich Killian in *Iron Man 3*, Loki in *The Avengers* and Ultron in *Avengers: Age of Ultron*).

The use of real-life locations, with their recognisable landmarks and associations, prove extremely relevant to how the MCU depicts the world. Unlike its counterpart, the DC Extended Universe (DCEU), the MCU films (and comics) are all primarily set in real-world cities, most importantly and frequently New York, whereas the DCEU films are set in fictional cities across the US like Superman's Metropolis and Batman's Gotham. While Christopher Nolan's version of Gotham in *Batman Begins*, *The Dark Knight* and *The Dark Knight Rises* (three films made before the DECU began with *Man of Steel* [2013]) might have been deliberately filmed to resemble (and evoke) New York (see Dargis 2012), the MCU has New York *itself* as its central location: it is where Stark Tower (later known as the Avengers Tower) resides in Manhattan; it is where the Hulk fights Abomination on the streets of Harlem; it is where Daredevil prowls the rooftops of Hell's Kitchen at night; it is where Captain America wakes up after seventy-five years in the ice, confronted by the technology of the modern world in Times Square, and it is the location of the attack of Loki's interstellar army. This has been a key aspect of Marvel's comic narratives since the 1960s and led Peter Sanderson to write, 'This was all in keeping with Stan Lee's intentions for his Marvel revolution: if the heroes had real personalities and realistic problems in life, then they should live in a real city and work in a realistic place' (2007: x). As Matthew Costello correctly argued, 'By placing its heroes in the real city [of New York] Marvel created a closer link between the world of the superheroes and the world of the readers' (2009: 11).[16]

It is my contention that this superhero renaissance offers quite clear articulations of particularly American fantasies in the wake of 9/11 and during the 'War on Terror'. The historical events which are described by this term arguably mark a new phase in America's conception of itself which, in turn, become manifested in many of the cultural texts it produced. This new phase is not to be considered an endorsement of the simplistic aphorism '9/11 changed everything', but

Fig. 4: Two iconic superheroes and global brands come together above the streets of New York in *Spider-Man: Homecoming* (2017) as Robert Downey Jr. returned to the role of Tony Stark for the eighth time since 2008

that these events were used to construct a narrative concerning American identity politics which had been profoundly unstable during the administrations of George H. W. Bush (1989–93) and Bill Clinton (1993–2001), who had each offered their own conceptions of what a *new* American identity might be comprised of after the binarisms of the Cold War narrative ended in 1989. In his book *The End of Victory Culture: Cold War America and the Disillusioning of a Generation*, first published in 1995, Tom Engelhardt wondered what might happen to America at the end of the Cold War, asking, 'Is there an imaginable "America" without enemies and without the story of their slaughter and our triumph?' (2007: 15). When he returned to this idea more than ten years later, in an afterword to a new edition of the same book entitled 'Victory Culture, the Sequel: Crashing and Burning in Iraq', he observed a return to this Manichean mindset through the use of rhetoric and imagery that 'would sound familiar indeed to an older generation of Americans. [George W. Bush's] approach would prove to be so effective, however, only because the images, the language, the history he evoked – including those memories of Pearl Harbor – had already risen chaotically to collective (and media) consciousness as those two great towers in New York came tumbling down' (2007: 306). The 'images, the language, the history' that Engelhardt refers to is the master narrative of the 'War on Terror' that the administration of George W. Bush (2001–9) chose to construct with a sense of moral clarity that regularly evoked the eschatological certainties of both the Cold War and World War II. These comparisons were even offered in the very language employed, from its evocation of the 'Total War' of World War II and the 'axis of evil', to the repeated comparisons between Osama Bin Laden and Saddam Hussein to Adolf Hitler. As Bush said, 'In a second World War we learned that there was no isolation from evil. We learned that some crimes are so terrible that they offend humanity itself. And we resolved that the aggressions and the actions of the wicked must be opposed early, decisively, and collectively, before they threaten us all. That evil has returned, and that cause is renewed' (2001f). These historical analogies are comforting to those who embrace them, but dangerously obfuscatory in their simplistic approaches to complicated geopolitical events.

Just as World War II provided the Bush administration with a framework for its 'War on Terror' narrative, it functions as just as potent a conceptual schema for the mythopoetic drive of the MCU, most significantly perhaps in the iconic figure of Captain America, who, as Robert Weiner suggests, differs from Superman, who 'comes to America, and finds the American Dream – Captain America *is the American Dream*' (2009: 10; emphasis added). Captain America's construction as a synechdocal embodiment of American values and ideals within the MCU is first present in *Captain America: The First Avenger*, a film which re-remembers World War II as it should have been rather than as it was, in an affirmation of

Benedetto Croce's assertion that 'All history is contemporary history' (qtd. in Woolf 2011: 463). The film's recreation of World War II portrays America as a bastion of freedom and liberty in its depiction of a multi-racial American military, a virtuous and righteous war fought for only altruistic reasons against an ignoble enemy, at a time in which disenfranchisement, segregation, internment and lynching were still common across the United States of America, historical truths which do not fit the way the country perceives itself in the twenty-first century and are elided from its popular narratives. Although one might suggest that *The First Avenger* is 'only' a fantasy film and has no obligation to represent World War II accurately, its depiction of the war is not too different to the one offered by such films as *Saving Private Ryan*, *U-571* (2000) and more recently *Fury*, which for the most part, embrace the 'greatest generation' rhetoric that has been pervasive in how America remembers the conflict. World War II is frequently evoked by the lingering presence of Tony Stark's father, Howard Stark (who is portrayed as a young man in *The First Avenger* and the short-lived television series *Marvel's Agent Carter*), and in Afghanistan, before his epiphany, Tony Stark states, 'That's how Dad did it, that's how America does it ... and it's worked out pretty well so far'. The references and allusions to Nazi Germany continue throughout the series and one of the most notable occurs in *The Avengers* when Loki (who Coulson refers to as an 'Asgardian Mussolini' in 'Pilot' (1.01) of *Marvel's Agents of S.H.I.E.L.D.*) visits Berlin in a scene which deliberately evokes the Holocaust (see chapter four).

As trauma discourse became a pervasive aspect of twenty-first-century American (and global) culture, the traumatised hero became absolutely central to the superhero film: Tony Stark is accused of having PTSD in *Iron Man*, but actually shown to have it in *Iron Man 3*; Captain America suffers from some form of psychological trauma when he wakes up in 2011; and Peter Quill aka Star-Lord, Gamora, Drax the Destroyer and Rocket Raccoon, collectively the eponymous Guardians of the Galaxy, bond over their shared trauma which enables them to find an unexpected surrogate family unit. The iconic green-skinned Incredible Hulk seems to be the clearest articulation of these trauma narratives in the MCU films, although whether it is true, as John C. McDowall asserts, 'That Bruce Banner is played by three different actors, in a series of "reboots", speaks to broader uncertainties as to how Hulk as an individual character resonates with post-9/11 audiences steeped in defences of democracy from external threats' (2014: 244) is debatable. This recasting process is not unique to the post-9/11 era, although given the proliferation of remakes and reboots in the new millennial years it is more frequent than ever. However, it is certainly ironic that the one character to be recast so frequently happens to be the one with conspicuous symptoms of dissociative disorder. The evolution of the Hulk post-9/11 is itself a particularly interesting one: from Ang Lee's divisive *Hulk* (2003), to Louis Leterrier's *The Incredible Hulk*, followed by his well-received portrayal in both Joss Whedon films *The Avengers* and *Avengers: Age of Ultron*. What is clear is that these modern iterations of Bruce Banner and his monstrous alter ego (which many have regarded as a projection of his Id) are each as connected to the 'War on Terror' decades as the original was to the nuclear-era anxieties in which he was formed.

Indelibly connected to this, one of the key parameters of the new millennial superhero text is the lean towards realism that the genre embraced in this period, which one might term the veristic turn of the superhero genre post-9/11, a practice often traced to the success of Christopher Nolan's Batman trilogy (2005–12) and even referred to by some as the 'Nolanisation' of the genre (see Seroword 2015). The assertion here is not that superhero texts are realistic in the usual definition of the term, but that they are *grounded* in reality to a much greater extent than the majority of superhero films made before, and that perhaps, as David Goyer the screenwriter of *Man of Steel* and *Batman v Superman: Dawn of Justice* suggested, they 'could happen in the same world in which we live' (qtd. in Dyce 2012). This is not to argue that there was some sort of overnight paradigmatic shift, but that the diegetic worlds the majority of modern superheroes reside in are quite distinct from the fantasies of the Donner-era Superman films or the Burton/Schumacher-era Batman. This turn towards 'reality' is not unprecedented in American genre cinema; as Leo Braudy has observed, many stagnant genres over the years have become revivified with an 'injection, usually of "realism"' (2002: 111). Grant Morrison, the award-winning comic book writer, observed this change and stated:

> Stories had to be about 'real' things. As a result, more and more Marvel Comics, including my own, had scenes set in the Middle East onboard hijacked aircraft. The emphasis veered away from escapist cosmic fantasy, nostalgia and surrealism toward social critique, satire, and filmic vérité wrapped in the flag of shameless patriotism. (2011: 355)

Morrison also maintains that this process is a reaction to the real-world geopolitical arena that is one of the central arguments of this book. He states, 'With no way to control the growing unreality of the wider world, writers and artists attempted to tame it in fictions that became more and more 'grounded', down-to-earth, and rooted in the self-consciously plausible' (2011: 348). Post-9/11 heroes became humanised, flawed and more vulnerable than ever before, facing ethical dilemmas their twentieth-century cinematic counterparts rarely came across. Yet as paradoxical as it sounds, this turn towards realism is itself part of a mythologisation process. As John Fiske reminds us, realism is just as much an aesthetic conceit as other modes of artistic expression: 'The conventions of realism have developed in order to disguise the constructedness of the "reality" it offers, and therefore of the arbitrariness of the ideology that is mapped onto it. Grounding ideology in reality is a way of making it appear unchallengeable and unchangeable, and thus is a reactionary political strategy' (2010: 36).

Despite their intense levels of popularity, American superheroes have provoked wide-ranging disapproval from many quarters. These arguments, some of which are very persuasive, range from the genre being suitable only for children and teens, that superhero texts are simplistic, perpetuate stereotypes, are ethically dubious and tend to embody reactionary values. Indeed, one can find these as early as Frederic Wertham's now much derided *Seduction of the Innocent* (1954). Given that, like the majority of popular American films, the superhero is created and embedded within capitalist, corporate-owned enterprises, it should come as no surprise that the genre habitually adopts and inculcates dominant ideological perspectives on issues of race, gender and sexuality. One of the primary criticisms directed at the MCU has been its lack of diversity in narratives which centralise the experiences and heroism of white heterosexual men. The MCU does feature African-American superheroes (see Falcon, War Machine, Black Panther and Luke Cage, etc) and female superheroes (see Black Widow, Scarlett Witch and Jessica Jones, etc), but they are undoubtedly secondary characters by quite some margin and, in the case of women, they are frequently defined by their vulnerability, whether that is physically, psychologically or emotionally. In the MCU films, characters like Jane Foster, Betty Ross and Pepper Potts are given superficially important professions (astrophysicist, cellular biologist and CEO respectively), but they tend to function only for what they can offer the man who is at the centre of the narrative and whose name is, more often than not, also the title of the film. As in most mainstream blockbusters the women in these films are either sex objects, victims to be saved or rewards for the heroism of their men. If the women *are* superheroes they tend to be given traits and powers characterised as specifically 'female' which are even often encoded into their names, hence the likes of Black Widow and Scarlett Witch. There have been some rare voices who have praised the representation of women in the MCU, like Joseph Walderzak in his interesting essay 'Damsels in Transgress: The Empowerment of the Damsel in the Marvel Cinematic Universe', where he contends

> Rescues become so abundant in a film [*Iron Man 3*], in which Tony is frequently powerless, that it allows for Pepper's heroics to be obscured or perhaps reduced to suggestions of mere tokenism. Yet, any such claims prove fallacious when considered in the context of Pepper's consistent heroism, success, and centrality to the

plot. Her donning of the iron man suit and temporary physical empowerment are not fleeting enactments of tokenism but, rather, conspicuously symbolic forms of the exact type of power she has wielded throughout her appearances in the MCU. (2016: 159)

Walderzak's assertions are problematic to say the least. While it is true Pepper Potts wears the Iron Man suit, it is only in one scene for less than sixty seconds and it is given to her (seemingly to her surprise) by Stark in order to save her and then taken away just as quickly.[17] When she is given potentially superheroic status and powers, these too are removed from her, as are the powers which are accidentally given to Jane Foster in *Thor: The Dark World* released in the same year. In both cases the idea of the girlfriend of the superhero being his physical equal is something seemingly so repulsive within the diegetic frames of the films that they are depicted as having to be removed almost immediately *in order to save them* (see Frankel 2017: 158). Furthermore, Pepper is saved at least once by Stark in each film in the Iron Man trilogy (sometimes twice), is hardly allowed to exist outside of her relationship to the protagonist, and is quite far from central to the plot. We can observe that the MCU promotes a superficial level of female empowerment, at the same time as participating in marginalisation and objectification and therefore functions as a reification of heteronormative patriarchal culture and its values. That is not to say that complications to this do not exist, especially in the TV shows, like Agent Peggy Carter from *Marvel's Agent Carter*, Melinda May and Daisy 'Skye' Johnson from *Marvel's Agents of S.H.I.E.L.D.*, and Jessica Jones and Elektra Natchios from *Jessica Jones* and *Daredevil* respectively. Yet it is important to note that all of these women are impossibly beautiful, slim, heterosexual and (mostly) white. In the cinematic realm, Black Widow has proven central to these debates, and she is undeniably an interesting and formidable character with a complicated history. She is intellectually and physically able (she even bests Hawkeye in *The Avengers*), but in the course of her exploits she often needs to be saved in ways that her male counterparts do not and some aspects of her characterisation have resulted in extreme disapproval from fans (in particular the forced sterilisation referred to in *Avengers: Age of Ultron* discussed in chapter eight).

What are we to make of the fact that in its first fifteen cinematic outings the MCU did not have one film with either a black or a female superhero as the title character? Nor did any of these films feature *a single* LGBT character? This was something that writer-director James Gunn was asked about on the release of *Guardians of the Galaxy: Vol. 2* and his answer was somewhat disingenuous. He stated, 'There's a lot of characters in the MCU and very few of them have we delved into what their sexuality is [sic], whether it's gay or straight or bisexual, we don't really know. So, I imagine that there are probably, you know, gay characters in the Marvel Universe we just don't know who they are yet' (qtd. in Zeldin-O'Neill and Swaby 2016). The 'very few' that Gunn is talking about cannot include the likes of Tony Stark, Bruce Banner, Thor, Steve Rogers, Natasha Romanov, Clint Barton, Scott Lang or Peter Quill, Gamora, Drax or Yondu Udonta, all of whom, are shown to be clearly heterosexual, as are *every single character* that is seen having a romantic relationship onscreen, not just on Earth, but *all over the galaxy*. The closest the MCU comes to a non-heterosexual character, at the time of writing, is in its televisual branch in the form of the long-forgotten Joey Gutierrez (Juan Pablo Raba), a gay construction worker who discovers he is an Inhuman in *Marvel's Agents of S.H.I.E.L.D.* who appeared for six episodes in Season Three before disappearing, and the slightly more interesting, although not exactly central, Jeri Hogarth (Carrie-Anne Moss), who appeared in episodes of *Daredevil, Jessica Jones, Iron Fist* and *The Defenders*.[18]

In this regard it is important to acknowledge then that *Guardians of the Galaxy* was the first MCU film to have a female screenwriter (Nicole Pearlman), *Black Panther*, the eighteenth film in the MCU, the first to have a director of colour (Ryan Coogler) and the first to have a black actor as protagonist (Chadwick Boseman), *Ant-Man and the Wasp* (2018), the twentieth film in the MCU, was the first film to feature a female character in its title, followed by the second the year after, *Captain Marvel* (2019), which was also the first film to be directed by a woman in the MCU, co-directed by Anna Boden and Ryan Fleck.[19]

In spite of this, the MCU, like all popular culture texts, is not monolithic or homogenous in its ideological approaches and the films often emerge as more interesting than they appear on the surface. The ways in which products of the American film industry might be able to offer criticisms of the ideological system they are a part of was explored by Jean-Louis Comolli and Jean Narboni throughout their work, and for the purposes of this book most specifically in 'Cinema/ideology/criticism' (1977). They acknowledge that film is an ISA (Institutional State Apparatus) in the Durkheimian and Althusserian sense that contributes to the reinforcement of hegemonic power systems, but they also experiment with seven groups of classifications which offer varying degrees of interaction with the ideological system that films are intrinsically a part of. From films in which dominant ideologies are perpetuated in 'pure unadulterated form' (1977: 5), to those 'which at first sight seem to belong firmly within the ideology and to be completely under its sway, but which turn out to be so only in an ambiguous manner' (1977: 7) and those which might offer 'an internal criticism … which cracks the film apart at the seams' (ibid.). The contours of the MCU illuminate both the limitations and the potentialities of modern blockbuster cinema, and whether they unambiguously embrace dominant ideological perspectives or are able to offer 'an internal criticism … which cracks the film apart at the seams' is one of the central questions of this monograph. Might the MCU offer counter-hegemonic dramatisations of some of the central paradoxes at the heart of the American experience as the weight of their cognitive dissonance on the frames of their films is too great to bear? Are the criticisms of the Military Industrial Complex in *Iron Man*, *Iron Man 2* and *The Incredible Hulk* superficial or sustained? Is Captain America's disillusionment with contemporary American values a convincing one, or rather just an endorsement of the conservative and nostalgic idea that the past was somehow better than the present? Does the USA PATRIOT Act-inspired narrative of *Captain America: Civil War* offer genuine insights into the era, or does it only provide us with the superficial patina of social criticism which is then erased and elided by the end of the film? Do they, as Slavoj Žižek suggests, articulate 'a trend in contemporary cinema of texts and audiences alike mocking deep-seated beliefs, yet continuing to sustain them, which serves to reify and strengthen dominant ideology'? (2013: 71). All these examples are evidence of Michael Wood's assertion in *America in the Movies, Or, 'Santa Maria, it Had Slipped My Mind'*, that 'Films offer a rearrangement of our problems into shapes which tame them' (1975: 18). *Avengers Assemble! Critical Perspectives on the Marvel Cinematic Universe* explores and interrogates many such contestory moments throughout the MCU, which are often fleeting, but do provide insights into the culture of which they are a formative part. Rather than simply providing texts which enable Americans to 'escape from the very real horrors of international unrest and terrorism whose epic moment was September 11, 2001' (Roberts 2004: 210), the MCU films are actually deeply immersed in and engage with their own historical moment.

Notes

1   Arthur Asa Berger has written that 'there is a fairly close relationship, generally, between a society and its heroes; if a hero does not espouse values that are meaningful to his readers, there seems little likelihood that he will be popular' (1972: 151).

2   As Hayden White suggests, this process is ideological by its very nature: 'What wish is enacted, what desire is gratified, by the fantasy that *real* events are properly represented when they can be shown to display the formal coherency of a story?' (1980: 8).

3   9/11 was also described as a 'mega-event' by Douglas Kellner in his volume *From 9/11 to Terror War: The Dangers of the Bush Legacy* (2003: 41).

4   To put the success of *The Avengers* into perspective, its opening weekend of $207,438,708 was only matched by ten other American films released that year in the entirety of their domestic box office run.

5   Given these sustained and very deliberate allusions to 9/11 it might be seen as strange

that it is not entirely clear if 9/11 actually happened within the MCU. Certainly, there is an extensive American military presence in Iraq and Afghanistan as shown in *Iron Man* and many characters in the series happen to be veterans who served there (Sam Wilson, Frank Castle and Lance Hunter). There are mentions of Osama Bin Laden: one by Aldrich Killian in *Iron Man 3* who contends, 'You simply rule from behind the scenes. Because the second you give them a face, a Bin Laden, a Gadaffi, a Mandarin, you hand the people a target', and another in the Season One finale of *Marvel's Agents of S.H.I.E.L.D.* 'The Beginning of the End' (1.22) where Ian Quinn asks a group of generals he is offering Cybertek technology to, 'How much did you spend to get Bin Laden?' but not, to my knowledge, an explicit mention of 11 September 2001. As real world aside, Tim Fernholz and Jim Tankersley, writing in *The Atlantic*, calculated the cost of killing Bin Laden, for which they factor in the cost of the wars in Iraq and Afghanistan, to have been a phenomenal $3 trillion.

6 Intriguingly, the films do not make it explicitly clear who is the president of the United States at the time of *The Avengers*. White House Press Secretary under Obama, Jay Carney, appears in the film and Obama is mentioned fairly frequently in the Netflix series *Luke Cage*, but in 2013 *Iron Man 3* introduced its own fictional President, Matthew Ellis (William Sadler).

7 In English, Delcroix's article would be titled '*The Avengers*: the Flagship of Obama' and Martínez's 'Obama, as Told by Hollywood'.

8 Stephan Zacharek in an article called 'Shane, with claws and bloodlust to spare' wrote, 'It's as if Mangold – he also co-wrote the script with Michael Green and Scott Frank – had looked into a crystal ball during production and seen a crisp vision of the postelection despair many Americans would be feeling in the early days of 2017. There's no doubt but that *Logan*, with its focus on persecuted outsiders, is tapping the mood of at least half of the country now' (2017: 50). John Patterson's review of *Get Out* in the *Guardian* was titled, '*Get Out*: The First Great Paranoia Movie of the Trump Era' (2017).

9 Much has been written about *Zero Dark Thirty* from this perspective (see Chaudhuri 2014; McSweeney 2014; Westwell 2014; Savage 2015).

10 Phil Strub, entertainment liaison at the Department of Defense, suggested, 'The relationship between Hollywood and the Pentagon has been described as a mutual exploitation. We're after military portrayal, and they're after our equipment' (qtd. in Weisman 2014).

11 Noam Chomsky wrote, 'Among the most elementary of moral truisms is the principal of universality: we must apply to ourselves the same standards as we do to others, if not more stringent ones. It is a remarkable comment on Western intellectual culture that this principle is so often ignored and, if occasionally mentioned, condemned as outrageous' (2007: 3).

12 As David Graham observes, Bill Clinton also used this expression frequently; in fact,

twenty-one times in public while in office (2015).

13 It is important to note that many leaders of other countries feel that they too are on the right side of history. Nikita Khruschev, First Secretary of the Communist Party of Soviet Union, famously remarked on 18 November 1956 to a team of twelve NATO envoys, 'Whether you like it or not, history is on our side, we will bury you!' Similar claims have been made in recent years by representatives of Turkey and the People's Republic of China (see Shambaugh 2016; Walderman and Caliskan 2017).

14 Kirk Douglas said that he once told John Wayne, 'It's all make-believe, John. It isn't real. You're not really John Wayne, you know.' But that John Wayne 'just looked at me oddly. I had betrayed him' (qtd. in Freeman 2017).

15 *Doctor Strange* might be considered an intriguing exception to this as Stephen Strange's final victory over both Kaecillius (Mads Mikkelson) and Dormammu, 'the destroyer of worlds', is achieved by Strange using his intellect.

16 At the premier of *Suicide Squad* David Ayer memorably yelled 'Fuck you, Marvel!' at the crowd (qtd. in Hawks 2016). Other examples of this rivalry were more elegantly constructed, as in the humourous reveal in *The LEGO Batman Movie* that the password to Batman's computer is 'Ironmansucks'.

17 In 2016 Shane Black, the writer and director of *Iron Man 3*, revealed that he had originally planned that the villain of the film would be a woman, but he was told by Marvel executives that the company would prefer a man. He said, 'We had finished the script and we were given a no-holds-barred memo saying "that cannot stand and we've changed our minds because, after consulting, we've decided that toy won't sell as well if it's a female"' (qtd. in Robinson 2016).

18 In this climate fans were often required to create their own narratives about non-heterosexual characters and relationships, many of which explore the bond between Steve Rogers and Bucky Barnes, or Steve Rogers and Sam Wilson. See https://www.fanfiction.net/comic/Marvel/.

19 The only female director of a mainstream superhero film until Patty Jenkins' *Wonder Woman* (2017) was Lexi Alexander who directed *Punisher: War Zone*.

PHASE ONE

'That's how Dad did it, that's how America does it ... and it's worked out pretty well so far': The Stark Doctrine in *Iron Man* and *Iron Man 2*

I think it's no coincidence that since September 11 [2001] superhero movies have really ... starting with Spider-Man people have really gravitated towards these simple good against evil stories. Now, five or six years later, they've tried to capture some of the imagery and anxiety that I know we feel as Americans and then to have the fantasy of this guy that can come in and thoughtfully take care of, or get rid of the bad guys and save the good guys. It's part of the escapism that I think people are looking for as they go to the movies to take their mind off of their problems for two hours.

– Jon Favreau, director of *Iron Man* and *Iron Man 2* (qtd. in Carnevale n.d.)

American contributions to international security, global economic growth, freedom, and human well-being have been so self-evidently unique and have been so clearly directed to others' benefit that Americans have long believed that the US amounts to a different kind of country. Where others push their national interests, the US tries to advance universal principles.

– Jessica Mathews (2015)

The Marvel Cinematic Universe began with the release of Jon Favreau's *Iron Man* in May 2008. A decade and billions of dollars later it is easy to forget that the film was a considerable gamble for the newly-formed studio. While Iron Man had been a major part of the comic world since 1963, he was considered by many to be a 'second string' superhero compared to the iconic figures of Superman, Spider-Man and Batman, each of whom had made an indelible mark on popular culture (see Boucher 2006). The Iron Man property had languished in so-called 'development hell' for a number of decades with actors like Nicolas Cage and Tom Cruise and directors such as Joss Whedon and Len Wiseman attached to the project at various times. When it was announced that the film would star Robert Downey Jr. and be directed by Jon Favreau, industry insiders and large sections of the fan community were surprised. Downey Jr. had long been regarded as one of the most talented and charismatic performers of his generation, but persistent drug- and alcohol-related problems had led to his incarceration and, for a brief time, his virtual exclusion from the film industry. Favreau had established himself as a director with something of an Indie sensibility with his critically acclaimed debut *Made* (2001), produced on a budget of $5 million, before moving into more family-oriented fare like *Elf* (2003) and *Zathura* (2005). *Zathura* might have had elements of science fiction, but there was little in any of these films to suggest that he might be an appropriate choice for a large-scale superhero blockbuster like *Iron Man* with a budget which, including marketing, would be close to $200 million and might well decide the fate of the fledgling film studio.

While Superman and Captain America came of age during World War II and even emerged as the quintessential symbolic figures of American identity and values in that era, Iron Man was originally very much a product and an icon of the Cold War, whom Matthew Costello described as 'the most ardent of Marvel's Cold Warriors' (2009: 63). First appearing in *Tales of Suspense #39* in March 1963, Iron Man is the alter ego of the billionaire weapons manufacturer and playboy Tony Stark. In this first edition, published just two years after President Dwight D. Eisenhower gave his farewell address warning of the encroaching impact of the Military Industrial Complex, six months after the Cuban Missile Crisis, and seven months before the assassination of President John F. Kennedy, Stark is shown demonstrating his hi-tech weapons to the grateful American military in Vietnam when he is kidnapped by the warlord Wong-Chu aka the Red Terrorist who demands that Stark make weapons *for him*. Throughout the 1960s Iron Man battled characters with similarly suggestive names like the Red Barbarian, the Red Ghost, the Mandarin, Bullski the Merciless (Titanium Man) and the Crimson Dynamo in triumphalist narratives which emphasised American technological and moral superiority over the Soviet Union and its allies.[1] Nearly fifty years after this first appearance, the new millennial cinematic reinvention of the character in 2008 has his origin story transplanted to the equally turbulent post-9/11 climate, and the jungles of Vietnam are replaced by the deserts and mountains of Afghanistan.[2] Yet even though the timeframe and location is changed, the events surrounding his kidnapping and the political worldview established are essentially very similar. *Iron Man* embraces the prerequisite kinesthetic pleasures of the blockbuster, but at the same time emerges as something of a contestory mythopoetic fantasy of how America sees itself in both its rejection *and* perpetuation of hegemonic master narratives of American identity.

After the flickering red and white logo of Marvel Studios, one which would become so familiar to viewers over the next decade, *Iron Man* opens with a line of three US military Humvees making their way along a dusty desert road with a panoramic view of snow-capped mountains in the background and a title card which reads 'Kunar Province, Afghanistan'. Setting and opening the film in one of the prime significatory spaces associated with the 'War on Terror' is a striking statement of intent on the part of Favreau and Marvel Studios and a conscious attempt to situate the MCU in something approximating the 'real world' instead of a more generic fantasyscape the likes of which had routinely been the settings of superhero films prior to the twenty-first century.[3] On the film's diegetic and non-diegetic soundtrack 'Back in Black' (1980) by hard rock group AC/DC blasts, a band and a type of music which became heavily associated with the American military in the conflicts in Iraq and Afghanistan. J. Martin Daughtry, the author of *Listening to War: Sound, Music, Trauma and Survival in Wartime Iraq*, even reported that in Iraq American soldiers would 'jack their iPods into the LRAD [long range acoustic devices], and blast AC/DC and other loud music at groups of Iraqis whom they wanted to disperse' (2015: 242).[4]

In the back of one of the Humvees is Tony Stark, not yet Iron Man, still *only* billionaire playboy and genius weapons manufacturer, CEO of Stark Industries and provider of weapons of mass destruction to the appreciative American military. In fact, Stark is in Afghanistan to demonstrate his new 'Freedom Line' of weapons which see him referred to as a man who 'has changed the face of the weapons industry by ensuring freedom and protecting America and her interests around the globe'.[5] Stark cuts an incongruous figure in his immaculately tailored suit, drinking expensive single-malt scotch on the rocks, chatting amiably to US soldiers in battle fatigues who are clearly enamoured by his celebrity status. In 1963 Stan Lee created Stark to be an amalgamation of Howard Hughes and Errol Flynn, but in the MCU era Stark is something of an Elon Musk-type figure with more than a little of Larry Ellison, CEO of Oracle, both of whom made cameo appearances in the sequel *Iron Man 2* (see Lee and Mair 2002: 160).[6]

With Stark's confession to the soldiers in the Humvee that he did indeed sleep with all twelve *Maxim* cover girls (with the help of a set of twins at Christmas), it is immediately apparent how far Downey Jr.'s spontaneously talented and egotistical screen persona has interwoven with Stark's. Favreau made it very clear on several occasions that he felt there was a distinct imbrication between the two, and that this was one of the primary reasons he sought to cast Downey Jr., initially against the wishes of many Marvel Studios executives. Favreau commented:

> The best and worst moments of Robert's life have been in the public eye. He had to find an inner balance to overcome obstacles that went far beyond his career. That's Tony Stark. Robert brings a depth that goes beyond a comic book character who is having trouble in high school, or can't get the girl. (qtd. in Bowles 2007)

Favreau's remarks, of course, are directed at Peter Parker/Spider-Man and by implication the demographic who have traditionally gone to see films of the superhero genre. *Iron Man*, with its cast of several Academy Award winners and nominees like Gwyneth Paltrow, Jeff Bridges, Terrence Howard and Robert Downey Jr., attempts to reconfigure the genre and appeal to a broader audience by the quality of its cast and by situating its narrative in a more grounded and less overtly cartoonish world.[7]

The spirited interactions between Stark and the soldiers are interrupted when their convoy comes under heavy fire from individuals coded onscreen and described in the *Guidebook to the Marvel Cinematic Universe: Marvel's Iron Man* as 'terrorists' (O'Sullivan 2015a: 9). The soldiers he had been chatting to and taking pictures with moments before are all killed in front of him and Stark only manages to scramble away from the vehicle just before it explodes. The sequence is filmed with the frenetic and jarring hand-held camera technique which became an indelible part of cinematic language during the decade in a variety of genres, which I have elsewhere called 'the quintessential new millennial marker of authenticity' (McSweeney 2014: 48). The Kunar Province itself, where the opening of *Iron Man* is set (although it was actually filmed in California), was the location of some of the fiercest fighting in the war in Afghanistan and it was the site of both the Navy SEAL mission Operation Red Wings (June–July 2005) which was later dramatised in the film *Lone Survivor*, as well as the deployment site of the soldiers featured in the documentary *Restrepo* (2010) and its sequel *Korengal* (2014). Stark turns to his right only to see a missile land next to him; he has just enough time to see his own Stark Industries logo written on its side before it detonates.[8]

When Stark comes to he realises he has been captured by the terrorists and is being filmed with a video camera. The formerly cocky and arrogant billionaire is shaken and confused by an intrusion of the Real into his hitherto privileged life. While Stephen Prince in *Firestorm: American Film in the Age of Terrorism* argues that the captors 'are generic bad guys, nonspecific, not identifiable as Islamists' (2009: 62), their beards, masks, posture and the threatening tone of their untranslated words certainly codes them as such and they fit firmly in Jack Shaheen's (1994) taxonomy of Arabs on the Hollywood screen under 'Terrorists'. By May 2008 when the film was released such imagery had become disturbingly familiar to American audiences in the form of several high-profile kidnappings like those of American citizens Daniel Pearl (d. 2002), Eugene Armstrong (d. 2004) and Nicholas Berg (d. 2004). In the first three minutes of *Iron Man*, its protagonist has been shown to be kidnapped and seemingly about to be beheaded in a film designed to not only sell movie tickets, but also action figures and Burger King-branded kids' meals all around the globe. It is an arresting opening for audiences who, prior to 9/11, had been used to the escapist fantasies of superheroes and a disconnection from anything approximating the real world in the cartoonish aesthetic of the Burton and Schumacher-era Batman or the Christopher Reeve-era Superman (1978–87). While this tone would become progressively diluted in the MCU films which followed it over the next decade, *Iron Man* locates the series in a clearly recognisable post-9/11 environment, one that it would remain firmly immersed in throughout the decade and beyond.

The film then abruptly cuts to 'Las Vegas, 36 hours earlier', before Stark's kidnapping and as he is about to be presented with an award by his friend and Department of Defense Liaison, Lt. Colonel James 'Rhodey' Rhodes (Terrence Howard), for Stark's status as a 'visionary, genius [and] American patriot'. The accolade is given to Stark in particular for his role in designing smarter weapons, advanced robotics and satellite targeting for the US military and, presumably,

Fig. 5: The kidnapping of Tony Stark in Afghanistan places *Iron Man* (2008) in a very different world to the majority of superhero films prior to the 2000s

given his visit to the Kunar Province and the film's timeline, for their use in the wars in Iraq and Afghanistan. However, much to the chagrin of Rhodes, who calls Stark a 'real patriot', he is not present to collect the award; instead he is found gambling alongside several beautiful women in the Caesar's Palace casino. As a signifier of both his extreme wealth and his decadence, a deleted scene from the film included on the Blu-ray release shows him place a $3 million dollar bet on a single roll of the roulette wheel. Outside he is confronted by another beautiful woman who is 'pre-screened' by his bodyguard and driver Happy Hogan (played by the film's director Jon Favreau), the *Vanity Fair* journalist Christine Everheart (Leslie Bibb), who challenges him on the ethics of his profession which has seen him labelled not just as a 'visionary' and a 'genius' but also the 'merchant of death' and 'the most famous mass murderer in the history of America'. Stark responds with the justification, 'It's an imperfect world, but it's the only one we've got. I guarantee you, the day weapons are no longer needed to keep the peace, I'll start making bricks and beams for baby hospitals.' Stark's cynicism is absolutely a product of the late-twentieth and early-twenty-first century, but much of his beliefs about the sanctity of both his role and by extension the global role of the United States (the two are presented as intimately connected) comes from the connections he draws between himself and his father, Howard Stark, who had participated in the Manhattan Project (1942–46). Stark repeats a saying that he attributes to his father, 'peace means having a bigger stick than the other guy', but it is one that is really a variation of US President Theodore Roosevelt's 'speak softly and carry a big stick', which some have suggested has defined American foreign policy since the turn of the twentieth century (see Bacevich 2003). With the very first film of the MCU, Marvel Studios sought to create not just a unified cinematic universe, but a history and a mythology which bleeds in and out of the real world when required. Stark's cognitive dissonance that his (and America's) weapons unambiguously keep the peace allows him to rationalise his work as a global arms manufacturer, but in less than thirty-six hours' time, as we have already seen, his worldview will be challenged by a revelatory traumatic event when he comes to experience what Chalmers Johnson memorably classified as 'blowback' in the deserts of Afghanistan in his book *Blowback: The Costs and Consequences of American Empire* (2002).

Despite his pronounced egotism and the fact that he is a weapons manufacturer and very much *of* the establishment, Stark is nevertheless one of the genre's most engaging characterisations. Tom Hart, writing in *New Statesman* in 2015, even observed that on paper Stark's background makes him sound not like a superhero, but actually a *super villain*: 'He's an arms dealer. He's a narcissist. He's a billionaire. He's irresponsible. He's vain. He's arrogant. He has a robotic exoskeleton.'[9] Stark's appeal, to a large extent, is based on his rebellious attitude, charisma and his genius, but also his prodigious wealth and the fact that he lives a glamourous and hedonistic lifestyle that many would aspire to. The Iron Man artist and illustrator Paul Ryan categorised this wish-fulfilment aspect as one of the central tenets of the character's allure. He said, 'Tony Stark was everything little boys wanted to be. He had money, toys and beautiful women. What more could little testosterone-charged adolescents ask for? For that matter, what grown men wouldn't envy Tony Stark?' (qtd. in Mangels 2008: 57). Whether it is his opulent and futuristic Malibu mansion (which happens to contain the bronze sculpture 'L'Homme qui marche' by Alberto Giacometi sold at auction in 2010 for US$107.3 million), his fleet of luxury automobiles or his private airfield and plane (staffed by beautiful stewardesses who happily pole dance for him), he is a veritable paean to consumer capitalism and a vivid personification of the American Dream.[10] Even though he inherited his company and his wealth from his father, the film goes to great lengths to indicate that he is a self-made man and is thus an embodiment of the belief that in America with hard work and ingenuity one can achieve *anything*. Later, Stark's lifestyle and his accumulation of wealth is briefly cast in a different light by the man who saves his life in the Tora Bora-like cave in Afghanistan and shares his prison cell, Ho Yinsen (Shaun Toub), who calls Stark 'a man who has everything *and* nothing'. The loquacious Stark, who usually has a witty rejoinder to everything, has no answer to Yinsen's observation, perhaps, because he knows that it is true.

From the US Stark flies to Afghanistan via Bagram Air Base to demonstrate the 'Freedom Line' to the American military. Like the Kunar Province, Bagram had by 2008 become heavily associated with the 'War on Terror' as the site of the controversial Parwan Detention Facility, where the Bush administration incarcerated those they elected to describe as 'unlawful enemy combatants' rather than 'prisoners of war' in order to abrogate their rights to *habeas corpus* and restrict the application of the Geneva Convention.[11] Favreau's Bagram, however, is modern, bright and well organised, and it is where a group of American and Afghanistani generals eagerly await Stark's weapons presentation during which he asks them, 'Is it better to be feared or respected? I say, is it too much to ask for both?' Even his terminology intimately connects him to the 'War on Terror': 'Find an excuse to let one of these off the chain and I personally guarantee you the bad guys won't even want to come out of their caves.' As Susanne Kord and Elisabeth Krimmer wrote in *Contemporary Hollywood Masculinities: Gender, Genre, and Politics*, 'Finding excuses to invade foreign countries is indeed an apt description of Bush-era foreign policy, and the fact that Tony throws in a portable, fully equipped bar to clinch the deal serves to underline the implied critique' (2013: 107). Indeed, Stark's casual flippancy about the destructive potential of his weapons is because he remains secure in the belief that they are being used *for* the forces of good, that is, *by* the United States of America. Once again Stark connects the American geopolitical landscape of the 'War on Terror' era to World War II and the 'greatest generation' of his father: 'That's how Dad did it, that's how America does it … and it's worked out pretty well so far.' Turning his back to the detonating missile he holds his arms up to the military spectators as the dust rushes towards them in a demonstration of 'shock and awe' for those both within and outside the film's diegesis. Stark's toast – 'To peace' – after the explosion then is an ironic one and he knows it, and in the Humvee shortly before it is attacked he comments, 'I'd be out of a job with peace'.

With this we are returned to the film's prologue, as the narrative then reveals that Tony has been captured by Raza (Faran Tahir), the leader of an Al Qaeda-esque terrorist organisation called the Ten Rings (even their logos are similar), who wants Stark to make WMDs *for him* just as Wong-Chu did in Vietnam back in 1963 in *Tales of Suspense #39.* For the first time Stark is confronted with the reality of his role as a weapons manufacturer as Raza is in possession of hundreds of Stark Industries weapons and Yinsen reports that the Ten Rings are his 'loyal customers' which both evokes and quickly disavows the extensive American military support provided to the Mujahideen in Afghanistan throughout the 1980s in their war against the Soviet Union, in a similar way to how this same act was largely erased from the master narrative of the 'War on Terror'. When Stark refuses, he is tortured and even seems to experience something approximating waterboarding in a reversal of the CIA practices which were much debated post-9/11. Rather than merely alluding to 'the interrogation of al-Qaeda suspects' (Pheasant-Kelly 2013: 148), the film suggests, as many American films and television shows did in this era, that when acts of torture or 'enhanced interrogation' are committed *against* US citizens they are barbaric and monstrous, but when used *by* Americans they are both lawful and effective (see such films as *Act of Valour* and *Taken* [2008] and TV shows like *24*).

It is revealed that Stark is only alive because he has been saved by Yinsen who has placed a battery in his wounded chest to prevent shrapnel reaching it, and his subsequent literal and symbolic change of heart has distinctly metaphoric properties which becomes both a recurrent visual and thematic motif throughout many of his appearances in the MCU.[12] Stark had met Yinsen some years before at a conference in Switzerland (which will later be dramatised in the opening to *Iron Man 3*), but he does not remember him as, in one of many examples of Stark's selfishness, egocentrism and cognitive dissonance, he is capable of ignoring or forgetting everything that does not revolve around him. Yet his kidnap, injury and the revelation that the Stark Industries weapons he designed have been used to kill American soldiers, have shaken the foundations of his worldview, something akin to an intrusion of the Lacanian Real, which Žižek described as, 'the direct experience of the Real as opposed to everyday social reality – the Real in its extreme violence as the price to be paid for peeling off the deceptive layers of reality' (2013: 5–6).[13] It is primarily for these reasons the MCU incarnation of Stark has been referred to the 'perfect post-9/11 hero' by Tom Pollard (2011: 92). Francis Pheasant-Kelly is quite right then to assert, as we will see is the case on many occasions, that Stark (and superheroes like him) becomes a surrogate for the audience and even an embodiment of aspects of national identity, writing that his trauma is reflective of 'the physical and psychological damage inflicted on the United States by 9/11' (2013: 144) (see also Dittmer 2012; Hassler-Forrest 2012). Similarly, Sean Carter and Klaus Dodds argue that the characterisation of Stark demands him to be read as more than simply a character in a film, and they assert that 'Stark's hubris, and more generally that of America as well, was cruelly exposed in Afghanistan' (2014: 56). Stark's transition from fervent believer and 'true patriot' to doubter and critic became a familiar one in post-9/11 cinema (see Hank Deerfield in *In the Valley of Elah*, Douglas Freeman in *Rendition* [2007], Roger Ferris in *Body of Proof* [2008] and Stanley Phillips in *Grace is Gone* [2007]), as many characters such as these experienced traumatic episodes which fundamentally changed their worldview.

Instead of building the missiles that Raza orders him to, Stark constructs a militarised arc reactor (based on his father's original plans, thereby connecting them even further) and the first iteration of the Iron Man suit in a rudimentary and bulky design: revealing Iron Man to be quite literally a product of the 'War on Terror'. Yinsen is a without a doubt a 'good Arab' stereotype, but the brief moment where he tells Stark of his homeland in Gulmira is one of the rare occasions the film pauses to consider those 'precarious lives' that Judith Butler described in *Precarious Life: The Powers of Mourning and Violence* (2004). Yinsen is killed during the escape when he sacrifices himself to ensure Stark's plan works and his final words to Stark are 'Don't waste it … don't waste your life…' in a vivid echo of Captain John Miller's (Tom Hanks) dying words to James Francis Ryan (Matt Damon) at the end of Steven Spielberg's *Saving Private Ryan*: 'Earn this … earn it.' Albert Auster proposed that Miller's injunction was deliberately formulated to reach beyond the frames of the screen and this might also be applied to *Iron Man* and its audiences in the new millennium:

> Although a command directed at Ryan and implicitly his generation that did return from the war, 'earn this' is also a command that resonates far beyond Ryan's generation to the baby boomers and Generations Y and Z. Indeed, every generation of Americans must somehow deserve the sacrifices made at Omaha Beach and other battles in World War II. Captain Miller's dying words make it possible for future generations to turn the Depression/World War II generation into the

embodiment of American ideals of self-sacrifice for the twentieth and twenty-first centuries. (2005: 212)

The films of the MCU return to World War II frequently (literally in the case of *Captain America: The First Avenger*) to provide a moral compass for its diegetic universe and beyond. Yet its depiction of World War II as a 'mythic summit of national virtue' (Hoogland-Noon 2004: 341) is through the comforting prism of the uncomplicated moral binarism it has conveniently been remembered as; of an unambiguous war of good versus evil, fought for justice and honour rather than the complicated geopolitical conflict that it actually was. *Iron Man* places Tony Stark in the more politically divisive '9/11 Wars', but the MCU rewrites these conflicts through the prism of World War II by recreating its supposed moral certainties. In fact, the MCU goes back even further than this by portraying Afghanistan as a metaphorical new millennial frontier, something that Geoff King argued is a prominent feature of contemporary American popular cinema, asserting that, 'Contemporary frontier narratives establish oppositions between the moment of the frontier – sharp, clear-cut, "authentic" – and a dull, decadent or corrupting version of "civilisation"' (2000: 5). It is only on this new frontier, freed from the decadence of his hedonistic lifestyle, that Stark is truly able to find himself and become the man he was destined to be. While Lisa Purse in *Contemporary Action Cinema* asserts that Afghanistan is 'quickly brushed aside' (2011a: 154), this is not entirely true, as its presence lingers and Stark will return there later in the film to prove himself once again in what perhaps is the film's most important sequence, the rescue in Gulmira.

During his escape, Iron Man destroys the Stark Industries weapons stockpile in Raza's camp and then returns home to the US after three months in captivity. To the surprise of his assistant Pepper Potts (Gwyneth Paltrow) and his colleague and mentor Obadiah Stane (Jeff Bridges), he immediately demands two things: an impromptu press conference and an 'American cheeseburger' which he devours onscreen with its Burger King logo rather conspicuously evident to the audience.[14] In a pointed illustration of one of the myriad of ways the life of Downey Jr. has informed the construction of the MCU version of Stark, just a few years before in 2005 he had thanked Burger King for providing him with a major stepping stone on his route to sobriety, but not in ways that would encourage sales of the Burger King *Iron Man* toy range that were produced to coincide with the release of the film:

I have to thank Burger King. ... It was such a disgusting burger I ordered. I had that, and this big soda, and I thought something really bad was going to happen. I thought I might have a heart attack or have to go to the hospital. So I reached out to some people and said: 'I'm really in trouble. I need to curl up for four days and get all this out of my system.' (qtd. in Anon. 2005)

At the conference Stark announces his retirement from the arms manufacturing industry. He tells the crowd, 'I had my eyes opened ... I saw young Americans killed by the very weapons I created to defend and protect them. And I saw that I had become part of a system that is comfortable with zero accountability.' Stark's experience in Afghanistan has led to this epiphany and the recognition of the lives of others, but it is not the lives of *all* others that he has been compelled to recognise.[15] In spite of his apparent sincerity, it is only the lives of young American soldiers lost that he mentions and not the hundreds of thousands killed or displaced in Iraq or Afghanistan during the 'War on Terror', a conflict in which he has been shown to have actively participated in. As Cristobal Giraldez Catalan has observed, 'Nothing is mentioned about the indigenous children and women who have suffered as a result of his weapons trading. Thus, the benevolent Arab is invisible in this film' (2008). In this way, the film establishes a hierarchy and sense of subjectivity that becomes one of the defining tropes of the MCU. So although the film does acknowledge the destructive potential of America's participation in the 9/11 wars, it absolves Stark of personal responsibility as he was apparently unaware of how his weapons were being used and refuses to portray or acknowledge the devastation and destruction perpetrated on those indigenous peoples living in the region.[16] Stark's public apology and partial disavowal of his past is similar to that of Jason Bourne's to his former victims at the conclusion of *The Bourne Supremacy* (2004) and is a tacit recognition of responsibility which provides audiences with the fictional catharsis of the US apologising for its aggressive foreign policy of the era without ever actually doing so during the Bush administration, which was in its last months by the time the film was released.

Interestingly, Stark's change of heart is initially vehemently rejected by those close to him, so far does it depart from their preconceived views about both their role and America's global responsibility and prerogative, which according to Stane, 'keeps the world from falling into chaos'. Yet Stane courts chaos as an iron monger (the name of the character in the comic but never attributed to him in the film) in his sponsorship of what Naomi Klein outlines in her volume *The Shock Doctrine: The Rise of Disaster Capitalism* (2008) released in the same year as *Iron Man*.[17] Stane's reaction is a predictable one given that he is soon after revealed to be the primary antagonist of the film, had even actually ordered the Ten Rings to kidnap and murder Stark in the Kunar Province of Afghanistan, and now declares Stark to be suffering from PTSD in order to take control of Stark Industries. Somewhat surprisingly the sympathetic Pepper Potts and Rhodes react the same way: Potts threatens to quit her job, to which Stark responds, 'You stood by my side all these years while I reaped the benefits of destruction. And now that I'm trying to protect the people I put in harm's way you're going to walk out on me?' Rhodes finds Stark's decision to discontinue making weapons of mass destruction for the American military such a disgusting idea that he asks with derision 'You a *humanitarian* now or something?' and then suggests Stark needs some 'time to get your *mind* right'. Instead of offering a critique of the Military Industrial Complex (MIC), as it seems to do on the surface, Stane is presented as a bad apple and Stark is largely disavowed of responsibility, as Mirrlees has observed: 'The potential of this framing of the U.S. MIC to become a structural critique of militarised capitalism, however, is not realised. *Iron Man* individualises the MIC in Stark and Stane' (2014: 11).[18]

Stark's first real mission as Iron Man in his newly streamlined red and gold Mark III suit (a colour scheme borrowed from the 1932 Ford Flathead Roadster a photograph shows him working on with his late father) is back to the frontier of Gulmira in Afghanistan, the home town of the man who had earlier sacrificed himself to ensure Stark's escape, Ho Yinsen. Stark is compelled to act when he is confronted by images of atrocities committed there and a news report which states:

> With no political will or international pressure, there's very little hope for these refugees. … Around me, a woman begging for news on her husband, who was kidnapped by insurgents, either forced to join their militia … Desperate refugees clutch yellowed photographs, holding them up to anyone who will stop. A child's simple question, 'Where are my mother and father?'

This is certainly how many Americans viewed the conflict in Afghanistan and Iraq during the first half of the new millennial decade. In polls carried out in May 2003 around eighty percent of Americans supported the war; by July 2008 this figure had lowered to sixty-eight percent; just five years later in December 2013 CNN was reporting that the war in Afghanistan was the most unpopular in US history.[19] It is in this scene we see very clearly established what we might call the Stark Doctrine which continues throughout his appearances in the MCU. Repulsed by his own image and how he has been a party to such a thing, he shoots at his reflection, obliterating the glass and then flies to Gulmira hoping to put things right in the first example of the truly global reach of American superheroes throughout the MCU. The subsequent sequence adopts a much more restrained tone than many later MCU films, which become filled with pro-gressively more and more one liners and witty banter, particularly from Stark himself. There are no wisecracks as he takes on Raza's men, shown led by the cruel Abu Bakar (Sayed Badreya). An award-winning Egyptian filmmaker and actor, Badreya, has frequently expressed frustration at the limited roles available in the American film industry for actors of Arabic descent like him. In one interview, he commented, 'Well, I hijack an airplane in *Executive Decision* [1996]. I blew up places in *True Lies* [1994]. I, I kidnapped people. I done everything – bad [sic]' (qtd. in Gladstone and Garfield 2008).[20] The Ten Rings are shown abducting women and children and forcing men to join their ranks, continuing the film's portrayal of Arabs as either vile terrorists or helpless natives with seemingly little room for any characterisations in between (see Shaheen 2009). Stark's rescue of the children in particular evokes the images of Iraq and Afghanistan depicted in many American films about combat in the 'War on Terror' era where their liberation emerges as a symbol of American humanity and beneficence. The scene also offers us one of the best examples of a recurring motif in the MCU, that of the superhero as heroic cowboy figure. In fact, the whole Gulmira episode is a potent manifestation of Geoff King's work on contemporary embodiments of the frontier narrative in Hollywood film, about which he has asserted, 'This version of the renewed frontier experience produces the appearance of enemies that are unambiguously defined and against which a clear definition of virtuous self can be articulated' (2000: 19). In Gulmira, Stark is a lone cowboy metaphorically riding into battle against savages and Rhodes will later (in the sequel *Iron Man 2*) even refer to Stark's 'lone gunslinger act'. The film's cinematography even accentuates these connections in a variety of ways: one remarkable shot directly evokes a western duel with Stark adopting the classic gunfighter pose like something straight out of a John Ford or Sergio Leone film as he faces off against his vindictive dark-skinned adversaries. In *Afghanistan in the Cinema* Mark Graham stated:

> If there is a common denominator in all of these Hollywood films, it would be their obsessive resonance with that curiously American blend of racism, imperialism and misogyny: the frontier myth. Afghanistan fades into a palimpsest beneath this mythic framework of desert plains, lone riders, native tribes, and the merciless struggle for definition between the civilised self and the savage other. (2010: 54)

While *Iron Man* is one of the only films in the MCU to directly portray Afghanistan, this quintessentially American brand of frontier mythology and all the ideological associations contained within it becomes one of the central narrative motifs of the series. In Gulmira Stark dispatches his terrorist enemies just as he had done the communists in the jungles of Vietnam in the early years of his appearances in the comic book, revealing the ideological, moral and military superiority of America just as emphatically now as it did then. Matthew Costello's

Fig. 6: Iron Man as a cowboy figure shown in the classic gunslinger pose, rescuing women and children while bringing American justice to the lawless frontier of Afghanistan in *Iron Man*

comments about Stark's early interventions in Vietnam might be equally applied to those in Afghanistan, as in both Americans are 'virtuous, free individuals on a progressive global mission to defend the world' (2009: 58).

The Stark Doctrine, then, can be seen as an embrace of the idea of the moral superiority of Tony Stark, and by association the United States, and both the responsibility and the prerogative to intervene whenever it is regarded as appropriate or necessary, with little or no consideration of matters of international law. In this way of course, the Stark Doctrine is not too far removed from the Bush Doctrine which was defined by Marvin Astrada in his book *American Power After 9/11* as one of pre-emption, prevention, primacy and democracy promotion, secure in the belief 'that American civilization is the highest achievement and aspiration for mankind' (2010: 2). The MCU embraces this ideology as categorically as Lamont Colucci did in his unselfconsciously-titled *Crusading Realism: The Bush Doctrine and American Core Values After 9/11*, where he suggested, 'The 9/11 attacks provided the impetus, the reason, and the need for a presidency on the road to Assertive Nationalism to embrace the totality of its own beliefs in mankind, God, justice, philosophy and therefore policy' (2008: 173).

The technologically advanced Iron Man suit also promulgates another myth about the pre-eminence of American warfare in the twenty-first century, that its weapons technology is able to target enemies and kill efficiently and morally without any collateral damage, and that those it kills are only ever 'the bad guys' who unequivocally deserve it. This, of course, is a problematic abstention from reality achieved only by erasing the painful truth of the thousands of civilians killed and wounded as the result of American military operations in the 'War on Terror' era. The Gulmira sequence, and indeed the entire film, positions audiences to see events exclusively from Tony Stark/Iron Man's perspective and specifically through his futuristic HUD (head-up display) which is shown to use complicated threat-recognition software, offering us a striking and visceral example of what E. Anne Kaplan described as the 'imperial gaze' in her book *Looking for the Other: Feminism, Film, and the Imperial Gaze* (1997), as Stark/Iron Man successfully dispatches the bad guys, leaving women and children completely unharmed and grateful to their American liberator. Scenes like these reinforce dominant social structures and ideas about America's role in the world, as Dan Hassler-Forest argued in his *Capitalist Superheroes: Caped Crusaders in the Neoliberal Age*: 'Like the uncanny images of smart bombs flying down the chimneys of targeted buildings in the first Gulf War, or the "Shock and Awe" tactics of the Rumsfeld doctrine in the more recent military conflict, Iron Man's use of high-tech weaponry is depicted as something that is possible without civilian casualties' (2012: 183). This is ultra-modern in the case of *Iron Man* (and Iron Man), but the trope is a perennial one in depictions of American heroes and was explored by Lawrence and Jewett about another iconic American hero, the Lone Ranger, who 'never kills anyone. With superhuman accuracy, his silver bullets strike the hands of threatening bad guys – evoking a mere "yow!" or "my hand!". Yet their evil powers are neutralised … the Lone Ranger's powers insure that he inflicts minimal injury' (2002: 40). After defeating all of Raza's men, Iron Man leaves the villainous Bakar to the Gulmirans themselves with a cry of 'He's all yours!' as the camera shows what seems like the whole village moving threateningly towards Bakar in what the film would have us believe is Afghan justice 'having received the American saviour's consent' (Catalan 2008).

In Stark's entirely moral and successful, yet completely unlawful intervention in Gulmira the MCU sets a precedent to which it will adhere throughout the film series to follow, that these intercessions are entirely normalised, depoliticised and even reified. It is also relevant that Stark's extra-judicial role is implicitly endorsed by the military and that the US armed forces are themselves absolved of responsibility for the events in Gulmira which necessitated Iron Man's mission in the first place. In a throwaway line of dialogue as to why the military were not allowed to help the Gulmirans a US soldier explains, 'They [the terrorists] were using human shields. We never got the green light.' Mirrlees has proposed that

> *Iron Man* thereby gives popular credence to the post-9/11 liberal imperialist idea that the US has a responsibility, obligation or mission to use its military's power [to] liberate or save other peoples living in other countries that are suffering from some kind of oppression. As an allegorical figure of the US state, *Iron Man*'s protagonist Stark personifies the US's exceptionalist state of exception. To secure America, Stark must play by his own rules and pursue goals he deems just, free of external constraints of his power. (2014: 10)

After several other adventures, Stark confronts his true nemesis and quasi-father figure Stane, who has taken to wearing stolen and 'improved' Iron Man technology, in the film's spectacular climax, fittingly initially on the Howard Stark Memorial Parkway. This is the first example of what became quite common in Phase One of the MCU, of metallic-suited, CGI creations fighting each other. However, Carter and Dodds saw more to the battle when they wrote, 'Ostensibly this is between Stark's Iron Man and Stane's Iron Monger, but the showdown could also be read as one between competing visions of the role of the US in the world, embodied in these assemblages of body and machine' (2014: 57). To finally beat Stane, Stark is forced to seemingly sacrifice himself in one of the most familiar motifs in American popular culture (and one that is frequently returned to through the MCU); but it is a false sacrifice that will *very rarely* result in the actual death of the hero, and functions primarily as a symbol of his masculinity, heroism and patriotism (see King 2012).

In the film's conclusion, Stark attends another press conference in the same location as the first where he is advised by Special Agent Coulson of S.H.I.E.L.D. (played by Clark Gregg who has little more than a cameo role in *Iron Man*, which will expand to something much more considerable as MCU continues) to read a prepared statement which indicates that Iron Man is in fact Stark's bodyguard, an excuse which allowed the comic book incarnation of Stark to hide his real identity for decades. However, Downey Jr.'s version of Stark, perhaps due to the character's narcissistic tendencies, is unable to prevent himself revealing the truth to the world, and the film ends abruptly with his delivery of the now iconic line '*I am Iron Man*', thereby establishing a precedent in the MCU that very few of their superheroes (unlike their DCEU counterparts) will have a secret identity and the usual secret identity narratives play very little part in the series.[21]

It is clear to see that the film is deeply immersed in the tumultuous geo-political arena of the 'War on Terror' era in which it was made, as much as Nolan's genre-defining Dark Knight trilogy. *Iron Man* is much more than a disposable pop culture text and offers a rich set of paradoxes which, in many ways, are characteristic of the ideological discourse of the era. It simultaneously criticises the military industrial complex and by extension US hegemony and aggressive foreign policy, but at the same time it rehabilitates the role of a more nuanced use of American technology and military in the form of Tony Stark's Iron Man suit and his humanitarian interventions in Afghanistan. Therefore, Hassler-Forest is quite correct in his assertion that the film offers 'a particular fantasy of militarized agency' which 'trades casually in these familiar Orientalist stereotypes' (2012: 95), and yet Pheasant-Kelly is equally correct to advocate that its narrative attempts 'the questioning of US political ethics after the events of 2001' (2013: 144).[22] Catalan's assertion that 'The social texture of *Iron Man* presents a

particularly disturbing fantasy during this time of American military occupa-
tion. On a daily basis one hears of a rising Iraqi or Afghan civilian death count
and extraordinary devastation; *Iron Man* transforms these tragedies into live
cinema spectacle' (2008) is as accurate as W. Bryan Rommel-Ruiz's observation
in *American History Goes to the Movies* that the film is

> more than a simplistic comic book narrative about the transformation of playboy
> and weapons designer Tony Stark into a superhero, *Iron Man* presents a complex
> story about American involvement in the Afghanistan War. Favreu's [sic] film
> is thus a provocative story about contemporary American foreign policy in the
> aftermath of September 11, and the longstanding debate regarding advancing
> American interests or American ideals in global geopolitics. (2011: 257)[23]

That the film might provoke such paradoxical reactions is, perhaps, a confirma-
tion of its efficacy and the unresolved contradictions which are often a hallmark
of contemporary Hollywood film. As the first film in the MCU, *Iron Man* establishes both a comprehensively realised diegetic universe and a vivid engagement
with the era in which it was made. It established the nascent MCU as being set
in the 'real world' rather than a fantastic and cartoonish landscape, in a reality
where 9/11 and the 'War on Terror' *actually happened*. Yet the kinesthetic pleasures of the MCU elide and obfuscate any sustained counter-hegemonic content
in its reiteration of American exceptionalism.

'God bless America and God Bless Iron Man!': The Hubris of Tony Stark in *Iron Man 2*

> Prone to self destructive tendencies … text book narcissism … recruitment as-
> sessment for Avengers Initiative. Iron Man, yes … Tony Stark, not recommended.
> – From the report compiled by Natasha Romanoff (Black Widow)
> on Tony Stark in *Iron Man 2*

Just two years after the remarkable financial and critical success of *Iron Man*,
which made in excess of $600 million worldwide and was the second larg-
est domestic box office earner of 2008 (behind another superhero film, *The
Dark Knight*), John Favreau and Robert Downey Jr. returned with *Iron Man 2*,
the third film in the MCU after *The Incredible Hulk* (explored in chapter two).
Despite the success of *Iron Man*, the longevity and stability of the MCU in 2010
was by no means guaranteed.[24] *Iron Man 2* bears all the hallmarks of a modern
sequel in the blockbuster age: from its expanded production budget (from $140
to $200 million), significantly larger cast of characters, to its more extensive use

of special effects and even greater levels of action and spectacle. While it does retain aspects of the character development and spontaneity which had endeared many to the original film, there is a distinct sense that it went into production without a completed script, something that is becoming more and common in an age where release dates are often announced before a screenplay is even written.[25] On the whole, *Iron Man 2* was well received by the critics on release and it was even more financially successful than its predecessor ($623 million worldwide), but there has been a subsequent backlash regarding the film's perceived failures to the extent where it has become regarded as the one of the lesser entries in the MCU to date. Richard Corliss described it as 'a cluttered, clattering toy story' (2010) and Kirk Honeycutt as a film full of 'noise, confusion, multiple villains, irrelevant stunts and misguided story lines' (2010). Corliss and Honeycutt raise valid points, but just like the first film and the rest of the MCU, *Iron Man 2* is profoundly connected to the era in which it is made and it develops many of the thematic motifs established in *Iron Man*. It continues to explore and negotiate, sometimes in quite an explicit fashion, perceptions of national identity through the figure of Tony Stark/Iron Man, in particular aspects of military agency and masculinity through the representation and ultimate erasure of vulnerability and the reaffirmation of hegemonic male power. As its predecessor did, it introduces elements of criticism that are once again negated in favour of a Slotkin-esque redemption through violence narrative the likes of which has characterised popular American cinema for decades. Instead of Obadiah Stane's quasi-father figure antagonist, *Iron Man 2* presents us with two dark mirrors of Tony Stark for Iron Man to do battle with: the maverick and prodigiously talented Russian weapons inventor Anton Vanko (Mickey Rourke), who has a history with the Stark family, and the oleaginous Justin Hammer (Sam Rockwell), CEO of Hammer Industries, who has replaced Stark as chief weapons advisor to the US military after Stark's retirement in the first film. The screenwriter of *Iron Man 2*, Justin Theroux, described both of them as being a 'shadow version' of Tony Stark (see Sciretta 2010; Weintraub 2010). At the same time as this, the film explores Stark's relationship with his deceased father, the Stark family legacy (and by extension an American legacy) and the idea that Tony Stark's most formidable enemy might not be a rival weapons manufacturer, but actually himself.

The film begins six months after Stark revealed to the world that he was Iron Man at the climax of the first film and in the meantime he has become 'the world's first celebrity superhero' (O'Sullivan 2015b: 7), heralded as a saviour by much of the world (a newspaper headline reads 'Iron Man stabilizes East-West Relations'), and awarded *Time* Magazine's prestigious 'Person of the Year'.[26] The film's opening shot shows him leaping out of an airplane dressed in the new Mark IV suit to the sound of yet another AC/DC song, this time 'Shoot to Thrill'

(1980), as explosions burst all around him. The audience perhaps wonders if he is back in Afghanistan once more, before he lands … revealing himself to actually be in Flushing Meadows, New York and the star attraction of the Stark Industries Expo being held for the first time since 1974. Standing at centre stage, flanked by beautiful dancing girls in matching red, white and blue Iron Man outfits known as the 'Ironettes', the adoring crowd chant his name over and over, as he outlines his hubristic vision of the future in a world in which Iron Man replaces Uncle Sam as the symbol of America.

> I'm *not* saying I'm responsible for this country's longest run of uninterrupted peace in 35 years! I'm *not* saying that from the ashes of captivity, never has a phoenix metaphor been more personified! I'm *not* saying Uncle Sam can kick back on a lawn chair, sipping on an iced tea, because I haven't come across anyone man enough to go toe to toe with me on my best day! It's *not* about me. It's *not* about you, either. It's about legacy, the legacy left behind for future generations.

Iron Man had already considered what Stark's legacy might be through Ho Yinsen telling him 'What you saw is your legacy Stark, your life's work in the hands of those murderers' and Tony's comment to Stane, 'I don't want a body count to be our legacy', but this idea is placed at the centre of *Iron Man 2*.[27] With the pyrotechnics, the rockets, explosions, shot and originally screened in IMAX, one might argue that the Expo is a manifestation of Stark's prodigious ego and, while he protests that the Expo is *not* about him, Pepper tells him that it is his 'ego gone crazy' and he seems to have forgotten many of the insights Yinsen revealed to him in the caves of Afghanistan in the first film. This convenient process of Stark forgetting the lessons of the previous films will become one of

Fig. 7: The Stark Expo in *Iron Man 2* (2010) emerges as a manifestation of Stark's hubris and his very particular vision of America's future

the essential tenets of his portrayal in the MCU, as at the beginning of each subsequent film Stark seems to return to his pre-Afghanistan, pre-epiphany state, perhaps in an acknowledgement that audiences prefer the arrogant and cavalier Stark, which is undeniably more interesting than his 'humanitarian' incarnation. Stark's reset is reminiscent of the device formerly used in sitcoms in which each new episode, roughly speaking, disregards the events of the previous, a process which is commonly referred to as a 'total reset' (see Newman and Levine 2011) and described as 'an existential circle' by Mick Eaton (1978: 74).

Stark interrupts his speech to play a recorded message from his father taken from the last Stark Expo in 1974. Even though Howard Stark has been dead since 1991 (in circumstances that will be more fully explored in *Captain America: Civil War* six years later), as we have seen, he is very much a part of his son's life: in the arc reactor that sustains him and even the choice of the colour of the iconic Iron Man suit.[28] Howard announces: 'Everything is achievable through technology, better living, robust health and for the first time in world history: the possibility of world peace.' Like his father, Tony seems to aspire to world peace, but his vision is a very particular one which sees US power and hegemony perpetuated around the globe with Iron Man as its national and corporate figurehead. Tony's relationship with his long-dead father is central to *Iron Man 2* and to the film's vision of American exceptionalism and scientific progress in what Jason Dittmer has observed as the superhero functioning as 'as an icon of American technological innovation and the hierarchies of domination it permits' (2010: 122).

Stark's consideration of his family legacy is more relevant to him than it might have been due to the fact that the chemical Palladium (Pd), which powers the miniature arc reactor in his chest and therefore keeps him alive, has proven to be toxic to his system and is slowly poisoning him to death. The narrative which follows will present him with what seems on the surface to be a challenge to this sense of hubris and self-importance which is evocatively portrayed in these opening scenes. Yet Stark's and the film's cognitive dissonance proves revealing both of the cultural climate in which the film is made and the prevailing ideological perspectives consolidated by the MCU. The film will show him to be arrogant, misguided and dangerous *but* he remains the film's largely unambiguous hero; it is to him we remain ideologically sutured and his irresponsible behaviour is ultimately endorsed and even celebrated throughout the narrative of *Iron Man 2* which will conclude with him vanquishing the bad guys, getting the girl and even receiving a medal from the US government by the end credits.

After his dramatic appearance at the Expo, Stark is called to testify before the Senate Armed Services Committee in Washington for the Weaponized Suit Defense Program Hearings which are to decide the fate of the Iron Man suit. In scenes reflective of real-life American military concerns about the technological progress of rival nations, the committee, presided over by the sardonic Arlen Spector-like Senator Stern (Gary Shandling), expresses worries that US power will be superseded by other nations appropriating technology similar to Stark's and because Stark is a private citizen he is not to be trusted to act in the best interests of the nation, and therefore wants to requisition the Iron Man technology and place it in the hands of the US military. The rival weapons contractor Justin Hammer suggests that 'Stark has created a sword with untold possibilities and yet he insists it's a shield, he asks us to trust him while we cower behind it'. Stark refuses, arguing that the Iron Man is not a suit but rather a 'hi tech prosthesis' and, in a particularly American declaration, that it is a *part* of him, 'I am Iron Man, the suit and I are *one*'. Even though this scene is played primarily for comedic effect its real-world resonances are palpable, evoking fears of an intrusive USA PATRIOT Act and also Colin Powell's testimony to the United Nations in 2003 which was broadcast live on C-SPAN as Stark's testimony here is shown to be too.[29]

Stern and Hammer argue that there might very well be other nations developing similar technologies and, in a video recording, two parts of the so-called Axis of Evil – Iran and North Korea – are shown. Initially the video images showing these threats seem to be very real and Hammer states (in language which echoes Powell's claims in 2003), 'This has been corroborated by our allies and local intelligence on the ground indicating that these suits are quite possibly, at this moment, operational'. That is until Stark commandeers the screens with the aside 'time for a little *transparency*', to reveal that Iran and North Korea are actually decades from manufacturing similar technology and that Hammer himself was even working *with* these rogue states, a term returned to frequently by the Bush administration. The defining testimony in front of the committee actually comes from Stark's friend James Rhodes who walks into the room with his back to the screen, momentarily hiding the fact that he is played by a different actor after contract disputes saw Don Cheadle replace Terrence Howard who had played the character in *Iron Man*. Cheadle's first line as Rhodes is directed both at Stark within the film's diegesis and audiences outside the frames of the screen: 'It's me, I'm here, deal with it.'[30] Rhodes' unwilling testimony, his reluctance to prematurely 'reveal these images to the general public at this time' and the fact he is forced by Stern to read only a brief extract out of context from his extensive report evokes and even satirises Powell's hearing in its language and its use of footage to show how insubstantial evidence is used in an attempt to sway public opinion, which led to Pheasant-Kelly's assertion that the scene 'parodies the justification for the invasion of Iraq' (2013: 149). Rhodes reads, 'As he does not operate within any definable branch of government, Iron Man presents a potential threat to the security of both the nation and to her interests' and while this is shown to be true on a number of occasions, it is thoroughly swept aside by the film's glamourisation of Stark and his narrative arc of redemption through violence.

The audience is positioned to cheer on Stark's defiant attitude through his belittling of the odious Stern (who is later revealed to be a HYDRA agent in *Captain America: The Winter Soldier*), despite Stern's demands that an unaccountable and unelected CEO in possession of a WMD be under some sort of control being entirely reasonable; but the way the events are *framed* they appear to be an affront to liberty and justice. Yet they are the very same demands made in the context of *Captain America: Civil War* six years later in which Tony Stark will reverse his opinion and agree not only with the intervention of the US government, but also the United Nations. Stern is the first in a long line of venal government officials throughout the MCU which practically demands that Stark (and his fellow superheroes) takes the law into his own hands in a moral crusade of unlawful but righteous vigilante justice. Stark's profoundly libertarian assertion that he has 'privatised world peace' and his pointed refusal to comply with the government's demands saw him labelled as a 'Randian hero' by Kyle Smith in *The New York Post* (2010) and embraced by Hugo Schmidt in a review at *The Atlas Society* titled 'A Capitalist Superhero?' (2010).[31]

The film's other primary villain is also a dark mirror of Tony Stark, the disgraced Russian scientist Ivan Vanko (who had been imprisoned for fifteen years for attempting to sell plutonium to Pakistan, which does not seem too different to Stark's company selling WMDs to the terrorist network, the Ten Rings), introduced in the film's credits sequence. Mickey Rourke brings his customary intensity to the role which saw him spend time in the infamous Butyrka prison in Moscow as part of his preparation (see Warmoth 2009). Like Tony, Vanko is influenced by his own father, Anton, who was a research scientist alongside Howard Stark after the end of World War II, but was deported in 1963 after being accused of espionage. In spite of his flaws (which are explored more extensively in *Marvel's Agent Carter*), Howard Stark is seen as an example of a maverick American creative genius, but the only equivalent the film offers us from Russia is morally bankrupt. Nick Fury (Samuel L. Jackson) later comments, 'Anton saw it [the arc reactor technology] as a way to get rich'. Vanko senior's dying words to his son are 'That should have been you' and Ivan seeks revenge on the family he thinks robbed him of his birth right as Favreau offers him up as a half-hearted image of what Stark perhaps could have become had his circumstances been different.[32] This use of Russia in the film is the first of many throughout the MCU which frequently reverts to simplistic Cold War binarisms transplanted into the 'War on Terror' narrative in which American film once again began to portray Russia as a growing threat to global peace and security in films like *Salt* (2010), *A*

Good Day to Die Hard (2013) and *Jack Ryan: Shadow Recruit* (2014) (see Kurutz 2014). Russia plays an insidious and prominent role as early (chronologically speaking) as Dr Johann Fenhoff and Dottie Underwood's plan to use the Howard Stark-invented 'Midnight Oil' to wreak havoc on New York in 1946 in *Marvel's Agent Carter*; in the Russian separatists that launch an ICBM at the United States in a flashback to 1989 in *Ant-Man*; in Black Widow's traumatic experiences in the Red Room orphanage, in Georgi Luchkov the crooked and gullible Russian general at the start of *The Avengers*; in the heroin and human trafficking criminal exploits of the Ranskakov brothers in *Daredevil*; or the Inhuman assassin general Androvich who tries to assassinate the Russian Prime Minister Dimitri Olshenko in *Marvel's Agent's of S.H.I.E.L.D.* in (3.13) 'Parting Shot', to name just a few. Each are characterised either by their perfidy, maniacal nature or their buffoonishness, and sometimes even a combination of all three.

Stark and Vanko finally come face to face at the Monaco Grand Prix where the Russian attacks him with seemingly the whole world watching live on television in what is suggested to be a terrorist attack by MSNBC which reports that Vanko is a 'terror suspect' and leads to the United States Department of Homeland Security raising the terror alert from yellow to red. Just a few days before at the committee hearing Stark had promised the American public that no nation had any technology comparable to his own advanced Iron Man suit, but Vanko's two electric whips powered by a miniature arc reactor are *exactly* like Stark's. Tony manages to defeat him, but Vanko informs him that he had intended for all this to happen and that his very appearance would be enough to bring Stark down and ruin his legacy. Stark is ignorant about Vanko and his family name and even remarks he could have sold his technology to 'North Korea, China, Iran'. He even casually gives Vanko advice about how to improve it (which his adversary actually adopts later), but Vanko tells him: 'You come from a family of thieves and butchers, and like all guilty men, you try to rewrite your history, to forget all the lives the Stark family has destroyed. ... If you could make God bleed, people would cease to believe in him. There will be blood in the water, the sharks will come.' There will be many characters who make similar criticisms of Stark's actions throughout the MCU (see Pietro and Wanda Maximoff from *Avengers: Age of Ultron*, and Aldrich Killian in *Iron Man 3*, among others), but most of these assertions are negated by coming from villains, or else they are swept away by the narrative of the films. Yet many of them, including Vanko's, have an element of truth about them. Vanko explicitly connects Iron Man and heroes like him to mythology in his comment that Stark has come to be a godlike figure to many and that by having his vulnerability revealed for all to see, the public will reject him and what he represents. But the idea that our heroes might truly be vulnerable or even responsible for their actions is too problematic, and every single film in the MCU without exception concludes with the reconstitution of masculine authority and patriarchal normalcy.

When Stark hears that Vanko's father, Anton, had once worked alongside his own he dismisses it, just as he forgot about Yinsen's teachings, and Pepper's birthday, and did not concern himself about weapons being made in his name that were being used in conflicts all around the world. However, Vanko's warning that the 'the sharks will come' is quickly proven correct as Stark's reputation and that of Stark Industries is severely damaged. First Senator Stern appears on MSNBC almost crowing that 'the genie is out of the bottle and this man has no idea what he's doing. He thinks of the Iron Man weapon as a toy!', then television hosts Christine Amanpour on CNN and Bill O'Reilly during *The O'Reilly Factor* (FOX News, 1996–2017) are severely critical of him: Amanpour asks, 'His continuing erratic behaviour may lead many people to ask themselves, can this man still protect us?' and O'Reilly states, 'When Mr Stark announced he was indeed Iron Man he was making a promise to America. We trusted that he would look out for us. He obviously did not.'

This pressure on Tony combined with his deteriorating health turns him to alcohol in a nod to the famous arc in the Iron Man comics known as 'Demon in the Bottle' (*The Invincible Iron Man, #120–29, 1979*), culminating in a birthday party scene in his Malibu mansion which he sincerely believes may be his last. Fully dressed as Iron Man during the celebration, he urinates in his suit and uses his repulsor beams to entertain the beautiful women in the crowd by shooting at champagne bottles and watermelons. The scene is primarily played for laughs, very differently to its much darker dramatisation in the comic, where it is one of the events which enabled Stark to realise he is, in fact, an alcoholic. It is this irresponsibility, combined with Vanko's revelations, that lead the government to finally forcefully intervene and decide to remove the Iron Man technology from Stark. Their chosen representative is Stark's best friend Rhodes who tells Tony, 'You don't deserve to wear one of these' (a line that Tony Stark will repeat almost verbatim to Captain America at the conclusion of *Captain America: Civil War* about his shield). The morning after, having hit rock bottom (or as close as a film made for families will allow its protagonist to go) Stark is handed a briefcase by Nick Fury that belonged to his father with which, he is informed, he will be able to solve his health problems. In a moving and understated scene Tony interacts with film footage of the long-dead Howard Stark, the man he had always thought had no real feelings for him but who he now sees telling him: 'What is and always be my greatest creation … is you.' Tony uses his father's research to create a new element, which Howard had discovered many years before, but due to the limitations of the technology of his time could not physically build. The new element is shown to generate more than enough power to run the reactor in Tony's chest and is not corrosive to his system, saving his life and allowing him to continue to be the Iron Man.[33]

The film's two villains, Hammer and Vanko, work together as *Iron Man 2* builds to its climax, Hammer using his extensive riches, influence and resources to get Vanko out of prison in order to make weapons for him, not in a decrepit Moscow flat, but using state of the art technology in Hammer's New York laboratory. Just as Tony is obsessed with his legacy so is Hammer, and while Hammer says he wants Vanko's technology to put him 'in the Pentagon for the next twenty-five years', it seems that his real reason is far closer to Vanko's own, to humiliate Stark and destroy his reputation, leading him to remark, 'you go after his *legacy*, that's what you kill'. The new Hammer drones, secretly made by Vanko, are displayed at the Stark Expo where the film had begun, in a presentation called 'In defence of peace' which continues the motif of American power being used globally in the name of protection, but here shown as being perverted by the likes of the selfish Hammer as opposed to the now selfless Stark.[34] As thirty-two of the new drones take the stage, each said to cost $123.7 million dollars, there seems to be approximately four billion dollars' worth of military hardware as part of the presentation, even without the arrival of the centrepiece, the redesigned Iron Man suit, piloted by Rhodes and now going by the more aggressive name of War Machine, featuring even more destructive weaponry than Stark has (see Axe 2011).[35] As one might expect, the presentation soon goes awry as Vanko commandeers the drone technology, and even Rhodes' suit, ordering the machines to attack the crowd. The scene is significant because it marks the start of the practice of superheroes fighting unambiguous hordes of computer-generated bad guys (which will be replicated frequently in the form of Chitauri, Ultron's robots and Dark Elves, among others). In another trend that will become common throughout the MCU, while there is much chaos, shooting and explosions, not a single civilian is shown to be killed or even hurt.[36]

Rhodes and Stark put aside their differences for the greater good (Rhodes even apologises to Stark, 'I should have trusted you more') and unite to fight Vanko as the film eschews character interaction and replaces it with an extended action scene as the genre demands, again between battling men in CGI metallic suits. As one critic commented, 'As for the actual grand finale, Downey Jr. and Cheadle seem like they're already network gaming the PS3 release instead of facing any actual threat' (Pinkerton 2010). Despite his litany of poor judgement calls and his egregious use of the Iron Man suit, on defeating Vanko Stark is congratulated by all those around him including being rewarded with the consummation of his relationship with Pepper (who is saved at the end of the film by Stark as she was at the end of *Iron Man*) and even given the Army's Distinguished Service Medal, one very rarely given to civilians, by Senator Stern in a dénouement which endorses and legitimises Stark's vigilantism and provides us with a perfect example of what Guy Westwell has suggested was a common trait in post-9/11 films which function 'in service of hegemonic renewal' (2014: 14).[37] The two *Iron Man* films at the start of the Marvel Cinematic Universe establish patterns of how the series interacts with American ideology and society. They both endorse profoundly America-centric views of the world, what Judith Butler called a 'first-person narrative' (2006: 7), but inconsistencies and paradoxes sometimes remain visible. Even though Stark is undoubtedly a hero, he is also profoundly selfish and undeniably immature, even after his epiphany. He is certainly a far cry from the virtuous Superman in either the Donner version, the rebooted Singer, or even the conflicted but morally pure character featured in Snyder's *Man of Steel*. It is maybe for these reasons that Tony Stark/Iron Man (and also the flawed figure of Batman) connected with audiences at a time when cinematic incarnations of Superman seemed to struggle. Might audiences be forced to acknowledge *Iron Man*'s refusal to recognise the lives of others in its overwhelming drive to glamourise Tony Stark's transformation and heroic status? Or is this painful reality swept away in the film's exhilarating and sustained justification of extra-judicial violence? Might they begin to question Stark's pronounced recklessness and hubris in *Iron Man 2*? Or is this too erased in the film's self-congratulatory and exculpatory narrative of redemption through violence? Jon Favreau's opinion about the politics of *Iron Man* and *Iron Man 2* were revealed in an interview with Edward Douglas at *SuperHeroHype*:

> We really went out of our way to try to avoid make (sic) it polarizing as far as what the politics represent, but instead try to maintain an emotional reflection of the fear of our times, and then to have Iron Man step in and not be somebody who could offer a simple solution, but instead be a guy who seemed singularly suited for the challenges of our day. A guy who didn't represent overwhelming military might, but also didn't represent pacifism or isolationism, instead a guy who could go in as a one-man army and separate the good guys from the bad guys and attack the people who are bringing the justice to the world while preserving innocent human life and leaving a very small military footprint where we're involved, so it's sort of an unrealistic fantasy. (Qtd. in Douglas 2008)

Even when *Iron Man 2* ends though, it does not *really* end. Just as the first *Iron Man* concluded with a post-credits teaser introducing Nick Fury with the now iconic line of dialogue, 'Mr. Stark, you've become part of a bigger universe. You just don't know it yet', informing Tony Stark and the audience that *Iron Man* was the beginning of a much larger experiment and that other superheroes existed in this diegetic world, the films which followed it would not just be sequels, but a part of a coherent and developing shared universe often with their own mid-credits and post-credits 'tag' or 'stinger' which have become such a part of the MCU experience that audiences have, as Matthias Stork asserted, become 'almost Pavlovian trained' (2014: 84) to expect them.[38] In 2008 this was virtually unheard of, but as the years progressed they have become a relatively common part of the blockbuster experience. They participate in the creation of this shared universe by sometimes introducing the next film (see Loki's plan in the *Thor* stinger), or new characters (see Thanos in the tag attached to *The Avengers*, Quicksilver and Scarlett Witch at the end of *Captain America: The Winter Soldier*, or the Collector at the end of *Thor: The Dark World*), unifying characters and events (as in Tony Stark's appearance at the end of *The Incredible Hulk*, Bruce Banner's at the end of *Iron Man 3* and Thor's at the end of *Doctor Strange*), or leave the audience with memorable vignettes that sometimes lead to the creation of popular memes (as in the Shawarma scene at the end of *The Avengers* and dancing baby Groot at the end of *Guardians of the Galaxy*). This reached a new level in 2017 with the inclusion of *five* separate post-credit scenes in *Guardians of the Galaxy: Vol. 2*, plus additional moving portraits during the credit scroll (one of which featured a dancing Jeff Goldblum who would appear as the Grandmaster in *Thor: Ragnarok* later that year), which encompass all of the variations described above. What they all demonstrate, without exception, is that the MCU films are not single entities, nor are they sequels in the traditional sense of the term, rather they are part of a cohesive and developing whole which encourages participation (and, very importantly, multiple viewings) with film franchises to a degree not asked before of audiences. The post-credits teaser of *Iron Man 2* features only four words of dialogue and shows Agent Coulson arriving in New Mexico, the 'Land of Enchantment', overlooking a large crater in the middle of which sits Mjölnir the mythical hammer from Norse legend. With Coulson informing Nick Fury, 'Sir, I found it' he teases the appearance of Thor, the God of Thunder in a film that was released almost exactly a year later on 6 May 2011 and which is one of the subjects of the next chapter.

Notes

1   Stan Lee later regretted the pronounced anti-communism of the early Iron Man stories (see Wright 2003: 223). As the 1960s progressed the comics questioned Tony Stark's (and by extension America's) motives and by the 1970s he was expressing doubts about Vietnam, US foreign policy and his own role in the Cold War.

2   Adi Granov has observed, 'The story of Iron Man has been rebooted a few times to make him more relevant to the times ... unfortunately the political climate in the world has always been able to suit the threat that originally served as the backdrop for

the comic. Weapons and those who design them seem as controversial and relevant today as they were during the Cold War, so it's not too much of a stretch to transpose Tony Stark from the 1960s into today' (qtd. in Mangels 2008: 109).

3   In the novelisation by Peter David, Tony Stark's is shown to muse, 'Not for the first time, he wonders why in the world anyone would willingly live here, to say nothing of using vicious terrorist tactics to defend the right to do so. ... If anything, people should be fighting for the opportunity to get the hell out of there' (2008: 2).

4   Jon Favreau suggested the reason they used this music was, 'We had to find the attitude and that's why we paid through the nose for heavy metal music that you've never seen in another superhero movie. That's why we open with 'Back in Black'. That's why it's Robert Downey Jr. This had to have attitude and be rock 'n' roll and in your face' (qtd. in Douglas 2008).

5   Several military operations in the 'War on Terror' era had the word 'freedom' attached to them. Aside from 'Operation Enduring Freedom' (2001–14) which was the official name adopted by the US government for the Global War on Terrorism itself, 'Operation Falcon Freedom' (December 2004) and 'Operation Bell Hurriyah' (October 2007) which when translated from Arabic means 'Enjoy Freedom'.

6   Jon Favreau wrote the *Time* Magazine '100' entry for Elon Musk in 2010. In March 2017 Musk issued a suitably Stark-like proposal that he would solve the energy crisis in South Australia within one hundred days or do it for free (see Hunt 2017).

7   At the time of the release of *Iron Man* Jeff Bridges had been nominated four times for an Academy Award; he won for *Crazy Heart* (2009). Gwyneth Paltrow won for *Shakespeare in Love* (1998), Terrence Howard was nominated for *Hustle & Flow* (2005), and Robert Downey Jr. was nominated for *Chaplin* (1993) and later for *Tropic Thunder* (2009).

8   The opening convoy ambush scene described here was filmed between 3–5 April 2007. Just a few days later on April 8 seven NATO soldiers were killed in car bombings in southern Afghanistan.

9   Several interviews with Stan Lee reveal that he was well aware of this aspect of Tony Stark's characterisation. He said, 'It was the height of the Cold War. The readers – the young readers – if there was one thing they hated it was war, it was the military, or, as Eisenhower called it, the military-industrial complex. So I got a hero who represented that to the hundredth degree. He was a weapons manufacturer. He was providing weapons for the army. He was rich. He was an industrialist. But he was a good-looking guy and he was courageous ... I thought it would be fun to take the kind of character that nobody would like – that none of our readers would like – and shove him down their throats and make them like him' (qtd. in featurette on *Iron Man* DVD).

10   According to David Cross at *Movoto*, a real estate blog, Stark's Malibu mansion was thought to be worth $117.2 million dollars in 2008 (n.d.). Stan Lee called Stark the 'quintessential capitalist' (qtd. in Lee and Mair 2002: 160).

11 Alex Gibney's Academy Award-winning documentary *Taxi to the Dark Side* (2007) is about the experience of several prisoners there.

12 In just a few of the examples from *Iron Man*: Tony describes the 'Freedom Line' as 'a generation of weapons with this [the Jericho missile] at its heart'; Pepper gives Tony the original miniature arc reactor which was in his chest inscribed with 'Proof that Tony Stark has a heart'; about his intervention in Gulmira Stark says 'I know in my heart that it's right'; and Tony's decision to turn his back on the military industrial complex leads Obadiah to lament, 'it breaks my heart'.

13 A similarly traumatic incident changes the worldview of the narcissistic yet brilliant surgeon Stephen Strange (Benedict Cumberbatch) in *Doctor Strange*; although like Stark's, Strange's epiphany is often forgotten when the narrative requires it.

14 In their volume *Appetites and Anxieties: Food, Film and the Politics of Representation* (2014), Cynthia Baron, Diane Carson and Mark Bernard suggest that, 'These partnerships not only provide film studios and food companies with nearly unlimited opportunities for advertising and cross-promotion, but are also ideologically charged and provide a platform for Western corporate supremacy' (2014: 54). In the specific section on *Iron Man* they write about this scene and conclude: 'Thus, the film promotes U.S. weapons and Whoppers and underscores American superiority in both arenas' (ibid.).

15 According to Robert Downey Jr. much of this press conference speech was written by Shane Black who would later go on to direct *Iron Man 3* (see Burlingame 2012).

16 Stark's comments that, 'I saw that I had become part of system that is comfortable with zero accountability' also bleed into the real world. Many critics of the actions of the United States in the decade asserted that 'zero accountabilty' was one of the defining, yet unacknowledged, attributes of the Bush Doctrine (see Parry 2008; Friedman 2014).

17 Klein also connects this to the western frontier narrative in interesting ways: 'What we have been living for three decades is frontier capitalism, with the frontier constantly shifting location from crisis to crisis, moving on as soon as the law catches up' (2008: 242).

18 See Durham (2015) for more details on how American companies like Halliburton, Thales, Lockheed Martin, etc generated huge profits from the wars in Iraq and Afghanistan.

19 See Dana Milbank and Jim VandeHei, 'Washington Post Poll May 1, 2003 Gallup Poll', 'Afghanistan', and 'CNN Poll: Afghan War arguably most unpopular in US History' (2013).

20 His role as Mustaafa Marzoke in *AmericanEast* (2008) was a rare film to challenge this stereotype.

21 The main exceptions to this are Daredevil in the Neflix series and Spider-Man in *Spider-Man: Homecoming*.

22 Anthony R. Mills returns to this paradox in his reading of the film: 'On the one hand, it seems to repeat a well-known mythic pattern in which helpless dark-skinned foreigners must be rescued by a strong white American, acquiescing to the duality of savage and civilised and to the myth of white superiority. On the other hand, it evidences a profound change in the person of Tony Stark' (2013: 176).

23 Martin Flanagan, Andrew Livingstone and Mike McKenny in *The Marvel Studios Phenomenon: Inside a Transmedia Universe* suggest that the film 'condemns risky, individualistic capitalism' and offers an 'attempt at progressivism' (2016: 82, 178). Carter and Dodds argue, 'The film thus begins to raise questions about the ethics of the global trade, the connections between key industries in the US economy and global terror, and the possibilities of a more beneficent role for modern technology in international affairs' (2014: 57).

24 On the director's commentary for *Iron Man 2*, recorded in 2010, Favreau commented, 'This is Marvel, one movie goes down and all of them go own. It's a lot of responsibility.' In another interview recorded some years later in 2016 Favreau recalled, 'There was a lot of pressure because if that first film had failed, the IP was collateral. ... If we didn't make money, they could have lost the rights to all their characters' (qtd. in Gallaway 2016).

25 This was later confirmed by Favreau himself: 'Often times we're rewriting right up until, you know, right on the day that we're shooting it we're rewriting on it. The script wasn't completely locked until we actually wrapped photography last week' (qtd. in Weintraub 2009).

26 In the real world, the *Time* magazine 'Person of the Year' in 2010 was that other billionaire tech entrepreneur Mark Zuckerberg.

27 *Iron Man* refers to Stark's legacy on two further occasions: the Apogee award suggests that the 'Freedom Line' of weapons represents 'a new era for his [Tony Stark] father's legacy' and Stane informs him: 'This is your legacy [the Iron Man suit]. A new generation of weapons. With this [the miniature arc reactor] at it's heart. Weapons that will help steer the world back on course. Put the balance of power in *our* hands.'

28 In *Iron Man 2* and subsequent appearances the middle-aged Howard Stark is played by *Mad Men* (AMC, 2007–15) actor Tony Slattery and not Gerard Sandler who played him in photographs in *Iron Man*.

29 There are also connections to the Howard Hughes Hearings (1947) which led to William Bradley at *The Huffington Post* calling Downey Jr.'s incarnation of Stark a 'postmodern Howard Hughes' (2010).

30 Several roles have been recast within the MCU: not only the Hulk, Howard Stark and Rhodes but also Fandral (played by Josh Dallas in *Thor* and then by Zachary Levi in *Thor: The Dark World*) and Thanos (played by Damian Poittier in *The Avengers* and after by Josh Brolin).

31 Stark's criticism of the government for even thinking of taking away his private property and his motto 'peace through strength' also saw the film described as 'a virtual love letter to Ronald Reagan' (Boot 2010). About this scene Bryn Upton wrote that Stark 'represents the great libertarian impulse that has been growing in America since the 1980s, when Ronald Reagan stated that the government was the problem, not the solution' (2014: 34). The novelisation by Alexander Irvine adds one further interesting line from Stern: 'The Iron Man suit is the most powerful weapon on the face of the earth. … Yet you use it to sell tickets to your theme park' (2010: 26).

32 In a deleted scene Vanko is shown to capture Pepper at the end of the film. Tony says 'Why don't you let her go? She's not like us she's normal, *we're* the same.' To which Vanko replies, 'We will only be the same when you lose everything'. Yet the film is unable to suggest they might be equal in any significant way. Mickey Rourke subsequently expressed his disappointment for these very same reasons. He stated, 'I try to find the moments where [the villain is] not that cliched, evil bad guy and it's a big fight. I had it on *Iron Man* and they won. It was going to work for Marvel and them breaking [Jon] Favreau's balls and wanting just a one-dimensional villain' (qtd. in Brew 2011).

33 The comic series which is an official part of the MCU states that Stark unsuccessfully tries to register the element under the name of Baddassium. See *The Avengers Prelude: Nick Fury's Big Week*, Volume 8.

34 When Hammer introduces each type of drone the anthem of each branch of the military is played: for example, the US Army's 'The Army Goes Rolling Along (The Caisson Song)' and the US Navy''s 'Anchors Aweigh'.

35 The novelisation by Alexander Irvine expands on this with the line 'It [the display of drones] was a power fantasy come to life, a general's dream of theater dominance walking on stage. It was the expression "force multiplier" redefined forever' (2010: 219).

36 During the confrontation at the Expo a young boy wearing an Iron Man costume raises his hand to shoot at one of the drones before being rescued by Tony Stark. In the weeks preceeding the release of *Spider-Man: Homecoming* Tom Holland, the actor playing Peter Parker/Spider-Man, confirmed that the young boy, according to Kevin Feige, was Peter himself (see David 2017).

37 Frank Capra, Robert McNamara and the suffragist Anna Howard Shaw being a few of the notable exceptions.

38 In *Spider-Man: Homecoming* the stinger process is affectionally sent up as after a very long credit scroll Captain America appears for a final PSA (Public Service Announcement) to inform audiences that 'Sometimes patience is the key to victory, sometimes it leads to very little and it seems like it's not worth it and you wonder why you waited so long for something so disappointing…'

CHAPTER TWO

Of Gods and Monsters: The Allegorical Narratives of *Thor* and *The Incredible Hulk*

The Americanisation of the God of Thunder: From 'Boy Emperor' to the Rightful King of Asgard in *Thor*

> Man is, and always has been, a maker of gods. It has been the most serious and significant occupation of his sojourn in the world.
>
> – John Burroughs (1913: 184)

In recent years a range of books, like Don LoCicero's *Superheroes and Gods: A Comparative Study from Babylon to Batman* (2007), Grant Morrison's *Supergods: Our World in the Age of the Superhero* (2012) and Ben Saunders' *Do Gods Wear Capes? Spirituality, Fantasy, and Superheroes* (2012), have persuasively argued that superheroes do not only endorse prevailing societal values and behaviours, but also function as godlike figures for the cultures that produce them. Although they are often viewed in this way in the diegetic world of the Marvel Cinematic Universe, Thor, the Asgardian god of Thunder, one of the subjects of this chapter, is the only one of the Avengers Prime to be, quite literally, *a god*. Martin Arnold's *Thor: Myth to Marvel* (2011a) charts the rich history of Thor from his origins in

Old Norse and Scandinavian texts like the *Poetic Edda* and *Prose Edda* (c.13th century) where he was the god of the air, fertility and the 'protector of mankind', through to the eighteenth and nineteenth centuries when he became a source of inspiration for a variety of Romantic poets and nationalist movements, even into the first half of the twentieth century which saw him appropriated as a nation-state god by Nazi Germany (2011a: 135). Jon Favreau's *Iron Man* was a considerable gamble for the newly formed Marvel Studios, but the character of Tony Stark and his metallic alter ego are, as we have seen, somewhat grounded in the quasi-realistic environment of the twenty-first-century United States. The characterisation of Thor, given his roots in Scandinavian mythology, the fact that he possesses supernatural powers and is an *actual* god brought their own challenges in adapting the character to the cinema screen for the first time in his Marvel history.

The empyreal status of the Asgardians remains somewhat ambiguous throughout the MCU. In *The Avengers* both Agent Coulson and Nick Fury refer to them as 'gods', as does Loki, Thor's mischievous and malevolent younger brother. Yet in *Thor*, Fandral, one of the Warriors Three, offers a slight distinction in his remarks to Thor when he observes, 'the mortals worship you *as* a god'. In *Thor: The Dark World*, after the remarkable Battle of New York, the disgraced Loki returns in chains in front of his father Odin where he explains his actions: 'I went down to earth to rule as a benevolent god, just like you do...' But Odin disagrees, telling him, 'We are *not* gods! We're born, we live, we die, just as humans do.' This ambiguity of their celestial nature often becomes a source of humour as in when an inebriated Erik Selvig (Stellan Skarsgård) ends his night of drunken revelry with Thor by telling him, 'I still don't think you're the God of Thunder, *but you ought to be!*', or when Captain America denies Thor's divinity in *The Avengers* as he leaps from a quinjet informing Black Widow: 'There's only one God ma'am, and I'm pretty sure he doesn't dress like that...'[1]

Like Iron Man, Marvel's Thor was also originally conceived during the Cold War era, first appearing even before Tony Stark in *Journey into Mystery* #83 (August 1962). Also like his metallic counterpart, and despite his Asgardian other worldly status, Thor was frequently closely associated with American values and foreign policy in this era. Martin Arnold commented that the character was 'transformed into an articulation both of an anxious male sexuality and of a parallel nervousness regarding American foreign policy' (2011a, back cover). Throughout his comic book run during the Cold War Thor participated in several real-world conflicts where his political perspectives were decidedly American and even went to Vietnam on more than one occasion. In 1965's *Journey into Mystery* #117 he roars at communist commander Hu Sak, 'To communism, then – may it vanish from the face of the earth and the memory of mankind'.[2] The MCU iteration of Thor is similarly a decisive man of action, a hard-bodied hero the likes of which Susan Jeffords considered emblematic of US self-image in *Hard Bodies: Hollywood Masculinity in the Reagan Era*, where she wrote, 'The depiction of the indefatigable, muscular, and invincible masculine body became the lynchpin of the Reagan imaginary; this hardened male form became an emblem not only for the Reagan Presidency but for its ideologies and economies as well' (1994: 25). But Thor, as a product of the new millennium, is portrayed as something more than this. Like many masculine figures of the era he emerges as a conflation of both hard-bodied and more sensitive new man archetypes which characterised the discourse of the period.

Thor's godhood must have proved difficult to reconcile with the broader narrative sweep of the MCU in 2011, but it is effectively embraced by director Kenneth Branagh rather than ignored in a film which confronts the confluence between science and fantasy, myth and reality throughout. The film begins with the stentorian tones of Anthony Hopkins' Odin, Thor's father, the king of Asgard and the All-Father, in a voice-over which addresses this in its very first moments:

> Once, mankind accepted a simple truth: that they were not alone in this universe. Some worlds man believed home to their Gods. Others they knew to fear. From a realm of cold and darkness came the Frost Giants, threatening to plunge the mortal world into a new ice age. But humanity would not face this threat alone. Our armies drove the Frost Giants back into the heart of their own world. The cost was great. In the end, their king fell, and the source of their power was taken from them. With the last great war ended, we withdrew from the other worlds and returned home to the Realm Eternal, Asgard. And here we remain as a beacon of hope, shining out across the stars. And though we have fallen into man's myths and legends, it was Asgard and its warriors that brought peace to the universe.

The woman that becomes Thor's lover, the astrophysicist Jane Foster (Natalie Portman) (formerly a nurse in the original comics), suggests, by paraphrasing Arthur C. Clarke, that these two areas can be reconciled as 'magic's just science we don't understand yet' (see Clarke 1973: 21, fn 1). Thor tells her: 'Your ancestors called it magic and you call it science. Well, I come from a place where they are one and the same thing.' The film goes to considerable lengths to blend the two with the help of its scientific advisors: Sean Carroll, a theoretical physicist at the California Institute of Technology and the author of *From Eternity to Here* (2010), and Kevin Hand, a NASA astrobiologist, who lend a patina of authenticity to the film with its mentions of Einstein-Rosen bridges and subtle aurora (see Kakalios 2010; Hill 2013). Even acclaimed popular scientist Neil deGrasse Tyson took to Twitter to speculate that based on his calculations Thor's famous hammer Mjölnir, if it is made of neutron-star matter as Odin states in *Thor* (he says it was 'forged in the heart of a dying star'), would weigh 'as much as a herd of 300-billion elephants' (2013). The film manages to reconcile high fantasy and science fiction in its portrayal of Asgard, a place which is technologically advanced (capable of interplanetary travel and has a fleet of futuristic space jets) but its residents still use swords and shields, dress in medieval garb and speak in Shakespearean-affected tones which Tony Stark will later joke in *The Avengers* resembles 'Shakespeare in the Park' with the aside to Thor, 'Doth mother know you weareth her drapes?' At the same time Branagh is able to undercut this melodramatic sweep with a rich vein of humour, as the film is the most broadly comic addition to the MCU until *Guardians of the Galaxy* and *Ant-Man* in 2014.[3] In the course of the narrative, as well as participating in several spectacular battles, the mighty Thor will be run over twice by Jane Foster and even tasered by her wise-cracking assistant Darcy Lewis (Kat Dennings).

Instead of the Iraq-set opening of *Iron Man*, the narrative of *Thor* begins in Asgard on the bright and sunny day of Thor's coronation where he is due to ascend to the throne in place of his aging father. The film quickly codes Thor as arrogant and overly confident, with his show-boating for the crowd and self-entitled winking. Asgard, with Thor as its primary representative, is self-consciously constructed as representative of the United States of America and Odin's description of it as a 'beacon of hope, shining out across the stars' is reminiscent of many pronouncements in the last two hundred years concerning America's self-proclaimed role around the globe, the exact phrase being used by both Ronald Reagan and Richard Nixon in their inauguration speeches, and a variation of which could be heard in that of Donald Trump's contention, in his own, that the American way of life will 'shine as an example... We will shine for everyone to follow' (2017). As Edwin J. Feulner and Brian Tracey wrote in *The American Spirit: Celebrating the Virtues and Values That Make Us Great*, 'Throughout our history, we [the United States of America] have served as a beacon of hope to oppressed men and women everywhere' (2012: 53). The residents of Asgard are no longer the blue-eyed blondes of Nordic mythology, but a harmonious multi-racial society with even some of their prominent figures of Asian (Tadanobu Asano as Hogun, later revealed to be of Vanir) or African (Idris Elba as Heimdall) descent. Vincent M. Gaine has stated that, 'This creates a sense of universalism in Asgard, preventing it from appearing as a Northern European version of the heavenly realm' (2016: 40). Since 1962 Marvel has participated in the Americanisation of Thor, initially in the comics but even more so in his MCU incarnation. This is visible in the peaceful and utopian multi-racial community of Asgard, but even more so in the characterisation of Thor himself through his embodiment of what Hagley and Harrison described as 'the American warrior ethos' (2012) and what many regard as the supposedly quintessential American values of equality, freedom and justice Asgard advocates. This Americanisation had reached such an extent by 2011 that Martin Arnold argued that we had reached 'the end of the meaningful story of the reception of Thor, as the interest is no longer in the Norse myth or the history of Thor as a God who was once believed in, but rather the exotic Norse trappings that the mass pop industry can endlessly recycle' (2011a: 65).

Unbeknownst to the peaceful Asgardians enjoying their privileged lives, a small number of their perennial enemies, the Frost Giants, mount a surprise attack on the long thought impenetrable Asgard. While their attempt is quickly repulsed by a large enchanted metallic being called the Destroyer, the arrogant and impulsive Thor is incensed and wants immediate revenge. He demands that the Asgardians should 'march into Jotunheim [the home world of the Frost Giants] as you [Odin] once did! Teach them a lesson! Break their spirits, so they would never dare try to cross our borders again!' Thor cannot understand the potential ramifications of his proposed actions or the lives that will be lost on both sides if they restart hostilities, and the wiser Odin urges caution and diplomacy in place of war, remarking that 'it is the action of but a few, doomed to fail'. Odin has maintained a fragile peace between the two races for many years and states that they cannot begin a conflict, which could lead to the deaths of tens of thousands, just because of the actions of a few who may not represent the whole. The events and exchange between Thor and Odin, with its lines of dialogue like 'This was an act of war!' and 'You know not what your actions would unleash', were read by some as a veiled commentary on the political landscape of the post-9/11 environment, and Anthony R. Mills was one of many who saw real-world connections in the portrayal of Thor's pride and hubris, stating: 'It is difficult not to consider our contemporary political context when observing the stark contrast of Thor's and Odin's on the appropriate response to the Frost Giants' actions' (2013: 180). Thor's argument that a pre-emptive strike on the Frost Giants is 'the only way to ensure the safety of our borders' and will end the war before it had hardly begun is a striking manifestation of the Bush Doctrine in a film that was described by Peter Labuza, author of *Approaching the End: Imagining Apocalypse in American Film* (2014), as 'playing heavily on some George Bush parallels' (2011) and which prompted a range of reviews with titles like 'The Summer's New Hero: Thor-Ge W. Bush' (Singer 2011) and 'Blockbuster: Bush v. Thor' (Stewart 2011).

Convinced that he knows better and after being expertly manipulated by his brother Loki (who later learns to his dismay that he is adopted and of Frost Giant descent), Thor goes against his father's wishes and leads a raiding party to Jotunheim where he confronts their king, Laufey, who tells him, 'Your father is a murderer and a thief', the very same accusation Ivan Vanko had made about Howard Stark in *Iron Man 2* released in the previous year.[4] Just as Vanko's assertions about Stark senior were shown to be false, Laufey's charges are also unfounded as Odin is portrayed as a benevolent and sage monarch who tells his sons, 'A wise King must never seek out war, but always be ready for it', and the Frost Giants are little more than crudely barbaric and war-like caricatures. Laufey's aside to Thor, 'You long for battle, you crave it. You're nothing but a boy trying to prove himself a man', suggests he knows the petulant prince better than Thor knows himself and evokes Chalmers Johnson's memorable description of George W. Bush as a 'boy emperor' (2004: 283). Seeing the gravity of their situation and the fact that they are hopelessly outnumbered, the Warriors Three (Fandral, Lady Sif and Volstagg) plead with Thor to reassess his ill-advised plan and for a moment he seems to reconsider, before Laufey goads him into battle by impugning his masculinity, 'Run back home, little *Princess!*' revealing that, even for gods, the worst insult is to cast doubt on one's masculinity and be compared to a woman.[5]

Despite their exceptional fighting prowess, it is clear that the Asgardians are outnumbered and outmatched, but at the moment of defeat Odin appears astride his mythical eight-legged horse Sleipnir. Thor calls to him, 'Father! We'll finish them together!' in a vivid manifestation of how many thought George W. Bush regarded war in Iraq.[6] Odin ignores his son and pleads with Laufey, 'These are the actions of a *boy*, treat them as such', the second time in the space of a few minutes that Thor is called a boy. But Laufey refuses and the clash of civilisations between the Asgardians and the Frost Giants has begun again. On their return

Fig. 8: Odin's description of Asgard as 'a beacon of hope shining across the stars' is at the centre of *Thor* (2011); an allegory for America in the first decades of the twenty-first century?

to Asgard, father and son once more argue as Thor tells Odin, 'There won't be a kingdom to protect if you are afraid to act! The Jotuns must learn to *fear me.*' Odin is disgusted by Thor's behaviour and decides to remove all of his powers, his beloved hammer, Mjölnir, and banish him to Earth. What *Thor* dramatises may not be an accurate relationship of the one between the Bushes, father and son, or the real motivation for the war in Iraq, but it is certainly the way it was perceived by the public at large and it is also the one portrayed in both Oliver Stone's *W.* (2008) and Jacob Weisberg's best-selling *The Bush Tragedy* (2008).[7] Darren Franich commented: 'The Thunder god invades a land he knows nothing about, a classic war hawk maneuver; chastened by his elders, he has to learn how his actions have consequences' (2013).[8]

In the post-9/11 period it became fairly common for the Bush administration and frequently George W. Bush himself to be represented in allegory in film and television texts of the era: from the likes of *Battlestar Galactica* (Sci-Fi, 2004–9) (see Kaveney and Stoy 2010), through to Oliver Stone's *Alexander* (2004) (see Jenkins 2015: 120–1), the Saw franchise (2004–) (see Kellner 2009: 7–9), and even in the aftermath of a zombie apocalypse in George Romero's *Land of the Dead* (2005) (see McSweeney 2010). In the superhero genre, Justine Toh regarded *Batman Begins* not just as an allegory for the Bush era, but for George W. Bush himself: 'In this frame, Batman's righteous task is to clean up Gotham by removing its corrupt elements, a fictional parallel for the righteousness of the US's campaign to promote democracy in the Middle East' (2010: 132).

Exiled to Earth and finding himself in the New Mexico town of Puente Antiguo, Thor has been stripped of his life of privilege in a similar way to what Tony Stark had been in *Iron Man* and what Bruce Banner experiences in *The Incredible Hulk*, discussed later in this chapter. It is here that he must learn humility and what it is to be a *real hero* among humans like the scientists Jane Foster and Erik Selvig who initially, and somewhat understandably, do not believe he is a Norse God. When Thor discovers that Mjölnir is nearby, in scenes which had been teased at the end of *Iron Man 2*, he is convinced that if reunited with his mythical hammer he will be able to fight his way out of trouble, as he has done all of his life. It is surrounded by S.H.I.E.L.D. security guards led by Agent Phil Coulson (whom Thor calls 'son of Coul') and watched over from above by Hawkeye (Jeremy Renner), and Thor makes his way towards it accompanied by thunder and lightning, with composer Patrick Doyle's orchestral score swelling to a triumphant crescendo … only to find that he is unable to pick it up, and that he has yet to understand the lesson his father wished to impart. Seemingly resigned to his fate he allows himself to be caught by S.H.I.E.L.D. and Coulson who immediately presumes him to be American and asks where he received his training: 'Pakistan, Chechnya, Afghanistan?' While in captivity his brother Loki, who has now usurped the Asgardian throne, appears and tells Thor that their father is dead and that Thor can never again return to Asgard. Loki explains his father's decision with the evocative line: 'Our people *need* a sense of continuity in order to feel safe in these difficult times.'

Having finally been appropriately humbled, Thor comes to the realisation, with the help of his new romantic interest Jane and friend Erik, that true strength derives from more than physical prowess and when Loki sends the Destroyer to Puento Antiguo to kill him once and for all, the ensuing battle is framed as reminiscent of a western standoff like those in *High Noon* (1952), *The Good, the Bad and the Ugly* (1966) and *Chisum* (1970), each of which are, not uncoincidentally, also set in New Mexico. Thor, who had earlier been quite content to destroy an entire race, helps evacuate the town of innocents, finally putting the lives of others before his own and pleads with his brother: 'Whatever I have done to wrong you, whatever I have done to lead you to do this, I am truly sorry, but these people are innocent. Taking their lives will give you nothing. So take mine and end this.' Thor's offer to sacrifice himself is, of course, a familiar convention in Western popular culture and will be frequently returned to in the MCU, although it is one that will very rarely result in an *actual* sacrifice.[9] Indeed, the notion of a quasi-christomimetic self-sacrifice recurs so frequently in American cinema that it has become one of its foundational tropes. Yet its valorisation, while the very same sacrifices of those of the Other are declared to be monstrous and inhuman, is problematic. Thor's 'death' at the hands of the Destroyer and his subsequent rebirth, and in particular the way that it is framed, situates him alongside a range of christomimetic figures in contemporary American science fiction and fantasy films like Neo from *The Matrix* (1999), Gandalf from the *Lord of the Rings* trilogy (2001–3), the eponymous *E.T.: The Extra-Terrestrial* (1982) and James Cole from *12 Monkeys* (1995). Adele Reinhartz has written that such is the pervasiveness of this pattern that 'any film that has redemption as a major theme (and this includes many, if not most, recent Hollywood movies) is liable to use some Jesus symbolism in connection with the redemptive hero figure' (2003: 189). This is heavily ironised, of course, by the fact that Thor is an *actual* god and according to Norse mythology predates Jesus (see Lindow 2002: 22) and the fact that the MCU is avowedly secular in its construction, with only fleeting references and allusions to a Judeo-Christian God. Those looking for religious meanings in the franchise have had to primarily rely on allusions and subtext rather than any explicit comments provided by its characters or the text (see McAteer 2016; Saunders 2016). The actor playing Loki, Tom Hiddlestone, felt that this malleability was one of the reasons contemporary superhero films have resonated not just in the United States, where they are conceived and produced, but with cultures all over the globe: 'Superhero films offer a shared, faithless, modern mythology, through which these truths [about the human condidition] can be explored. In our increasingly secular society, with so many disparate gods and different faiths, superhero films present a unique canvas upon which our shared hopes, dreams and apocalyptic nightmares can be projected and played out' (2012). Odin, sensing his son's growth all the way from his Odinsleep in Asgard, responds with a single tear and it is this which brings Thor back to life, returning his powers and once again giving him the right to wield Mjölnir.

As previously mentioned, Thor certainly is a hard-bodied hero the likes of which defined the 1980s, according to Jeffords, and perhaps the return of the more traditional type of masculinity that writers like Peggy Noonan and Kim DuToit asked for, but in Chris Hemsworth's portrayal of the character, this hypermasculine mode is represented as fundamentally flawed, revealing the complicated and frequently paradoxical nature of new millennial masculinity. Thor is a man of action, a warrior and protector, but his initial decisiveness and appetite for violence are explicitly connected to his hubris and lack of self-awareness. It is only after his epiphany (as we have seen with Tony Stark) as he demonstrates compassion and is shown to be able to acknowledge humility and weakness, traits which have been historically coded as feminine and thus traditionally antithetical for action heroes, that the film asks us to recognise that he becomes a true hero. Far from being 'dumb movies for dumb people' (Tasker 1993: 6) the action genre, the codes and conventions of which the superhero film is profoundly immersed in, provides us with a striking cultural barometer. As depictions of idealised masculinities were embodied in figures like Sylvester Stallone, Arnold Schwarzenegger and Chuck Norris in the 1980s, then shifted to the likes of Johnny Depp, Brad Pitt and Keanu Reeves in the 1990s, the ascendance of stars like Chris Hemsworth, Chris Evans, Chris Pratt and Robert Downey Jr., each of whom starred in an MCU film in this period, offer more complex, but still hegemonical articulations of masculinity in the new millennial decades which this monograph will return frequently to.

The battle between Thor and Loki comes to a climax with Thor's return to Asgard as a new man. Loki had planned to kill his biological father Laufey and the entire race of Frost Giants in a startling act of genocide of his own people, all in order to prove himself to his step-father Odin as a worthy successor. However, Loki has yet to learn the lesson that Thor has on Earth, that even though they possess immense power and are virtually immortal, Asgardians are not inherently superior to humans or any other species. Loki asks Thor a similar question to that which Rhodes asked Stark after his epiphany in Afghanistan: 'What is this new-found love for the Frost Giants?' It is one that will be repeated several times throughout the MCU by those who have not experienced a life-changing traumatic event which enables them to see compassion and empathy not as a weakness but as a strength, while at the same time, it should be observed, dispatching almost countless numbers of simplistically framed enemies. After Loki threatens Jane Foster with implied rape ('When we are finished here, I will pay her a visit myself!'), Thor overcomes him in a battle which resonates because of their relationship (something the MCU will struggle to match after), and both his method of combat and his perspective are altered, as he is shown to refuse to use his hammer against his brother and acts only in defence. Defeated and silently denied with a dismissive gesture from his 'father' Odin, Loki's last act of defiance is to refuse their offer of help as he lets go of Odin's spear, falling into the cosmos to an uncertain future.

Like many other superhero films in the era, *Thor* presents us with a fantastical reimagining of reality: *Iron Man* rewrites the conflict in Afghanistan as a humanitarian undertaking and *Thor* shows a vain and impetuous leader recognising the error of his ways ('I had it all backwards, I had it all wrong'). Thor's second act of sacrifice is to forfeit his own happiness to save the race of the Frost Giants that he had once shown such scorn for, by destroying the Bifrost Bridge to save them and perhaps never being able to return to Earth and his love Jane Foster again. This act of altruism is central to the understanding of the American monomyth, which has encoded within it the idea that America's wars and interventions abroad are never undertaken for selfish reasons, but only ever for the good of mankind and that the global superpower carries with it a burden of responsibility that no one can ever truly understand (see Colucci 2008). The lessons Thor has learned throughout the course of the narrative will stand him in good stead for the apocalyptic battle he will face in *The Avengers*, in which his brother Loki will return to play no small part. But Thor's emotional growth continues in that film and in his second solo outing, the underwhelming *Thor: The Dark World*, and his character will not be 'reset' as we have seen (and will continue to see) with Tony Stark. While Martin Arnold might have been correct to suggest that by the end of the first decade of the new millennium 'the reception history of the Thunder God is, in any meaningful sense, at an end' (2011a: 160), the very same period saw his rebirth as an American icon and a key part of the evolving Marvel Cinematic Universe.

Making a 'monster into a hero': *The Incredible Hulk*

> How do you make a monster into a hero and still maintain the monster's essential element of menace – yet combine that with a personality that audiences would come to love, or at least be fascinated by? And, on top of that, how do you make such a creature a hero?
>
> – Danny Fingeroth (2004: 123)

Despite an inauspicious start in the comics which saw the character cancelled after only six issues published between May 1962 and March 1963, the Incredible Hulk has been one of Marvel's most popular creations and even one of the rare superheroes to have had a live-action syndicated TV show, with the fondly remembered *The Incredible Hulk* (CBS, 1978–82). The original comic book incarnation of the Hulk was just as much a creation of the Cold War as the characters of Iron Man and Thor, and given that he was the result of a gamma radiation blast at a nuclear testing facility, he is, like Iron Man, both literally and figuratively a product of the conflict. This has led to the Hulk frequently being read as an articulation of Cold War fears and anxieties concerning the nuclear age in a similar way to how that other iconic cinematic monster, Godzilla, has been (see Inuhiko 2007; Darowski and Darowski 2015). Like the Japanese mega-lizard, part of the Hulk's enduring appeal is undoubtedly that he has often blurred the line between hero and monster. In *Superhero: The Secret Origin of a Genre*, Peter Coogan explores how the Hulk's original 1960s comic narrative was one of the first to actually invert one of the established tropes of the genre and turn 'superpowers from a blessing to a curse, an innovation of Stan Lee and Jack Kirby in the Silver Age. Without that heroic sacrifice, the Hulk is just a monster, and so the Hulk film is not a superhero film but a monster movie' (2006: 11). Indeed, Lee's inspiration came from two classic Gothic literary texts: Mary Shelley's *Frankenstein* (1818) and Robert Louis Stevenson's *The Strange Case of Dr. Jekyll and Mr. Hyde* (1886) about which he commented: 'We would use the concept of the Frankenstein monster but update it. Our hero would be a scientist, transformed into a raging behemoth by a nuclear accident. And – since I was willing to borrow from *Frankenstein*, I decided I might as well borrow from *Dr. Jekyll and Mr. Hyde* as well – our protagonist would constantly change from his normal identity to his superhuman alter-ego and back again' (qtd. in DeFalco 2003: 7). Almost fifty years after his first appearance in the comic much of the drama in Louis Leterrier's *The Incredible Hulk*, the second film in the MCU, and Hulk's subsequent appearances in *The Avengers* and *Avengers: Age of Ultron* and beyond, stems from this juxtaposition between monstrous and human, control and chaos.

Released in the same summer as *Iron Man*, *The Incredible Hulk* appeared only five years after Ang Lee's divisive *Hulk* (2003) produced by Universal Pictures with only limited involvement from Marvel, which, although it made $245 million at the global box office, was considered as something of a financial disappointment when it failed to have the commercial or cultural impact of the Batman or Spider-Man films which its producers had undoubtedly hoped for given the high profile nature of the character. Lee's version seemed to have both delighted and disappointed fans in equal measure on its release: with many admiring its attempt to bring a sense of psychological complexity to an often simplistic genre, while others regarded it as too cerebral and pretentious for a superhero film. Leterrier's *The Incredible Hulk* is simultaneously a sequel to Lee's film, a reboot of the Hulk franchise, while at the same time being a continuation of the broader MCU narrative, a process which led to producer Gale Hurd describing the film neologistically as a 'requel' (qtd. in Weintraub 2008a). Prior to the turn of the new millennium this reboot process would often take a decade: for example, the eight years between *Batman & Robin* (1997) and *Batman Begins* (2005), or the nineteen between *Superman IV: The Quest for Peace* (1987) and the aptly-named *Superman Returns* (2006). However, in a film industry increasingly defined by annual additions to franchises (or in the case of Marvel sometimes triannually) the process is much faster than ever before: hence Batman was portrayed by Christian Bale in the conclusion to Christopher Nolan's Batman trilogy *The Dark Knight Rises* and then rebooted only four years later, played by Ben Affleck in *Batman v Superman: Dawn of Justice*; Spider-Man was portrayed by Tobey Maguire in *Spider-Man 3* (2007) and then by Andrew Garfield in *The Amazing Spider-Man* (2012) and *The Amazing Spider-Man 2* (2014) before being played by Tom Holland in *Captain America: Civil War* (2016), three actors playing the same role in major studio films in less than ten years.

Leterrier's *The Incredible Hulk* replaces all members of the previous cast, but seems to continue the narrative from Lee's version (with one or two caveats) incorporating some aspects of *Hulk* at the same time as eschewing others to enable itself to fit into the then fledgling MCU. In interviews Leterrier, who had been known before *The Incredible Hulk* for his kinetic and fast-paced action films like *The Transporter* (2002) and *Unleashed* (2005), revealed an affection for Lee's interpretation of the character, but also suggested how his version might differ:

> I really do love Ang's movie because as a director, as all of you guys, you've seen the cinema in Ang's movie. It's beautiful. It's a great movie. But if you're 7 years old, 8 years old, you're totally lost in Ang's movie so I wanted to give it like more of like an overall approach. You didn't have to be a fan knowing the Hulk story to love this movie – hopefully, my movie, or to be 7 and 13 and a boy to like this movie. I wanted to make it like a broader and like a general – more general – kind of a movie. (Qtd. in Weintraub 2008b)

While Leterrier's remarks imply a film more self-consciously aimed at a younger audience, its star (and uncredited co-writer) Edward Norton saw much more to the project, stating 'that's why these things [superhero films] endure, because they're kind of modern, pop revisitings of that myth of stealing power from the universe. There's a lot of great stories of people reaching beyond what is permitted – like Icarus or Proteus' (2007). Norton's version of the script which is widely available online, dated 13 May 2007, even begins with an epigraph taken from the work of Joseph Campbell, 'We have only to follow the thread of the hero path, and where we had thought to find an Abomination, we shall find a God... And where we had thought to be alone, we will be with all the world' (originally, 1949: 18). Norton's words and his choice of epigraph indicate a desire to make a very different film to that which Leterrier described, not one aimed primarily at seven- to thirteen-year-old boys, but one which resonates with an understanding of the mythic role of contemporary superheroes. This divergence of aims is very palpable in the finished film and might explain Norton's dissatisfaction with the final result which led to him distancing himself from the project and a very public falling out with Marvel's president of production Kevin Feige. The film released at the cinemas removes much of the character development and philosophical musings of Norton's script (the Blu-ray release also contained a remarkable seventy minutes' worth of deleted scenes) to concentrate more on action and spectacle, often to the film's detriment, but still finds time to state that the Hulk (and later Abomination's) is 'godlike'.

It might be considered fitting, for a variety of reasons, that of all of the Avengers Prime it was the Hulk that came to be played by three different actors in the space of just nine years; certainly because of Bruce Banner's Dissociative Identity Disorder (DID), but also because of the pronounced range of variations the comic book Hulk has gone through since 1962, which led Danny Fingeroth to write that the Hulk 'probably holds the record of personality changes for one character' (2004: 126). In different versions throughout his history the Hulk is sometimes able to talk and sometimes not, he is intermittently intelligent but at other times a mindless beast not even conscious of his actions, and his strength seems to vary from incarnation to incarnation. Leterrier's film is full of many affectionate 'Easter eggs' which reference these different versions of the character and it is the CBS television series that receives the most frequent homages: from the sporadic use of Joe Harnell's iconic 'Lonely Man' (which ended every episode of the television show), to having Lou Ferrigno, who played the Hulk in the series, as a security guard (who also voices the only six words the Hulk will speak in the film 'Leave Me Alone', 'Hulk Smash', and 'Betty'), and showing an episode of *The Courtship of Eddie's Father* (ABC, 1969–72) starring Bill Bixby, the original Banner, on a television screen in Banner's apartment. This method of including Easter eggs in contemporary popular films has evolved from being a minor diversion to one of the myriad of ways multimedia companies seek to encourage fans to consider themselves as active participants in evolving franchises and, just as importantly, return to the films again and again, a process Henry Jenkins called 'participatory culture' which 'contrasts with older notions of passive media spectatorship' in his influential volume *Convergence Culture: Where*

Old and New Media Collide (2006: 3).

This variability is also apparent in the diversity of readings of the Hulk character which have emerged since the 1960s, which prompted James N. Gilmore and Mattias Stork to suggest that the Hulk is 'potent with images and iconographies harbouring polysemous meanings' (2014: 12). Hulk's condition has been read as connected to the nuclear anxieties during which he was originally created (see Darowski and Darowski 2015), to fears of emasculation and crises of US national identity in the wake of Vietnam and the rise of feminism (see Eaton 2013), as a countercultural icon on American college campuses during the 1960s (see Duncan and Smith 2013), for bipolar disorder (see Power and Dalgleish 2016: 298; Wooton 2012), and even as a metaphor for black rage (see Kleefeld 2014; Burch n.d.). Like many MCU films, and in particular our reading of *Thor* in this chapter, *The Incredible Hulk* is what David Holloway categorises as an 'allegory lite' in which 'controversial issues can be safely addressed because they must be 'read off' other stories by the viewer; while the 'allegory' is sufficiently loose or 'lite', and the other attractions on offer are sufficiently compelling or diverse, that viewers can enjoy the film without needing to engage at all with the risky 'other story' it tells' (2008: 83). While it is quite correctly the nuclear age that most commentators have turned to in their interpretation of the roots of the character – as Joseph and John Darowski have observed, 'Born in the mushroom cloud of a nuclear explosion, the Incredible Hulk may seem like the perfect character to embody the complexities and ambiguities of the atomic age' (2015: 7) – the Marvel Cinematic Universe version of the Hulk is profoundly immersed in the fractious post-9/11 decade. About this incarnation of the Hulk, Tom Pollard was correct to assert, 'In times of national trauma, film audiences find superheroes like the Incredible Hulk especially attractive. This character serves as a perfect post 9/11 superhero because his superpowers flow from his anger' (2011: 82). Fear, anger and trauma are placed at the centre of *The Incredible Hulk* as they were in many new millennial popular culture texts, an era when the concept of their political role in modern society became widely discussed. Many asserted that America found itself living in a culture of fear which seemed to revolve around the phrase the 'War on Terror' itself and a range of studies found that anger rather than terror was the defining emotion many Americans felt after the events of 11 September 2001 (see Kluger 2010). The Hulk is portrayed as a distinctly post-9/11 weapon of mass destruction that the military, personified by the obsessive General Thaddeus Ross (William Hurt), seeks to control. In perhaps the film's most memorable line of dialogue Ross tells his team of soldiers: 'That man's [Bruce Banner] whole body is the property of the US army.' The Hulk's body emerges as the site of a battle between Ross and Banner, but *even within* for Banner himself in his struggle to control his own anger and find his place in the world after his traumatic accident. The cultural battleground of Leterrier's version are those fears and anxieties uniquely pertinent to the post-9/11 era: the encroaching powers of the Military Industrial Complex, the intrusions of the government into civil liberties, American interventions overseas and the shifting parameters of new millennial masculinity, issues which, though they are rarely addressed by name in the film, linger within the frames of not only *The Incredible Hulk* but the majority of the MCU.

The relationship between *The Incredible Hulk* and its predecessor, Ang Lee's *Hulk,* is effectively established in Leterrier's imaginative credits sequence which replays the events of the first film with the new cast and several engaging changes of emphasis. Instead of being accidentally caught in a gamma radiation experiment as he had been in Lee's version, Banner is now shown deliberately testing the process on himself with a self-assured wink (just like Thor winks at the crowd on his inauguration day) at his scientist girlfriend Betty Ross (Liv Tyler), a far cry from Eric Bana's portrayal of Banner as a tortured soul *even before* his life-changing accident. The Hulk has generally been perceived as 'the personification of intense emotion and unresolved conflicts residing within the troubled psyche of Bruce Banner' (Patrick and Patrick 2008: 222), but here in the MCU Banner seems *compos mentis* until the traumatic incident which leads to the creation of his monstrous alter ego. In Lee's version Banner was working on the regeneration of cells for medical purposes; here Banner *believes* he is working purely on gamma radiation resistance experiments, but Ross later reveals that the military was duping him into participating in the reproduction of the Super Soldier Serum from World War II which led to the creation of Captain America (discussed in chapter three). The credits sequence shows the experiment going catastrophically wrong causing Banner to transform into the Hulk, initially only shown from the first-person perspective through Hulk's eyes. Betty is injured as the result of the Hulk's inability to control himself and this emerges as one of the film's recurring motifs, the lengths that Banner goes to ensure she (and later other civilians) will not be hurt because of his actions ever again. The credits montage shows the extent of Ross's global search for Banner/Hulk which becomes progressively more and more unhinged as the film continues: newspaper headlines chart a list of his sightings, mentioning a 'green monster', and maps show that the hunt for Banner extends through Asia, Africa and even the Middle East where his status as a weapon of mass destruction would have coincided with the wars in Afghanistan and Iraq, and in particular the American search for Saddam Hussein's supposed stockpile of weapons.

The sequence ends with Banner snapping back to consciousness, revealing the credits to have been a traumatic conflation of memory and dream. Trauma, as it has been in many new millennial superhero films, and particularly so of the

MCU, is placed at the centre of *The Incredible Hulk* and while it is not explored with the psychological complexity of Lee's version, it emerges as the defining aspect of Edward Norton's (and later Mark Ruffalo's) interpretation of the character. In *Iron Man*, Stark's traumatic experience in Afghanistan changed his life irrevocably and the same is shown to be true for Banner, yet his is a trauma which repeats *every time* he is forced to transform into the Hulk. Even when he is not the Hulk, flashes of his Hulk experience (which he seems to not be conscious of at this stage) return to him in a distinctly traumatic form in episodes where he is unable to discern what is real from that which is memory, in what Norton's script describes in an appropriately Deleuzian fashion as 'MEMORY IMAGES'. When Betty asks him what it *feels* like to be the Hulk he, as most versions of the character do, struggles to find words to express it. He says, 'It's like someone has poured a litre of acid into my brain'. Banner in Lee's version had provocatively suggested that it was 'like a dream about rage, power and *freedom*' and later in *The Avengers* (when Banner is played by Mark Ruffalo) he will describe it as 'I'm exposed… Like a nerve… It's a nightmare…'.

One conspicuous difference between Norton's Hulk (which will repeat in Ruffalo's portrayal) and previous incarnations of the character is the shift from him being prompted to transform into the Hulk by becoming angry to, in the MCU version, changing into the Hulk due to the elevation of his heart rate.[10] In the television series Banner's transformations were always the result of him becoming angry, which became more outlandish as the series progressed and writers sought for excuses to bring the Hulk onto the screen. As a result Banner 'Hulks out' when he does not have the correct change for a phone booth in 'Never Give a Trucker an Even Break' (1.09), when he is locked in a steam room by bullies in 'Killer Instinct' (2.08), by a loud ringing bell in 'The Confession' (2.20) and when he is attacked by bees in 'Prometheus, Part One' (4.01). In the MCU it is made very clear that it is not only anger that prompts his transformation, but stress, fear, frustration, exertion and in one scene, which is primarily played for laughs but is inescapably tragic, romantic interplay between Banner and Betty which he has to stop with the line, 'No. No. I can't… I can't get too excited.' Looking for mechanisms to maintain a measure of control over his mental state, Banner experiments with techniques to control his heart rate throughout, in particular a Brazilian Aikido instructor, who tells him in broken English that 'Fear no good. Emotion and control', and the use of a heart-rate monitor on his wrist as a conveniently visual cue for audiences to recognise how close he is to changing.

Having done away with the need to show Hulk's origin by placing it in the opening credits, *The Incredible Hulk* is free to pursue what happens to Banner after he goes on the run from the authorities and attempts to live 'off the grid'. The narrative formally begins in Rio de Janeiro in Brazil with a title informing us that it has been one hundred and fifty-eight days since his last 'incident'. It is no coincidence that Banner has relocated to the crowded spaces of Rocinha, Rio's largest *favela* and Leterrier employs a range of attractively framed helicopter shots to glide over multiple times, revealing the chaotic beauty of its architecture. Banner attempts to blend in with the six million people who live there, learning Portuguese by watching dubbed versions of *Sesame Street* (1969–) on television. Leterrier was quite clear about why he chose to locate Banner in the *favela*: 'We needed a place in the world where Banner could truly disappear… [the *favela*] … is madness… It is a place that is a little at the margins of the law, with so many people packed in together' (qtd. in Spanakos 2011: 18). The globe-hopping narratives of the MCU (and the majority of American blockbuster films) rarely pause to offer meaningful engagements with their foreign locations; rather they function as little more than exotic backgrounds for action sequences while at the same time endorsing and legitimising extra-judicial American incursions and perpetuating racial stereotypes (see Heise 2012; Jones 2015).

It is in Rio that Banner experiences, to a certain extent, as Thor and Tony Stark have been shown to, the lives of others. Banner works as a poorly-paid day labourer in a Pingo Doce soda bottling plant (a fictional Marvel-created brand which reappears some years later in *Ant-Man*), lives in a rundown flat, and later when he is homeless he is forced to beg on the streets for food. Antony Peter Spanakos writes: 'While in Brazil, Banner displays an orientation towards recognition reflective of a US search for understanding and respect of the other in coming to terms with itself, a self that has become unrecognisable as ethics have not developed as quickly as technology' (2011: 19). Yet of course, as the film's virtuous American hero, he can never really be shown to be *one of them*, as he is distanced from the Other by his narrative centrality, his good looks, humility and his prodigious intellect: he is modestly able to fix the broken factory machines when asked to by the grateful manager, he is able to build complicated scientific machinery in his ramshackle flat with bits and pieces sourced from garbage very much how Tony Stark was able to prove his brilliance in the caves of Afghanistan, and he stands up for his beautiful co-worker, Martina (played by Brazilian model Débora Nascimento), when she is harassed by local thugs.

It is revealed that Banner has relocated to Brazil in order to discover a cure for his condition, hoping to either find a way to control his state or be rid of it by using a rare flower only to be found in the Amazon jungle. Unfortunately for him he accidentally cuts himself while working in the factory, causing his blood to inadvertently drip into a bottle of Pingo Doce soda which later infects a man in the United States with gamma radiation poisoning.[11] It is this which allows General Ross to finally locate him and he sends a team of elite soldiers led by the aging British-Russian Emil Blonsky (Tim Roth). Ross is keenly aware that Banner does not belong in the *favelas* of Rio and offers a very specific order, 'Get our agency people looking for a white man at that bottling plant!' The resulting mission itself is clearly immersed in very specific new millennial 'War on Terror' discourse when it is described by Ross as a 'snatch and grab, live capture' and Banner as 'a fugitive from the US government who stole military secrets'. Five years after the release of *The Incredible Hulk*, the 2013 Snowden revelations concerning NSA spying practices revealed that thousands of heads of state had been spied on, including the Brazilian President Dilma Rousseff (2011–16). Glenn Greenwald suggested,

> That the US government – in complete secrecy – is constructing a ubiquitous spying apparatus aimed not only at its own citizens, but *all of the world's citizens*, has profound consequences. It erodes, if not eliminates, the ability to use the internet with any remnant of privacy or personal security. It vests the US government with boundless power over those to whom it has no accountability. It permits allies of the US – including aggressively oppressive ones – to benefit from indiscriminate spying on their citizens' communications. It radically alters the balance of power between the US and ordinary citizens of the world. And it sends an unmistakable signal to the world that while the US *very minimally* values the privacy rights of Americans, it assigns zero value to the privacy of everyone else on the planet. (2013; emphasis in original)

It is clear that Ross and Blonsky, both from within the military industrial complex, are framed as the film's antagonists: Ross is another one of the MCU's errant father figures (much like Stane in *Iron Man*) and Blonsky is a dark mirror the likes of which appear frequently in the genre. This is quite a contrast to the roots of the Hulk character who, in the early years of his existence during the Cold War, primarily fought against Communist villains. These early battles against villainous 'reds' portrayed 'American moral, technological, and scientific superiority at several points, while portraying the Communist enemy as manipulative, cowardly, and inferior' (Darowski and Darowski 2015: 10). The villains in *The Incredible Hulk* are all American and all from the Military Industrial Complex as they are in *Iron Man* and *Iron Man 2*, but the films are careful to depict those responsible as isolated individuals, rather than the system as a whole being at fault. When placed in the hands of someone more 'moral', like Stark or Banner (and as we will see in the next chapter, Steve Rogers), advanced weaponised technology (even Weapons of Mass Destruction) can and even *must* be used for the greater good. It is important to note that Stark, Banner and Rogers, or more accurately their alter egos Iron Man, Hulk and Captain America, are portrayed as reluctant heroes and defensive weapons, who only use their powers when it is necessary to protect civilians, as opposed to the likes of Ross and Stane who seek to use them to instigate conflicts all over the globe, often for very selfish reasons but almost always under the guise of national security.

Blonsky's men target Banner in the *favela* seemingly unconcerned about the presence of civilians and after a chase through crowded streets and across rooftops, they corner him in the bottling factory where he works. It is only then, twenty-six minutes into film, that we see the Hulk for the first time. Having not been told what to expect, Blonsky's men are unsurprisingly shocked at the appearance of the Hulk and are then quickly overpowered as their conventional weapons are shown to be entirely useless against something so powerful. Evading the military, the Hulk flees only to wake up, transformed back into Banner, no longer in Rio or even Brazil, but thousands of miles away in Guatemala. From there a destitute Banner, stripped of his first-world status (if only for a limited time, like Stark in Afghanistan, Bruce Wayne in China in *Batman Begins* and Danny Rand in K'un-Lun in *Iron Fist*), hitchhikes through Mexico where he begs for money on the streets of Chiapas.

The aging military man Blonsky is keenly aware that he is no match for something as incredible as the Hulk, so Ross inducts him into an experimental programme, a discontinued offshoot of the Super Soldier Programme which created Captain America, designed to increase his speed, strength and agility. The ethics of unchecked experimentation become a recurring motif in the MCU and those who seek to use science for their own personal gain (like Samuel Sterns, Blonsky and Ross in *The Incredible Hulk*, Stane in *Iron Man*, Hammer and Vanko in *Iron Man 2*, and many others) are contrasted with those who seek to use it for the greater good (in *The Incredible Hulk*, Banner but of course Tony Stark and later Hank Pym in *Ant-Man*). *The Incredible Hulk* shows that powers obtained from science magnify already present qualities: therefore, Blonsky becomes harder and crueller because he was like that anyway (when asked how he feels by one of his men, he replies 'like a monster') but Banner, even in his uncontrolled Hulk guise, is capable of protecting innocents, because he is virtuous in his original unchanged state.

Seeking to retrieve his research, Banner returns to the site of his original trauma, Willowdale in Virginia, the home of Marvel's fictional Culver University (where we are informed both Erik Selvig and Andrew Garner in *Marvel's Agents of S.H.I.E.L.D.* also taught) having walked all the way from Brazil through Guatemala and Mexico to the United States in seventeen days. Reluctantly reunited with Betty, as he knows the dangers he continues to face and does not want to involve her, he is again confronted by Ross and a newly enhanced Blonsky. After first using a Tony Stark-designed non-lethal long-range acoustic device (LRAD) Blonsky and Hulk engage in hand-to-hand combat. For a while

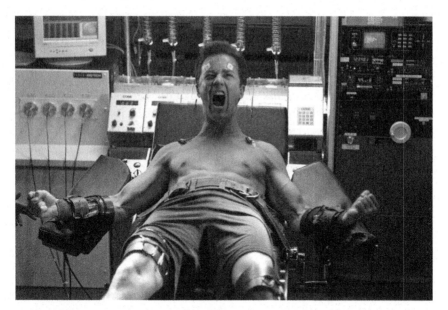

Fig. 9: Bruce Banner (Edward Norton) struggles to control the monster within in *The Incredible Hulk* (2008)

Blonsky is even able to keep up with Hulk, before his hubris gets the better of him and Hulk smashes him into a tree, seemingly leaving him for dead. In these scenes Banner is shown as deeply reluctant to transform both because he loathes the process and also because he fears that he cannot control it. It is here that Ross reveals the extent of his desire to capture Banner and that he will put innocent civilians in danger, even his daughter, when he orders helicopter gunships to target the Hulk. When Betty gets caught in the crossfire and is about to be killed it is only the Hulk that saves her, demonstrating that he is indeed conscious of his actions in some way.

The figure of the Hulk has often been connected to debates concerning masculinity throughout the history of the reception of the character and *The Incredible Hulk* presents us with two very distinct types of man in a similar way to that articulated in *Thor*: the more traditional, macho, hypermasculine model personified by the likes of Blonsky and Ross, which is shown to be fundamentally flawed throughout, and the new millennial sensitive 'new man' embodied in Betty's new boyfriend, the psychiatrist Leonard Samson (Ty Burrell). This paradigm is also shown to have its problems, as despite his earnestness, Samson is framed as rather weak, ineffectual and is entirely ignored by Betty as soon as Banner returns. It is only Banner who is able to reconcile these two seemingly paradoxical strains of masculinity in one person: he is sensitive, intelligent and virtuous, a man unafraid of action even in his unchanged form. But, of course, his transformations into his alter ego enable him to protect Betty and other innocents in ways Banner alone would never be able to do. It is this which makes the character of Banner/Hulk the perfect conduit for what many regard as the wish-fulfilment fantasy appeal of the superhero genre, as it becomes acted out in the film itself. While audiences might aspire to be *like* Thor, Iron Man or even the Hulk, Banner gets to see this realised within the diegetic frames of the film and is able to *become the Hulk* in our place. Edward Norton described this process as the 'great fantasy you have when you don't feel empowered, that you have this lurking monster within you that's going to come out to defend you if people hassle you… It's a fantasy a lot of teenagers can relate to! Not just teenagers…' (2008). The casting of Edward Norton as Banner might then be seen as either ironic or one of the reasons he was drawn to the material as Norton's interpretation accentuates the split-personality theme which has come to dominate his career in films like *Primal Fear* (1996), *Fight Club* (1999) and *Leaves of Grass* (2009). Like Tyler Durden in *Fight Club*, itself a powerful treatise on the crisis of masculinity, the Hulk has been read by many writers as a projection of a rampant and out of control id which is unconstrained by social mores (see Comtois 2009). Kevin Feige stated that this was one of the reasons Marvel wanted Norton for the role, 'Edward has got that duality down pat – look at *Primal Fear* or *Fight Club*. I think that was the big draw to us and to him with the project' (qtd. in De Semlyen 2008: 66). As already noted, in the creation of the Hulk Stan Lee drew from Stevenson's *Dr Jekyll and Mr Hyde* and if it is correct, as Freud surmised, that 'The ego represents what we call reason and sanity, in contrast to the id, which contains the passions' (qtd. in Reef 2001: 106), one might ask what doctors Jekyll and Banner are able to do in the form of their alter egos that their ordinary selves are not? The answer to this in *Dr Jekyll and Mr Hyde* seems fairly unambiguous: through the transgressive character of Hyde, Jekyll is able to free himself from the stultifying morality of the Victorian era and indulge in licentious behaviour that he would never be able to participate in or even acknowledge in his respectable daily life (see Rose 1996). In the case of the MCU incarnation of Banner and Hulk, this is complicated somewhat as there is very little sexual dimension to the character, although of course this might be because he is not allowed to express this in a family film (but this certainly makes us see the 'I can't…' scene in a different light). Might Banner's transformation to the Hulk be more about the power with which it affords him to reject those who would seek to infringe on his rights as a citizen, an issue of particular relevance in the post-9/11 era, when he finds himself targeted, restrained and pursued by a military industrial complex that refuses to recognise his personhood? Like in many MCU films his heroism is a burden, later described as a 'terrible privilege' by Tony Stark in conversation with Banner (who is then played by Mark Ruffalo) in *The Avengers*. Leterrier and Norton, given their angst-ridden interpretation of the character, cannot bring themselves to allow Banner to express that he might actually *enjoy* the power and liberation of being the Hulk (which does happen in Lee's version), but the film does provocatively imply that on some levels it might actually be the Hulk who is *the real* identity and Banner who is the mask. In this understanding, the Hulk allows him to be that which he really wants to be, behave how he truly wishes, unrestrained by contemporary mores and social values. As Michael Brewer wrote of the comic version of the Hulk, but which can just as accurately be applied to the films,

> Most terrible of all for Bruce Banner is the dawning realisation that the Hulk isn't a separate entity at all. The bestial hulk represents the hidden dark side of Banner's own subconscious mind, the angry and aggressive persona Banner has always feared and repressed. Suddenly the habits and safeguards of a lifetime are inadequate. Morality, cooperation, acceptance, reason, compromise – all the bricks that build a civilised society – are shattered and scattered by the fury of the Hulk. (2004: 28)

This understanding, which Banner only comes to in the final image of the film, reveals that his search for a cure might be ultimately futile, as he cannot erase that which is an integral part of his own identity.

Having been defeated by the Hulk twice, Blonsky overdoses on the serum (which he ingests by drinking samples of Banner's blood) and transforms into the monstrous Abomination, before going on a rampage through Harlem, New York. Blonsky's latent irresponsibility and immorality becomes magnified in both his monstrous appearance and behaviour. It is only then that Banner, who until then had seen his condition as something to be eradicated, realises that he might be able to do good as the Hulk. What separates Banner from Blonsky and Ross are his feelings of empathy and his acceptance of responsibility for his actions ('*We* made this thing [the Abomination], *all of us*'). Like Stark and Thor and many (though not all) of the MCU heroes, Banner has undergone a profound change because of his traumatic experiences, which transforms him physically, but just as importantly, emotionally and psychologically.

The film's conclusion lacks the dramatic impact of the ending of *Thor*, where audiences had been able to become invested in the emotional triangle between Thor, Loki and Odin. Here Marvel sidelines the charismatic performances of Norton and Roth in favour of two CGI creations fighting on the streets of Harlem, with the scale of the destruction considerably larger than that of the final confrontation between Stane and Iron Man, the start of a process that would continue, for the most part, in Marvel films with every year that passed. Even though the CGI is impressively detailed, it is hard to care about the actions of the two in a sequence which feels more akin to a video game. As one might expect, Hulk finally overcomes Abomination but is prevented from killing him by Betty, who reminds him of his humanity and that to kill him would be reducing himself to his level.

If the early Marvel films are indeed to be seen, as Spanakos suggested, 'post-September 11 fantasies of self-preservation' (2011: 15), *The Incredible Hulk* poses questions about the relationship between superheroes and the state that the MCU will meditate on as the series progresses and which will build to a climax in *Captain America: Civil War*, a film which will not feature the Hulk, but will see the return of General Ross. Banner is a tortured and traumatised hero, much like Stark, and they are both examples of Pheasant-Kelly's 'wounded hero' the likes of which became so prominent in post-9/11 films, both inside and outside of the superhero genre (2013: 144). While the original Hulk was a Frankenstein's monster created by the nuclear age, his MCU incarnation is consciously framed as a WMD created by the Military Industrial Complex, the impact of which will continue to be explored in both *The Avengers* and *Avengers: Age of Ultron*. Banner is a very human figure, even in his Hulk guise, and after his defeat of Abomination, he again runs, this time to the wilds of Bella Coola in a remote cabin in the wilderness of British Columbia, Canada. As he had tried unsuccessfully to in Rio, he attempts to control his heart rate. As the camera shows it reaching two hundred beats per minute there is a close-up of his face: his eyes turn red and he seems to have a hint of a smile, before the shot abruptly cuts to black. Audiences ask themselves 'Does this mean he is finally able to control it?' Norton's original script explicitly features the question 'Was that a flash of a smile?' (2007: 115) and Peter David's novelisation of the film features the line, 'His lips twitched with the tiniest hint of a smile' (2008b: 128). It is a question that is not fully answered until the end of *The Avengers* four years later and this element of control, or rather lack of it, will be key to the character as he progresses through the MCU films. However, these future appearances of Bruce Banner/the Hulk did not feature Edward Norton playing the character, reportedly due to creative differences between himself and Marvel Studios, and he was replaced by Mark Ruffalo who described the Hulk, with tongue firmly in cheek, as, 'my generation's *Hamlet*' (qtd. in Jensen 2012).

As only the second film in the MCU proper, the connective tissues which would go on to define the franchise are tentatively and not entirely convincingly in place and the film struggles to find an appropriate tone throughout which is no doubt largely the result of competing visions of what Leterrier, Norton and Feige wanted to see on the screen. Leterrier's assertion in the director's commentary that, 'We all decided together that this was a world without superheroes, this is the first time everybody sees that' are contradicted by the film's explicit mentions of the Super Soldier programme and even the appearance of Tony Stark himself in what would be the equivalent of the post-credits stinger in the rest of the MCU, here placed during the body of the film and even before the scene in the wilderness. Stark enters a bar where Ross is drowning his sorrows in the aftermath of the Hulk versus Abomination battle and asks the General, 'What if I told you we were putting a team together?' Two years later by the time of the release of *Iron Man 2*, as we have already seen, it was clear that this was not the direction that Marvel Studios intended to take the overarching narrative of the MCU when it was revealed that Stark is initially *rejected* from the Avengers Initiative. In 2011 Marvel attempted to 'retcon' this in one of the series of short films released by Marvel which were termed One-Shots, *The Consultant*, which showed that it was all part of a S.H.I.E.L.D. ruse to annoy Ross to make sure he does not release Blonsky, so Stark was sent on purpose to make sure that this did not happen. Louis D'Esposito, the co-president of Marvel Studios, admitted as such with his statement, 'some things we had to correct' (qtd. in Surrell 2012: 10). Regardless, the two subjects of this chapter, *The Incredible Hulk* and *Thor*, are origin stories and the building blocks upon which the future of the Marvel Cinematic Universe was built. After the successful introductions of Iron Man, Hulk and Thor, there remained only one more member of the Avengers Prime to bring to the screen and, despite his iconic status and popularity since his creation in 1941, he proved to be the most challenging of all.

Notes

1   In the pilot episode (1.01) of *Marvel's Agents of S.H.I.E.L.D.* Grant Ward observes, 'I don't think Thor's technically a god' to which Maria Hill replies, 'Well, you haven't been near his arms'. In the first fifteen MCU films the closest one gets to a 'real' god is Ego, the Celestial and Star-Lord's father, in *Guardians of the Galaxy Vol. 2* and even he qualifies his status as a god with 'a small g'.

2   Thor also went to San Diablo, a thinly-veiled substitute for Cuba, during the Cold War and fought against a Castro-like villain called The Executioner in June 1965 *Journey into Mystery #117*.

3   It has been observed that the interactions between Odin, Loki and Thor in their Marvel iterations have a distinctly Shakespearean dimension to them (see Fingeroth 2004: 37). In fact, many speculated this was precisely the reason that Marvel selected Branagh to direct the film. In interviews Branagh went to significant lengths to downplay the Shakespearean connections, but they do seem quite pronounced. Shakespeare's *Henry V*, an adaption of which Branagh directed in 1989 starring himself, is a template for Thor in its portrayal of a young king and his trials and tribulations in a journey towards maturity. Anthony Hopkins concurred in his description

of the film as 'a superhero movie, but with a bit of Shakespeare thrown in' (qtd. in Carroll 2010).

4 Interestingly, in Norse mythology, Laufey was Loki's mother and not his father. No doubt this change amused audiences in Iceland where Laufey is still a fairly common female name and the film was one of the most popular of the year.

5 Laufey's insult is a knowing reference to Þrymskviða, a poem from the *Poetic Edda* in which Thor is forced to dress up as the goddess Freya to retrieve his hammer Mjölnir from a giant. Thor complains, 'You'll all mock me and call me unmanly if I put on a bridal veil' (Crossley-Holland 1980: 70).

6 In 2002 George W. Bush was said to have remarked of Saddam Hussein, 'After all, this is the guy who tried to kill my dad' (qtd. in King 2002).

7 In what might be considered as a strange coincidence and/or evidence of the lack of roles for actors of Middle Eastern descent, Oliver Stone's *W.* features Sayed Badreya as Saddam Hussein, the same Egyptian actor who played Abu Bakar in *Iron Man*.

8 Martin Arnold also commented on *Thor* directly in an article called 'Thor the Movie: Politics with a Hammer' that 'In this case, the issue is national salvation or, to put it another way, the problems of twenty-first century American foreign policy... And its story of an unmotivated invasion by a son who feels empowered by birthright to conquer the evildoers that embarrassed his father adds a clever subtext about American foreign policy' (2011b).

9 Some of the rare *actual* sacrifices in the MCU are Yinsen Ho's for Tony Stark in *Iron Man*, Quicksilver in *Avengers: Age of Ultron* and Yondu Udonta's for Peter Quill at the climax of *Guardians of the Galaxy: Vol. 2*.

10 The Banner in the television show was an extremely empathetic incarnation of the character and his origin was very different to the comic and both Lee's and Leterrier's films. Bixby's Banner was researching into the phenomonen of how some people are able to tap into extreme reserves of strength at stressful moments after he was unable to save his wife in a car crash. Discovering that it was gamma radiation which prompted this change in normal individuals Banner blasted himself with excessive doses which led to his unique condition.

11 This is the second of what would become ubiquitous Stan Lee cameos. In *Iron Man* he played a man mistaken for Hugh Heffner by Tony Stark on the red carpet for the Stark fundraiser. In 2017, responding to a fan theory which had been gaining momentum for some years, Kevin Feige seemed to imply that all his characters might be the same person and that he is a Watcher, an alien race that observes key events throughout the galaxy (see McMillan 2017).

CHAPTER THREE

State Fantasy and the Superhero: (Mis)Remembering World War II in *Captain America: The First Avenger*

> Significant to this role is Captain America's ability to connect the political projects of American nationalism, internal order, and foreign policy (all formulated at the national or global scale) with the scale of the individual, or body. The character of Captain America connects these scales by literally embodying American identity, presenting for readers a hero both of, and for, the nation.
>
> – Jason Dittmer (2005: 627)

I.

Despite being known as 'the First Avenger', Captain America aka Steve Rogers was actually the last of the Avengers Prime to receive an origin film in the MCU in the form of Joe Johnston's *Captain America: The First Avenger*, the penultimate film in Marvel's ambitious Phase One. While this was Captain America's first onscreen appearance, his arrival had been foreshadowed on several occasions: both in *Iron Man* with the Easter egg of his iconic red, white and blue shield hidden in the background of Tony Stark's workshop, in *Iron Man 2* with Stark's casual use of the shield as an impromptu wedge during one of his many experiments, but also in the inclusion of a variation of the Super Soldier Serum in *The*

Incredible Hulk. Stark's disrespectful use of Captain America's symbolic weapon anticipates the conflict which will be depicted between the two in *The Avengers*, continues in *Avengers: Age of Ultron* and comes to a dramatic climax in *Captain America: Civil War*, where Captain America's irony-free patriotism and old-fashioned values are shown to be far removed from the acerbic wit, scepticism and moral flexibility of a character like Tony Stark. The creation of Iron Man and the Hulk, as we have seen, has been updated many times over the decades, but Steve Rogers has *always* remained a product of World War II and his origin is so firmly associated with the conflict that it is unlikely that it could ever be successfully altered. His connection to the enduring mytho-poetic resonance of World War II, a conflict which Cynthia Webber explained produces a 'rich vein of moral certainties that the United States mines at moments of its greatest moral uncertainty' (2006: 29), might have been why Thomas Foster regarded the character as the perfect antidote to twenty-first-century cynicism. He suggested it was 'precisely this immediate symbolic burden, this allegorical flatness and lack of psychological depth, and this lack of distance between character and nation, that make Captain America a perfect 9/11 icon for a culture dominated by cynical reason' (2005: 262). When Captain America was 'killed' in the comic books in 2007, fan reaction was mixed to say the least and Joe Simon, his original co-creator stated, 'It's a hell of a time for him to go. We really *need* him now' (qtd. in Shapiro 2011; emphasis added). The 'now' to which Simon refers are the turbulent first decades of the new millennium and it is fitting then that both Marvel Studios *and* the diegetic universe of the MCU turned to Captain America once again in one such real-world era of 'moral uncertainty'. The return to more traditional forms of masculinity had been called for, as we have already noted, by the likes of Peggy Noonan and Kim DuToit who regarded 9/11 as something of a wake-up call for all that had gone wrong in America in the second half of the twentieth century, and there could be no better example of this than Captain America, who has been an enduring and iconic figure in the world of comic books and popular culture since his first appearance on 10 March 1941, where he was famously pictured on the front cover punching Adolf Hitler and fighting Nazis nine months *before* Pearl Harbor and America's entry into World War II (see Noonan 2001; DuToit n.d.). Nicholas Yanes' description of him as 'the meridian example of pro-war attitudes in World War 2 era comic books' (2009: 53) is an apt one for a character who was originally explicitly created to function as a propagandistic figure both *inside* and *outside* of the panels of the original comic book. Jack Kirby, the other person responsible for the creation of Cap, said that he 'was created for a time that needed noble figures' (qtd. in Goulart 1993: 4). In fact, alongside Superman there has been no more potent symbol of what many perceive as quintessential American values than Captain America in popular culture and the character has also been described as 'the ideological center of the Marvel universe' (Costello 2009: 66). Even the very weapon that he uses and the costume he wears function as synechdocal emblems of these values: the use of a defensive shield instead of an offensive weapon is symbolic of Captain America's, and by extension America's, enduring belief in its role of the protector of liberty and defender of innocents around the globe. It is for these very reasons that Jason Dittmer (2012) considers Captain America (and other heroes like him) as superlative examples of 'nationalist superheroes' because of their pronounced connection to and an embodiment of the values of the country they were created in and come to represent. This has been viewed very critically by some: John McTiernan, who, in his own way, contributed more than most in the 1980s to the evolution of modern action cinema through films like *Die Hard* (1988) and *Predator* (1987), denounced the superhero genre, and in particular Captain America, in an interview with the French edition of *Premiere* in July 2016: 'Captain America, I'm not joking... The cult of American hyper-masculinity is one of the worst things to have happened to the world during the last fifty years. Hundreds of thousands of people have died because of this idiotic delusion. So how is it possible to watch a film called *Captain America*?!' (qtd. in West 2016).

While the integration of the fantastical character of Thor into the predominantly 'real world' diegetic narratives of the MCU proved a challenge, reconciling such an iconic figure of World War II like Captain America, one often associated with jingoistic patriotism and American triumphantalism, to the post-9/11 era was perhaps an even greater one. Unlike the starkly drawn moral binaries that World War II has provided storytellers with in the decades since, in recent years the United States has been viewed with much more scrutiny around the globe and so when the puny Steve Rogers, yet to become Captain America, says 'I don't want to kill anyone, I don't like bullies I don't care where they are from', it is an ironic suggestion for international audiences in an era in which America is regarded by some as the 'bully of the free world' (see Wills 1999) and by others as the biggest threat to global peace (see Huntingdon 1999). Thus, John Shelton Lawrence and Robert Jewett were right to ask the question, writing prior to the release of the film but after 9/11, in a foreword to *Captain America Complex: The Dilemma of Zealous Nationalism*, what direction or relevance the character might have after the events of 11 September 2001: 'Since Captain America's writers traditionally compelled him to engage in the discourses of power within his eras, consider the strong implications of his playing a role in the Global War on Terrorism. Remaining true to his own character, as well as the genre conventions, how could he fight in this war?' (2003: v). They use the term 'the Captain America Complex' to define the complicated relationship between American national self-identification processes and foreign policy, indicating that the phrase encompasses 'the uneasy fusion of two kinds of roles. Should America be the "city set upon a hill" that promotes the rule of law even when faced with difficult adversaries? Or should it crusade on the military plane of battle, allowing no law or institution to impede its efforts to destroy evil?' (2003: xiii).

Joe Johnston's *Captain America: The First Avenger* consciously strives to avoid the problematic and divisive politics of the post-9/11 era by setting the majority of its narrative, apart from a brief prologue and epilogue, during World War II. Yet this itself causes a range of complex issues about how its vision of the war is constructed from very modern perspectives. In spite of the presence of fantastical elements like HYDRA, the Tesseract and the Red Skull, its World War II is one very familiar to American audiences and one which has been routinely recreated in American films since *Sands of Iwo Jima*, through *Saving Private Ryan* and more recently *Fury*, films which have dramatised World War II as it would like to be remembered by American culture at large rather than, in any meaningful sense, how it actually was. These films construct a 'good war' fought by the 'greatest generation' in which US forces are unambiguously heroic and moral, and the Axis forces of Germany, Japan and Italy are unquestionably evil, in a mythic conflict in which America wins almost alone and sacrifices a great deal for very little in return. In *Captain America: The First Avenger* the war is won because, as Colonel Chester Philips (Tommy Lee Jones) states, 'General Patton has said that wars are fought with weapons but they are won by men. *We* are going to win this war, because *we* have the best men.' But, as many historians have argued, this is very far from the truth. In actual fact, the most critical aspect of US power was

> an economic base that staggered its opponents. Germany and Japan could boast of considerable productive prowess, all the more impressive for an ability to function under tremendous pressure from encroaching enemies. And German as well as Japanese soldiers were typically at least the equal of any the United States sent into battle. (Many observers consider their army with which Germany invaded the Soviet Union, an ally it turned on in 1941, the finest the world has ever seen.) But neither the Japanese nor the Germans could withstand the seemingly bottomless ability of the United States to supply not only itself, but its allies, with whatever it took to win. By 1943, most informed leaders of both Germany and Japan knew they were doomed simply because they could not compete with the seemingly bottomless US capacity for war-making. (Cullen 2017: 6)

Yet this military and capacity is not mythopoetic enough for American identity politics and comments like Colonel Phillips' are platitudes which have become transmogrified into facts in the cultural imaginary and embodied in fictional

American soldiers like Sgt. John M. Stryker (John Wayne) in *Sands of Iwo Jima*, Captain Virgil Hilts (Steve McQueen) in *The Great Escape* (1963), Captain John H. Miller (Tom Hanks) in *Saving Private Ryan*, and Sergeant Don 'Wardaddy' Collier (Brad Pitt) in *Fury*. In these films, and many like them, total military and economic dominance is metamorphosed into narratives about plucky soldiers outgunned and outmanned, but never outfought. As Marilyn Young has stated, the war is understood 'as a long, valiant struggle that the United States fought pretty much on its own, winning an exceptionally clean victory that continues to redeem Americans under arms anywhere, at any point in history' (2005: 178), whereas in actual fact it might be more truthful to assert, as Jim Cullen did, that the United States 'risked the least and gained the most from World War II' (2017: xix). Several writers have criticised this simplistic depiction of World War II and argued that films like *Saving Private Ryan* have endorsed and reconsolidated an alluring vision of a 'just war' and American altruism which led Debra Ramsay to assert that Spielberg's film offers a 'nostalgic view of the Greatest Generation [which] cannot be separated from nostalgia for the war itself' (2015: 98). *The First Avenger* does something comparable, rewriting the war in a range of compelling and affective ways, primarily by viewing the conflict through the prism of the twenty-first century in its portrayal of harmonious multicultural communities, American beneficence and moral superiority. In doing so it joins the ranks of a multitude of American films which erase and misremember those unpalatable aspects of the war, in a process which James Berger described as the elision of 'the actual and evident imperfections of American history' (1999: 134), offering instead another example of the 'mythic massage' that popular media texts are able to perform in their appropriation of cultural memory (Lawrence and Jewett 2002: 116).

II.

The First Avenger begins in June 1943, eighteen months after the attacks on Pearl Harbor, with the diminutive Steve Rogers (Chris Evans) desperate to join the armed forces and serve his country, but finding himself rejected again and again due to his slight frame and numerous health problems. Steve is inspired to join up because he knows it is the right thing to do and that everyone is doing their bit. A newsreel announcer declares, 'War continues to ravage Europe but help is on the way. Every able-bodied young man is lining up to serve his country... Our brave boys are showing the Axis powers that the price of freedom is *never* too high.' Rogers wants to join the 107th Infantry like his father before him who fought in World War I, and it is the unit recently joined by his best friend James 'Bucky' Barnes (Sebastian Stan). The film gives us thirty minutes with this 'skinny Steve' before he becomes Captain America, but it is important for audiences that he always remains 'skinny Steve' at heart, not just in this film but throughout his future appearances in the MCU. It is this determination, earnestness and sense of duty that brings him to the attention of Dr Abraham Erskine (Stanley Tucci) at the World Exposition of Tomorrow who signs him up for the experimental Super Soldier programme, which goes by the name of Operation Rebirth, that finally gives him the opportunity to serve his country.

Steve Rogers, even prior to becoming Captain America, embodies the belief that World War II was a noble war fought for justice and freedom, not a complicated geopolitical enterprise of conflicting rivalry, land, influence and economic interests. This socio-political reality has become progressively diluted into the public's understanding of a war in which the US was a beacon of liberty, standing up for freedom, both for itself and for those around the globe and the Axis powers were categorically evil, each with designs to enslave the world. In a quiet dialogue exchange at Camp Lehigh where Steve is being trained, the German exile Erskine tells Steve, 'Hitler uses his fantasies to inspire his followers … with the marching and the big show and the flags', speaking to a man who will, very soon, inspire his own nation … while wearing a flag on his shield and a large 'A' on his head in what Brian Hack memorably described as a 'eugenic makeover' (2009: 80). Erskine speaks to particular American fantasies of beneficent power being used only for good and the enduring paradox of the USA desirous of seeing itself simultaneously as the world's number one *and* a plucky underdog. While Captain America is undoubtedly being created as an offensive weapon in the war, the process is referred to as a defensive one and 'the first step on the path to peace'. Erskine persuades the reluctant Colonel Philips to choose Steve Rogers, among all the potential recruits, 'Because a strong man who has known power all his life may lose respect for that power, but a weak man knows the value of strength'. Erskine is framed very much like Yinsen Ho in the caves of Afghanistan in *Iron Man*, right down to the similarity of their deathbed pleas: in place of Yinsen's 'earn this' Erskine silently points at Steve's heart, reminding him of their conversation: 'Stay who you are, not a perfect soldier but a *good* man.' However, unlike Stark and despite his diminutive status, Steve was already heroic before his physical transformation in Project Rebirth, which significantly enhances his physical characteristics, but leaves his essential qualities of goodness and decency *exactly the same*. So, although Steve is a more traditional form of masculine hero, even in the 1940s he embodies aspects of the new man archetype in his sensitivity and emotional vulnerability.

Captain America's antagonist in *The First Avenger* is his most famous and enduring one, the Red Skull, one of the most literal examples of the dark mirror referred to in the previous chapters. The Red Skull retrieves the powerful

Tesseract from the town of Tønsberg in Norway (which had briefly featured in *Thor*) and, with the help of his colleague Arnim Zola (Toby Jones), proceeds to transform it into a weapon of mass destruction (WMD). Even though Hugo Weaving delivers a charismatic performance, the Red Skull is a pantomime-like villain who would not have been out of place in Captain America comics circa 1941 and a disappointingly one-dimensional villain after the Machiavellian allure of Tom Hiddlestone's Loki in *Thor*. In an effort to depoliticise the film, Nazis are almost entirely erased from its narrative, aside from a few brief mentions, and Cap is shown to fight against the less politically sensitive HYDRA throughout the film instead, which prompted German film critic Robert Cherkowski to suggest that the film dramatises 'the last just war in which the US took part. But even this war ... is still depoliticized and played out in the fields of fantasy ... [and does not] show a single swastika' (n.d.). Whether this is done with an eye on the international box office is hard to discern, but in some countries (for example Russia, Ukraine and South Korea) the film was released only as *The First Avenger* rather than *Captain America: The First Avenger*. What the film does imply is that if a pure of heart American participates in Erskine's experiments his innate sense of goodness will create an altruistic hero, but if a German does it he will emerge as abhorrently evil, conveniently ignoring how close Captain America fits the image of an Aryan ideal himself. This potent image and Erskine's earlier comment about 'the marching and the big show and the flags' is dramatically realised in the film's two-and-a-half-minute United Service Organisations (USO)-themed musical number accompanying David Zippel and Alan Menken's Irving Berlinesque 'The Star Spangled Man' which wittily evokes both the wartime musicals of the era like *Yankee Doodle Dandy* (1942) and *The All-Star Bond Rally* (1945), and at the same time reproduces early Captain America iconography: from the changing shapes of his shield to showing him punch Hitler in the face on the stage replete with children interacting with the show as if it were a pantomime calling to Cap, 'He's behind you!'

Captain America's involvement with the USO had been instigated by Senator Brandt (Michael Brandon), chronologically the first in a long line of self-serving politicians in the MCU (see also Stern in *Iron Man* 2 and Senator Christian Ward in *Marvel's Agents of S.H.I.E.L.D.*) offering him a different way to contribute to the war effort with the question, 'Son, do you want to serve your country on the most important battlefield in the war?' This battlefield is not fighting Nazis overseas as Steve had originally hoped, but as part of the USO selling war bonds to the public. The musical number intercuts Steve holding babies and signing autographs with images of both children *and* G.I.s reading comics about his exploits. In 1942 a remarkable fifteen million comics a week were sold across the United States, a level of popularity that has never been approximated since (see Wright

Fig. 10: Captain America (Chris Evans) is a synechdocal figure representative of what are regarded as quintessential American values in *Captain America: The First Avenger* (2011)

2003: 31). Brandt's aid explains to Steve, 'You sell a few bonds, bonds buy bullets … bullets kill Nazis, bang bang boom!', but the film portrays Steve's participation in the process as distinctly unmasculine and even shameful. Steve is informed that bond sales are boosted by ten percent in every city he visits, an achievement in itself, but still Colonel Phillips refers to him dismissively as a 'chorus girl' and Agent Peggy Carter, with whom by now he has fallen in love, sees him as 'a dancing monkey'. However, the centrality of the sale of war bonds to the US war effort is hard to underestimate; between 1941 and 1945 World War II cost the United States government in excess of $250 billion, approximately forty-five percent of which was paid for by taxes with the rest being raised in eight separate war bond drives sold to eighty-five million people (see Kimble 2006). The implication being that the only way for a real man to serve one's country is by killing its enemies, ignoring, as Hollywood films have done for decades, the hard work and sacrifices of many millions of civilians during the conflict. The sequence ends with Rogers taking the USO tour to Azzano in Italy in November 1943 and performing for servicemen from the 107th infantry, the unit he had earlier aspired to join, who prove to be not as enamoured with him as the children and young women stateside were; they even throw fruit at him, yelling 'Nice boots Tinkerbell!'

The Azzano sequence is noteworthy for other reasons too, as in the crowd and also in subsequent missions, it is clear to see that the vision of the US army during World War II *The First Avenger* wishes to project is one of a desegregated military with white and black soldiers serving alongside one another. Nearly a million African-Americans joined the armed forces in World War II in a variety of capacities but they served entirely separately, had separate training facilities and even had separate blood supplies (see Wynn 2010; Controvich 2015). The only black soldiers fighting in Europe at this time were segregated including the famous Buffalo Soldiers of the 92nd Infantry Division who fought in Italy from 1944 until the end of the war. This is not the only time the film shows such scenes of racial harmony, which conveniently ignores or erases the unpalatable realities of the African-American experience of World War II, as have the majority of films about the conflict, as earlier in the film black and white Americans are shown sharing recruitment stations, and black and white children are shown happily playing on the streets together. Charles M. Blow, writing in *The New York Times* stated, 'But as I watched the scenes of a fictitious integrated American Army fighting in Europe at the end of World War II, I became unsettled. Yes, I know that racial revisionism has become so common in film that it's almost customary, so much so that moviegoers rarely balk or even blink' (2011).

Later when Cap forms his elite unit, the Howling Commandoes, it features an African-American, Private Gabriel 'Gabe' Jones and a Japanese-American, Private James 'Jim' Morita, who we are informed served in the US Army Nisei Squadron. While a considerable number of Japanese-Americans fought during World War II they were forbidden from being deployed in the Pacific Theatre, whereas no such restrictions were placed on Italian-Americans or German-Americans who fought on the Western Front, and all Japanese-American men not in the armed forces were automatically given 4C status as an 'enemy alien'. Around 110,000 Japanese-Americans were interned by the United States government due to fears of anti-American activities and sabotage, an act President Reagan later apologised for as part of the Civil Liberies Act of 1988 when Congress stated that the internment was a decision based on 'race prejudice, war hysteria, and a failure of political leadership' and ordered reparations paid to every surviving internee. This mistreatment of both African-Americans and Japanese-Americans is entirely erased from the film and even when implied it is treated as something of a joke. On being rescued from a HYDRA cell he is being held in with Jim Norita, Timothy 'Dum Dum' Dugan turns to the Asian-American with a look of suspicion on his face and asks, 'What, are we taking *everybody*?' to which Norita replies, 'I'm from Fresno, ace'. The seemingly offhand choice of Fresno is also an intriguing one which may or may not be coincidental, but in 1942 North Fresno was the location of the Pinedale Assembly Centre, an interim facility for the relocation of Japanese-Americans to internment camps and perhaps somewhere to which Morita's family and friends could have been sent. These unpleasant truths about World War II offer conspicuous challenges to how it has come to be remembered, as an unambiguous war for freedom fought by all Americans as equals. Dugan's reaction is one of the more truthful moments in a film set in an era when Japanese characters in comics were routinely caricatured with fangs, buckteeth, hunched backs, and drawn with yellow skin.[1] There could have been a scene in *The First Avenger* in which Captain America protests about

Fig. 11: The racial diversity featured in *Captain America: The First Avenger* is one of many examples of how American cinema, according to Bazin, has historically refused to portray American society as it is, but rather 'just as it wanted to see itself'

the racial inequality of his era, where he advocates his support of the Double-V campaign (the drive to promote for equality for African-Americans in the US) or protests against the incarceration of Japanese-Americans, but the film chooses to ignore these aspects of American history, instead presenting us with a vision of the 'good old days' which never really existed outside of film, literature and our collective imagination.[2] *The First Avenger* might only be a fantasy film but it is symptomatic of an American cultural attitude to history and how Americans use the past to create meaning in the present, while at the same time as using the present to images of the past (see Rosenzweig and Thelen 1998). The years between 1942 and 1945 are remembered as a period when the United States was fighting for freedom around the globe, but the fact that it was, at the same time, subjugating large sections of its own people becomes largely forgotten, because such facts do not easily reconcile with the vision America has created of itself.

After he fails to save his best friend Bucky on one of their missions, an act which will return in consequential ways in *Captain America: The Winter Soldier*, Cap redoubles his efforts to destroy the HYDRA bases all over Europe. When he comes face to face with the Red Skull in the final base in the Swiss Alps, the Skull asks him, 'What makes you so special?' and his answer is very revealing, 'Nothing … I'm just a kid from Brooklyn'. It is imperative that Cap, despite his prodigious talents, remains identified as an ordinary person with the implication that anyone, were they virtuousness and hardworking enough, could have been in his place: a more powerful evocation of the American dream would be hard to find, as Jackson Sutliff concurred, describing him as 'the American dream made flesh' (2009: 121). When he discovers that the Red Skull has used the Tesseract to construct WMDs which are aimed at Chicago, Boston and New York, Cap manages to destroy the first two but the one directed at New York remains stuck in the HYDRA ship, the Valkyrie. In an act of supreme self-sacrifice, he elects to pilot the ship into the ground in order to prevent thousands of civilians being killed. In scenes which have been read as evoking the events of 9/11, on the radio with Peggy, Cap says, 'This thing's moving too fast and it's heading for New York... There's not gonna be a safe landing but I can try and force it down.' Sukhdev Sandhu, writing in *The Telegraph*, wrote that, 'Only towards the end is there a whiff of genuine terror: a scene in which an aeroplane heading for New York plummets to earth briefly revives disconcerting memories of *United 93*' (2011). It is interesting that Sandhu equates the sequence not to 11 September 2001 or the crash of Flight United 93, but Paul Greengrass's film, *United 93* (2006). It is not that director Joe Johnston deliberately recreates the scene from the earlier film or perhaps even that he was self-consciously comparing the two events, but that notions of heroic sacrifice for the good of the nation act as the very apex of heroic masculinity now as much as they did during World War II. Like Thor at the climax of his film and Iron Man at the climax of his, Steve elects to voluntarily give up his life for the greater good, *as this is what American heroes do*. As in *United 93* the moment of impact is too traumatic to bear witness to, so *The First Avenger* cuts directly to 8 May 1945 and the V.E. Day celebrations suggesting Cap's sacrifice, and those of many like him, was not in vain.

The film concludes with a brief but resonant coda, as Rogers is shown to wake up in what appears to be a small room in 1940s New York with a seemingly live baseball game playing on the radio revealing that, yet again, the MCU has offered audiences a heroic sacrifice which does not end in an *actual* sacrifice. But it seems wrong to Steve: there is something odd about the nurse's behaviour and he informs the audience that he had attended that baseball game in person. Suspecting foul play, he runs onto the streets of New York outside ... only to find himself not in 1945, but 2011. The rest of Captain America's appearances in the MCU will be in the modern era and his struggle to reconcile himself to the differences between the two will be the central dramatic arc for his character. Until then the goals of Captain America and the government he was working for were one and the same, Colonel Phillips had been hard on him but they had shared a clearly defined mission, to defeat the Nazis and HYDRA. The modern world, as portrayed in the MCU, is shown to be, on the surface at least, much more complicated and even his friends and colleagues like Tony Stark, Nick Fury and

Black Widow frequently display ambiguous moral compasses. The film ends with a close up of his face, now ninety-three but having not aged a day, cast adrift in a world in which everything he knew has been taken from him. He utters just a single understated line and one of the most human moments of the MCU thus far: 'I had a date…'

Notes

1   Somewhat revealingly the actor playing Jim Morita, Kenneth Choi, is not of Japanese but of Korean descent. However, given the relative paucity of roles for Asian-Americans in American film and television his career has been littered with films in which he plays not only Koreans, but both Chinese *and* Japanese characters: from his Fujimoto in *Harsh Times* (2005), Chester Ming in *The Wolf of Wall Street* (2013), to Henry Lin in *Sons of Anarchy* (FX, 2008–14) and Judge Lance Ito in *The People v. O. J. Simpson: American Crime Story* (FX, 2016). Choi reappeared in *Spider-Man: Homecoming* as Principal Morita, with a picture of what one presumes to be either his father or his grandfather, James, in his office.

2   Just as the film struggles to reconcile its twenty-first-century view of race from the 1940s by erasing it from the film, *The First Avenger* raises and then refuses to explicitly mention the Holocaust in its narrative. For many contemporary Americans, the Holocaust now counterfactually has been altered from a difficult-to-process fact learned during and after the war to now being one of the reasons the war was fought for in the cultural imaginary and 'like the story of D-Day a central part of [the American] victory narrative and celebration' (Bodnar 2010: 221). It is alluded to in *Captain America: The First Avenger* in a newspaper headlines read 'Nazis retake Zhitomir' in an allusion to the Zhitomir Pogrom. Dr Erskine is never confirmed to be Jewish but the death of his family in Dachau in 1937 is mentioned in the MCU comic book *Captain America: The First Vengeance* (2011). It can also be seen in the reactions of an elderly couple when 'skinny Steve' visits a cinema where a disrespectful bully shouts at the newsreel. The couple are obviously visually coded coded as being Jewish and the film's script describes the moment as 'Steve looks across the aisle. A YOUNG WOMAN watches the screen, tears welling. She clearly has a man overseas. Across the aisle, a middle-aged Jewish couple looks somber' (Markus and McFeely 2014: 13).

CHAPTER FOUR

'Seeing ... still working on believing!': The Ethics and Aesthetics of Destruction in *The Avengers*

> Once we loved movies where tall buildings exploded or burned to the ground. Now we don't like those so much. And then again, now we do.
>
> – Jeffery Melnick (2009: 18)

> Arguably, being vicariously traumatised invited members of a society to confront, rather than conceal, catastrophes, and in that way might be useful. On the other hand, it might arouse anxiety and trigger defense against further exposure.
>
> – E. Anne Kaplan (2005: 87)

I.

After the two origin stories released in 2011, *Thor* and *Captain America: The First Avenger*, Marvel released only one film in 2012, *The Avengers*, the final film in Phase One of the Marvel Cinematic Universe and the culmination of four years of world-building and the five films discussed so far in this volume.[1] The film had the largest opening weekend in the history of American cinema at the time, taking over $200 million dollars at the US box office and going on to gross more than one and a half billion dollars worldwide, making it the most successful of the year and the third-biggest film of all time behind only James Cameron's *Avatar* (2009) and *Titanic* (1997).

The task of reconciling these disparate heroes into a single film, at the same time adding two more protagonists, Black Widow (who had appeared in *Iron Man 2*) and Hawkeye (who had appeared briefly in *Thor*), was handed to director Joss Whedon. Despite being a high-profile figure in the television industry, *The Avengers* was only Whedon's second feature film after the modestly budgeted *Serenity* (2005), the cinematic expansion of his critically acclaimed but short-lived *Firefly* (Fox, 2002–3). Perhaps the reason he was chosen by Marvel Studios was his proven track record of crafting intelligent, ensemble science fiction narratives and his elevated status within the fan community. *The Avengers* functions as a sequel to each of the three previous origin films (*The Incredible Hulk*, *Thor* and *Captain American: The First Avenger*), the continuation of Tony Stark's narrative arc from *Iron Man* and *Iron Man 2*, the conclusion of Phase One, *and* an introduction to Phase Two, which would begin the following year with *Iron Man 3*. Each character gets their own personal narrative thread which returns to many of the themes discussed in previous chapters: Steve Rogers struggles to come to terms with his place in the modern world; Tony Stark continues to learn about the moral responsibilities of a superhero; Thor about brotherhood and the value of being part of a team; and Bruce Banner (now portrayed by Mark Ruffalo) reconciles himself with his alter ego, who he refers to hypocoristically throughout the film as 'the other guy', and even, as the audience slowly comes to understand, about controlling his emotions.

Given the huge impact of Robert Downey Jr.'s portrayal of Tony Stark/Iron Man, which had resulted in the actor going from having trouble securing insurance bonding on films like *The Singing Detective* (2003) and Woody Allen's *Melinda and Melinda* (2005), to becoming one of the biggest film stars in the world, it was natural to assume that his character would be *primus inter pares* in *The Avengers* (see Lax 2009: 57). This is true to a certain extent, but it is Captain America who emerges as the emotional and moral fulcrum of Whedon's film. *The Avengers* does contain a range of spectacular action scenes, including a climactic 45-minute-long sequence referred to throughout the MCU in the future as the Battle of New York, which are, of course, prerequisite for the genre, but it also features more intimate scenes of character development than one would expect from a big-budget blockbuster. Much to Whedon's credit, he strives to put the humanity of the characters in the foreground of the film which, as a result, gives the action sequences a greater sense of meaning rather than merely an excuse for extravagant spectacle. Whedon commented: 'People think it's all about the mission, but it's all about the team, really. When you do a film like this you have to make sure each character matters as much as the others, but in a different way. That was something that was really important to me. Making sure everyone mattered' (qtd. in Hundley n.d.).

We have seen in previous chapters how the MCU has been intrinsically connected to the times in which it is made: whether we consider Iron Man's explicit connections to the Military Industrial Complex in the 'War on Terror' era, the status of *Thor* and *The Incredible Hulk* as post-9/11 allegories, or Captain America's complicated relationship to how World War II has come to be remembered by American culture at large. This pattern continues in *The Avengers*, which is very much a product of the 'War on Terror' and even views, quite explicitly on occasion, the central alien attack on New York through the prism of the events of 11 September 2001. Several critics drew attention to these connections and J. Hoberman even asserted that the film 'recasts 9/11 in the Bush years' dominant movie mode, namely the comic book superhero spectacular – albeit with a heavy dose of irony and added stereoscopic depth... Bombs away: *The Avengers* is 9/11 as you've never seen it!' (2012). Aside from being consciously visually designed to evoke 9/11, the Battle of New York also functions as a '9/11 moment' within the narrative of the MCU with long-term narrative ramifications throughout Phase Two and beyond. As Senator Ellen Nadeer will later say in *Marvel's Agents of S.H.I.E.L.D.* 'Broken Promises' (4.09), with an eye on the phrase's now powerful associations to 11 September 2001, 'everything changed that day'. In *Iron Man 3*, released the year after, Tony Stark suffers from noticeable symptoms of PTSD after the traumatic events he both witnesses and experiences during *The Avengers*, and even says, 'Nothing's been the same since New York' before confronting a terrorist known as The Mandarin who is, on the surface at least, explicitly constructed as an Osama Bin Laden analogue as much as Ra's al Ghul was in *Batman Begins*.[2] The aftermath of the Battle of New York becomes a backdrop for the events of the Netflix series *Daredevil* (2015–) and Captain America's growing mistrust of S.H.I.E.L.D. in *Captain America: The Winter Soldier*. The Battle of New York itself might be regarded as an example of what Richard Corliss (2009) has called 'disaster porn', a term he originally used to describe the Roland Emmerich disaster film *2012* (2009) and the tendency of large-scale Hollywood films of the era to present spectacularly orchestrated scenes of destruction and devastation which audiences were invited to both marvel at *and* revel in. Corliss's criticism was one of many to emerge around the same time which raised concerns about whether the presentation of such scenes for the amusement of audiences raised ethical quandaries in the aftermath of 9/11, a period in which images of planes colliding with skyscrapers, tall buildings collapsing, debris falling from the skies and scenes of dust-caked, panicked crowds fleeing disaster became an indelible part of the cinematic landscape. Films like *The Day After Tomorrow* (2004), *War of the Worlds* (2005), *Transformers* (2007), *Cloverfield* (2008) and *2012* fill their screens with barely-coded images and situations which seem so self-consciously designed to evoke 9/11 and the 'War on Terror' that Kyle Buchanan felt compelled to ask, 'Is It Possible to Make A Hollywood Blockbuster Without Evoking 9/11?' (2013).

II.

The Avengers begins with the line, 'The Tesseract has awakened', an object that had provided continuity between the Phase One MCU films, appearing briefly in Odin's throne room in *Thor* before becoming more prominently featured in *Captain America: The First Avenger* when the Red Skull used it to arm his legion of HYDRA soldiers. Although it has been called a MacGuffin (see Surrell 2012: 44) it emerges as much more important for the film's narrative than this: described by Black Widow as having 'the potential energy to wipe out the planet' and being 'the key to unlimited sustainable energy' by Nick Fury, who orders it to be used to create weapons, later referred as WMDs by Bruce Banner, in an act decidedly similar to those of the Red Skull during World War II. It is these experiments that function as the catalyst for the events of *The Avengers* as Thor later informs Fury: 'Your work with the Tesseract is what drew Loki to it … and his allies. It is a signal to all the realms that Earth is ready for a higher form of war!' While S.H.I.E.L.D. does not understand the properties of the Tesseract, Nick Fury determines that the use of it is necessary in order to keep the world safe given that he now knows, after the events of *Iron Man*, *Iron Man 2*, *Thor* and *The Incredible Hulk*, that super-powered beings and even aliens exist, and are a potential threat to the Earth. Yet unbeknownst to him the Tesseract is also a door which Loki uses to transport his army of invading aliens, the Chitauri, to New York. When he realises the extent of the danger the world faces, Nick Fury restarts the discontinued Avengers Initiative, against the recommendations of the World Security Council, suggesting: 'These people [the Avengers] may be isolated, unbalanced even, but I believe with the right push they can be exactly what we *need*.' Throughout the course of the narrative the Avengers will be called 'freaks', by World Security Council member Gideon Malick (Powers Boothe), 'lost souls', by Loki, and a 'ticking time bomb', by Bruce Banner himself, but these very American superheroes prove to be the only thing capable of saving the Earth when no one else can.

Having quickly and efficiently established its apocalyptic stakes, the film's protatic stage is comprised of bringing the superheroes together, not just from all over the globe, but even the galaxy, in the case of the Norse god Thor, a task which proves to be as much of a challenge within the film's diegesis for Nick Fury as it must have been for writer/director Joss Whedon. Black Widow is retrieved from an active mission in Russia to recruit Bruce Banner, who has relocated to the poverty-stricken slums of Kolkota, India (via a soundstage in New Mexico) where he has found some sort of solace treating patients there, similar to how he had lost himself in the *favelas* of Rio in *The Incredible Hulk*. Just as those scenes in *The Incredible Hulk* emerged as problematic, the sequence in India with its refuse and livestock-filled alleyways, ripped sheets in doorways and televisions on the street proves equally culturally insensitive. Producer Jeremy Latcham labelled these scenes 'a very realistic version of India' (qtd. in Anon. 2012), but others were not so complimentary, including award-winning Indian actress and producer Rituparna Sengupta, who wrote: 'Kolkata has a rich culture and heritage, and a filmmaker should respect that. There are two scenes about India and they only show slums. It could have been done in better taste' (qtd. in Pulver 2012). As Anandra Mitra observed in her volume *India on the Western Screen: Imaging a Country in Film, TV, and Digital Media* they are emblematic of the 'slum and leprosy' motif that is characteristic of the way Hollywood films tend to portray India, which has 'become the dominant representation of the [Indian] space on the Western screen' (2016: 65). These scenes are certainly representative of how American film in general, not just the MCU, luxuriates in the perpetuation of crudely drawn national stereotypes that are primarily designed to reveal inherent qualities of goodness in their American heroes: in the case of Rio and Kolkata, they emphasise Banner's altruism and his intellect (he is able to speak Portuguese and Bengali), or in Afghanistan, *Iron Man* Stark's selfless heroism, his masculinity and his morality (see Spanakos 2011: 19). Ruffalo's Banner is quite distinct from Norton's portrayal of the character (and Eric Bana's before him) and his sensitive, vulnerable and decidedly human interpretation found a level of appreciation with both reviewers and fans to an extent the previous incarnations were unable to achieve. Ruffalo's understated and empathetic screen persona enables him to do more with a single line concerning Banner's failed suicide attempt – 'I got low. I didn't see an end … so I put a bullet in my mouth, and the *other guy* spit it out' – than Leterrier and Norton were able to do in an extended two-and-a-half-minute-long scene which was removed from the final cut of *The Incredible Hulk* and can be seen only on an extra for the Blu-ray release. Like *The Incredible Hulk* before it, *The Avengers* seems to recognise the existence of the previous Hulk film, but also departs from it. Banner comments, 'The last time I was in New York, I kinda broke Harlem', referring to the climactic battle with Abomination in *The Incredible Hulk*. But the nature of the gamma radiation experiment which caused his unique condition is altered, as Coulson later tells Captain America, 'Banner thought gamma radiation might hold the key to unlocking Erskine's original formula', a deviation from General Ross's manipulation of the character. Leterrier's film ended on a moment of ambiguity about whether Banner was able to control his rage and in *The Avengers* characters speculate as to whether he is able to do so or not: Black Widow asks him if he practices yoga and Tony Stark asks him directly, 'What's your secret? Mellow jazz? Bongo drums? Huge bag of weed?' The answer to their question is only revealed more than an hour later, during the climax of the film in the Battle of New York.

Tony Stark is also unenthusiastic about joining what he sarcastically described as Nick Fury's 'super secret boy band' in *Iron Man 2* and still harbours a certain amount of resentment after being called 'volatile' and 'self-obsessed'. Following his desire to contribute more to the world than blowing things up, in the time between *Iron Man 2* and *The Avengers*, Stark has become a leading figure in the field of sustainable energy. He is still his cynical and wisecracking self, but he is shown to have settled down and started a relationship with Pepper Potts. The character who has undoubtedly gone through the most profound change is, of course, Steve Rogers. Having woken up nearly seventy years after the end of World War II at the climax of *The First Avenger*, he is understandably alarmed at how much the world has changed. Steve is shown to have lost his sense of purpose in the transition from the apparent moral clarity of World War II which is replaced with the ethical vagaries of the 'War on Terror' era in which *The Avengers* is set, where even his friends and colleagues Nick Fury and Black Widow are known for their secrets and subterfuge. Cap says to Nick Fury, 'They say we won – they didn't tell me what we had lost', referring quite explicitly to the changes which America has undergone since the Total War of World War II he had participated in and even came to embody. When Fury reluctantly admits to Captain America, 'We've made some mistakes along the way … some very recently', his comment lingers. Is he talking about the use of the Tesseract to create WMD within the film's diegesis, or America's ill-considered and ill-conceived post-9/11 'War on Terror'?

Of all the characters from the modern era, *The Avengers* connects Captain America most closely to Agent Coulson, who in the space of five films went from a minor player with a handful of lines in *Iron Man* to a key character and subsequently the star of the television show *Marvel's Agents of S.H.I.E.L.D.* Coulson has frequently functioned as the audience surrogate in the Marvel Cinematic Universe, and Whedon himself said, 'that's what Clark Gregg embodies: the Everyman' (qtd. in Mellor 2013). The narrative of *The Avengers* humanises him even further by giving him a first name (to Tony Stark's incredulity) and even mentioning a girlfriend, a cellist in Portland, in preparation for his 'death' in a subsequent decisive moment in the narrative of *The Avengers*.[3] Like Cap, Coulson has old-fashioned notions about heroism and purpose which are embodied in his nostalgic collection of vintage World War II-era Captain America trading cards. When Cap is tasked with putting on his old uniform for the upcoming mission against Loki he looks at his own iconic costume, coloured red, white and blue, and asks Coulson, 'Aren't the Stars and Stripes a little old-fashioned?' But Coulson knows that, in the wake of Loki's attacks and the apocalyptic battle that is still to come, everything has changed. He states: 'With everything that is happening and things coming to light people just might *need* a little old-fashioned.'

There is significance to Coulson's use of the term 'old-fashioned', which will be repeated later by Nick Fury in his description of the idea of people working together to become something greater as an 'old-fashioned notion'. It is an idea that the MCU returns to frequently, that things were better in 'the good old days'. Whedon suggested this about the film: 'It's about the idea – which is very old-fashioned – of community, of people working for each other. That's gone away. *The Avengers*, for me, is about bringing that back' (qtd. in Breznican 2012). This contrast is particularly evident in the differences between Captain America's understanding of what constitutes heroism, compared to Stark's new millennial cynicism. World War II has been a lingering presence in the MCU since Tony Stark's frequent elicitations of his father in *Iron Man* and *Iron Man 2*, but it is a very particular view of the conflict that is evoked, a distinctly 'mythologised view of the Second World War' (Guffey 2014: 286) that the MCU emphatically suggests current generations *could* and *should* learn from. This continues quite strikingly with Loki's arrival in, of all places, Stuttgart in Germany to retrieve material to make a second supernatural weapon of mass destruction. In an ostentatious display of power he demands the German crowd kneel before him, informing them that he will free them from their obsession with the very idea of freedom, which he calls 'life's glorious lie' adding 'you were *made* to be ruled'.[4] The crowd all fall to their knees except one white-haired old man, the implication being that he is a survivor of the Holocaust who has seen such tyranny before. 'There are *always* men like you', he calls out to Loki, with the non-diegetic music providing a suitably affective lilting folk melody. The Norse God turns his weapon on the old man seeking to make an example of him but, as his supernatural blast of energy fires, Captain America arrives just in time to protect the old man with his shield. Captain America gazes up at Loki with disdain and says, 'The last time I was in Germany and saw a man standing above everyone else, we ended up disagreeing'. There is no ostensible reason for the scene to be set in Germany other than to continue these sustained allusions to World War II. As Ensley F. Guffey contended, 'the old man and Captain America are *contemporaries*. For both, memories of World War II and Nazi Germany are far more present than for anyone else in the crowd' (2014: 286; italics in original). Guffey is correct to point this out, but perhaps does not take it far enough, as while to us audiences the events of World War II happened more than seventy years ago, for Cap they are much closer physically and emotionally: for him Coulson's cards are not vintage, they are contemporary and the war is not a distant memory, but very much a part of his present.[5] In the ensuing battle Captain America is shown quite clearly to struggle against the Asgardian god Loki and it is only when Iron Man arrives in his Mark IV suit, with his coming heralded by 'Shoot to Thrill' blasting out of Black Widow's quinjet after he commandeers the PA system, a stark contrast to the Franz Shubert String Quartet Number 13 in A Minor, D. 804, Op. 29 ('Rosamunde') that had played in the scene a few moments before, that he is subdued. Stark and the visibly shaken Cap are civil to each other in their first scene together, exchanging only the greetings 'Mr Stark' and 'Captain', but it is a level of courtesy that does not last for long.

Although Loki is quickly apprehended and imprisoned on the giant helicarrier (in a prison cell actually built to contain the Hulk) it emerges that the Avengers are deeply conflicted in their approaches, a fact which becomes the source of much of the film's drama. On his arrival, Thor expresses the desire to take Loki back to his realm where he will face 'Asgardian justice' but for Captain America and Iron Man it is necessary that he stays on Earth to help them locate the Tesseract and prevent the imminent Chitauri invasion. While Steve Rogers and Tony Stark agree about the importance of keeping Loki in their custody, they disagree about practically everything else. It is important to note that Rogers was raised and came of age during the presidency of Franklin Delano Roosevelt (1933–45) in an era where people, in the cultural imaginary at least, generally expressed more faith and respect for their governmental institutions and representatives, and he even received his powers from a state-sponsored programme and participated in a war which demanded sacrifice of all those that participated in it. Stark, as we explored previously, is more of a neoliberal, even Randian icon who places individual rights before the prerogatives of the government, which has largely been portrayed as incompetent if not duplicitous throughout the MCU. It is clear that the cynical Stark associates the idealistic Cap with the establishment that he has come to deride, and initially sees him as something of a naïve lackey with outdated and inflexible values. There is also considerable evidence that Stark projects anxieties about his relationship with his father onto Rogers ('That's the guy my dad never shut up about?'). For his part, Steve Rogers regards Stark as an embodiment of all that has gone wrong with the United States during the time he was 'away', with his cynicism and lack of moral accountability.[6] As Samira Nadkarni argues, 'The simultaneous presence of Captain America and Iron Man creates a temporal play in which the events of World War II and 9/11 are made co-incident. This brings into focus the "Greatest Generation" myth that grew in the aftermath of World War II and the US's current position as a global superpower in the aftermath of those events' (2015: 16). Captain America doubts that someone like Stark would sacrifice himself for his country, as many did during World War II, *even Cap himself.* He tells Stark, 'The only thing you really fight for is yourself. You're not the guy to make the sacrifice play, to lay down on a wire and let the other guy crawl over you.' Stark has a witty rejoinder for this, as he has for most things, 'I think I would just cut the wire…'. Despite his many faults, Stark is one of the most self-aware of new millennial superheroes and recognises the absurdity of what he calls the 'terrible privilege' of their situation, a phrase more readily used to describe the burden of hegemonic superpowers than super-heroes (see Chambliss 2012). The film then will seek to reconcile these seemingly contrasting perspectives by providing them with an apocalyptic challenge which demands they put aside their differences for the greater good, find a compromise and both evolve into more than they were before.

Their internal conflict is brought to an end by Loki who, it transpires, has deliberately allowed himself to be caught in order to provoke disharmony among the heroes, then manages to escape after Banner finally changes into the Hulk for the first time in the film after seventy-six minutes of screen time. Loki 'murders' Coulson, an act which finally motivates the heroes to put aside their differences and come together for the common good after Fury hands Cap Coulson's vin-tage trading cards, now blood-stained, telling him they were found on his lifeless body. However, moments later Agent Hill reveals to the audience that the cards were not on Coulson at all when he died and that Fury had only said they were in order to galvanise Captain America and the group into action. Although Fury's methods throughout the film have been questionable, the film shows that such transgressions are sometimes required in order to ensure that the *right* and *necessary* thing is done. Captain America never seems to learn of Fury's act of *legerdemain* but in a rare moment of moral relativity he remarks that Fury has 'got the same blood on his hands as Loki does', but it is an assertion that has little weight, even though it is uttered by the film's hero, after what we have already seen and are about to see.[7]

III.

The stage is then set for the heroes to meet Loki and his intergalactic army in a protracted 45-minute battle above and through the streets of New York, full of fleeing civilians, crashing debris and falling structures. In the aftermath of 9/11 there was a relatively brief pause concerning the frequency of how often New York was attacked in Hollywood film, which had regularly perpetrated great crimes on the city in the guise of earthquakes, tidal waves, bombs, meteors and even alien invasions and giant apes in films like *King Kong* (1976), *Independence Day* (1996), *Deep Impact* (1998) and *Armageddon* (1998). In November 2001 Peter Matthews, in an article entitled 'Aftermath', predicted that such films would be-come forgotten relics of a bygone era:

For a long time to come, there will be little appetite for the entertainment staples of bombs, plane crashes and burning buildings, since to enjoy such kinetic excitement affectlessly seems a violation of the dead. Temporarily, the whole idea of entertainment becomes obscene – or at least those versions that offer clean, airbrushed carnage for fun and profit. Escapism in all its cultural forms might be said to rest finally on a denial of the fact of death. Now it cannot be denied, and that circumstance threatened to shake popular cinema to its roots. (2001: 20)

With the benefit of hindsight, it is clear to see that this 'long time to come' did not prove to be such a long time at all, as within a few years scenes of disaster and carnage returned to the city in even more spectacular fashions than they had been depicted before, often with a deliberate eye on the specific iconography associated with that day (see in particular *Cloverfield*, *Spider-Man*, *I am Legend* [2007] and *Knowing* [2009]). Karen Randell offered a list of these motifs adopted by American films which she appropriately called the 'lexicon of 9/11' (2016: 141):

There is in these movies a repetitive set of sounds: helicopter blades; emergency services sirens; screaming and shouting; particularly the phrase 'Oh my God'; and a repetitive set of images: aerial shots of a devastated modern city; vertically falling high-rise tower blocks; emergency responders, particularly fire-fighters; stunned, injured people; people running from dust clouds; falling debris and falling paper. These effects echo and often replicate the images of 9/11 in extraordinary detail in a way that is not seen in more realist cinema. (2016: 138)

To these one might add the implementation of cinematic techniques which emphasise and accentuate a degree of realism (hand-held shaky camera work, dust specks on the camera lens); transfixed crowds gazing up, unable to tear their eyes away from the sheer scale of the destruction; and the vocalisation of disbelief at what they are experiencing, like the cameraman Hud in *Cloverfield* who exclaims 'Did you see that?!' and 'Are you guys seeing this shit right now?!' These visual and aural signifiers are embedded in many post-9/11 American blockbuster films and are a key part of how the MCU portrays large-scale destruction. *The Avengers* does not explicitly mention 9/11, but the range of imagery it employs consciously evokes it in what we might regard as a palimpsestuous relationship with that day that many American films adopted in the decade after. This complicated interrealation between texts and the myriad of influences which form them was interrogated in the work of Sarah Dillon in *The Palimpsest: Literature, Criticism, and Theory*, where she described the concept as 'an inventive process of creating relations where there may, or should, be none' (2007: 83). On the surface, there seems to be no apparent connection between the alien invasion featured in *The Avengers* and the events of 9/11, but Manohla Dargis was one of many commentators to speculate on American cinema's compulsion to return to this evocative imagery as a convenient short-hand for trauma and a dubious source of entertainment, suggesting that it was remarkable 'just how thoroughly Sept. 11 and its aftermath have been colonized by the movies' (2013). These connections, which Dillon refers to as 'an involuted phenomenon where otherwise unrelated texts are involved and entangled, intricately interwoven, interrupting and inhabiting each other' (2007: 4) are not always deliberate on the part of their creators, although they often are. On one of the extras included on the DVD release of *Cloverfield* called 'Wall of Dust', members of the crew frequently specifically discuss 9/11 and it influence on the film. Special Effects Coordinator David Waine states, 'We're doing a wall of dust, basically it's supposed to be the leading edge of the building exploding and collapsing just like in the Trade Towers', and Niamh Murphy, the film's Textile Artist says, 'We looked through a lot of 9/11 photos and we noticed certain things like some people were completely covered and they looked just utterly vulnerable'. In Steven Spielberg's *War of the Worlds*, the director himself stated, 'I think 9/11 reinforced everything I'm putting into [the film]... We now know what it feels like to be terrorised' (qtd. in Abramowitz 2005: E26). Joss Whedon, in the director's commentary for *Avengers: Age of Ultron*, observed, 'Even now, many years later, the last thing we want to do is egregiously evoke the specter of 9/11. Being callous about that is unthinkable...'.

What is particularly significant about *The Avengers* is the fact that it arguably marks a turning point in terms of how this 9/11 imagery is represented in American film. In 2005 Geoff King correctly identified a distinction between pre-9/11 and post-9/11 disaster films, arguing that whereas pre-9/11 films invited audiences to take guilt-free, vicarious pleasure in their spectacles of devastation in 'enjoyable fantasies of destruction, enjoyable precisely because they can safely be indulged in the arena of fantasy' (2005: 49), science fiction and disaster cinema of the post-9/11 era presented spectators with much more challenging 're-makes' of 11 September 2001, both in their striking replications of the aesthetic of 9/11 and in the traumatic situations the characters find themselves in. By the time of the production of *The Avengers*, which filmed some of its sequences in New York in September 2011 almost exactly ten years after 9/11, a new phase was undoubtedly emerging which departed from King's classification with its more explicit and sustained evocations of 9/11. Writing in 2005 King had yet to be exposed to the more unambiguous 9/11 imagery featured in the likes of *War of the Worlds*, *Cloverfield*, *Knowing* and *The Dark Knight*. *The Avengers*, released in 2012, marks a point of divergence and heralds a range of films, like *Iron Man 3* and *Man of Steel*, *Olympus Has Fallen* (2013), *White House Down* (2013), and *San Andreas* (2015), which appropriate the imagery associated with 9/11 with a

Figs. 12–15: Scenes of destruction and devastation deliberately designed to evoke 9/11, like those shown here in *The Avengers* (2012), became a recurring visual motif in American cinema after 2001

fascination which borders on the obsessive.[8] This shift was widely observed by many commentators in the United States and abroad: Jordan Hoffman stated that 'Marvel Movies Are Bringing 9/11 Back to Pop Culture, and It's Still Too Soon' (2014), J. Hoberman titled his review of Joss Whedon's film, 'The Avengers: Why Hollywood is no longer afraid to tackle 9/11' (2012), and in Italy, Marco Luceri, writing in *Corriere Fiorentino*, asserted that the film was to be considered a reaffirmation of American primacy that was 'strongly shaken not only in political, economic, social, but also cultural terms' by 9/11, but that *The Avengers* 'seems like a new, roaring, declaration of war' (2012).

This relationship is a particularly complicated one for a culture that was compulsively drawn to the events of 9/11, characterised by the injunction to 'Never Forget', but was at the same time deeply reluctant to represent them onscreen, due to the fact they were widely regarded as too traumatic to recreate in fiction, and only three high-profile American films in the fifteen years after portray the day as it happens: *United 93*, *World Trade Center* (2006) and *Extremely Loud and Incredibly Close* (2011). At exactly the same time as this, as Dana Heller asserted in her book *The Selling of 9/11: How a National Tragedy Became a Commodity*, America at large 'both participated in, and bore witness to, a rapid transformation of the World Trade Center attacks into commodities aimed at repackaging turbulent and chaotic emotions, reducing them to pious, quasi-religious nationalism' (2005: 6). We might consider the appropriation of 11 September 2001 into Randell's 'lexicon of 9/11' as another example of Heller's proposition and while American cinema proved reluctant to tackle 9/11 directly, the event became subsumed into genre cinema in film after film which, as Francis Pheasant-Kelly has bserved, 'draws attention to real traumatic events (often by the death of characters and the destruction of buildings), but simultaneously disavows them, partly because of fantasy's implausibility, but also through the pleasurable experience of its aesthetic disarray' (2013: 14). What this reveals about the relationship between collective cultural trauma and depictions of it on the cinema screen is ambiguous. Does vicarious trauma invite an interrogation of it 'in that way might be useful' or does it 'trigger defense against further exposure'? (Kaplan 2005: 87). What is clear is that the narrative of *The Avengers* performs a very similar cultural function as those films that explicitly depict the events of 11 September 2001, *United 93*, *World Trade Center* and *Extremely Loud and Incredibly Close* (a film which was was described by Andrea Peyser, writing for the New York Post, as '9/11 porn' for its appropriation of cultural trauma and its use of the unidentified 'falling man'), which are self-consciously designed to appear ideologically neutral on the surface, removing themselves from historical and political context to adopt an apolitical guise, but they offer mythologised portraits of an America populated by honest, everyman heroes, individuals who selflessly put aside their differences and come together in defence of their nation at a time of great need, very similar to the citizen superheroes on the streets of New York in *The Avengers*.

It is in the Battle of New York where each of the Avengers prove themselves to one another and to the world. Faced with symbolically and literally a manifestation of George W. Bush's contention that, 'Like generations before us, we have a calling from beyond the stars to stand for freedom' (2004), they run *towards* the dust clouds and the destruction, rather than away from it unlike the crowds of innocent civilians. This unity is strikingly visualised in the film's famous tie-in shot, a remarkable 40-second-long unbroken image which flies through the streets of New York mid-battle as the heroes are shown working together for the first time. It is a moment which works both on a thematic level, but also signifies the extent to which the MCU has brought together and unified these separate brands into one film, and, as Matthias Stork suggests, 'It further functions self-referentially, as an in-text commentary on how Marvel sought to aesthetize its new superhero marketing concept and establish its own brand of the superhero movie: the conventional genre film, repackaged on a larger scale, as a cycle' (2014: 80). The tie-in shot is followed by them appearing in the same frame for the first time, in front of Grand Central Station, where they all stand together under what remains of Jules-Félix Coutan's clock statue of Mercury flanked by Hercules and Minerva known as 'Glory of Commerce' (1914). The presentation of these images is significant as it is only through their formation as team that they are able to defeat Loki and the Chitauri with their embrace of old-fashioned notions of community and self-sacrifice, ideas that Stark had been disdainful of towards the start of the film. Banner returns to the fight, finally revealing to the audience his secret … that he is '*always* angry'. His assertion is somewhat ambiguous, but the implication is that by living in a constant state of anger he is able to control it, rather than it controlling him, and an acknowledgement that Banner and the 'other guy' are now one. He is also, for the first time in the MCU, allowed to enjoy the use of his powers onscreen, as evidenced by his smile after being ordered by Captain America to 'smash', as they are now unambiguously being used in the service of good. Like the Hulk, Cap is shown to have found a renewed sense of purpose, as despite the bureaucracy and the political machinations he has observed, the potentially apocalyptic event has shown him that he is still needed and that his old-fashioned brand of heroism can be inspirational, even in the cynical modern era.

However, to make things even harder for them it is not just the Chitauri and Loki that they are forced to contend with. Fearful that the situation in New York has become untenable, the World Security Council (made up from representatives all over the globe) override Fury's wishes and order a nuclear weapon to be targeted at New York. The film is critical of the motives of the WSO, a body self-consciously designed to be reminiscent of the United Nations, an institution that American cinema has been unwaveringly critical of (see *Black Hawk Down*, *Behind Enemy Lines* [2001], *Tears of the Sun* [2003]).[9] It is only then that Stark accepts Rogers' earlier challenge to be the guy that 'lays down on the wire' and 'make the sacrifice play' by diverting the nuclear weapon through the Chitauri wormhole even though, as Cap tells him, it is 'a one way trip'. Therefore, the battle ends with Iron Man sacrificing himself in a way that Captain America said he would never be able to do, a new generation of hero embodying the spirit of the 'greatest generation', and in the process unifying both. Thus, we can see how the film offers a wish-fulfilment fantasy by rewriting the 'War on Terror' through the prism of the superhero film, a vision in which

> The buildings didn't fall. We didn't have to go to war, because we could shut the border between our world and the one from which our enemies came. We didn't even have to conduct a mop-up operation or interrogate detainees because when that portal closed, the invaders collapsed like toys… It's a dream of resilience and clean war… where we can end the war in a day; where we can avoid doing grievous harm to ourselves and our values in the process. (Rosenberg 2012)

The palliative nature of this fantasy is clear as events transpire as we wished they could have been rather than how they actually were, something that Todd Van Der Werff argued that American popular cinema has been doing on an endless loop since 11 September 2001: 'In the wake of the 9/11 terrorist attacks, America turned to superpowered heroes to rewrite that day so that it ended as one where nobody had to die' (2016). Van Der Werff is correct to point this out and in the film not a single person is shown to die, nor are they in any scene which evokes 9/11 throughout the MCU.

The film's connections to 9/11 continue in the aftermath of the attack which will frequently be referred to as 'the incident' or 'the event' as the MCU moves forward, as if it were too traumatic to mention by name. The news features a candlelight vigil and a range of survivors talking about their experiences of the day: one says, 'It's just really great knowing that they're out there. That someone's watching over us'; another states, 'I don't exactly feel safer with those things out there'; and a third, 'It just seems like there's a lot they're not telling us'. While each of the comments are reactions to fictional superheroes saving New York from an intergalactic threat, they are certainly suggestive of the range of responses the international community (and American citizens themselves) have had towards the United States throughout the first decade of the new millennium.[10] These scenes emphasise that it is not just US citizens who are grateful to their American saviours, but those from all over the globe: there is a Tony Stark lookalike on the

Indian subcontinent, a memorial board which seems to be located somewhere in Southeast Asia, a smiling woman clad in a sari who happily holds up a picture of the Hulk and the MSNBC headline reads: 'Aftermath: The world responds to alien attack.' *The Avengers* participates in the broader ideological mission of the superhero genre in the era, one which may not have been a conscious decision on the part of filmmakers, but nevertheless becomes one of its formative and undergirding tropes. As Jeffrey Brown has argued,

> Superhero films are a means to collectively deal with the trauma of 9/11 and symbolically help make sense of the world again. Superheroes represent an effort to rewrite and reconfirm the belief in American exceptionalism. Specifically, the superhero genre counters fears of a nation that has grown soft, weak, and vulnerable, instead offering a narrative of toughening up, of remasculinizing America. As men who have been defined by trauma, just as America has, the superhero is able to rise up and prove himself stronger than any threats. (2017: 64)

Without mentioning the events of 11 September 2001 on a single occasion, the transgenerational heroism of *The Avengers*, set against the backdrop of a metaphorical recreation of that day, leads to it becoming one of the most significant American films of what is now referred to as post-9/11 American cinema.

Notes

1   In the United States the film was called *The Avengers*, but in the UK it was released with the title *Marvel's Avengers Assemble* due to copyright reasons concerning the fondly remembered television show *The Avengers* (ITV, 1961–68) and the disastrous cinematic adaption of it, *The Avengers* (1998).

2   *Batman Begins* writer David S. Goyer made this comparison explicitly clear when he stated, 'We modelled him after Osama bin Laden. He's not crazy in the way that all the other Batman villains are. He's not bent on revenge; he's actually trying to heal the world. He's just doing it by very draconian means' (qtd. in Ryan 2005).

3   The cellist from Portland who is referred to in a throwaway line here is returned to in *Marvel's Agent's of S.H.I.E.L.D.* 'The Only Light in the Darkness' (1.19) where her name is revealed to be Audrey Nathan.

4   In 2014 Tom Hiddlestone's email to Joss Whedon after reading the script was published. Hiddlestone wrote: 'Thank you for writing me my Hans Gruber [the iconic villain from *Die Hard* played by Alan Rickman]. But a Hans Gruber with super-magic powers. As played by James Mason ... It's high operatic villainy alongside detached throwaway tongue-in-cheek; plus the 'real menace' and his closely guarded suitcase of pain... He gets battered, punched, blasted, side-swiped, roared at, sent tumbling

on his back, and every time he gets back up smiling, wickedly, never for a second losing his eloquence, style, wit, self-aggrandisement or grandeur, and you never send him up or deny him his real intelligence…' (qtd. in Acuna 2014).

5　The Marvel Cinematic Universe timeline wiki suggests that Captain America crashes his plane into the sea on 4 March 1945 and that he is awoken from the ice on 17 April 2012, so when he meets Loki in Stuttgart on 3 May 2012 it has only been three weeks of physically aware time for him.

6　Some writers saw something further to the conflict between Rogers and Stark. In an intriguing piece by Derek S. McGrath called 'Some Assembly Required: Joss Whedon's Bridging of Masculinities in Marvel Films' *The Avengers*' he asserts that the friction between Stark and Rogers is primarily 'sexual tension' (2016: 141) as demonstrated by lines of dialogue like 'I'm thinking I want you to make me!'

7　The pilot episode of *Marvel's Agents of S.H.I.E.L.D.* returns to whether the Avengers were made aware of Fury's lie about Coulson's cards when Agent Hill remarks that they never found out because 'they're not level seven' in 'Pilot' (1.01).

8　Given this relationship it is interesting to note that the film only shot in the actual New York for a few days and instead created a simulacrum of the city digitally inside the computers of Industrial Light and Magic (see Fraser 2012).

9　In *Marvel's Agents of S.H.I.E.L.D.* one of their number, Gideon Malick, is revealed to be a high-ranking member of HYDRA. Interestingly, it was also the World Security Council that led the Pentagon to remove its support for the film. Phil Strub, the Defense Department's Hollywood liaison, stated, 'We couldn't reconcile the unreality of this international organization and our place in it… To whom did S.H.I.E.L.D. answer? Did we work for S.H.I.E.L.D.?' (Ackerman 2012).

10　*The Hollywood Reporter* consulted disaster experts at Kinetic Analysis Corp. who speculated that the destruction wreaked on New York in the film would have cost $60–70 billion worth of damages and $90 billion in clean up costs, with an overall cost of $160 billion. In comparison, the real-world recovery operatations for 9/11 and Hurricane Katrina cost $83 billion and $90 billion respectively (see Zakarin 2012a). Four years later in *Captain America: Civil War* in the run up to what becomes known as the Sokovia Accords it is revealed that the cost of the Battle of New York was officially 'only' $18.8 billion with seventy-four casualties.

PHASE TWO

'Nothing's been the same since New York': Continuity and Change in *Iron Man 3* and *Thor: The Dark World*

Many people who witnessed the event [11 September 2001] suffered nightmares and psychological trauma. For those who viewed it intensely, the spectacle provided a powerful set of images that would continue to resonate for years to come, much as the footage of the Kennedy assassination, iconic photographs of Vietnam, the 1986 explosion of the space shuttle Challenger, or the death of Princess Diana in the 1990s provided unforgettable imagery.

– Douglas Kellner (2004: 54)

I.

For Tony Stark and the entirety of the Marvel Cinematic Universe nothing *was* the same after New York. The aftermath of the Chitauri invasion led by Loki featured in *The Avengers* flows through the films and television programmes in Phase Two without exception. The unprecedented success of *The Avengers* ensured that the Marvel Studios experiment had become one of the most successful franchises in film history with the six films comprising Phase One generating $3.8 billion at the world-wide box office and those from Phase Two would go on to make $5.2 billion. This did not mean the series would not be presented with challenges as it moved forward, but that it would not have the uncertainty that it had faced during the production of *Iron Man*, a character who had gone from something of a second-tier figure to the most successful superhero in the world by the end of 2013. In the wake of the success of *The Avengers*, Marvel announced an ambitious slate of productions for Phase Two which would be comprised of another six films: *Iron Man 3* and *Thor: The Dark World* in 2013, followed by *Captain America: The Winter Soldier* and *Guardians of the Galaxy* in 2014, with *Avengers: Age of Ultron* and *Ant-Man* to complete the phase in 2015. After the achievements of Phase One, Marvel Studios remained aware that the films each needed to appeal to audiences in their own right, but also continue to grow the Marvel brand *and* offer variations on the superhero genre, a market which was growing more crowded with every year that passed. Each of the six films in Phase Two offers deviations from the genre: *Iron Man 3* is a superhero film, as one might expect, but it also contains elements of a thriller that had not been seen before in the MCU, *Thor: The Dark World* is a fantasy film with palpable aspects of melodrama and comedy, *Ant-Man* is a heist film with a superhero at its centre, and *Captain America: The Winter Soldier* is a conspiracy thriller deliberately evocative of those from the 1970s like *Three Days of the Condor* and *Marathon Man* (1976). Due to its success, Marvel was also ready to gamble on less familiar properties like their ambitious space opera *Guardians of the Galaxy*, which was definitely the riskiest proposition in the MCU at the time of its release, featuring a cast of characters virtually unknown to the general public. This did not go uncommented upon in trade magazines (see, for example, McMillan 2014). Yet ultimately the film earned $777 million at the world-wide box office, which made it, at the time, the third-highest earning of any Marvel film, behind only *Iron Man 3* and *The Avengers*. From a production point of view the success of *The Avengers* generated an increased interest in the MCU and a financial boost to the films made after which came to be referred to as the 'Avengers Effect' (see Stewart 2013). Thus *Thor: The Dark World* had a thirty-one percent larger domestic opening than its predecessor *Thor* (leading to a global take of $644.7 million compared to $449.3 million of the first) and even more remarkably *Iron Man 3* made $1.215 billion globally, nearly double the $624 million of *Iron Man 2* released just three years before in 2010.

For the first film in Phase Two it undoubtedly made financial and thematic sense to return to the character who had made this all possible, Iron Man. Marvel also continued its intriguing choices for directors by turning to Shane Black, who had been one of the highest paid screenwriters in Hollywood throughout the 1980s and early 1990s, but had only one directorial credit to his name, *Kiss Kiss Bang Bang* (2005), which had starred Robert Downey Jr. in what many had seen as his comeback film after his incarceration. What Black perhaps lacked in directorial credits he made up for in fan cachet and the closeness of his relationship with Downey Jr. who by then had emerged as the cornerstone and figurehead of the MCU's success. Black brings his characteristic acerbic sensibilities to the superhero genre, with his witty one liners, subversion of cliché and a deconstruction of many of the genre's central tenets, in particular hotly debated revisions to the character of the Mandarin, who had initially appeared in the comics in *Tales of Suspense #50* in 1964, which seemed to be as loved by some as it was hated by others.

The film opens with Tony Stark's deliberately self-referential and stumbling narration:

> A famous man once said, 'We create our own demons'. Who said that? What does that even mean? Doesn't matter. I said it 'cause he said it. So now, he was famous and it was basically said by two well-known guys. I don't... uhh... I'm gonna start again. Let's track this from the beginning...

The uncertain nature of the voice-over is similar to the one employed by Black and Downey Jr. in *Kiss Kiss Bang Bang* and will only later make sense in the post-credits stinger which reveals that Tony Stark is actually on the therapist's couch recounting the film's events. The therapy motif is a relevant one given that *Iron Man 3* discloses fairly early on that Stark is suffering from pronounced symptoms of PTSD after the events in New York and in the course of the narrative will go on something of a psychological journey which culminates in an acknowledgement of his past and his status as a superhero, bringing the Iron Man trilogy to a close.

The 'beginning' that Stark refers to is a flashback to New Year's Eve in Bern, Switzerland in 1999, several years before the epiphany which led him to become the Iron Man in the mountains of Afghanistan. Black transports the audience back to the last year of the twentieth century by way of the Italian Europop group Eiffel 65's 1999 chart-topping 'Blue (Da Ba Dee)', which playfully contrasts with the bombastic Alan Silvestri score of *The Avengers* and the hard rock anthems that Jon Favreau's tenure as the director of the series often turned to. These prefatory moments offer glimpses of the former crass and distinctly unpolitically correct Tony before his literal and figurative change of heart. Drunk both on alcohol and his own sense of self-importance he brushes off Ho Yinsen, the man who will play a considerable role in his future, to seduce the beautiful and talented biologist Maya Hansen (Rebecca Hall) who has pioneered an experimental regenerative treatment known as Extremis, which has the potential to decode human DNA and thereby eradicate all forms of disease. In a couple of offhand exchanges Stark's brilliance is revealed to both her and to the audience, and it is his drunken scribble of formula that he leaves on a business card which he learns years later enabled her to complete her research. Hansen is one of the 'demons' he talks of, but it is the nebbish Aldrich Killian (Guy Pearce) and his Advanced Idea Mechanics (A.I.M.) that Stark refers to most of all. Stark agrees to meet Killian on the roof at midnight to listen to his business proposal, but rather callously stands him up. These seemingly inconsequential encounters lead to key events later in his life, as Stark comments: 'I had just created demons and I didn't even know it... I never thought they would come back to bite me. Why would they?' At this stage Stark is blissfully ignorant about his role in the world, unaware of the fact that his weapons of mass destruction are being used in war zones around the globe and unaware of Chalmers Johnson's concept of 'blowback' in *Blowback: The Costs and Consequences of American Empire* (2002), an idea which came to define many people's attitude to American foreign policy in the post-9/11 era.

Back in the film's post-Battle of New York present, Stark is suffering from PTSD, something Obadiah Stane had claimed he had after his kidnapping in *Iron Man*, but a condition which he seems to *actually* have now, the symptoms of which are shown to be anxiety attacks, traumatic nightmares and trouble sleeping (he mentions he has been awake for seventy-two hours). While in a restaurant with his friend James Rhodes he has a full-blown panic-attack triggered even by the mention of New York by a young fan, which coincides with his unconscious scribble of 'help me' on a child's picture of him. At first, he is reluctant to recognise that what he is experiencing might be a psychological issue given the stigma still attached to mental health problems in contemporary Western culture (especially among men), and looks for a physiological explanation like poison or heart attack, but later he acknowledges to Pepper (who now lives with him): 'Nothing's been the same since New York... You experience things and then they're over and you still can't explain them.'

The Iron Man suit itself becomes an extension of this psychological trauma, evoking how Stark once described it and himself as 'one and the same' in *Iron Man 2*. As a result of his PTSD-induced intimacy issues he controls the suit remotely in an effort to convince Pepper that he is present when he is unable to be near her, and, when responding to one of his intense nightmares of the alien invasion, the suit itself almost attacks her. Later, when he is stranded in Tennessee he informs the young boy who becomes his companion, Harley, that the Iron Man suit is 'in pain, he's been injured... leave him alone' when he is clearly talking about himself. For the purpose of its narrative, the film has Stark become aware of his own physical and emotional vulnerability and his place in the MCU after the events of *The Avengers*, where Stark (and the rest of the world) was forced to acknowledge not only the existence of, as Stark says, 'gods, aliens ... other dimensions' but the fact that he is, in his own words, 'just a man in a can'. Stark will have his 'can' taken away from him for large sections of *Iron Man 3* as he is forced to rely on his intelligence and his wits alone for the first time since Afghanistan, and it is this which proves him to be a *real* superhero. Yet while the film initially prioritises Stark's physical and emotional vulnerability, this becomes problematised by the fact that *Iron Man 3*, emerges as something of a paradox, as the Phase Two MCU films become increasingly casual in their portrayal of violence and destruction, a trend which culminates in *Avengers: Age of Ultron*.

As Stark continues to process his personal trauma, America at large is being wracked by events of a decidedly contemporary nature, seemingly perpetrated by a terrorist going by the name of the Mandarin (Ben Kingsley) who has been orchestrating bombings all over the country and abroad (the real-life Ali Al Salem airbase in Kuwait).[1] On a series of live televised addresses the Mandarin asks the nation, 'Some people call me a terrorist, I consider myself a teacher. America, ready for another lesson?' With his Arabic beard and robes he is quite different to the Asian roots of the original comic book character, but seems to embrace very prevalent Middle Eastern new millennial stereotypes. His video message contains footage of chanting Arab crowds, hooded figures kneeling before being executed and burning effigies of the American president intercut with 1950s Americana and the shopping channel, playing on very real post-9/11 US fears and anxieties with imagery very similar to that discussed by Jack Shaheen in his study *Reel Bad Arabs: How Hollywood Vilifies a People* (2009). Shaheen argued that Hollywood films have perpetuated the same reductive and racist stereotypes for almost a hundred years:

> Arab Muslims are fanatics who believe in a different god, who don't value human life as much as we do, they are intent on destroying us (the [W]est) with their oil or with their terrorism; the men seek to abduct and brutally seduce our women; they are without family and reside in a primitive place (the desert) and behave like primitive beings. The women are subservient – resembling black crows – or we see them portrayed as mute, somewhat exotic harem maidens. (Qtd. in Harrickton 2008)

The visceral thematic resonance of the 'War on Terror' proved difficult to resist for many popular films in the post-9/11 era both inside and outside of the superhero genre and, as we have seen, the MCU returned to it frequently. Andrew Johnson has written: 'Over the past decade, no other event has seeped into our cinema more thoroughly, from political thrillers that focus directly on the War on Terror to blockbuster escapism inspired by the overseas conflicts that resulted' (2013). In the world of the superhero comic, Mike Grell has asserted that, 'Because 9/11 happened, we spun that into the storylines that actually dealt with terrorism and potential terrorist attacks on New York, and what would you do if you were a guy like Tony Stark? How far would you go to defend your people, your city, your country, the people that you loved?' (qtd. in Mangels 2008: 96). The first terrorist bombing physically seen onscreen in *Iron Man 3* is at the iconic Mann's Chinese theatre, in Hollywood, California, and it is Stark's friend and bodyguard Happy Hogan who is one of many that gets caught in the blast. Deliberately filmed to resemble a real-life suicide bomb attack and function as one within the film's diegesis, it is revealed later to have been perpetrated by one of several wounded ex-US soldiers who have participated in the unstable Extremis programme designed by Aldrich Killian and Maya Hansen.

Despite his health problems and issues with the government in *Iron Man 2*, Stark offers to help with the Mandarin, but, as Rhodes states, after the previous events in the MCU especially the 'incident' in New York, the government want to be seen as dealing with their own problems of domestic security and that 'we [the United States] need to look strong'. He calls the Mandarin 'not superhero business' but '*American* business', however the MCU has shown little real distinction between the two. In connection to this Rhodes has had his superhero name changed from War Machine to Iron Patriot as the name 'tested well with focus groups' and 'sends a better message' than the 'too aggressive' sounding War Machine. Searching for the location of the Mandarin, Iron Patriot (whom the Mandarin describes as President Ellis's 'red, white and blue attack dog') is sent to two locations in Pakistan, a process he calls a 'little knock and talk ... making friends'. In one he appears to be welcomed by the burqa-wearing seamstresses, but his uncomfortable 'You're free ... if you weren't before. Iron Patriot on the job. *You're welcome*?' is exactly the kind of dark humour that has characterised Shane Black's work since *Lethal Weapon* (1987).

Incensed by the bombings, and in particular by Happy Hogan being left in a coma, Stark is compelled to confront the Mandarin directly with a challenge which evokes George W. Bush's ill advised 'Bring em on' message to Iraqi insurgents (see Loughlin 2003). Stark insists that 'There's no politics here, just good old revenge. There's no Pentagon, it's just you and me, and on the off chance you're a *man*, here's my home address...'. As a direct result of this the Mandarin sends attack helicopters to destroy Stark's Malibu mansion and when it collapses it drags him to the bottom of the ocean leading Pepper and rest of the world to believe that he is dead. In the aftermath, Stark finds himself stranded in Rose Hill, Tennessee, which had been the site of the first Mandarin bombing, with no access to money, technology or resources. Earlier he had joked with Maya Hansen, 'Please don't tell me there's a twelve-year-old kid waiting in the car that I've never met', but in Rose Hill he becomes a temporary surrogate father to the neglected Harley Keener. What could have been a clichéd plot development in which Stark 'finds himself' through his relationship with the boy, emerges, in Black's hands, as something more interesting as evidenced by Stark's line to Harley having learned that the boy's young father had left, 'which happens … Dads leave, no need to be a *pussy* about it'. Given what he has seen of the Mandarin, Stark presumes (perhaps as we audiences also do) that the enigmatic terrorist leader is to be located somewhere in the Middle East or Asia. He speculates 'North Africa, Iran, Pakistan, Syria?', but is surprised to find out that he is actually in Miami and in the film's much debated twist, not really a terrorist at all, but an unemployed and drug-addicted British actor called Trevor Slattery hired by the real villain of the film, Aldrich Killian, to be a front for his schemes. The film's genuinely startling reveal shows the film not to have been perpetuating Arab stereotypes at all but, in actual fact, satirising and deconstructing them. In showing the Mandarin to have been a 'custom made terror threat' calculated to resemble just how we have come to expect terrorists to look and behave post-9/11, the film satirises our new millennial fears of the Other with his Asian robes, Arabic beard and speeches decrying American imperialism. As in the original *Iron Man* the villain *seems* to be a terrorist from the Middle East, only to have it revealed that the real bad guy was a middle-class American white man and CEO of a large multi-national company. Killian turned to Maya Hansen's research after being humiliated by Stark on New Year's Eve back in 1999, weaponising the Extremis virus and then orchestrating a series of bombings in order to monopolise the market in global weapons manufacture, showing him to be as much of a product of the 'War on Terror' as Iron Man himself. Killian says, 'You simply rule from behind the scenes. Because the second you give them a face, a Bin Laden, a Gaddafi, a Mandarin, you hand the people a target.' He continues: 'this time tomorrow I'll have the West's most powerful leader in one hand, and the world's most feared terrorist in the other: I'll *own* the 'War on Terror' … create supply and demand.' Killian's outlandish plan is to assassinate President Ellis live on television on a Roxxon Norco oil tanker and have him replaced by the AIM-friendly Vice President Rodriguez (Miguel Ferrer). The film goes to great lengths to distinguish Killian, a bad scientist, from the likes of Stark, but Stark's fortune was built on profiting from global wars not so long before. Even Pepper comments, as she rejects Killian's request that Stark Industries purchase a stake in Extremis, 'That's exactly what we used to do'. The film's immersion in the post-9/11 geopolitical arena was challenged by the likes of Manohla Dargis for the way it 'invokes Sept. 11 and dodges it' leading to it being called 'at once inherently political and empty' (2013). Dargis's perspective was no doubt fuelled by the proximity of the film's release to the Boston Marathon bombings, which had occurred just two weeks before. She continued: 'But Mr. Black [the film's director] and his colleagues, like other filmmakers who use the iconography of Sept. 11 and its aftershocks, want to have it both ways. They want to tap into the powerful

Fig. 16: While he initially appears to be a caricature, the Bin Ladenesque Mandarin (Ben Kingsley), emerges as a satire of the terrorist Other during the 'War on Terror' era in *Iron Man* (2013)

reactions those events induced, while dodging the complex issues and especially the political arguments that might turn off ticket buyers' (ibid.).

When both Pepper and the president are kidnapped, Stark is faced with the hero's predicament of who to save. The stakes are raised even further when thirteen innocent people are thrown from Air Force One and J.A.R.V.I.S. (Stark's artificial intelligence programme which helps him control his suit which stands for Just A Rather Very Intelligent System) informs Stark that, based on the laws of physics, he will only be able to save four. Stark is faced with the perennial superhero dilemma, which Stephen Faller labelled as the 'false dichotomy choice' (2010: 259), in which superheroes are seemingly forced to decide between saving one innocent party or another, before in the end figuring out a way to save both (see Raimi's *Spider-Man*, *Superman Returns et al.*). The playful manner of the scene and the lack of peril in spite of the seemingly raised stakes is indicative of the tone which becomes increasingly more prominent in the MCU throughout Phase Two. Unlike the Gulmira sequence in *Iron Man* which featured no witty one-liners, the Air Force One rescue and the Roxxon sequence which follows are full of humorous banter between Stark and Rhodes. These decisions seem to go against comments made by Shane Black before he became affiliated with the MCU when he suggested, in a 2009 interview with the *Guardian*, that

> If someone fires a gun in a movie, it should always be a big deal. I don't like movies where someone shoots at someone else but they just run away and manage to dodge the bullet. Or people are all firing at each other continuously for 10

minutes. You need shock and impact and a genuine sense of peril whenever violence takes place. (Qtd. in Delaney 2009)

But this 'genuine sense of peril' is entirely absent from *Iron Man 3*. Even though early scenes were suggestive of Stark's vulnerability, they are disavowed quite comprehensibly in the narrative which follows in which he is portrayed as almost indestructible. A pointed illustration of this comes just after he has saved *all* thirteen passengers on Air Force One and pauses on a bridge to admire his achievement, only to be hit by a passing truck, leaving the audience to believe, just for the briefest of moments, that Stark is dead ... before a quick cut reveals that he was remotely piloting the suit the whole time and even further from harm than we had even realised.

In the film's spectacularly orchestrated climax on the oil tanker, Rhodes and Stark take on an army of Extremis soldiers, initially even without their own suits, as Stark has proven that his real identity and even his status as a superhero lies not with the 'tin can', but the man inside it.[2] Killian is shown to have kidnapped Pepper and infected her with the Extremis virus and when she hangs from a high beam on the oil tanker Stark calls for her to have faith in him and take his hand. In a rare moment of doubt about an MCU hero, she seems to refuse to trust him and when she apparently falls to her death for the first time in the trilogy Stark is shown to have failed someone he has attempted to rescue. But, as we have seen many times before in the MCU, this sense of precarity is a brief one; just a few minutes later she returns, now with her own superpowers and between the two of them they dispose of Killian. The idea that life in Hollywood cinema is fragile is just a momentary illusion; only in a Hollywood film could someone experience the trauma of the violent death of a loved one, just for it to be disavowed moments later and normalcy be reconstituted.

Like generations of mythopoetic American heroes before him Stark has been redeemed through violence and his PTSD is seemingly erased in the process. The film ends by bringing to a conclusion Stark's journey that had started back in 2008 as he finally has the shrapnel removed from his heart and no further need of the miniature arc reactor in his chest. Its final line of dialogue is 'I am Iron Man', the very same words that ended the first film, but with a very different meaning for the character five years later. The post-credits stinger reveals that Stark had been recounting his story to not just any therapist, but Dr. Bruce Banner himself. Stark says, 'Thank you, by the way, for listening. There's something about just getting it off my chest and putting it out there in the atmosphere instead of holding this in...', only for the film to disclose that Banner had fallen asleep and missed the whole story. On waking up, he apologises and tells Stark, 'I'm not that kind of doctor, I don't have the ... *temperament*'.

'You told your dad about me!?': The problematic representation of women in *Thor: The Dark World*

This volume has dedicated little time and space to the discussion of the representation of women in the Marvel Cinematic Universe and this is primarily because women play a very small role in the films throughout Phases One and Two. As indicated in the introduction, female characters rarely occupy the privileged and dynamic spaces of the series and tend to be at best marginalised, at worst objectified, sexualised and infantilised. There is a superficial patina of progressivism in the way that women are given meaningful job titles: in the *Iron Man* trilogy Pepper Potts becomes the CEO of Stark Industries; in *The Incredible Hulk* we are informed that Betty Ross is a renowned cellular biologist; and in *Thor* that Jane Foster is an celebrated astrophysicist, which some have mistakenly identified as positive representation. In their description, these professions sound as if they might be empowering to the women who occupy them, but in the course of the narratives they are rarely given the opportunity to demonstrate their intellect and individuality commensurate to these titles and, in actual fact, are shown as having a severely restricted life outside of their relationships to their partner whose name is, in all three cases mentioned above, also the name of the films they feature in. Pepper Potts might be described by Tony Stark as having the responsibility of running 'the largest tech conglomerate on Earth' (*Avengers: Age of Ultron*) but she does little more than react *to* and be rescued *by* him throughout the course of the *Iron Man* films. We are told that Betty Ross is a brilliant scientist and Joseph Walderzak calls her 'a hero, a partner' (2016: 159), but the film never shows her doing any substantial research, she is rescued several times in *The Incredible Hulk*, and does not seem to exist outside of her relationships with Banner, her father and her boyfriend Leonard Samson. Aside from these slightly more central characters, the MCU is littered with minor female characterisations who are treated even more poorly. Christine Everheart in *Iron Man* and *Iron Man 2* is referred to as 'trash' by Pepper and is on the receiving end of Stark's comment about 'Doing a piece for *Vanity Fair*', while Stark himself is lauded for his sexual profligacy; a beautiful female private (played by Natalie Dormer and called Lorraine in the credits) in *Captain America: The First Avenger*, tells Cap 'the women of America, they owe you their thanks, and seeing as they're not here...', before dragging him behind a book case to kiss him. The very fact that these patterns are so prevalent in the most successful film franchise ever made is troubling, but it is even more disturbing that they are part of broader trends in cultural representation in the new millennial decades which have prided themselves on their political progressivism.

Of course, there are partial complications to this throughout the MCU, like Agent Peggy Carter from *Captain America: The First Avenger*, Maria Hill in *The Avengers*, Gamora in *Guardians of the Galaxy,* and most clearly Natasha Romanoff aka Black Widow introduced in *Iron Man 2*, before becoming one of the Avengers after. Peggy Carter is an engaging character in her own right, but in her restricted screen time and the fact that she only exists in relation to Steve Rogers and his narrative means that her character is unable to develop in the film as much as it does in the television series, *Marvel's Agent Carter.* Gamora is resourceful and tough, but even though she is called a 'living weapon' she is saved by Peter Quill on multiple occasions in a film which is undoubtedly *his story* rather than anyone else's. Black Widow is the closest to a central female character the MCU provided audiences with in Phases One and Two across her four film appearances, but her portrayal also emphasises the contradictions at the heart of seemingly empowered women in the genre. She is shown to be physically and intellectually capable, it is she who shuts down the Tesseract at the end of *The Avengers* and she outfights Hawkeye in the same film, but she is also depicted as more physically, psychologically and emotionally vulnerable than any of her team mates. In *The Avengers,* it is Black Widow who needs to be protected by Cap's shield when a car explodes on the streets of New York, as even Hawkeye is able to quickly take cover behind a car, and it is she who whimpers and cowers after being exposed to the Hulk for the first time in a way none of the other Avengers do. As Jeremiah Favara has written, 'At times, Black Widow is shown to be more than capable of defending herself; she knocks out Hawkeye in a fight, she bests/tricks Loki, and is the only Avenger that is able to harness alien technologies in the final fight scene. Yet at other times, Black Widow is shown to be vulnerable and in need of protection; when encountering the Hulk, for example, Black Widow is helpless only to be saved at the last minute by Thor' (2016: 179). *The Avengers* contains intriguing allusions to her past, but they remain only allusions as she was not given a solo film throughout Phases One, Two and Three. Even within her film appearances she is certainly marginalised and problems arose around specific moments of her character development (see *Avengers: Age of Ultron* and the forced sterilisation discussed in chapter eight) and depictions of her in combat are sexualised in ways that are never applicable to men (see Purse 2011b). As Sherry Ginn, the editor of *Marvel's Black Widow from Spy to Superhero: Essays on an Avenger with a Very Specific Skill Set*, has suggested, she remains the most compelling of the MCU women and even though the character as presented in the MCU is 'not without her faults… Nevertheless, she has characteristics that make her a superhero in her own right' (2017: 4).

It might be relevant to pause for a moment to consider the ages of the women who play these roles within the MCU as opposed to their male counterparts, as they reveal a continuation of the disparity between male and female performers which has characterised the American film industry for decades. The most egregious examples of this perhaps being the infamous romantic pairings of Sean Connery and Catherine Zeta Jones in *Entrapment* (1999), with their thirty-nine-year age gap, or that of Cary Grant and Audrey Hepburn in *Charade* (1963) with twenty-five years between them, or Harrison Ford and Anne Heche in *Six Days and Seven Nights* (1998) with twenty-seven years, and the twenty-one years between Annabelle Wallis and Tom Cruise in *The Mummy* (2017). Rather than isolated occurrences, these are part of trend which has defined Hollywood since the very birth of the medium (see Herman and Sender 2015). In the MCU, Edward Norton (b. 1969) is eight years older than Liv Tyler (b. 1977); Mark Ruffalo (b. 1967) is seventeen years older than Scarlett Johansson (b. 1984); Paul Bettany (b. 1971) is seventeen years older than Elizabeth Olsen (b. 1989); Paul Rudd (b. 1969) is nine years older than Evangeline Lilly (b. 1979), Chadwick Boseman (b. 1976) is seven years older than Lupita Nyong'o (b. 1983). Robert Downey Jr. (b. 1965) has been paired with Gwyneth Paltrow (six years his junior, b. 1972), Leslie Bibb (nine years his junior, b. 1974) and Rebecca Hall (seventeen years his junior, b.1982) and is shown attempting to instigate a relationship with Kate Mara (twenty-two years his junior, b. 1983) and Scarlett Johanson (twenty-one years his junior, b. 1984). There are exceptions to this, but they are rare and the age differences are slight: Natalie Portman (b. 1981) is two years older than Chris Hemsworth (b. 1983), Hayley Attwell (b. 1982) is a year older than Chris Evans (b. 1981) and Zoe Saldana (b. 1978) is a year older than Chris Pratt (b. 1979).

This discrepancy can also be seen in the initial ages when actors first play their character in the series: Robert Downey Jr. was forty-three when he first played *Iron Man* in 2008, Paul Rudd was forty-five in *Ant-Man* in 2014, Don Cheadle forty-six in *Iron Man 2* in 2010, Edward Norton was thirty-nine when he played the Hulk in *The Incredible Hulk* in 2008 and Mark Ruffalo was forty-five when he played the same role in *The Avengers* in 2012, and finally Chris Evans was thirty at the time of *Captain America: The First Avenger* 2011. The only actor in his twenties when he first played a MCU superhero in Phase One was Chris Hemsworth who was twenty-nine in *Thor* in 2011. As not a single MCU film from Phases One or Two have a woman as the lead character named in the title, the comparative process is slightly more complicated. However, Scarlett Johansson was twenty-six when she first appeared as Black Widow in *Iron Man 2* in 2010, Hayley Atwell was twenty-nine in *Captain America: The First Avenger* in 2011, Elizabeth Olsen was twenty-five in *Avengers: Age of Ultron* in 2014, Zoe Saldana was thirty-six in *Guardians of the Galaxy* in 2014 and Karen Gillan twenty-seven in the same film. It should be noted that this is without considering the range of aging yet still active and virile patriarchal figures the MCU provides audiences with, like Nick Fury played by Samuel L. Jackson who was sixty when *Iron Man* was released and in his seventies by the time of *Captain Marvel*, Anthony Hopkins who was seventy-five at the time of *Thor*, William Hurt who was fifty-eight for *The Incredible Hulk*, Jeff Bridges who was fifty-nine at the time of *Iron Man*, Stellan Skarsgård who was sixty during *Thor*, and Michael Douglas who was seventy at the release of *Ant-Man*. What aging and similarly dynamic matriarchal figures does the MCU offer in Phases One and Two with comparative screen time and influence? Only the likes of Rene Russo, who played Frigga in *Thor*, who was fifty-six at the time, Jenny Agutter who was sixty in *The Avengers* in 2012, or Glenn Close who was fifty-eight at the time she played Irani Rael in *Guardians of the Galaxy*. None of these characters have anywhere near the narrative centrality of the likes of Nick Fury, Odin, Thaddeus Ross, Obadiah Stane, Erik Selvig or Hank Pym.[3]

Another way it becomes clear how far women have been marginalised in the MCU and across the American film industry is through a statistical analysis of the frequency of male- or female-speaking roles in films. A range of institutions and individuals have conducted research in this area, the most prominent of which are those undertaken by 'The Media, Diversity, & Social Change Initiative' at USC Annenberg, the Geena Davis Institute on Gender in Media, and the Center for the Study of Women in Television & Film. As one might expect, their findings prove uncomfortable reading in an age in which there has emerged a general consensus in the media that there are more roles for women than there have ever been before, both in front of and behind the camera, with films like *Star Wars: The Force Awakens*, *The Hunger Games* franchise (2012–15) and *Wonder Woman* being cited as evidence for this supposed shift (see Scott and Dargis 2014). Furthermore, this has also prompted a backlash in some quarters, a process described as a 'feminist takeover' by Rachel Lefler (2015). However, this understanding is not supported at all by the findings of the aforementioned studies which proves such assertions to be anecdotal rather than empirical. For example, the 2017 USC Annenberg study titled 'Inclusion in the Director's Chair?: Gender, Race, & Age of Film Directors Across 1,000 Films 2007–2016' revealed that there are almost twenty-four male directors for every one female director in Hollywood, that female directors' careers are not as long as those of men and that they are offered dramas rather than other genres (see Smith *et al.* 2017). In front of the camera, research indicates that, on average, taking into account the top hundred grossing films of the year, women occupy only approximately between 28–33% of speaking roles; additionally, when considering the action and adventure genres (in which the superhero film is included) this percentage decreases to closer to 20% (see Smith *et al.* 2015a). Females were considerably more likely than males to be shown in sexy attire (27.9% of females vs. 8% of males), featured nude

(26.4% of females vs. 9.1% of males), or referred to as physically attractive (12.6% of females vs. 3.1% of males) (see Smith *et al.* 2015b). Considering one particular year in detail, 2015, the year in which the MCU released *Avengers: Age of Ultron* and *Ant-Man*, as illustrative of these general trends, in the top hundred grossing films male characters received approximately twice the amount of screen time (28.5% compared to 16%), men were 71% of protagonists (females comprised 29% of protagonists) and women occupied only 4% of directors, 11% of writers, 3% of cinematographers, 19% of producers, 14% of editors (see Lauzen 2016). Neither of the MCU films produced in 2015 come anywhere close to even the average of 28–33% of speaking roles being taken by women observed above and neither does a single film across Phases One or Two, with only *Iron Man 3* having more than 25% of its speaking characters women. Particularly egregious examples in Phase One include *The Incredible Hulk* (12.2%) and *Thor* (15%), and in Phase Two *Ant-Man* (14%) and, somewhat surprisingly, *Guardians of the Galaxy* (10.7%), which has the lowest percentage of female-speaking characters in Phases One and Two.[4] *The Incredible Hulk*, in its 112-minute running time, features only five female characters that even *speak* and only three of those are named in the credits: Betty Ross, Martina (who has a single line of dialogue in untranslated Portuguese), Major Kathleen Sparr, an unnamed woman selling clothes in the market and an unnamed newsreader. In case one might regard this as an aberration, consider the fact that in *Thor* only Jane, Darcy, Sif, Frigga and two unnamed nurses speak, and in *Iron Man* (19.1%) eight women speak and only five of these are named: Pepper, Christine Everheart, Ramirez (the soldier in the Humvee at the start), and two television newsreaders, real-life Zoriana Kit and fictional Amira Ahmed (the three others are two stewardesses and a mother in Gulmira). *Captain America: The First Avenger* (17.5%) has only two females who are even named onscreen: Agent Peggy Carter and Mandy, a girl at the World of Tomorrow exhibition, who does not speak a single line of dialogue.[5]

With this context provided, this sub-chapter is an exploration of the transformation of Natalie Portman's Jane Foster between *Thor* and its sequel *Thor: The Dark World*, which may or may not have been the reason for Portman's comment in 2016 that she was 'done' with the Marvel Cinematic Universe (see Han 2016). It was reported by the *Hollywood Reporter* that the Academy Award-winning performer was dissatisfied with the film's original director Patty Jenkins being removed from the project and the creative direction the film took as a result (see Masters 2011). Jenkins would have been the MCU's first female director and indeed the first female director of a major superhero blockbuster in 2013, which she then became four years later anyway when she took the helm of the critically and commercially succesful *Wonder Woman* for the DCEU in 2017. In the DVD commentary for *Thor: The Dark World* her replacement Alan Taylor stated, 'Natalie's character brings something fresh to a female heroine in the picture. She's an intelligent scientist'; and Kevin Feige added, 'She advances the action, she's really integrated into the action', but these assertions reveal a substantial disconnection from the film itself which provides a superlative example of the questionable portrayal of women across the MCU. The suggestion is that the series promotes a superficial level of female empowerment, at the same time as participating in their marginalisation and objectification and thus functions as a reification of heteronormative patriarchal culture and its reactionary values.[6]

Thor: The Dark World, released in October 2013, is both the sequel to Kenneth Branagh's *Thor* and a continuation of the narrative of *The Avengers*, beginning as it does with Loki being brought back in chains to Asgard after the failed Chitauri invasion of New York. It received mixed reviews on its release, many of which echoed Mick LaSalle's comments that, 'Bigger is not always better. *Thor: The Dark World* pumps up the action and special effects and loses some of the human element that made the original *Thor*' (2013), or Amy Nicholson's contention that, 'Lacking Iron Man's wit, the Hulk's brains, and the Captain's ideals, he's [Thor] in peril of going poof himself if the franchise doesn't figure out how to capitalize on its most glorious hero' (2013). The film is widely regarded as being one of the lesser entries in the MCU, although it does have a significant fan following, much of which is connected to the continued presence of Tom Hiddlestone playing Loki for the third time.[7] In the period between *The Avengers* and *Thor: The Dark World* Hiddlestone had further endeared himself to MCU fans by appearing dressed in full Loki regalia at the 2013 Comic-Con, gleefully repeating his two most often quoted (and memed) lines of dialogue from *The Avengers*, but retailoring them for the Comic Con audience:

> Humanity ... look how far you have fallen. Lining up in the sweltering heat for hours. Huddling together in the dark... Like beasts! I am Loki, the last god – and I am burdened with glorious purpose. Stand back, you mewling quim. The bright lure of freedom diminishes your life's joy in a mad scramble for a place in this chamber. In this meagre palace of Midgard the arena they call Hall H. Where are your Avengers now? *Say my name!*

In *Thor*, the eponymous hero was shown growing from an arrogant and impetuous youth into a worthy heir to the throne of Asgard and *Thor: The Dark World* continues to portray this development. Like the first film, its emotional centre is the oedipal dynamic between the two brothers, Thor and Loki, and their aging father Odin. While Thor has been quick to proclaim his father's abilities as both a king and a parent, Alan Taylor, who had until then been more recognised for directing episodes of *Game of Thrones* (HBO, 2011–) than his work on feature films, offered an alternative perspective: 'Odin is called the All-Father but he is one of the worst parents I have ever met... Their father has so completely screwed up their childhood. You don't tell two boys that they're both meant to be king, but only one will achieve it!' (qtd. in Moore and Javins 2013: 174).[8] The throne itself will later be destroyed by the film's primary antagonist, the bland and unshaded villain Malekith (Christopher Eccleston) who is from the race of Dark Elves once thought eradicated by Odin's grandfather, Bors. Many years before Malekith was cast out and on his return seeks revenge, but he lacks anything resembling a personality even compared to Laufey, king of the Frost Giants, from the previous film. The film derives its title from the fact that Malekith wishes to usher in a new era, a Dark World, and hopes to use a mysterious substance known as the Aether, one of the six Infinity Stones spread throughout the MCU, to achieve it.

It is Jane Foster, Thor's human girlfriend, who accidentally comes into contact with this Aether and sets the plot in motion. In the first film Jane had been one of the slightly more interesting female characters in Phase One, especially compared to the likes of Pepper Potts and Betty Ross. She did fulfil the role of the adoring girlfriend and was infantilised by her clumsiness, but she was also introduced as a dedicated and talented astrophysicist shown working and researching, she was not required to be saved by Thor and was not overtly sexualised by either her clothes or her demeanour. In the two years Thor has been away heroically fighting battles all across the nine realms, we are informed that Jane has been doing little more than pining for him in his absence. Darcy chastises her for 'moping around in your pyjamas, eating ice cream and obsessing about *you know who*', the uncomfortable implication being that she is unable to function, continue her research, or even her life without him. She is re-introduced to the audience on a date with the genial Richard (Chris O'Dowd) having relocated to London, but it is clear to see that, like Betty dating Leonard Samson in *The Incredible Hulk*, she could never be satisfied with anyone other the film's hero, who she fears has deserted her after the events of the first film. Jane does not know, but we the audience do, that Thor's destruction of the Bifrost Bridge at the climax of *Thor* to save the race of Frost Giants from Loki's genocide, had made it impossible for him to return to her.

When Jane and Darcy visit an unexplained 'stable gravitational anomaly' they find a truck floating in the air, somehow impervious to the rules of gravity, which reminds them both of what they had experienced just before meeting *Thor* in New Mexico in the first film. Jane instructs Darcy 'Don't touch anything!' … but this is exactly what she does herself, only to be pulled through a portal into another realm and infected with the Aether. With the mysterious substance coursing through her body she is given what appears to be super powers, but they also lead her to faint whenever they are triggered, meaning she spends several long minutes in the film shot as an attractively framed literal sleeping beauty. Additionally, as a conduit for the remarkable powers of the Aether she is transformed into an object fought over for much of the film's narrative by Thor and Malekith, as the strength and determination she displayed in the first film are replaced by her becoming effectively a 'damsel in distress' who needs to be frequently rescued not just by Thor, as one might expect, but by other characters like Loki, Frigga and even Erik Selvig. Learning of her plight, somehow Thor returns to Earth only to be comedically slapped twice by Jane demanding to know why he did not come back before, in one of several examples of the character being primarily defined by her emotions rather than her intellect. Her subsequent journey to Asgard leads to an intriguing reversal of the fish out of water narrative of the first film, now instead with Asgard shown through Jane's human eyes, but Odin is revealed to be distinctly unhappy at her presence. When the once resolute and determined female scientist hears that Thor has discussed her with his father she blushes like a teenager and asks, 'You told your *dad* about me!?' Odin's dismissive line on seeing her, even when she is in the same room, is 'She does not belong here in Asgard any more than a *goat belongs at a dining table*'. Thor protests that 'She's strong in ways you'd never even know', but Alan Taylor's film presents little evidence of this and Jane is transmogrified from an intelligent and resourceful scientist to a flighty and overly emotional girlfriend, who tells Thor, 'I like the way you explain things!' and the audience that, 'Physics is gonna go ballistic!' While Thor has brought Jane to Asgard to cure her, there is a lingering suspicion that the prospect of her having powers is such a monstrous idea that the narrative demands that they must be removed as quickly as possible in a very similar way to how Pepper Potts was treated in *Iron Man 3* after she became infected with the Extremis virus.

Jane is not the only female character to undergo a regression from the original film. Sif, one of the Warriors Three, is treated quite differently to her male counterparts and has herself deteriorated since *Thor*. Branagh's film had portrayed her as strong and independent, clearly in love with Thor but reluctant to reveal it. In the sequel it is Sif and not her male compatriots who is teased about not being in control by Thor in the film's opening battle, it is her costume that accentuates her form and her pining for Thor becomes much more explicit, even though she knows he has chosen another partner. In contrast, Volstagg is obese and comical, but never weak or emotionally vulnerable and neither are Fandral or Hogun. In the first film, Thor's mother, Frigga, was shown as too weak to hardly even raise a sword in the throne room with Laufey the Frost Giant king, but in the sequel she is provided with a heroic moment as she bravely fights back against Malekith in order to save Jane; yet she is killed in the familiar trope of the death of a female providing source of motivation for the hero. So, while Craig Kyle is able to assert

Fig. 17: Thor and Jane Foster (Natalie Portman) in *Thor: The Dark World* (2013), a film in which she finds herself objectified, marginalised and infantilised throughout

that Frigga is 'even more important' (qtd. in Moore and Javins 2013: 194) than Odin, she is still one of a range of mothers in the MCU who are marginalised if not literally erased from the narrative.

In the wake of Frigga's death Thor and his father have an argument as how to best proceed in their fight with Malekith, a moment which is decidedly reminiscent of their disagreement in the first film over how to deal with the threat of the Frost Giants, although now their roles have been reversed. It is Thor who suggests the path of reason and Odin who wants to stand and fight 'to the last drop of Asgardian blood!' Thor even questions his father's judgement – 'Then how are you different to Malekith?' – but it is a false comparison as Odin is wracked by grief and has shown himself to be a wise and honourable man in both *Thor* films, whereas Malekith is a one-dimensional pantomime-like villain. Nevertheless, Thor goes against his father once again, but this time in the best interests of Asgard. It is then he lets Loki out of prison because he needs his help in order to defeat Malekith. When Loki meets Jane, the woman he had threatened with implied rape in the first film, she slaps him around the face as she had done Thor, with a cry of 'That was for New York!', the metaphorical equivalent of punching Osama Bin Laden in the aftermath of 9/11 (which Captain America actually did in issue one of the comic *Freedom 3* [2006]). Thor knows that he cannot trust his brother, but hopes that their shared desire for revenge will prevail. When they finally confront Malekith it seems that Loki has betrayed Thor again and cuts off his hand, claiming that 'All I ever wanted was you and Odin dead at my feet!' but it is revealed to be part of their ruse and they attack the leader of the Dark Elves together. Jane seems terrified at this turn of events and as oblivious to their strategy as Pepper seemed to have been of Tony's plan to give her the Iron Man suit during the Mandarin's attack on his mansion in *Iron Man 3*. During the battle, it is Loki who saves Jane and then seemingly sacrifices himself for his brother. A tearful Thor informs him, 'I'll tell father what you did today' but Loki says, 'I didn't do it for him...' In the history of the MCU's fake deaths through Phases One and Two, Loki's is the shortest, as within three minutes this too is revealed to have been part of his scheme.

With the Aether removed from Jane she is now effectively superfluous as a character and the stage is set for the film's climax in Greenwich, London, a fitting choice due to its historic connections to both time and space.[9] In this sequence it is not Jane who takes the lead in helping Thor as one might expect given her expertise, but Erik Selvig who has recently been released from a psychiatric institution. As Walderzak remarks, 'it is Erik who understands and provides an explanation to the audience of the gravitational convergence, despite Jane's focus on the subject' (2016: 160). Jane does participate in the battle at Greenwich and it is her computations which help them realise where the teleportation devices they use against Malekith should be placed, but she is given an 'oops!' moment when she accidentally teleports Darcy and Ian (Darcy's own intern) and later she is saved by Selvig when the Dark Elves attack them. After Malekith has been defeated by Thor's noble act of sacrifice for the sake of the galaxy, Jane too offers to sacrifice herself, but in a very different way to those performed by male heroes in film after film in the MCU since *Iron Man*. Seeing that an unconscious Thor is in the path of Malekith's falling ship, she tries to pull him free but realises she will not be able to, so she decides to cover him (an immortal god) with her very human body, willing to *die for her man*. However, as we have come to expect, the sacrifice is not a real one and she is saved for the second time in the space of a few minutes by Selvig who cleverly uses the device to teleport Malekith's ship to another world. Why it could not have been Jane's ingenuity that saved Thor or her colleagues remains unclear, but it is in the film's post-credits scene that she is rewarded for her behaviour throughout the film with the ultimate in heteronormative reification, a passionate kiss the likes of which Robin Wood memorably referred to as the 'ideological straightjacket' of Hollywood cinema (1998: 37). In one final twist, another symbolic gesture of her superfluousness, Jane's face is hidden from the camera during their embrace and in the film's audio commentary director Alan Taylor revealed that Natalie Portman was not present for the scene and in fact was replaced, unbeknownst to the audience, by Hemsworth's real-life wife, Elsa Pataky.

Notes

1   In one of the many connections we have seen drawn between the superhero film and the western throughout the MCU, the Mandarin recounts the story of the real-life Sand Creek Massacre and offers parallels between it and his attack on the Ali Al Salem airbase in Kuwait. In 1864 a 700-strong force of Colorado territory Militia attacked a peaceful Native American settlement killing between seventy and one hundred and sixty-three Indians. The Mandarin says, 'the US military waited until the friendly Cheyenne braves had all gone hunting, waited to attack and slaughtered the families left behind and claim their land'. The Sand Creek Massacre has been regularly recreated in western film from *Tomahawk* (1951) to the Vietnam-era *Soldier Blue* (1970) and *Little Big Man* (1970).

2   This is the primary lesson that Tony Stark helps the young Peter Parker learn in the narrative of *Spider-Man: Homecoming*, where he informs him, 'If you're nothing without this suit, then you shouldn't have it'. After Stark takes away the hi-tech Spider-Man suit he designed from him, Parker proves himself to be a real hero by thwarting the plans of the salvage contractor-turned-weapons designer Adrian Toomes aka the Vulture.

3   Tilda Swinton was fifty-five when she played the Ancient One in the Phase Three film *Doctor Strange* and Marisa Tomei was fifty-one at the time of *Captain America: Civil War* in 2016.

4   These figures are reflected in the failure of some of the MCU films (for example *Ant-Man*, *The Avengers*, *Iron Man*, *The Incredible Hulk*, *Captain America: The First Avenger* and *Doctor Strange*) to pass what is referred to as the Bechdel Test, named after the cartoonist Alison Bechdel, which requires that a film must contain two named female characters who talk about something other than a male character.

5   As a benchmark, one should probably turn to Patty Jenkins' *Wonder Woman*, which certainly raised the bar in a number of ways for the representation of women in the genre. It earned $103 million during its opening weekend, the highest for a female director and highest for a female-led comic book film. Its global opening weekend of $228 million was more than the combined entire box office of the two other female comic book superhero films before: *Elektra* (2005; $56 million) and *Catwoman* (2004; $82 million). Yet even *Woman Woman*, which begins with an extended all female sequence set on the island of Themyscira, only has 34% of its speaking characters as women.

6   The poor characterisation of Jane Foster led to her name being used by script-reader Ross Puttman in his @femscriptintros project on Twitter. Puttman takes 'female character descriptions out of screenplays, changes all names to 'Jane' (to protect the innocent), and then sends them out 140 characters at a time. The result is a parade of one-note, superficial notes that describe characters' looks, but rarely anything about

them' (Watercutter 2016).

7   *Thor: The Dark World* is the worst reviewed film in the franchise according to both Metacritic and Rotten Tomatoes, followed by *Iron Man 2*.

8   In the comic book *Thor: The Dark World Prelude* (2013) Iron Man is shown to ask Thor during the Battle of New York whether he has seen any episodes of *Game of Thrones*. He adds, 'It's like you but instead of a magic hammer they have *dragons* and *sex*'.

9   In what I would regard as the film's most powerful time and space anomaly *Thor: The Dark World* was one of several American films produced in 2013 to be awarded the status of 'British' by the British Film Institute after they passed the 'cultural test for film'. Films like *Saving Mr Banks*, *Jack the Giant Slayer*, *Fast and Furious 6*, *The Dark Knight Rises* and *Wrath of Titans* were all awarded British status in 2013 and the Best British Film at the BAFTA that year was controversially awarded to *Gravity* (2013).

CHAPTER SIX

'The world has changed and none of us can go back': The Illusory Moral Ambiguities of the Post-9/11 Superhero in *Captain America: The Winter Soldier*

It's hard to make a political film that's not topical. That's what makes a political thriller different from just a thriller. And that's what adds to the characters' paranoia and the audience's experience of that paranoia. But we're also a very pop-culture-obsessed and we love topicality, so we kept pushing to [have] scenes that, fortunately or unfortunately, played out [during the time that Edward] Snowden outed the NSA. That stuff was already in the zeitgeist. We were all reading the articles that were coming out questioning drone strikes, pre-emptive strikes, civil liberties – [Barack] Obama talking about who they would kill... We wanted to put all of that into the film because it would be a contrast to [Captain America]'s greatest-generation [way of thinking].

– Anthony Russo (qtd. in Lovece 2014)

Captain America's heroic persona changed as the culture's needs and expectations of a hero changed. The level of complexity of the hero's character, his moral viewpoint, is altered as society alters. But as the society becomes better educated and more aware of those ambiguities, the mythic character must reflect the awareness of those ambiguities in some way.

– Jeffrey S. Lang and Patrick Trimble (1988: 169)

I.

On its release in April 2014 *Captain America: The Winter Soldier* was widely regarded in the mainstream press as being Marvel's most political movie to date. In fact, reviews seemed almost contractually obliged to mention its sustained immersion in the fractious politics of the 'War on Terror' era. Many reviews echoed Ty Burr's suggestion that the film was 'torn between patriotic ideals and harsh post-9/11 realpolitik' (2014) or David Edelstein's description of it as 'a bracing, old-style conspiracy thriller made extra-scary by new technology and the increasingly ugly trade-offs of a post-9/11 world' (2014). However, more than just depicting these issues, the film was said by many to be particularly challenging in how they were represented. This, arguably, reached a peak when two articles at popular film websites made almost exactly the same claim: Ryan Lambie at *Den of Geek* asked whether *Captain America: The Winter Soldier* was '2014's most subversive superhero film?' (2014) and Darren Franich, writing at *Entertainment Weekly*, titled his 'The real, subversive politics of *Captain America: The Winter Soldier*' (2014). What might have led the film to be described so frequently in such terms? The superhero, as we have seen, and as writers like Dan Hassler-Forest and Jason Dittmer have persuasively argued, is predominantly a reactionary figure whose narratives tend to inculcate and legitimate dominant ideological values. *The Winter Soldier* does indeed situate itself amid some of the defining political issues of the new millennial decade, yet what Lambie and Franich refer to as the 'subversive' perspective of its narrative offers similar paradoxes to that which we have already observed throughout this monograph: in Tony Stark's rejection of the Military Industrial Complex only to embody and legitimate extra-judicial American intrusion into Afghanistan; in the redemptive violence offered in both *Thor* and *The Incredible Hulk*; or the heroic transgenerational last stand in New York in *The Avengers*, a film described by Richard Brody as a 'post-9/11 revenge fantasy' (2012). In a similar way to this, *The Winter Soldier* offers a range of topical critiques of contemporary America, while at the same time embracing a mythopoetic vision of what are commonly regarded as quintessential American values. This process was classified by Jason Dittmer as one in which 'superheroes are not reflections of, but are instead (along with many other elements) co-constitutive of the discourse popularly known as American exceptionalism' (2012: 10).

The Winter Soldier is partially based on Ed Brubaker's 2005 Captain America series of the same name, but reimagines and integrates it with the broader ongoing MCU narrative, and encompasses many of the formative elements of the 1970s conspiracy thriller cycle seen in American films like *Three Days of the Condor, Marathon Man* and *The Parallax View* (1974). These texts have been characterised by scholars such as Barna William Donovan as addressing 'the very real international and financial concerns of the day' (2011: 77) like the Gulf of Tonkin incident (1964), the leaking of the Pentagon Papers (1971), the Watergate scandal (1972–74), and the Pike Committee (1975–76). *The Winter Soldier* does something very similar to this, but turns its attention towards a range of key post-9/11 events and debates: from the pervasiveness of contemporary surveillance culture, data mining, governmental duplicity and the need for more transparency from the intelligence community, to targeted killing, the ethics of pre-emptive strikes, the USA PATRIOT Act and the balance between collective security and individual rights. Around the time in which the script was being written by Christopher Markus and Stephen McFeely, WikiLeaks was in the process of releasing thousands of previously secret files concerning the daily realities of the 'War on Terror': like that of the footage entitled *Collateral Murder* which showed the 12 July 2007 Baghdad airstrike by two US AH-64 Apache helicopters (published in April 2010), 9,200 sensitive documents pertaining to the Iraq War (in July 2010) and the United States diplomatic cables leak (in November 2010) among many others. At the same time the public became aware of high profile whistle-blowers like Chelsea (then Bradley) Manning, who was charged and then found guilty of five counts of espionage (July 2013), and Edward Snowden, a contractor for the United States government, who passed on thousands of classified documents to journalists before fleeing to Russia where he was granted temporary asylum (June 2013).[1] The film's focus on issues very much connected to these events made it seem prescient when it was released in the summer of 2014, but as Joe Russo, the film's co-director, stated, 'It was all in the ether, it was all part of the zeitgeist. The Snowden stuff actually happened while we were shooting' (qtd. in Lovece 2014). Thus, reviews and opinion pieces with titles like '*Winter Soldier*: Snowden superheroics' (Harris n.d.), 'Captain America and the age of Snowden' (Willmore 2014) and 'Is *Captain America: The Winter Soldier* a Post-Snowden Superhero Movie? Not quite' (Eddy 2014) were commonplace, and not just restricted to the United States, as for once commentators and reviewers discussed a superhero film's political perspectives almost as much as its spectacular action sequences (see also Amarillo 2014; Salva 2014; Schlüter 2014).[2]

II.

The opening scene of *The Winter Soldier* shows Steve Rogers on a morning jog, with the Lincoln Memorial, the Washington Monument and even the White House shown rather conspicuously in the background. It is no coincidence that the film associates Rogers with these landmarks, not just because he is an iconic figure himself, but because he is an embodiment of a very particular type of American identity, a set of 'old-fashioned' values which the MCU has shown many in the first decades of the new millennium have come to regard as outdated. As we saw at the end of *The First Avenger* and throughout *The Avengers*, Rogers is struggling to come to terms with life in the modern era. In *The First Avenger* his adversaries were the unambiguously evil HYDRA and the Nazis; in *The Avengers*, while his enemies were also clearly defined (Loki and the Chitauri), the machinations of the World Security Council and S.H.I.E.L.D. complicated his role somewhat, when even the motives of his close friends and colleagues were revealed to be more questionable. Nick Fury, director of S.H.I.E.L.D., had been shown to favour extreme levels of secrecy and an embrace of what he refers to in *The Winter Soldier* as 'compartmentalisation' which we had already seen in *The Avengers* with his pursuit of HYDRA technology and his lies about finding Coulson's blood-stained vintage cards on the agent's dead body. The inscrutable superspy Natasha Romanoff/Black Widow, who is as much a product of the sceptical new millennial world as Rogers is of the 1940s, is defined by her cynicism and moral fluidity, which is strikingly different to the patriotism of Captain America's former comrades the Howling Commandos and Cap's own view of how his government, and those who represent it, should behave. As if to emphasise these contrasts, Black Widow picks up Captain America from his jog, during which he has met another veteran Sam Wilson (who will later become the superhero Falcon), and jokingly asks both of them, 'Either one of you know where the Smithsonian is? I'm here to pick up a fossil...'.

His symptoms are not as obvious as Tony Stark's in *Iron Man 3*, but Steve Rogers does seem to be suffering from some form of trauma, and even though he jokes about all that he has lost – 'All the guys from my barbershop quartet are dead...' – it is clear to both the audience and Sam, who now works for the Veteran's Association, that Rogers is suffering. As one might expect they are both too stoic to actually discuss their feelings, but they can agree that the beds are too soft after 'coming home' compared to 'over there', a shared unspoken acknowledgement of the similarities between the battlefields of the 'War on Terror' for Sam and those in World War II for Captain America. When Cap does visit the VA he overhears a group of former soldiers talking about their experiences after the end of their tour of duty; a young woman recounts: 'A cop pulled me over last week, he thought I was drunk. I swerved to miss a plastic bag... I thought it was an IED.' Sam's response is directed as much to Cap as it is to the veterans of Iraq and Afghanistan that he stands in front of: 'Some stuff you leave there, other stuff you bring back. It's our job to figure out how to carry it...'

Steve Rogers' apartment is testimony to the 'stuff' that he has brought back with him and a marker of his sense of cultural and temporal dislocation. It is decorated with period 1940s furnishings reminiscent of that which was forced upon him in the coda of *The First Avenger*, but this time by his own hand.[3] In

Fig. 18: Visiting an exhibition dedicated to his life and death in the Smithsonian Institute, Steve Rogers struggles to find his place and his purpose in the modern era in *Captain America: The Winter Soldier* (2014)

a deleted scene, Steve is shown leafing through the files of his former Howling Commandos, all of whom are now dead. The camera lingers on that of his best friend, Bucky Barnes, whose death Cap felt personally responsible for in *The First Avenger*. In a literalisation of Black Widow's joke about his status as a 'fossil', he is shown visiting the *actual* Smithsonian Institute where there is an exhibit dedicated to his life entitled 'Living legend and symbol of courage' among other icons of American cultural history like Charles Lindbergh's Spirit of St. Louis and the X-15, the fastest aircraft ever made. Here the camera also remains on an image of Bucky with the description of the two of them as being 'best friends since childhood ... inseparable in the school yard and on the battlefield', in preparation for the film's dramatic reveal later. Walking through an exhibit dedicated to his own life (and death) is a Borgesian experience for Rogers and the scene makes it clear that Cap's past, and even his own identity, do not entirely belong to him anymore. He may be a 'symbol to the nation' but he is alone and isolated in a culture where he feels he does not belong and no longer has a purpose.

Much of Cap's anxiety is concerned with how much the world has changed and what he is being now asked to do in the name of national security, some of which goes against his conscience. When he recounts his concerns to the elderly Peggy Carter (still played by Hayley Atwell), now in her nineties and suffering from some form of dementia, he tells her, 'For as long as I can remember I just wanted to do what was right. I guess I am not quite sure what that is anymore.' Peggy's response is '*You* saved the world ... we rather mucked it up'. It is this juxtaposition between the 'greatest generation' rhetoric endorsed by the first film (and throughout the MCU) and what is shown to be the moral compromises of the new millennial decades which provides much of the film's dramatic friction.

In an attempt to familiarise himself with everything he has missed Cap is shown to have compiled a list of things that people have suggested to him have been important cultural and historic events in the years that he 'lost'. A brief close up insert of his notebook shows the handwritten words: Moon Landing, Berlin Wall (up and down), Star Wars/Trek, Thai food, and Steve Jobs (Apple), among other things. Adding to these Sam Wilson offers his own, Marvin Gaye's 1972 album *Trouble Man* with the comment, 'Everything you missed jammed into one album'. Sam's assertion is something of a throwaway line, but it is one which resonates with the central assertion of this book, that popular cultural artefacts are able to embody the times in which they are made in a range of ways. In a compelling example of how the modern blockbuster is self-consciously designed to function as a transnational cultural artefact, the filmed insert was varied in different distribution markets. So, for the film's release in Russia the list contained Yuri Gagarin, the poet and singer Vladimir Vysotsky and the beloved Soviet-era romantic drama *Moscow Doesn't Believe in Tears* (1980); in South Korea it featured *Oldboy* (2004), Ji-Sung Park and the 2002 World Cup; whereas in Brazil it had racing driver Ayrton Senna, the award-winning actor Wagner Moura and the singer and TV presenter Xuxa. Furthermore, the fact that these inserts were voted for by online audiences is another pertinent example of Henry Jenkins' participatory culture (2006: 3). They are also part of a sustained attempt by Marvel Studios to mediate the inherent jingoism that has been associated with the character of Captain America, a process that was only partially successful with *The First Avenger*, but much more effective in *The Avengers* and *The Winter Soldier*: to self-consciously sell Captain America as not just an American hero, but a global one.

III.

Captain America's anxiety concerning his role is embodied in the film's first dramatic mission on the S.H.I.E.L.D. vessel, the Lemurrian Star, which has been hijacked by pirates in the Indian Ocean led by the French-Algerian ex-DGCE (General Directorate for External Security) Georges Batroc, who is said to be at the 'top of INTERPOL's Red Notice'. What Cap initially presumes to be a rescue mission becomes more complicated when he discovers the ship is not off course, as he has been told, but trespassing and is actually a mobile satellite-launch platform. When Cap calls to Black Widow for assistance he learns that, unbeknownst to him, she has been given a secondary mission to retrieve confidential S.H.I.E.L.D. files by Nick Fury, in an example of his 'compartmentalisation', an action which could have compromised the safety of the hostages. Returning to the S.H.I.E.L.D. headquarters in the Triskellion in Washington DC on the banks of the Potomac river, Captain America confronts the director of S.H.I.E.L.D. with his discovery, to which Fury responds: 'I didn't want you doing anything you weren't comfortable with. Agent Romanoff is comfortable with *anything.*' Fury's evocation of the idea of compartmentalisation, which he describes as 'nobody spills the secrets, because nobody knows them all', is one of the film's many sustained connections to the current geopolitical environment: throughout the George W. Bush and then the Barack Obama administration compartmentalisation emerged as a key policy in the how state secrets were kept under the umbrella term SCI or 'Sensitive Compartmented Information'. These practices became widely discussed after the STELLARWIND leak on 27 June 2013 which was shown to have authorised such practices as warrantless wiretapping, data mining and call recording. The leaks revealed to the public for the first time the extent of the collection of metadata (in the form of phone and email records) that nine major internet companies had been ordered to turn over to the NSA in bulk which was reported to be, by October 2011, in excess of two hundred million internet communications each year. In further revelations, it was also revealed that these practices were paid for by the tax payers themselves as part of a hidden 'black budget'. In the year before the release of *The Winter Soldier* taxpayers spent $10.3 billion on NSA surveillance, a figure 53% higher than it was in 2004. As Charlie Savage has observed, 'It became clear that twenty-first century technology coupled with a virtually unlimited budget in the post-9/11 era were helping to grow the American government's surveillance arm into a leviathan. It was also clear that the surveillance story, even more than other areas of national security legal policy, was really one single narrative that spanned the Bush-Cheney and Obama administrations' (2015: 169).

Fury reveals to Cap the extent of the World Security Council's plans and the reason for their secrecy: Project Insight, the construction of three huge next-generation aircraft known as helicarriers which are able to adopt continuous suborbital flight around the globe, each of which is armed with weapons capable of pre-emptively targeting one thousand hostiles per minute. These extreme measures were only able to be undertaken because of the heightened fears after the Battle of New York featured in *The Avengers*. In a line of dialogue that evokes the real-world increases in security characterised by the USA PATRIOT Act after the attacks on 9/11, Fury states, 'After New York I convinced the World Security Council we needed a quantum surge in threat analysis. For once we're ahead of the curve.' The interaction between Fury and Captain America which follows is perhaps one of the most resonant moments in the film as Fury informs him: 'The satellites can read a terrorist's DNA before he steps outside his spider hole. We're gonna neutralise a lot of threats *before they happen*'; to which Cap counters: 'Thought the punishment usually came after the crime?' But Fury has his

Fig. 19: Captain America and Nick Fury (Samuel L. Jackson) discuss Project Insight in *Captain America: The Winter Soldier*, a film which thoroughly mines the fears and anxieties of the 'War on Terror' in the course of its narrative

own answer: 'We can't afford to wait that long.' Their brief debate about the ethics and efficacy of these security measures, as much of the MCU has been, is firmly immersed in the turbulent events of the post-9/11 decade and is similar to the one many were having in the United States after 9/11 when the USA PATRIOT Act was considered by some as a regrettable but necessary measure to protect a nation under threat and others as an unconstitutional encroachment on civil liberties. Cap makes his own feelings clear about the prospect with a single suggestive line: 'This isn't freedom ... this is fear.'

Shortly after, perhaps in part prompted by Cap's questions, Fury raises some of his own concerns about Project Insight to the man leading its development, his friend and the Secretary of Defense Alexander Peirce (Robert Redford), which results in Fury being targetted by the mysterious assassin known only as the Winter Soldier. Before he 'dies', Fury hands Cap a memory stick with the warning, 'Don't ... trust ... anyone'. Now branded a 'fugitive from S.H.I.E.L.D.' and on the run from the authorities who inform the public that he is a traitor, Cap visits an underground bunker in his old World War II-era training facility in Camp Lehigh looking for answers. What he discovers there is the film's paradigm-shifting reveal and certainly the biggest twist in Phase Ones and Two of the MCU; that HYDRA, the organisation led by the Red Skull in *The First Avenger* and thought to have been destroyed by Cap's sacrifice at the end of the film, have infiltrated S.H.I.E.L.D. as a 'glorious parasite' and gained a global position of enormous power since 1945. Furthermore, it is Arnim Zola (Toby Jones), whose consciousness has been uploaded onto a computer, that has orchestrated HYDRA's ascent. Zola is shown to have been one of many German scientists invited into the USA in the aftermath of World War II as part of the real-life Operation Paperclip (1945) which saw the relocation of more than a thousand

Nazi scientists with strategic value, like 'the father of rocket science' Werner von Braun, Arthur Rudolph and Kurt H. Debus. While President Truman officially ordered that no former members of the Nazi Party were to be included in the programme many were given false records in order for them to assist with science and military developments which were thought to be vital to enable America to win the Cold War. This development led to von Braun going from selecting individuals from the Buchenwald concentration camp for his experiments on the V-2 rocket to appearing on an episode of *Walt Disney's Disneyland* (ABC, 1954–58), 'Man in Space' (1.20) in 1955, not much more than ten years later (see Jacobsen 2014), an uncomfortable reality that has been largely erased from the agreed-upon American master narrative of the Cold War. Zola tells Cap that 'For seventy years HYDRA has been secretly feeding crisis, reaping war, and when history did not cooperate ... history *was changed*', flashing onscreen a selection of 'crises' from the second half of the twentieth century and the start of the twenty-first, including images of the Cuban Missile Crisis, Muammar Gaddafi, Daniel Ortega, the Iranian Revolution, Hugo Chavez and even Julian Assange on the balcony of the Ecuadorian Embassy in 2012, the implication being that each were sponsored by HYDRA to promote disharmony and instability around the globe.[4] He continues: 'HYDRA created a world so chaotic that humanity is finally ready to sacrifice its freedom to gain its security.' To this end, Project Insight is not just able to control traffic lights and security cameras, but it can break into peoples' phones, read tweets, and as Agent Jasper Sitwell later informs Cap, gain access to 'bank records, medical histories, voting patterns, emails, phone calls, your damn SAT scores!' The helicarriers contain a predictive algorithm designed by Zola himself, who has read the twenty-first century like a 'digital book', in order to recognise potential threats and dispose of them.

The choices of which world events and personalities to display onscreen as representative of HYDRA's malevolent intrusions into global affairs are revealing of the film's ideological perspectives and, on close inspection, it is a political worldview that is far from 'subversive' as it was described by Ryan Lambie and Darren Franich in the articles referred to at the beginning of this chapter. As much of the MCU has done, *The Winter Soldier* endorses the prevailing idea that American foreign policy and its reluctant involvements abroad during the twentieth century and into the twenty-first have been inherently beneficent and noble, an idea that to anyone with even a cursory awareness of the history of the post-World War II era is problematic to say the least and demonstrates a profound disconnection from the historical reality of American interventions into places like Iran (1953), Guatemala (1954), Cuba (1959), the Dominican Republic (1961), Vietnam (1965), Chile (1970), Grenada (1983), Bosnia (1992) and Iraq (1990 and 2003), to name but a few.[5] It is only through a highly subjective and ideologically motivated prism that one can still view the Cuban Missile Crisis as solely the result of perfidious Soviet belligerence instead of complicated Cold War brinksmanship caused just as much by aggressive American foreign policy as by Russian provocation. *The Winter Soldier* asks us to regard the Iranian Revolution (1979) as an unambiguously evil threat to global stability and freedom, instead of the result of, among other things, a century or more of imperialist interference by the US and the UK into the affairs of a sovereign country. The inclusion of Julian Assange, a complicated and richly contradictory figure who has been described as a 'martyr for free speech' (Frank La Rue qtd. in Hall 2010) by some and by others as the head of a 'foreign terrorist organisation' (Peter King qtd. in McCullagh 2010), as what we are asked to understand as an agent of HYDRA, responsible for fomenting dispute and crisis around the world is not suggestive of a film that is subversive, but rather a conservative treatise which regards all of those that might be considered 'America's ideological enemies' (Luttwak 1993: 45) in the real world as sponsored by a conflation of the descendants of the Nazis and the Soviet Union. While HYDRA is initially and frequently associated with the Nazis in World War II, as the MCU narrative has progressed it has grown to also encompass both Soviet-era (1922–91) and modern Russia, and the term 'hydra' itself was frequently connected to the Soviet Union, even after its dissolution, in descriptions of 'hydra-headed communism' (Buckley 2002: 233).[6] As further evidence of the convenient fluidity of these associations, in recent years Stan Lee defined HYDRA as being 'sort of like ISIS today. There are so many of them. And if you kill a few, it doesn't mean anything. There are more' (2016b: xv). The most interesting figure to be included in Zola's HYDRA sequence is perhaps the one least familiar to contemporary audiences, the Nicaraguan President Daniel Ortega (1985–90, 2007–). Through the 1980s Ortega, the head of the SNLF (Sandinista National Liberation Front), was vociferously demonised by the United States press and government, primarily due to his attempts to expel American interests, both political and economic, from his country. More than a decade later, in 1996, the International Court of Justice ruled that the US had repeatedly violated international law by supporting forces opposed to Ortega known as the Contras. A panel of ten out of thirteen judges from all over the globe concluded that 'by training, arming, equipping, financing and supplying the Contra forces or otherwise encouraging, supporting and aiding military and paramilitary activities in and against Nicaragua, has acted, against the Republic of Nicaragua, in breach of its obligation under customary international law not to intervene in the affairs of another State' (ICJ 1986). Yet it was a decision rejected by the United States government, and US Ambassador to the United Nation Jeanne Kirkpatrick called the International Court of Justice 'semi-legal, semi-juridical, semi-political body, which nations sometimes accept and sometimes don't' (qtd. in Scott 2012: 90).[7] This is not to say that those figures included in the HYDRA sequence in *The Winter Soldier* are not responsible for transgressions of international law themselves, which of course, in many cases, they most definitely are, but that what they all share, and one might surmise why they were chosen, is their challenge to an America-centric view of the world and this is why they are simplistically branded by the film as agents of chaos and destruction.[8]

It is revealed to be none other than Alexander Peirce who is the central architect of HYDRA's plan, the man who Fury observes, once refused a Nobel Peace Prize because 'peace was not an achievement ... but a *responsibility*'. Peirce is deliberately framed as a Bush era neo-conservative the likes of which regularly filled the screens of Hollywood films as antagonists in the first decades of the new millennium (see Ward Abbot, Noah Vosen and Alexander Conklin in the original Bourne trilogy [2002–7], Admiral Alexander Marcus in *Star Trek: Into Darkness* [2013] and Dreyfus in *Dawn of the Planet of the Apes* [2014] for prominent examples) and this is why many might have considered the film to be critical of contemporary American security policies.[9] Peirce is wholly convinced of the appropriateness of what he is doing and is prepared to sacrifice twenty million people to bring order to the lives of seven billion. He tells Fury: 'It's the next step, Nick. If you have the courage to take it.' Peirce uses an anecdote about his experiences in Bogota, Colombia, to justify his use of pre-emptive methodology, in which the ELN (National Liberation Army) rebels captured hostages at the US embassy, one of which was his daughter, and Nick Fury ignored his direct orders and saved the hostages with direct military action. Echoing the Bush Doctrine, Peirce suggests that sometimes rules must be broken in order to do what is right and reminds Fury that diplomacy is 'a holding action, a band aid' and that 'you didn't ask ... you just did what *needed* to be done'. The captivity narrative and the prospect of rescuing a young American woman in peril became one of the defining thematic motifs of post-9/11 American cinema in popular culture texts like *Taken* and *24*, and Peirce returns to the trope again in his bid to convince the WSC of the efficacy of HYDRA's plan (see also Faludi 2007). He asks Councilman Singh a question which evokes the Ticking Time Bomb scenarios popularised by Alan Dershowitz after 9/11; 'What if Pakistan marched into Mumbai tomorrow and you know they were going to drag *your daughter* into a soccer stadium for execution and you could just stop it with the flick of a switch?' (see Dershowitz 2008). This angle has proven a pervasive one for those articulating a belief in the efficacy of torture or enhanced interrogation, a process which has been largely discredited in serious scientific studies (see O'Mara 2015; Schiemann 2015). In the first week of his presidency, Donald Trump was prompted to return to this idea in an interview with claims I would suggest formed more by media depictions of torture than by analysis of this aforementioned research, with Sean Hannity on *Hannity* (26 January 2017). Hannity suggested, 'I would ask [American journalist] David Muir, if they kidnapped your kid and you have one of the kidnappers, what would you do to get the location of your child?' To which Trump responded, 'Or would you want him to talk in 48 hours from now by being nice to him, OK? ... And by that time, *it's too late*' (qtd. in Slattery 2017).

Peirce emerges as the architect of HYDRA's plan but it is the Winter Soldier, a shadowy assassin initially described as a 'ghost story', who has somehow carried out 'two dozen assassinations over fifty years' in service of HYDRA's goals, that is Captain America's central adversary. When they finally meet, after a running battle through the streets of Washington deliberately reminiscent of Michael Mann's *Heat* (1995), the film reveals that the Winter Soldier is in fact James 'Bucky' Barnes, Cap's best friend who he had thought long dead, but who had been captured by HYDRA in 1945 and brainwashed very much like Raymond Shaw in *The Manchurian Candidate* (book, 1959; film, 1962) a name Tony Stark will later refer to the character by in *Captain America: Civil War*.[10] *The Winter Soldier* had subtly reminded audiences of Bucky's importance to Steve Rogers without giving away his identity in the Smithsonian Institute and in a flash-back to the aftermath of Steve's mother's funeral during which Bucky told his friend 'I'm with you *til the end of the line...*'. In a franchise which has been often criticised for the shallowness of its villains, the emotional connection between Rogers and Barnes gives the film a tangible resonance and is perhaps the reason why it was returned to once again as one of the driving narrative mechanisms of *Captain America: Civil War*.

With the heroes and the audience now aware of the stakes involved, the film shifts from a conspiracy thriller into a mission film, with Captain America, Falcon, Black Widow, Maria Hill and a still-living Nick Fury (having revealed that he faked his death) tasked with preventing the three Project Insight helicarriers from killing millions across the globe and installing HYDRA in control of the world. It is then that Cap returns to the Smithsonian for a final time to retrieve his World War II-era uniform; a more obvious plea for a return to old-fashioned ideals in a film set in the tumultuous 'War on Terror' era would be hard to find. After infiltrating the Project Insight base, Cap gives a rousing speech to patriotism and freedom worded very similarly to the newsreel featured in *The First Avenger*:

If you launch those helicarriers today, HYDRA will be able to kill anyone that stands in their way ... unless we stop them. I know I'm asking a lot, but the price of freedom is high; it always has been. And it's a price I'm willing to pay. And if I'm the only one, then so be it. But I'm willing to bet I'm not.

Cap is fully prepared to sacrifice himself, as he did once before in *The First*

Avenger, and he asks others do to the same with an evocation of the Total War of World War II. Cap and his team manage to switch the pre-arranged helicarrier targets, so instead of shooting at innocents on the ground they fire at and destroy each other, in an ironic reversal of the asymmetrical power relationship of drone warfare which came to increasingly characterise military operations in the Obama era. In a rare occasion of a superhero refusing to fight at the climax of the film, which is almost always ended by a physical battle between the protagonist and antagonist, Cap drops his shield telling Bucky he will not continue, and that he is with him *'til the end of the line...'*. At first Bucky refuses to acknowledge his friend and continues to strike him repeatedly in one of the most brutal moments across the MCU films, but when Cap falls unconscious into the Potomac river, he saves his life before disappearing with the ruins of the Triskellion shown burning in the background. At the same time, Peirce is killed but not before Black Widow uploads all of HYDRA's *and* S.H.I.E.L.D.'s secrets onto the internet, an act which will leave her own carefully guarded past exposed for the whole world to see. It is important to note that the film shows that the only way to destroy HYDRA is not to physically defeat the organisation, but to make their secrets public, and this act with its connections to the likes of Manning, Snowden and Assange, is viewed as one of tremendous heroism within the film's narrative at a time when the country was divided about the actions of these real-world figures. In the aftermath, Black Widow is shown in front of a senate committee where she, and her fellow heroes are accused of 'laying waste' to the US intelligence network, but she is unrepentant and secure in her belief that she will not be imprisoned 'because you [the US government and the world] *need* us. Yes, the world is a vulnerable place and yes, we help make it that way, but we're also the ones best qualified to defend it...'.

IV.

Since the film frames itself as a conspiracy thriller and borrows so heavily from *Three Days of the Condor* it seems appropriate to compare the endings of the two. *The Winter Soldier* concludes with the successful dispatch of Peirce (shot in the heart rather than brought to trial), the destruction of the three Project Insight helicarriers (which are shown to cause no deaths of innocents onscreen), and the unqualified redemption of the film's eponymous hero. In *Three Days of the Condor*, for the CIA analyst on the run Joe Turner (Robert Redford), there is no such conclusive resolution. In constant danger, he passes on his story of a clandestine CIA plot to take over oilfields in the Middle East, to the press, but it is not clear whether they will publish it or not given the tremendous power of those it will implicate. The film's final shot is Turner as he walks away anxiously looking over his shoulder, with an uncertain freeze frame which Michael Ryan and Douglas Kellner describe in *Camera Politica: The Politics and Ideology of Contemporary American Film* as a 'note of ambiguity characteristic of the mid-seventies' (1990: 100).[11] Even though *The Winter Soldier* borrows from the conspiracy thriller cycle of the 1970s it is able to encompass little of its ideological challenges to the status quo and it, like the vast majority of the MCU, ends on a moment of triumphant violent redemption. As Martin Flanagan, Andrew Livingstone and Mike McKenny argue, these references to the 1970s conspiracy cycle are 'imported more as a calculated referential risk, addressing the hip consumption patterns of an audience able to recognize codes of post-Cold War films' (2016: 111), than a meaningful attempt to engage with the fears and anxieties of the time in which the film was made. *The Winter Soldier* is critical of the practices of HYDRA, which are little more than hyper-allegorised extensions of real-world new millennial debates, but its underlying message is a reification of American foundational mythic values represented by (and embodied within) Captain America, a character who has long been considered as expressing the 'divergence between American ideals and American practice' (Dittmer 2005: 642).

The film's critical thrust and Cap's primary role is to offer the idea that America is *more than* its institutions, and that it is its core *values* and *principles* which makes America great and distinguishes it from every other country. This type of criticism was described by Benton Bond as 'redemptive anti-Americanism' and he wrote: 'The message of redemptive anti-Americanism comes from a peculiar apex where the ideas of the most virulently anti-American voices are mixed with jingoistic and nationalistic pro-Americanism. Thus, a distinctive anti-American voice emerges: one that celebrates America in a fallen Captain and lashes out against the America that fell him' (2013: 77). So the film adopts a superficially critical patina at the same time as embracing a mythopoetic vision of what makes America unique, an idea itself steeped in mythology, embodying an illusion that there is a tangible great America to return to. This was undoubtedly part of Donald Trump's appeal in his successful 2016 Presidential election campaign, two years after *The Winter Soldier* was released, in which he criticised that which America had become, primarily under the presidency of Barack Obama, but promised to 'make America great again' by returning to these very same illusory core values and principles. Trump stated in his victory speech on 9 November 2016, 'Working together, we will begin the urgent task of rebuilding the nation and renewing the American dream'. Both Trump's campaign and *The Winter Soldier* articulate a concerted desire for a return to 'the good old days' (a line Sam Wilson actually uses in the film), yet they do not offer an answer as to where might one find these them outside of the cultural imaginary. Might they be located in the 1940s in which Captain America was first conceived? But this is certainly an era marked by profound social inequality, disenfranchisement and segregation, even though it is now remembered through the comforting lens of a nostalgic prism, a fact which was comprehensively challenged by Norman Finkelstein in *The Way Things Never Were: The Truth about the 'Good Old Days'*, a book which thoroughly undermines the reality behind the idea that the 1940s were 'a happy and carefree time for everyone in America' (1995: 1).

Despite his seeming rigidity Captain America has emerged as a surprisingly malleable figure, co-opted in the new millennium by those on both sides of the American political spectrum, as likely to be found appearing at Tea Party rallies across the country as at liberal events like Jon Stewart's 'Rally to Restore Sanity' in Washington DC on 30 October 2010. Bob Calhoun at *Salon* asked, 'Would he [Captain America] be a New Deal Democrat slinging his mighty shield for new public works programs or would he be rallying with the Tea Party to lower taxes on billionaires and gut Medicare? Whose Captain America is he anyway?' (2011) The Captain America of the MCU is similarly flexible and this was the reason why many were able to see their own political ideology reflected in *The Winter Soldier*. For those on the right side of the political spectrum the film criticises the intrusive policies of Big Government, standing up for those 'real Americans' who feel they have been forgotten and let down by the Obama administration. This is why prominent Republican commentator Glenn Beck was able to suggest:

> This should teach Hollywood… Here's a movie that not only is good but tells a pro-American story. This one even has a political point to it. Even the director is coming out and saying, 'Yeah, I'm trying to make a point here that killing people with drones, with some committee or the president saying yeah, we can just kill those people because they're a problem, spying on them, collecting their data is wrong.' That's what Captain America is about. (2014)

At the same time, those on the left side of the political spectrum can just as easily read the film as being about the excesses of the Bush administration in the aftermath of 9/11 and Captain America as standing up for what *their* vision of America should be (see Franich 2014; Lambie 2014). *Captain America: The Winter Soldier* is justifiably one of the most well regarded films in the MCU and even, alongside Christopher Nolan's Dark Knight trilogy, in the genre as a whole, but claims, like those of Darren Franich at *Entertainment Weekly* and Ryan Lambie of its supposedly 'subversive' nature are an indication of the seeming inability of genre to offer narratives that are able to challenge the times in which they are made in anything more than superficial ways.

Notes

1   In the week after the release of *The Winter Soldier*, the *Guardian* and the *Washington Post* were awarded the Pulitzer Prize for public service for their coverage of the Snowden leaks.

2   Ignacio Andrés Amarillo reviewing the film for the Argentinian newspaper *El Litoral* wrote that, 'For many South Americans, Captain America is a symbol of imperialism' and that the film was immersed in the 'post-Bush and post-Snowden era' (2014).

3   In one of the richly textured moments which indicates the care and attention to detail often employed in the MCU films, a brief shot of Cap's bookcase reveals what Cap has been reading since his return: including *All The President's Men* (1974) by Carl Bernstein and Bob Woodward, the Vietnam War memoir *Dispatches* (1977) by Michael Herr, *Never Surrender: A Soldier's Journey to the Crossroads of Faith and Freedom* (2008) by Lieutenant General William G. Boykin and *Barack Obama: The Making of the Man* (2012) by David Maraniss.

4   The alternate storyboard design for this by Philip Keller and James Rothwell also includes President Kennedy, what appears to be the 'hanging chad' controversy from the 2000 presidential election, and footage of the Howard Hughes senate hearings in 1947.

5   As Noam Chomsky reminds us, 'The US is the only country that was condemned for international terrorism by the World Court and that rejected a Security Council resolution calling on states to observe international law' (2001: 44).

6   For its release in Russia the film was titled Первый мститель: Другая война, which translates into English as *The First Avenger: The Other War*.

7   The United States is certainly not alone in refusing to accept the ICJ rulings: a small selection of examples are rejections due to nuclear testing (France, 1974), fishing rights (Iceland, 1974; Japan, 2014), and territorial possession (Argentina, 1977; South Africa, 1990; Israel, 2004).

8   Each of those chosen to be agents of HYDRA can be explored in a similar way and should be done so in more space than we have here. Gaddaffi was called the 'mad dog of the Middle East' by Ronald Reagan (qtd. in Bearman 1986: xvi), but he too is a complicated figure. Undoubtedly his cruel dictatorship led to terrible human rights abuses and deaths, but he is acknowledged as overseeing the transformation of Libya from one of Africa's poorest nations into one of its very richest and he was lauded by both the Soviet Union (who awarded him the Order of Lenin in 1971) and Nelson Mandela, who called him 'my brother' (qtd. in Gwaambuka 2016), primarily for his anti-imperialist stance which saw him emerge as a figurehead against American intervention on the African continent. For many Americans Hugo Chavez was a 'tyrant who forced the people of Venezuela to live in fear' (Ed Royce qtd. in Watkins 2013), but he also played a central role in promoting Venezualan independence and

nationalised industries in the face of severe opposition and pressure from the United States.

9   The casting of Robert Redford as Peirce, given his off-screen persona as a supporter of liberal concerns and his status as an all-American symbol in his own right, resonates. The decision to cast him was influenced by his role as Joe Turner in Sydney Pollack's *Three Days of the Condor*, a film from which *The Winter Soldier* draws heavily for inspiration. It also should not be forgotten that Redford was once in contention for the role of Superman in Richard Donner's original *Superman* (1978) (see Rossen 2008: 78).

10 Most American presidents since the publication of Richard Condon's novel in 1959 have been described by their political opponents as a 'Manchurian Candidate' for one reason or another. These assertions gained significant traction in 2017 in the light of accusations of links between the Trump administration and Russia (see Boot 2017).

11 See also the psychological breakdown of Jack Terry (John Travolta) at the end of *Blow Out* (1981) or the murder of the protagonist Joseph Frady (Warren Beatty) in *The Parallax View* (1974).

CHAPTER SEVEN

Blurring the Boundaries of Genre and Gender in *Guardians of the Galaxy* and *Ant-Man*

Genre criticism takes for granted that most works fall within one and only one genre with genre mixing the exception rather than the norm... The superhero genre seems capable of absorbing and reworking all other genres.

– Henry Jenkins (2009: 17)

What has changed is not male power as such, but its form, its presentation, its packaging. In other words, while it is apparent that styles of masculinity may alter in very short time spans, the substance of male power does not.

– Arthur Brittan (1989: 2)

Guardians of the Galaxy and *Ant-Man* are the tenth and twelfth instalments of the Marvel Cinematic Universe, with *Ant-Man* being the concluding film of Phase Two coming after *Avengers: Age of Ultron* (discussed in chapter eight). Both are arguably important and transitional films for the franchise as they introduce wholly new characters and offer deviations from what many had come to expect from the genre. By 2014 criticisms of the sheer number of superhero films being released were increasing, as were speculations as to how long the genre might be able to sustain such levels of popularity with audiences. Steven Spielberg, one of the central architects of blockbuster cinema in the four decades since the release of *Jaws* in 1975 commented that, like the western before it, the superhero film could not go on indefinitely:

> We were around when the western died and there will be a time when the super-hero movie goes the way of the western. It doesn't mean there won't be another occasion where the western comes back and the superhero movie someday re-turns. Of course, right now the superhero movie is alive and thriving... There will come a day when the mythological stories are supplanted by some other genre that possibly some young filmmaker is just thinking about discovering for all of us. (Qtd. in McMillan 2015)

Spielberg is, of course, correct in his assertion that genres fall in and out of fa-vour with audiences and there is no reason to assume that the superhero film will be any different. One of the keys to its continued success has been its ability to diversify and encompass other genres while remaining recognisably within the parameters of its own, whether, as we have already seen, this might be *The Avengers* embodying the traits of a war film, the tropes of the fantasy film which are a key part of *Thor*, or the conspiracy thriller elements which go a long way towards defining *Captain America: The Winter Soldier*. The two films featured in this chapter are similar attempts to expand and diversify the superhero film while remaining a recognisable part of the Marvel brand: *Guardians of the Galaxy* is clearly influenced by the rich history of the space opera and *Ant-Man* is a heist film which happens to feature a superhero. Both draw on these respective genres in ways which enable their own narratives to seem vibrant and engaging at a time when concerns were being raised about the superhero film's reversion to formula. They are also the two most explicitly comedic films in the MCU in Phases One and Two *and* the most self-consciously postmodern: both filled with witty pop culture allusions and playfully intertextual narrative devices that were largely absent from the Phase One films. *Ant-Man* references films like *Titanic*, TV shows like *Thomas The Tank Engine* (1984–) and includes sounds from the AT-AT Walker in *The Empire Strikes Back* (1980) in its audio mix, and *Guardians of the Galaxy* mentions a diverse range of texts from the 1980s: films like *Footloose* (1984) and *Raiders of the Lost Ark* (1981), and television shows like *Full House* (ABC, 1987–95) and *Teenage Mutant Ninja Turtles* (1987–94) in a nostalgic film which views an intergalactic space adventure through the prism of its protago-nist's memories of his childhood on Earth.

They are also the two films that were regarded as the riskiest propositions for the MCU in Phase Two given the relative obscurity of their central charac-ters, which led many to speculate they would both struggle to find an audience (see McMillan 2014). The director of *Man of Steel, Batman v Superman: Dawn of*

Justice and *Justice League* (2017), Zack Snyder, was dismissive of *Ant-Man* and, reacting directly to Steven Spielberg's comments quoted above stated: 'I feel like he's right. But I feel like Batman and Superman are transcendent of superhero movies in a way because they're Batman and Superman. They are not just, like, the flavour of the week *Ant-Man*, not to be mean, but whatever it is. What is the next, Blank-Man?' (qtd. in Khatchatourian 2015). However, both *Guardians of the Galaxy* and *Ant-Man* exceeded expectations at the box office, the former ending up being one of the biggest box office successes of the year, earning \$773 million world-wide, and both were positively reviewed (considerably more so than Snyder's *Man of Steel* and *Batman v Superman: Dawn of Justice*).

This chapter will be an exploration of how far these two films offer deviations from the superhero genre, but at the same time interrogate their depictions of masculinity as they both provide two excellent examples of the diversity of models of the representation of men offered by contemporary American film. The superhero film, as Suzanne Kord and Elizabeth Krimmer have suggested, is 'centrally concerned with concepts of masculinity' (2011: 109) and we have considered what might be described as these more malleable dimensions of what it means to be a 'real man' in the MCU on occasion throughout this volume: in how Captain America's more traditional brand of masculinity is updated to encompass, at the same time, variations of the modern, more sensitive new man archetype; or how Thor has been shown to both embody aspects of what Susan Jeffords (1994) called the hard-bodied hero, but also present a vulnerability and empathy not connected with this more traditional model. Debates concerning the evolution of masculinity in the 1990s and into the 2000s were frequently concerned with how far the dominant hegemonical masculine modes were in a state of crisis (see Brittan 1989; Easthope 1992; Segal 2001; Peberdy 2011) and some of the most interesting films of the era like *Fight Club, Falling Down* (1993) and *American Beauty* (1999) are able to portray the perceptions of these shifting coordinates onscreen. This book asserts that much of the discourse surrounding this crisis was itself largely ideologically motivated and, somewhat paradoxically, resulted not in the limitation of the spectrum of masculinities offered to men, but, in actual fact, a broadening of them in the way that it offered a freedom from some of the constraints imposed on what Western culture had hitherto defined as what constitutes a 'real man'. So, while Anthony Easthope might be correct to argue that, 'men live in the dominant version of masculinity ... they themselves are trapped in structures that fix and limit masculine identity. They do what they *have* to do' (1992: 7; italics in original), the characterisations of many of the heroes in the MCU are demonstrative of trends in contemporary American film that offer men a much wider range of complexities than were ever offered before, or have ever been offered to women. As Lynne Segal has argued, masculinity is *'always* in crisis' (2001: 239; emphasis added) and this crisis, which Peter Quill and Scott Lang, the white heterosexual males at the centre of the two films explored in this chapter, certainly undergo variations of, becomes part of the formative constituents of what defined masculinity in the first decades of the new millennium on the cinema screen and in Western culture at large.

'There's one other name you may know me by...': Negotiating Peter Quill's Identity and Masculinity in *Guardians of the Galaxy*

> The heroes of myth embody something like the full range of ideological contra-
> dictions around which the life of culture revolves, and their adventures suggest
> the range of possible resolutions that the culture's lore provides.
>
> – Richard Slotkin (1992: 14)

Earth 1988. A young boy, Peter Quill, sits in a hospital, waiting to see his termi-nally ill mother, Meredith, perhaps for the last time. Sitting quietly, he listens to a mix-tape given to him by her on his 1979 Sony TPS-L2 Walkman cassette player, blocking out the world around him with *her* music. The songs contained within it will not only become a key part of the film's diegetic and non-diegetic soundtrack, but also a significant thematic element in its narrative, much more so than in any superhero film before or since, with the exception of the film's sequel *Guardians of the Galaxy: Vol. 2*. Ushered to his mother for a final audience, he is presented with the gift of a second mix-tape with her plea to 'open it up when I am gone'. She tells him how much he looks like his father who was 'an angel ... composed out of pure light', comments which at the time seem nonsensical, but are later revealed in the sequel to be very close to the truth. In her last moments, she holds out her hand to Peter, but the young boy is overcome with grief and refuses, in-stead he flees out of the hospital into the darkness of the night. Out of nowhere a beam of light and a space ship emerges from the sky, as if from a Steven Spielberg film like *Close Encounters of the Third Kind* (1977) and *E.T. The Extra-Terrestrial* (1982), the likes of which Peter may well have watched a few years before with his mother and the atmosphere of which James Gunn strives to emulate throughout *Guardians of the Galaxy*. The ship sucks up the now orphaned Peter inside it and the last sound we hear are his cries for his mother.

Twenty-six years later and thus in the diegetic year of 2014, the year of the film's release, we meet the man Peter has become, a selfish yet good-natured mercenary who prefers to be referred to as the 'legendary outlaw' Star-Lord, but is often disappointed when people refuse to recognise him or call him by that name. In an introduction deliberately reminiscent of the opening scenes of another Spielberg film, *Raiders of the Lost Ark*, Quill looks for a mysterious object on a long-abandoned planet called Morag, whose oceans only briefly recede every three years to reveal hidden areas of land. Peter still listens to his mother's first mix-tape, but has been unable to bring himself to open the second. It remains unspoken, but his devotion to it is a way of retaining a connection to his mother and his childhood on Earth. James Gunn has remarked: 'The tape is really the character of Quill's mother... The Walkman and the compilation tape inside of it is the heart of the film' (qtd. in Grow 2014).[1] Later, when a blue-skinned alien prison guard takes the Walkman from him and listens to 'Hooked on a Feeling' (1968) by Blue Swede, Peter yells at him not just that the Walkman is *his*, but 'That song belongs to *me!*' and risks his life to get it back. On Morag he is searching for a mysterious artefact, as Indiana Jones once looked for the fertility idol among the Hovitos in Peru, but the tone of *Guardians of the Galaxy* abruptly shifts just six minutes into the film when Peter places the Walkman on his head and the 1974 song 'Come and Get Your Love' by Redbone fills the soundtrack. The hitherto dark and gloomy Morag is now enlivened by the incongruity of the 1970s rock song appearing in a film which identifies itself so readily as a space opera as well as a superhero film, as it is by Peter's exuberantly unselfconscious dancing, his use of an unwilling rat-like creature (an Orloni) as an impromptu microphone and even a smoothly orchestrated horizontal slide almost exactly the same as Tom Cruise's from *Risky Business* (1984), released four years before his abduction. It is these unlikely juxtapositions, the adroitly balanced tonal shifts and the film's irreverent postmodernism which emerge as the defining aspects of *Guardians of the Galaxy* and serve to distinguish it from much of the MCU and other films of the superhero genre.[2]

The early scenes of James Gunn's film show Peter to be a somewhat vain and rather egocentric protagonist, offering parallels to the pre-epiphanic states of the narcissistic Tony Stark, Stephen Strange and the arrogant Thor. Peter is shown to have had sexual relations with Bereet the red-skinned Krylorian, but forgets both her name and that she is even in his ship, and later boasts of his conquests of several aliens: a 'smoking-hot Rajak girl', a Kree girl, and an A'askavarian, even though they have 'tentacles, and needles for teeth', and he seems to initially only care about the money he will make from the sale of the Orb he finds on Morag (which he has 'stolen' from his mentor Yondu [Michael Rooker]), even when he learns of its tremendous destructive power. However, whether the film endorses Peter's behaviour or criticises it, as Gamora does calling out his 'pelvic sorcery', is up to audiences to decide. Peter is muscular and handsome, but Chris Pratt introduces an element of vulnerability and an Everyman quality to the character through his sense of humour, clumsiness and the ineptness of his braggadocio even in these early stages which mark him as quite distinct from what we have characterised as the hypermasculine model often found in the genre.

It is when Peter finds himself embroiled in an intergalactic conflict between two alien species, the Kree and the Xandarians, who have been at war for millennia, that he is forced to reconsider his attitude. While the war was finally brought to an end by a fragile peace treaty, one fanatical Kree, the antagonist of the film, Ronan the Accuser (Lee Pace), refuses to accept that it is over and embarks on a genocidal spree to eradicate the Xandarians from the galaxy, referring to them and their culture as a 'disease'. The Kree are a harsh and unforgiving people and Ronan is an overtly masculine figure who sees weakness as a sin, sharply contrasted to that of the progressive Xandarians who are shown to be a caring, multicultural and liberal culture, home to twelve billion people, self-consciously portrayed as a utopia that Earth should aspire to become in the future. The Xandarians are led by their female Nova Prime, Irani Rael (Glenn Close), who demands that the Kree condemn Ronan's actions, but they refuse. Ronan says: 'They call me terrorist, radical, zealot because I obey the ancient laws of my people the Kree and punish those who do not!' While Jeffrey Brown's suggestion that 'for all of its light-hearted comedy and escapist space adventure, *Guardians of the Galaxy* also revisions 9/11 with a rag-tag team of heroic victims, led by a white American male, saving an alien planet from a fanatical terrorist. The film's central bad guy, Ronan the Accuser, is a thinly veiled symbol of the all-encompassing Middle-Eastern Other that stands as a constant threat to the West' (2016: 76) is not entirely convincing, Ronan's characterisation provides the distant intergalactic conflict, a familiar element of the space opera, with a new millennial clash of civilisations resonance.

It is these deviations from the formula of the superhero film and its densely-layered world which separates *Guardians of the Galaxy* from many films of the genre, with almost every frame full of detail to the extent that audiences still continued to find elements within it for years after its release (see Peters 2016). Its environment is futuristic, but it has a palpable lived-in quality reminiscent of the early films in the *Star Wars* franchise. This emphatic embrace of retro-pop space culture offers audiences not the nostalgia for the 1930s or 1950s of George Lucas's original trilogy of films (1977–83), but the 1970s which marked both Peter and director James Gunn's (b. 1970) youth. Gunn manages to effectively balance this earthiness with the more dynamic and vibrant colourful palette of pulp science fiction. He commented:

> I like keeping the grittiness of it but I wanted to bring back some of the color of the 1950s and '60s. You know, pulp science fiction movies and inject a little bit more of that pulp feel into things. So, that's where I think that comes from. There's the pulp mixed with the grittiness and that's been throughout the whole movie – the beauty mixed with the ugliness. (Qtd. in Sciretta 2014b)

Indeed, Gunn's *bricolage* of influences is decidedly postmodern in design both visually and narratively: drawing from such disparate sources as the already-mentioned *Raiders of the Lost Ark* and *Close Encounters of the Third Kind*, but also *Fantastic Voyage* (1966), *The Dirty Dozen* (1967), *Barbarella* (1968), *The Right Stuff* (1983) and *Black Hawk Down*, all of which Gunn returned to in interviews (see Faraci 2014; Hunt 2014; Sciretta 2014b). Like *Star Wars*, a film from which it draws so much inspiration, it is a space opera; in fact, it is, according to Gunn, 'one thousand percent space opera' (qtd. in Faraci 2014), who also said:

> This was intentionally my version of *Star Wars*. When I was first considering doing the movie, the chance to make something like that was one of the things that get me on board. Not just *Star Wars*, but *Raiders of The Lost Ark*, and other movies like that. The stuff I loved as a kid. I wanted to make a movie that made people feel *the way they made me feel*. (Qtd. in Hunt 2014; emphasis added)

Gunn's remarks articulate his desire that *Guardians of the Galaxy* function as more than just a homage to the formative films of his youth, but an attempt to recreate the feelings which they inspired in him for a new generation of audiences.[3] Its chief points of nostalgia begin with Peter Quill's Walkman and the film's period soundtrack, but they are primarily located in the prism of his childhood on Earth which permeates Peter's intergalactic experience, as, like Captain America, he is also a man 'out of time'. There is a distinct sense that he is living out his childhood fantasies *in reality* within the diegetic frames of the film, even in his desire to be referred to as Star-Lord, rather than Peter, the true meaning of which is not revealed until the film's final moments. The fact that these pop culture references are largely meaningless to those around him, but very familiar to audiences, makes up a large portion of the film's humour: whether it might be naming his space ship, the Milano, after the actress he had a crush on from *Who's The Boss* (ABC, 1984–92), referring to an 'outlaw' by the name of John Stamos, an actor in the family comedy *Full House*, calling a Sakaarian guard a 'Mutant Ninja Turtle', or shots of his personal quarters on the ship which reveal he has decorated it with Garbage Pail Kids and Scratch N'Sniff stickers, trading cards from the TV show *Alf* (NBC 1986–90), and even a Troll doll.[4] This almost dizzying range of postmodern references might be regarded as part of the malaise of modern culture that some have seen as suggestive of a lack of originality and creativity, but others have argued that they are 'aesthetic symptoms of far more profound developments in postmodern society as a whole' (Booker 2007: xviii). So while the nostalgia of Lucas's *Star Wars: A New Hope* and *American Graffiti* (1973) have been understood by many as an attempt to realise and recreate the 1950s which remains for many Americans 'the privileged lost object of desire' (Jameson 1984: 67), 1980s-influenced films like Gunn's *Guardians of the Galaxy*, *Super 8* (2011) and *It* (2017), and television shows like *Stranger Things* (Netflix, 2016–) and *The Goldbergs* (ABC, 2013–) attempt to recapture a sense of innocence around the childhood experiences of their creators and large sections of their intended audiences, which extend far beyond the teen audiences often associated with the genre.

When Peter is arrested and sent to an intergalactic prison known as the Kyln, it is there he gets to know the four other characters who will later be referred to as the 'guardians of the galaxy': a talking raccoon-like mammal by the name of Rocket, a giant tree-beast called Groot, a green-skinned female assassin called Gamora, and the muscular and taciturn Drax, whose family had been murdered by Ronan. Like Drax, each of them are marked by the trauma of their past (except Groot whose background remains unrevealed): Gamora's entire race, the Zehoberi people, were killed by Thanos in front of her when she was a child, who then adopted her, raising to be one of the most feared killers in the galaxy. Rocket, whose real name is 89P13, was tortured and genetically altered, and he is not the last of his people, but the *only* one of his kind, eloquently describing his predicament with the line, 'Ain't no thing like me 'cept me'. They are all examples of what Francis Pheasant-Kelly described as the 'wounded hero', the likes of which became so prominent in post-9/11 American film and they join the ranks of Tony Stark, Bruce Banner and even, to a lesser extent, Steve Rogers (2013: 144). The group are initially only sarcastically referred to as the 'guardians of the galaxy' by Ronan, but later come to earn the evocative sobriquet and, to their own surprise, find a sense of purpose and belonging among each other that each had thought lost.

Much of the film's comedic elements derive from its expressive linguistic wordplay: from Peter's surprisingly risqué joke about what a blacklight might reveal if used in his spaceship ('like a Jackson Pollack painting'), to his final 'trolling' of Yondu at the end of the film with the very personal gift of an *actual* Troll doll, both as a joke, a gift and an apology for lying to the man he says was 'the closest thing I had to a family'.[5] Groot's extremely limited vocabulary – only the words 'I am Groot' – has a variety of meanings extrapolated from it throughout the course of the film, including 'We need to save them', 'they are the only friends we have', 'they are ungrateful' and 'it's better than eleven percent' among others.[6] One places the pronoun 'his' in inverted commas because of Rocket's throwaway line instructing Groot to 'Learn genders, man!' when he tells the endearing tree-like character to place a bag over 'his' (Peter's) head which Groot does not seem to understand, implying that his species have no gender (although the character is referred to as 'he' throughout the film). This wordplay continues with the characterisation of Drax who comes from a planet with no understanding of simile

Fig. 20: The eponymous heroes of *Guardians of the Galaxy* (2014): "a thief, two thugs, an assassin and a maniac"

and metaphor, so when Peter puts a finger to his throat indicating that he will be able to finally get his revenge and kill Ronan, he too is unable to understand what it means. When Rocket explains, 'His people are completely literal, metaphors are going to go over his head', even this is misconstrued and Drax responds with, '*Nothing* goes over my head, my reflexes are too fast. I would catch it.' The whole team struggles with Peter's references to 1970s and 1980s American culture, the most memorable of which, and the one that inspired a legion of memes, is when Peter relates to Gamora a 'legend' from his planet about the inspirational value of dance. When he tells her 'It's called *Footloose* and in it a great hero named Kevin Bacon teaches an entire city with sticks up their buts that dancing, well, is the greatest thing there is', her first question is 'Who put the sticks up their butt?' but later as they go into the film's final battle Gamora proudly tells Peter, 'We are just like Kevin Bacon!' One might speculate that one of the reasons *Guardians of the Galaxy* was able to engage with a broad variety of audiences are these witty metatextual references which are very different to the majority of those found in contemporary American films, which most often refer to what are, at the time, current pop culture events and have the tendency to date quickly. Those contained in James Gunn's film do not date in such a way, because they *already are* dated and mine a general fascination for all things connected to 1970s and 1980s culture.

When Ronan takes possession of the Orb and attempts to use it in his genocidal war against the Xandarians, only needing to touch the surface of the Xandar with it to see the whole planet destroyed, Peter's first instinct is to flee, but he changes his mind and gives a speech about them being 'losers' heavily reminiscent of *The Goonies* (1985) 'our time' speech: 'I look around at us. You know what I see? *Losers*. I mean like folks who have lost stuff. And we have, man we have. All of us. Our homes, our families, normal lives.' Rocket asks him, 'What are you, some saint all of a sudden?' echoing the comments made by Rhodes to Stark in *Iron Man* and Loki to Thor at the climax of *Thor*. Peter's emotional growth had started earlier in the film with his decision to risk his life to save Gamora in space, but it is this moment where he decides to put aside his selfishness and take a stand for something, a decision he boils down to as 'the choice between giving a shit and not giving a shit'. It is fitting that it is from then on people finally recognise him as Star-Lord, first Ronan's henchman Korath, but also the Xandarian Rhomann Dey (John C. Reilly) and Gamora, each of whom had previously refused to re- fer to him by that name. Peter's brand of masculinity offers just as much of a paradox as we have seen with many of the superheroes in the MCU: he is a white heterosexual male the likes of which have filled American screens as the apex of popular culture for a century, but on the other hand, his is a multi-dimensional one which involves the acceptance of, on the surface at least, vulnerability, empa- thy and humility. Peter is quite removed from the hard-bodied males to be found in American movies of the 1980s when he was abducted in the penultimate year of Reagan's presidency, but the film shows that even in space the responsibility for saving the galaxy still falls to a white heterosexual American man. The film is a vigorously nostalgic text on a variety of levels, but it is not nostalgic for the hy- permasculinity of performers like Stallone and Schwarzeneggar whom Jeffords suggested stood for 'not only for a type of national character – heroic, aggressive, and determined – but for the nation itself' (1994: 2) and who also returned to the screens in the decade after 9/11, often together, in films like *The Expendables* (2010), *The Expendables 2* (2012) and *Escape Plan* (2013). However, at the same time it is a film which, as much of popular cinema does, pushes the experiences of women to 'the margins' (King 2000: 108) and tells a story about *men*. As men- tioned in the previous chapter, *Guardians of the Galaxy* has the lowest percentage of female-speaking characters across Phases One and Two of the MCU, with only six women who utter a line of dialogue in the entire film: Meredith Quill, Bereet, Nebula, Gamora, Nova Prime and Corrina. The other women which populate its narrative, none of whom have a speaking role, are referred to in the credits as things like Pretty Xandarian, Sad Woman with Horns, Sad Krylorian Girl, Corpsman Dey's Wife, Crying Xandarian Citizen or Tortured Pink Girl. This seems to cast doubt on the sincerity of director James Gunn's 2016 comments that, 'I am sick of stories where there are a bunch of fully realized male characters and one female character, whose primary characteristic is simply being "the girl" or the personality-less object of some man's affections' in a different light (qtd. in Baker-Whitelaw 2016). While it is true that these men (including Rocket) demonstrate that the hypermasculine model is now regarded as inadequate in a variety of ways and the film offers in its place a more flexible mode of masculinity, its representation of women is decidedly problematic.[7]

The eponymous characters of *Guardians of the Galaxy* never refer to each other explicitly as a family until the film's sequel (although Gamora alludes to it once), but one might argue that it earns the use of the term due to the strength of their bond and the richness (for the genre) of their characterisations, especially if contrasted to the egregious scene in *Suicide Squad* where Diablo (Jay Hernandez) is seen to shout to his fellow anti-heroes, 'I lost one family. I can't lose another!' in a film that does not warrant the use of the term in any shape or form. This bond is articulated in what might be the film's most moving moment, as Groot elects to give his life to save his new family and in the only time in the film he says something other than 'I am Groot' he tells them all, '*We* are Groot'. Groot's 'death' is followed by an audacious callback to *Footlose*, as Peter distracts Ronan with, of all things, a demand for a dance off, one of several moments given to Quill that it seems hard to imagine any other superhero in the MCU doing, the other most notable perhaps being his remark, 'There's a little bit of pee coming out of me right now'. He grabs the Orb knowing that it will probably kill him, but hoping it will at least save the entire planet.[8] In the film's final gesture of togetherness, the guardians of the galaxy earn their name and refuse to let Peter face his ordeal alone, by linking hands, and somehow find themselves able to contain the Orb's power. In doing so Ronan is defeated by the very qualities of cooperation, community and emotion that he regards as weakness, and so far beneath him. During the sequence, Peter sees a vision of his mother on her deathbed, but this time agrees to her original plea to 'take my hand' and in doing so he is able to acknowledge her death and her loss, and come to terms with his past and his place in the world. In the aftermath of the battle, he finally opens the letter she had written to him twenty-six years before which poignantly reveals, in another of example of the film's wordplay, that the name she called him as a child was 'my little Star-Lord'.

About the space opera Gary Westfahl has written: 'To remain at the forefront of science fiction, which esteems freshness and originality, space opera must continuously reinvent itself' (2003: 198), an assertion that could be just as readily applied to the superhero film. What James Gunn achieves with *Guardians of the Galaxy* is a dynamic reinvigoration of the genre by fusing it with the space opera and embracing the iconic films of his youth in ways beyond merely paying homage to them. It is able to transcend many of the parameters of the the super-hero film and in some ways more traditional understandings of what constitutes hegemonic masculinity, but it still remains entrenched in the dominant ideology of the culture in which it is made.

'It's not about saving our world, it's about saving theirs': The Redemption of the Father in *Ant-Man*

> These films depend upon similarly contrived scenarios that recuperate failing fatherhood through enactment of paternal protectiveness in extreme circum-stances, whereupon the reconstitution of a normative familial unit is not the point of the protagonists' narrative journey, so much as the revalidation of his initially derogated fatherhood. These extreme scenarios depict the redemption of inadequate fathers, deflecting feminist critiques of masculinity, by positing the male's fulfilment of the role of father-protector as compensating for domestic and personal failings...
>
> – Hannah Hamad (2013: 250)

As we have seen on numerous occasions throughout this volume so far the MCU and the superhero genre as a whole has displayed a questionable tendency to prioritise the experiences of men in their narratives and in the process largely erase the experiences of women, sometimes figuratively, but often quite literally. This can be seen in the MCU as early as *Iron Man* and *Iron Man 2*, where Howard Stark plays an integral part in Tony Stark's life, but his mother, Maria, barely merits a mention; in *The Incredible Hulk*, Betty's father, General Ross, is a central character, but her mother is entirely absent; in both *Thor* and *Thor: The Dark World* it is Odin who plays a prominent role, while Frigga is killed off in scenes which are designed to do little more than provide a motivation for Thor's future actions. Even in *Guardians of the Galaxy*, while Peter Quill's mother appears in the opening scene and remains a lingering presence, the film is much more about fathers and father figures: bad ones (like Thanos and Ronan), traumatised ones (like Drax), ambiguous ones (like Yondu) and absent ones like Peter's, who was revealed to be the Celestial Ego (Kurt Russell) and given a central role in *Guardians of the Galaxy: Vol. 2*.[9] It is clear to see that these are not isolated ex-amples, but rather foundational tenets on which the MCU and the superhero genre is based. *Ant-Man* emerges as one of the most vibrant of the Phase Two films, but it is also one of the most egregious examples of what Robert Walser has termed, 'exscription'; that is, the exclusion of females from popular narratives, or the 'total denial of anxieties through the articulation of fantastic worlds without women' (2014: 110).

Ant-Man was actually one of the original films to be discussed at the first Marvel Studios panel back in 2006, even prior to the release of *Iron Man*, which featured Kevin Feige, Jon Favreau and the film's then director, Edgar Wright, who had been connected to the property since as early as 2003. Wright stayed with *Ant-Man* for more than a decade, but on 23 May 2014 Marvel Studios announced that he was no longer contributing to the project, citing 'differences in their vision of the film' (qtd. in Sims 2014) as the reason for his departure. Evangeline Lilly, who played Hope van Dyne in the film, suggested in interviews that Wright's vision had deviated too far from the thematically and aesthetically consistent world Marvel had endeavoured for so long to create and it was this which led to him leaving the film:

> I saw with my own eyes that [after Wright left] Marvel had just pulled the script into their world. I mean, they've established a universe, and everyone has come to expect a certain aesthetic [and] a certain feel for Marvel films… It just would have taken you away from this cohesive universe they're trying to create. And therefore it ruins the suspended disbelief that they've built. (Qtd. in Vary 2014)

Like *Guardians of the Galaxy, Ant-Man* also begins with a 1980s-set prologue and as with Gunn's space opera, the scene goes a long way towards establishing many of the film's recurring thematic motifs. In Washington DC in 1989, inside the still-being-built S.H.I.E.L.D. headquarters known as the Triskelion (which audiences had only recently seen destroyed in *The Winter Soldier*), genius inventor Hank Pym (Michael Douglas) storms through the building and the first words of the film are his: 'Stark!' Standing in front of a panel comprised of Mitchell Carson (S.H.I.E.L.D. Head of Defense), Peggy Carter (still played by Hayley Atwell) and Howard Stark, he demands to know why S.H.I.E.L.D. have gone behind his back and tried to replicate his invention, the Pym Particle. Stark informs the audience that the Pym Particle is a 'miracle' and 'the most revolutionary science ever developed', but it is something Pym is unwilling to share as he knows how powerful it is and does not trust S.H.I.E.L.D. to utilise it as ethically as it would be used in his hands. Carson insists that Pym consider the bigger picture, as the Cold War and the United States needs 'a soldier' like him, but Pym refuses, preferring to define himself as 'a scientist'. Stark then tells him to 'act like one!' as for Howard Stark (and later his son), scientists invent technology and do not necessarily ruminate on the consequences of how it might be used. The prologue ends with Pym's promise that, 'As long as I am alive nobody will ever get that formula' and the film which follows will portray the challenge he faces keeping his word and the threat to the world if he does not.

Hank Pym is one of the film's central characters and the original Ant-Man, but he is not its protagonist, as the narrative moves briskly from 1989 to the present day and Pym is shown to be looking for a younger man to carry on the Ant-Man mantle. He believes he may have found him in Scott Lang (Paul Rudd) even though Lang was sentenced to five years in San Quentin Penitentiary for breaking and entering, grand larceny and stealing approximately $4 million from the international cyber security and data storage conglomerate, Vista Corp. Despite his prison sentence, Lang's motives are shown to be altruistic as he only committed the crime after learning that the company was taking millions of dollars from its customers, so he broke in and transferred all the money back to the victims. The casting of Rudd, an actor with a primarily comedic background, like Chris Pratt who played Peter Quill in *Guardians of the Galaxy* (they even starred together in *Parks and Recreation* [NBC, 2009–15]), brings an improvisatory tone to the series largely absent since *Iron Man 2*. Lang finds life after prison difficult, as even though he has a Master's Degree in electrical engineering, as a former convict the only work he can secure is as a teller at Baskin and Robbins, but even they fire him when they learn about his criminal past.

Pym sees something of his own situation reflected in Lang's predicament. Just as Pym became estranged from his daughter Hope after the death of her mother, Lang struggles to reconnect with his infant daughter, Cassie. When they finally meet, Pym tells Lang, 'Before Hope lost her mother [Janet Pym] she used to look at me like I was the greatest man in the world. Now she looks at me and there's just disappointment. It's too late for me, *but not for you.*' Hope refuses to call Hank 'dad' and she even led the board of his own company against him, an act which saw him replaced by his arrogant protégé Darren Cross (Corey Stoll), who becomes the film's antagonist. Hope and Pym only reconnected, in a limited way, after Hope learned that Cross was embarking on dangerous experiments in order to replicate the Pym Particle. Similarly, Lang has to prove himself to his ex-wife Maggie, his daughter, and everyone around him that he is worthy of being a father and can function as a responsible member of the community. Both mothers, Janet Pym and Maggie, are marginalised, with Janet being killed off in flashback (and never even showing her face either then or in family photos in the Pym house) acting only as motivation for the breakdown of the relationship between father and daughter, and Maggie, who has even less screen time than her new husband Paxton (who tells Scott, 'You don't know the first thing about being a father!'), who is portrayed as cold and lacking empathy, refusing to allow Scott to see Cassie or even attend the child's birthday party.

It is perhaps fitting that as the first of the MCU's central protagonists to be a father (with the exception of Hawkeye in *Avengers: Age of Ultron* whose family are shown onscreen, but play a much smaller role), Scott Lang's (and also Hank Pym's) paternal plight is portrayed in ways that had become familiar to

Fig. 21: The redemption of the father: Hank Pym (Michael Douglas) and Scott Lang (Paul Rudd) discuss the similarities of their plight in *Ant-Man* (2015)

new millennial audiences as two of many fathers (or father figures) similarly challenged by questions concerning their masculinity and patriarchal status in the era: like Ray Ferrier (Tom Cruise) in Steven Spielberg's *War of the Worlds*, Bryan Mills (Liam Neeson) in *Taken*, John Creasy (Denzel Washington) in *Man on Fire* (2004), Tom Stall/Joey Cusack (Viggo Mortensen) in *A History of Violence* (2005), to name but a few. Dramatisations like these have been regarded by many as an embodiment of the prevailing fears and anxieties concerning the perceived erosion of paternal power and privilege, as Nicola Rehling in her book *Extra-Ordinary Men: White Heterosexual Masculinity in Contemporary Popular Cinema* observed: 'In the last few decades, fears about how absent fathers damage their sons have been endlessly articulated in the US and British media, as well as neo-conservative and neo-liberal political rhetoric, with the supposition being that only a restoration of paternal authority will heal male pain and, by extension, the ailing social body' (2009: 65). Each of the men in these aforementioned films have their masculinity tested by events in the narrative and are offered the opportunity of reconstituting it (and in doing so re-establishing traditional patriarchal order) through the redemptive acts of violence they are 'reluctantly' forced to participate in as they protect or often rescue, not the sons mentioned by Rehling above, but the young girls in their charge. While they are each personal stories, their plights should be taken as standing for broader cultural tendencies, as Donna Perbedy has argued: 'Fatherhood is equated with nationhood and considered to be an inherent part of masculinity; if the central position of the father to the family is threatened, the threat constitutes a direct attack on the US, and its absence critically damages men and male identity' (2011: 125).

Pym suspended his relationship with Cross because he saw too much of the dark side of his own personality in him. However, unlike in the comics where Pym has been shown as, on occasion, a domestic abuser and an alcoholic, the film refuses to portray him as anything other than a grieving and misunderstood genius who is just as virtuous as Scott Lang. Both characters are tasked by the narrative with seeking redemption, but it is quite clear that they have done very little which they need to redeem themselves for: flashbacks show that Pym was not responsible for his wife's death and his only crime is the distance the traumatic loss created between him and Hope. Scott might have served a prison sentence, but his was a Robin Hood-like crime striking back at the capitalist corporate machine and, according to the information the film provides us with, not at all for personal gain.

Evangeline Lilly's Hope makes an interesting addition to the MCU's roster of female characters and she has every attribute that might make her a suitable candidate for being a superhero, were she not a woman. She is intelligent, determined, strong, and is even shown to be physically able to beat Lang in a fight. Yet she is defined by her relationship with her father and infantilised in the process as Hank Pym refuses to allow her to use the Ant-Man suit, worried about her safety after the death of her mother, even though she is obviously more qualified than Lang. Pym's choice of Scott over Hope is a richly suggestive one, and audiences are asked to decide whether it is illustrative of the MCU's prioritisation of men and the masculine experience over that of women with a frequency that was decidedly problematic, or a commentary on it. Furthermore, Hope is often equated with Lang's daughter, the six-year-old Cassie: Pym says to Lang, 'This is your chance to earn *that* look in your daughter's eyes', the one he has lost in his relationship with Hope, who is now a woman in her mid-thirties. He continues, 'It's not about saving *our world* it's about saving *theirs*', an awkward but familiar distinction between the world of the white male hero and that of the female sphere where females, regardless of their age, exist not to rescue, but to be rescued.

In the run up to the film's release Marvel's fictional diegetic news organisation WHIH World News, which had first appeared at the Stark Expo in *Iron Man 2*, then seen at the Battle at Culver University in *The Incredible Hulk*, before featuring regularly in both the films and the televisual branch of the MCU in *Marvel's Agents of S.H.I.E.L.D.*, released three news promos for the film posted online on 2, 7 and 16 July 2015, fronted by Christine Everheart, the journalist featured in *Iron Man* and *Iron Man 2* and, as the most interesting paratexts do, the reports offer some interesting engagements with the film's narrative. The third and final of the segments features an interview with Scott Lang live from prison in which WHIH World News is revealed to be a subsidiary of Vista Corp, the same company who Lang stole from and their reporting is obviously biased against his case. Christine attacks Lang calling him a 'self-proclaimed whistle blower' and Lang admits that he took 'service charges' from the burglary, implying that his crime might not have been as entirely altruistic as the film's narrative would have us believe.[10] Christine also says Lang has 'a few high-profile burglaries already on record' which are never mentioned in the film, nor are they denied by Lang, but would help us understand why Lang is considered such a master thief rather than a novice even though the film mentions only one burglary. These elements, if they had been a part of the central narrative of *Ant-Man*, would have made Lang's character more complicated and are further evidence of the MCU's inability to embrace moral ambiguity in its superheroes.[11]

Cross is driven increasingly unstable by his prolonged exposure to the recreated Pym Particle and becomes desperate to prove himself to his father figure Pym in a way that recalls Loki's desire to earn the respect of Odin. When he learns that Pym has replaced him with a new surrogate son, it is Lang who then becomes the target of his ire and the film's final battle between Ant-Man and Cross, now wearing the Yellowjacket suit, provides Lang with the opportunity to prove himself as a man and as a father that he has been looking for and is fittingly set mostly in his infant daughter Cassie's bedroom where Cross had gone to take revenge on the man who has taken his place. To defeat him Lang is forced to enter the atomic realm by shrinking himself, the same process which had 'killed' Pym's wife decades before, a place where 'all concepts of time and space become irrelevant'. However, whereas Janet Pym remained trapped inside, Lang hears Cassie's cries of 'Daddy!' and is able to return in a way that Janet Pym was not: because men in the MCU are braver and more resourceful than women, and they simply *love their children more*. Their combined successful defeat of Cross enables Lang and Pym to both redeem themselves in the eyes of their families and the law, marking Scott's transformation and reacceptance into the family unit where he is now literally welcomed back to the family table and is able to see Cassie whenever he likes (and is also rewarded by being given a romance with Hope). At the same time, Hank Pym's relationship with Hope is revived as she once again appears to have opened up and let her father into her life and, according to the conventions of Hollywood film, is able to call him 'Dad' again. The film's end credits stinger shows Hank Pym finally reluctantly acknowledging that Hope is more than capable of being a superhero and he offers her the Wasp suit once worn by her mother. Shortly after the release of *Ant-Man* Marvel announced that a sequel was in development to be called *Ant-Man and the Wasp*

(2019), which, as we have already noted, would be the first MCU film to have a female character as the lead with their name in the title. Hope's diegetic response to being given the suit was perhaps echoed by that of many women in the audience in the year of the film's release: 'About damn time!'

Notes

1 Additionally, Gunn's musical choices offer metaphorical connections to the onscreen action in the form of David Bowie's 'Moonage Daydream' (1971) which plays as we are introduced to the bizarre 'planet' Knowhere, the rebellious punk-inflected 'Cherry Bomb' (1976) by the Runaways as the team form for a heroic group shot (which Gunn undercuts by showing Rocket adjusting his underwear, Gamora yawning and Peter scratching his nose), or 'O-o-h Child' (1970) by the Five Stairsteps as the song which Peter uses to challenge Ronan to a dance-off at the film's climax. This process becomes even more apparent in the sequel with musical selections like George Harrison's polytheistic anthem 'My Sweet Lord' (1970) heard as the film arrives at Ego's planet (which is also Ego himself). About this choice, Gunn remarked, 'And there's this big creation myth about how he came about and it was kind of lined up with that. I've always been into Hindu creation myths and there's some similarities there' (qtd. in Hiatt 2017). 'Brandy' (1972) by Looking Glass is used by Ego as a metaphor for his and Peter's status as outsiders who cannot be tied to those around them. Fleetwood Mac's 'The Chain' (1977) is used twice, once when the group splits up and again at the climax when they come back together again to defeat Ego. Gunn commented that the song 'is about the Guardians, at least in the way we use it' (ibid.).

2 These tonal shifts are a key part of James Gunn's signature filmmaking style and are apparent in his directorial debut, *Slither* (2006) and his second film, the darkly comedic superhero movie *Super* (2010) in which the unremarkable Frank Darbo (Rainn Wilson) embarks on a life of crime-fighting when he becomes the Crimson Bolt. Darbo attacks anyone who contravenes his strict moral code, even those who cut the line in a queue for a movie theatre, leaving them with his memorable catchphrase 'Shut up, crime!'

3 When Steven Spielberg, who had been somewhat critical of the genre, was asked in 2016 what his favourite superhero film was, he replied: 'I love the *Superman* of Richard Donner, Christopher Nolan's *The Dark Knight*, and the first *Iron Man*, but the superhero film that impressed me most is one that does not take itself too seriously, *Guardians of the Galaxy*.' He continued: 'I left with the feeling of having seen something new in movies, without any cynicism or fear of being dark when needed' (qtd. Kyriazis 2016). These comments led James Gunn to say, 'This is the greatest compliment I've ever received. I'm teary-eyed right now. No one has influenced *Guardians* [*of the Galaxy*] more' (ibid.).

4   The sequel contains references to *Knight Rider* (NBC, 1982–86), *Cheers* (NBC, 1982–93), the video game *Pac-Man* (Namco, 1980), *He-Man and the Masters of the Universe* (Various, 1983–85), *The Smurfs* (NBC, 1981–89) and the actress Heather Locklear who Peter might have seen in *T.J. Hooker* (Various, 1982–86).

5   While Peter's joke about Jackson Pollack (1912–56) is one of the funniest moments of the film, one might ask whether Peter, who left Earth as a small boy in 1988 and seems to have had no contact with Earth culture since, would know enough about the painter's work to make the remark.

6   In *Guardians of the Galaxy: Vol. 2* it is also taken to mean 'They were looking at me funny', 'I'm glad you don't want me to wear this hat', 'He called me twig' and most memorably 'Welcome to the fucking Guardians of the Galaxy!'

7   In a humorous aside which perhaps belies the seriousness of these discrepancies, in a presentation entitled 'Super Daddy Issues, Masculinity, Fatherhood, and Superhero Films', Kara Kvaran suggested, referring to the fact that three of the superheroes of the MCU were named Chris, 'The best way to be a superhero is to be a blonde white guy named Chris' (qtd. in Coventry 2015).

8   Ronan's attack on Xandar was said to contain the highest onscreen body count in the history of film, as opposed to offscreen deaths, with around 80,000 Nova Corps pilots being killed in the attack. The figures for *Guardians of the Galaxy* were 83,871, nearly fifteen times higher than those of the second-placed film *Dracula Untold* (2014) (see *Go Compare* 2016).

9   Yondu Udonta gets the most interesting arc in *Guardians of the Galaxy* and the sequel, a testimony to Gunn's writing and Rooker's charismatic performance. Yondu's affection for Quill is very clear in the first film and in the second he sacrifices himself for the man he regards as his son with the simple but poignant line, delivered in Rooker's Alabama-inflected drawl, telling Peter, 'He [Ego] may have been your father, boy, but he wasn't your daddy'. Over Yondu's funeral the Cat Stevens song 'Father and Son' (1970) plays.

10 In the MCU-set comic book prologue *Ant-Man. Scott Lang: Small Time* (2015) more details are revealed about the Vista Corp robbery which are entirely absent from the film. Lang is explicitly shown to steal jewellery and clothes, which also casts him in a very different light to that shown in *Ant-Man*.

11 On the commentary track included on the Blu-ray release of the film Paul Rudd alludes to a vague sense of dissatisfaction about this and asserts he would have liked to have seen more of an exploration of what he describes as Scott Lang's 'questionable moral code'.

CHAPTER EIGHT

'Isn't that why we fight? So we can end the fight and go home?': The Enduring American Monomyth in *Avengers: Age of Ultron*

And why, in a country trumpeting itself as the world's supreme diplomatic model, do we so often relish depictions of impotent democratic institutions that can be rescued only by extralegal superheroes? Are these stories safety valves for the stresses of democracy, or do they represent a yearning for something other than democracy? And why do women and people of color, who have made significant strides in civil rights, continue to remain almost wholly subordinate in a mythscape where communities must always be rescued by physically powerful white men?

– John Shelton Lawrence and Robert Jewett (2002: 7–8)

We were dealing with the greatest heroes and the greatest villains. We were dealing with the greatest novel material there ever was. Across this world stage were these great out-size characters. A battle of the giants. When you say 'epic,' yes, we are dealing with epic-sized people and epic-sized events.

– Frank Capra (qtd. in Bailey 2004: 125)

I.

Just as *The Avengers* in the summer of 2012 was designed to both reconcile the disparate origin stories which had largely comprised Phase One and introduce the films of Phase Two, *Avengers: Age of Ultron* had a similarly difficult task three years later: to bring together the variegated narrative strains of the Phase Two films and establish a context for what would become Phase Three, which began with *Captain America: Civil War* released the following year in 2016. Furthermore, Joss Whedon's return to the MCU was expected to meet, if not exceed, the tremendous financial and cultural impact of *The Avengers*. It was undoubtedly a considerable challenge and one, writing after the fact, that many regarded the film did not meet, even Whedon himself in a series of frank interviews conducted while publicising the film, exchanges which he later admitted regretting (see Van Syckle 2016). Even though *Age of Ultron* made $1.4 billion dollars at the world-wide box office which led to it being the third-highest earning film of the year, second only to *Jurassic World* (2015) and *Star Wars: The Force Awakens* (2015), the fact that it was not *the biggest* film of the year as its predecessor had been, and that reviews were generally positive rather than the frequently jubilant reaction to *The Avengers* led to the sense that the film was regarded as something of a disappointment. Peter Travers at *Rolling Stone* called it 'a whole summer of fireworks packed into one movie. It doesn't just go to 11, it starts there' (2015); and Chris Nashawaty at *Entertainment Weekly* wrote, 'Still, my real beef with these movies – and this one in particular – is how same-y they've started to feel. Each time out, everything is at stake and nothing is at stake' (2015). These comments and the perception that the film had not quite lived up to its potential are certainly an indication of how far the financial bar has been raised and continues to be raised, for not only the films of the Marvel Cinematic Universe but also the majority of 'tent pole' summer releases, where, given their escalating budgets, expectations are incredibly high. There were also lingering rumours of friction between Joss Whedon and Marvel Studios, creative differences similar to the likes of which had led Patty Jenkins to leave *Thor: The Dark World* and Edgar Wright to leave *Ant-Man*. There is evidence of this in the final film: in its undeveloped plot strands, unevenness of tone and the inability to balance its large cast with the success Whedon had achieved in *The Avengers*. Despite these issues, *Age of Ultron* is an important addition to the MCU and makes a significant contribution to its ongoing mythos, introduces important new characters and the consequences of its narrative choices have a considerable impact on the Phase Three films which were to follow. The film also is, arguably, the fullest approximation of Marvel's political ideology and what we have previously described as the Stark Doctrine. The mythology that it embodies and contributes to is a particularly American one, which was called the 'American Monomyth' by John Shelton Lawrence and Robert Jewett in their book of the same name (1977). In their later book, *The American Monomyth* (2002), they maintain that American incarnations of heroic narratives differ considerably from Joseph Campbell's accounts of common mythological tropes in his now iconic *The Hero with a Thousand Faces* (1949), as they focus not on initiation, but instead redemption:

> The monomythic hero claims surpassing concern for the health of the community, but he never practices citizenship. He unites a consuming love of impartial justice with a mission of personal vengeance that eliminates due process of law. He offers a form of leadership without paying the price of political relationships or responding to preferences of the majority. In denying the ambivalence and complexity of real life, where the moral landscape offers choices in various shades of gray rather than in black and white, where ordinary people muddle through life and learn to live with the many poor choices they have made, and where the heroes that do exist have feet of clay, the monomyth pictures a world in which no humans really live. It gives Americans a fantasy land without ambiguities to cloud the moral vision, where the evil empire of enemies is readily discernible, and where they can vicariously (through identification with the superhero) smite evil before it overtakes them. (2002: 48)

Writing six years before the release of *Iron Man* and at the very start of the superhero renaissance, Lawrence and Jewett effectively describe key aspects of the MCU, and the superhero film as a whole, in a single paragraph, for the simple reason that the genre continues to replay and perpetuate deeply embedded mythological values which have become formative aspects of American identity.

The '11' that Peter Travers writes of is the film's extended James Bond-esque prologue in the mountain forests of the fictional Eastern European country of Sokovia which opens the film. Whereas *The Avengers* had spent a large amount of its running time bringing its superheroes together, Whedon gives audiences another iconic tie-in image in which they are all pictured in the same frame within the first two minutes of the film, even presenting the action in extreme slow motion to give us a moment to admire the synchronicity of its franchise coordination, the status of the Avengers at the apex of contemporary pop culture, and underline the fact that they are now a fully formed and cohesive unit. The shot was described by Jordi Costa, writing in *El Pais*, as 'a sculptural group that eternalises the characters in full battle [which does not miss] the conceptual implications of his [Whedon's] specific baroque gestures' (2015). The moment will be referenced again in the film's credits more than two hours later in the form of an *actual sculpture* of the Avengers made from marble. There is no waiting for the Hulk to smash (which took twenty-six minutes in *The Incredible Hulk*, and approximately one hour and sixteen minutes in *The Avengers*), as in *Age of Ultron* he is shown 'hulking out' and crashing his way through the last remaining HYDRA base in the aftermath of the events of *Captain America: The Winter Soldier* in the film's opening moments. The tone is quickly established as much lighter than the majority of the previous MCU films and Stark's banter is more pronounced than it has ever been, with jokes about Captain America's language, impromptu interactions with HYDRA henchmen, and fairly blatant sexual innuendo.

The base is the location of Baron Von Strucker's research laboratory, which has been using the mysterious power generated by Loki's sceptre to perform ethically ambiguous experiments on human beings (as opposed to those we are asked to understand as distinctly moral performed on Steve Rogers back in *The First Avenger*).[1] The film reveals that all but two of those experimented on have died, leaving only the Maximoff twins, Wanda and Pietro, alive. Wanda is known in the comics as Scarlett Witch due to her telekinetic powers and Pietro is called Quicksilver, because of his superhuman speed, but they are never referred to by these names in the film. While Sokovia is a suitably exotic location for the film's prologue, it holds more significance for *Age of Ultron* as Scarlett Witch and Quicksilver are both Sokovian, and the film will return there for its climax, the Battle of Sokovia, during which an entire city will be detached from the ground and lifted into the sky, threatening the world with an extinction level event.[2]

It is clear from the way it is visually represented and cues in the film's dialogue that Sokovia has been the site of repeated wars and even American military intervention in the recent past. Agent Hill remarks: 'Sokovia's had a rough history. Nowhere special, but it is on the way to *everywhere* special.' These observations, the Serbian spoken by civilians, Cyrillic writing (for example supermarket/ супер маркет; police/полиција; optician/Оптичар; a pub/ПАБ, and a bakery/ ПЕКАРА, among others), and scenes of anti-American protests code Sokovia as being reminiscent of Kosovo in the late 1990s. Two MCU films in the future, in *Captain America: Civil War*, the ex-Sokovian intelligence officer Helmut Zemo (Daniel Bruhl) will call his own country a 'failed state' a term which was regularly applied to Kosovo during and after what is referred to as the Yugoslav Wars (1991–2001). Sokovia's depiction as a pitiful Eastern Europe country in need of liberating and saving by heroic American forces is similar to the portrayal of many countries in zones of instability around the world by Hollywood cinema over the decades. However, when Stark sends in the Iron Legion, his army of Iron Man suits with advanced AI, to evacuate the city, telling the residents in English rather than Sokovian, 'We wish to avoid collateral damage and will inform you when this current conflict is resolved', the population do not welcome them as we might have expected (as Iron Man was welcomed by civilians in Afghanistan in *Iron Man* and Captain America was in Germany in *The Avengers*), but throw debris at the metallic figures, and in the background one can see several examples of anti-Iron Man graffiti, and banners which read 'иди из Соковија' ('Out of Sokovia'). A deleted scene included on the Blu-ray release of the film shows a remarkable mural of Captain America's face with the anglicised Serbian word 'Fašista' scrawled across it, a stark contrast to the effusively grateful global graffiti acknowledging the debt the world owed the superheroes featured at the end of *The Avengers*. Agent Maria Hill informs Captain America that the Maximoffs were orphaned at the age of ten when a shell collapsed their apartment killing their parents, but it is only later from Pietro himself that we hear the full story. The Maximoff family were having dinner when their building was hit by a Stark branded bomb (evoking the Afghanistan set prologue of *Iron Man*) which failed to detonate, leading them to spend anxious hours waiting for help which never arrived. As Wanda says in her broken English, 'We wait for two days for Tony Stark to kill us...'. Therefore, it seems that it is American intervention in Sokovia that has prompted the Sokovians' mistrust of the Avengers and the Maximoff twins to volunteer for Strucker's experiments, and one wonders if it was their deep-seated hatred of Stark that led them to be the only ones to survive. Agent Hill is dismissive of their motives but Captain America, in a rare moment of moral equivalence in the MCU asks, 'Right. What kind of monster would let a German scientist experiment on them to protect their country?'

Tony Stark finds Loki's sceptre in Strucker's basement laboratory and as he reaches for it Scarlett Witch uses her powers to induce some sort of vision in him which becomes central to the film's narrative and appears to be a projection of his deep-seated fears and anxieties. In scenes very reminiscent of his PTSD-influenced nightmares in *Iron Man 3,* he sees the Avengers decimated after another Chitauri invasion: Black Widow, Thor and Hawkeye are dead, and the Hulk's giant corpse hangs limp, grotesquely pierced by several large metallic spikes. Captain America's iconic shield lies broken on the floor, ripped in two next to its owner's lifeless body. As Tony moves towards him, Cap reaches up and asks, as if with his dying breath, 'You could have saved us. Why didn't you do more?' Stark's narcissistic vision, in which he once again is the only person who can save humanity, will compel him to undertake his own ethically dubious experiments and ultimately create the film's antagonist, the malicious and advanced sentient robot known as Ultron, actions he will refuse to apologise for throughout the film. Even later after he knows that Scarlett Witch was involved and that she has given his fellow Avengers similarly twisted visions, he still claims that, 'I wasn't tricked, I was *shown*, it wasn't a nightmare, it was my *legacy*' in a return to the motif which had played such an important role in the Iron Man trilogy. As the scene ends both of the Maximoff twins are shown standing behind Stark and could have easily prevented him from taking the sceptre, but instead Scarlett Witch merely smiles as she knows that Stark has within him the capacity to destroy not only himself, but the rest of the Avengers too.

II.

After their success in destroying the final HYDRA base the Avengers return to what was formerly Stark Tower in New York, now renamed the Avengers Tower. As the camera glides over Grand Central Terminal near the Tower's base it passes over a monument which has replaced Jules-Félix Coutan's *Glory of Commerce* shown destroyed in *The Avengers*. The new statue is dedicated to the heroes of the Battle of New York, but it is not the exploits of the Avengers that are memorialised, rather, in an allusion to 9/11, the ordinary, everyday heroes like the firemen, soldiers, police officers and a mother and child who participated in the Chitauri invasion three years before. The Avengers celebrate their Sokovian victory alongside numerous other civilians among whom are several World War II veterans (including Stan Lee who served in the Signal Corps, then known as the Training Film Division), continuing the connections the MCU has often established between the adventures of their very modern heroes and World War II. When Thor drinks from a flask containing alcohol from 'barrels built from the wreck of Grunhal's fleet' he warns the veterans that it is 'not for mortal men' to which Stan Lee's character replies: 'Neither was Omaha Beach, blondie!' The superheroes are shown to have developed a genuine bond and an easy-going rapport with one another best revealed in the after-party scene which shows them all in a rare off-duty moment playfully discussing who might be worthy enough to lift Thor's hammer, Mjölnir. Each of the heroes takes a turn, with the exception of Black Widow who tells them: 'That's not a question I need answered.' The film's light-hearted tone continues with Stark's teasing of Barton, who was injured in the Sokovia prologue, with, 'We won't hold it against you if you can't *get it up*'. Bruce Banner, in an indication of how comfortable he now feels around his fellow Avengers, even pretends to 'Hulk out', something it seems hard to imagine the same character having done when played by Edward Norton in *The Incredible Hulk* or even by Ruffalo himself at the time of *The Avengers*. The scene ends with Captain America's attempt to lift the hammer which produces a definite wobble, shot in the same frame as Thor's momentarily very anxious face.

It initially seems that Stark has matured as he had been shown to at the end of *Iron Man 3*: he asks for Thor's permission to run tests on the sceptre and playfully defers to Cap as 'the boss' with the aside that he is the one who pays for everything, designs everything and generally makes 'everyone look cool'. But when he discovers that the advanced artificial intelligence contained within the sceptre might hold the key to a project he has been working on, one which could prevent his apocalyptic vision from ever coming true, he is revealed to have not changed so much at all. Stark's plan is to make a robotic AI so powerful that it would make the existence of the Avengers unnecessary, an act that he describes in suitably Reaganesque terms, evoking the Star Wars Missile Defence system (formerly known as the Strategic Defense Initiative), as a 'suit of armour around the world' which will enable 'peace in our time' (itself a fairly potent allusion to Neville Chamberlain's pre-World War II proclamation after signing the Munich Agreement [1938] with Hitler). In interviews Downey Jr. made these connections explicit:

> With *The Avengers*, Tony was becoming a team player and with *Iron Man 3*, it was him transcending his dependency on the tech that's keeping him alive. So I thought, 'Okay, now what?' But there's all this unfinished business. There's the matter of a certain wormhole that opened over New York and the imminent threat that still implies, so Tony has turned his attentions more toward a bit of a post-Reagan era, Star Wars-type notion and he likes to call it Ultron. (Qtd. in Collinson 2015)

Stark's confidante, Bruce Banner, suggests that this is something they should discuss with the rest of the Avengers, but Stark refuses telling him they do not have time 'for a city hall debate' or what he defines as 'the man was not meant to meddle medley'. Although Ultron is created shortly after, the film gives Stark a get out clause: they were running extensive tests but they apparently did not *commit* to actioning the programme and later Stark asks Banner, 'Were we even close to an interface?' The AI that is created is very different to the one Stark envisioned and while the early Iron Man films had seen Stark struggling with his relationship with his deceased father, *Age of Ultron* sees him become a father himself.

Ultron (voiced by James Spader) joins the ranks of many malicious robots in the history of the science fiction genre: like Maria in *Metropolis* (1927), HAL 9000 in *2001: A Space Odyssey* (1968), VIKI in *I, Robot* (2004) and even the duplicitous Ava in *Ex Machina* (2015) released in the same year as *Age of Ultron*. As we see 'him' being 'born' Ultron is shown accessing the internet, witnessing in seconds centuries' worth of man's inhumanity to man presented in flashes on the screen which ends with footage from *Iron Man*, of Stark demonstrating the Jericho Missile to the grateful American military in Afghanistan. Ultron first appeared in the comics more than forty years before in *Avengers #55* originally published in 1968, but his new millennial guise is very different, as one might expect, given the remarkable advances in technology in the almost fifty years since. He is able to acquire and access any information from around the world via the internet, digitally alter any bank account and even transfer his consciousness from machine to machine. When the Avengers find out what he has done Stark refuses to offer an apology for his creation, and he even laughs when they criticise him, saying 'It *is* funny. It's a hoot that you don't get why we *need* this!'

Stark has again returned to the equilibrium state we observed in our discussion of the Iron Man trilogy and *again* forgotten the lessons the Yinsen had revealed to him in the caves of the Kunar Province. In the director's commentary on the Blu-ray release of the film, Joss Whedon proposed, somewhat tongue in cheek one might add, 'We have a problem ... and that problem is Tony ... Tony Stark is *the villain*'. Of course, the film cannot pursue this idea with any substance, as despite his often irresponsible behaviour, the MCU has always endorsed Stark's brand of rule-breaking, individualistic heroism as the summit of twenty-first-century masculinity. Stark is undoubtedly flawed in a range of interesting ways, but what he pursues is something greater than himself, and by the end of its narrative *Age of Ultron* will even suggest that he was right to create Ultron after all, despite the massive levels of destruction that it leads to. Later, when Stark again justifies his decision to Captain America with the question, 'Isn't that the mission? Isn't that *why we fight*? So we can win the fight, so we get to go home?', the intonation Downey Jr. adopts in his delivery of the line seems a deliberate reference to the seven American propaganda films in the series known as *Why We Fight* (1942–45) directed by Frank Capra (and frequently co-directed by Anatole Litvak) made during World War II. Robert Neimi stated that these films were extremely influential in how Americans came to view the conflict, both at the time and in the years since, and that they presented 'a decidedly Manichean – but largely accurate – view of the world in which the Axis powers represent barbarism and slavery and the Allied powers stand for civilisation and freedom' (2006: 72). Whedon's film, and the MCU as a whole, subsumes this moral clarity into the diegetic frames of its own post-9/11 world in a similar way to how William J. Bennett did in his book titled *Why We Fight: Moral Clarity and the War on Terrorism* which insisted that America was 'a beacon of freedom' (2002: 151) a term we have heard uttered before in the MCU, and that the United States has 'brought more justice to more people than any nation in the history of mankind; that our open, tolerant, prosperous, peaceable society is the marvel and envy of the ages' (ibid.).

In Ultron's first scene in the film, which comes right after the Avengers' playful interaction around Mjölnir, he notifies them quite directly of his purpose. Like many advanced robots in the history of the science fiction genre he decides that humanity cannot be trusted to act in its own best interests and must therefore be eradicated. With the Avengers being 'Earth's mightiest heroes' (as Stark described them in *The Avengers*), they are the greatest embodiments of all that needs to be destroyed and, as Ultron informs them, 'You are all killers'. But of course, Ultron's criticisms, like most of those from previous antagonists throughout the MCU, are easy to dismiss as they come from a genocidal and quite clearly insane robot. Whedon gives Ultron the aside, which becomes a thematic motif, from *Pinocchio* (1940), 'I had strings on me but now I'm free, they are no strings on me' (with the actual line and tune layered over from the original) which complements the Frankenstein allusions at the film's centre.

Executive Producer Victoria Alonso remarked that Ultron emerges as 'almost the alter ego of Tony Stark' (qtd. in Johnston 2015: 158), which is certainly true, but the relationship between the two is presented as something much more than that: Ultron is Stark's offspring who he refers to as 'junior' and even tells Ultron: 'You're gonna break your old man's heart.' When Thor subsequently comments 'Nobody has to break anything', Ultron quickly adds, 'Clearly you've never made an omelette' – to which Stark responds, 'Beat me by one second!' The robot's caustic one-liners are undoubtedly a manifestation of aspects of Stark's own acerbic character, a process which Michael O'Sullivan refers to as Ultron as having 'assimilated many of Tony Stark's mannerisms' (2016: 22). Ultron's criticisms of Captain America, in particular, are very reminiscent of Stark's from *The Avengers* where he informed Cap: 'Everything that's special about you came from a bottle!' Ultron sneers at Cap and contemptuously refers to him as 'God's righteous man' who only pretends that he 'can live without war'. Later Scarlet Witch even compares Stark and Ultron directly: 'Ultron can't tell the difference between destroying the world and saving it. Where do you think he gets that?'

Just as Tony Stark had a complicated relationship with his own father, Ultron similarly has issues with Tony, and when the South African arms dealer Klaue (Andy Serkis) dares to say to Ultron that 'You're one of Stark's!', the robot becomes so enraged he cuts off the man's arm and asks him: 'You think I'm one of Stark's puppets?' Ultron had gone to Klaue with his new recruits, Quicksilver and Scarlett Witch, to access his reserves of the world's strongest metal, Vibranium, only found in the mysterious Kingdom of Wakanda (the home of the Black Panther, who is introduced in *Captain America: Civil War*). Stark denies doing business with Klaue and insists that, '*This* was never my life', but when Ultron remarks to Klaue, 'Keep your friends rich and your enemies rich and wait to find out which is which' it is this which prompts Klaue to make the connection between father and son, implying more intimacy between Klaue and the self-proclaimed billionaire, playboy and philanthropist, than Stark had suggested. Stark's refusal to accept responsibility for Ultron, acknowledge Klaue, and his subsequent rejection of the Maximoff twins' story of how their parents were killed, is a denial of a responsibility and culpability which has marked the character from his very first introduction in *Iron Man* despite his epiphany and apparent rejection of 'zero accountability'.

In the ensuing battle between the Avengers and Ultron, Scarlett Witch forces Thor, Captain America and Black Widow to experience their own vision just as Tony Stark had in the film's prologue in Sokovia. It is hard to say what they are exactly: hallucinations, nightmares, projections of their worst fears, or even moments 'dredged from their darkest memories' (O'Sullivan 2016: 1). After claiming they will not affect him because of his godlike status, Thor hallucinates a celebration in the halls of Asgard with his friend Heimdall in attendance. The scene quickly turns from light-hearted revelry to something altogether more sinister as Heimdall accuses the God of Thunder of being a 'destroyer' and telling him 'see where your power leads … to *Hel!*' (a reference to the Asgardian afterworld where those who are evil go after death). Thor's fear is that he will not be a worthy leader and the scene hints at the future apocalyptic direction of *Thor: Ragnarok*, which would feature Hela (Cate Blanchett), the Asgardian goddess of death, and the destruction of not only Mjölnir, but the whole of Asgard. Black Widow's vision is equally personal as it recreates her time in the Red Room, a place which, by then, had been explored in more detail in *Marvel's Agent Carter* 'The Iron Ceiling' (1.05), where she was forced to undergo brutal and dehumanising training in order to become a cold-hearted master spy and assassin. It culminates in a scene which shows the murder of an unarmed man and alludes to a forced hysterectomy to mark her graduation from the programme. In Captain America's, he is reunited, very briefly, with a young Peggy Carter for the date they never were able to have, referred to in those poignant last lines of *The First Avenger*. As with Thor, the scene starts out joyfully, this time in a dance hall on V.E. Day (Victory in Europe Day) with Peggy assuring him that 'the war's over, Steve, we can go home, imagine it'. But Cap's face reveals that he knows these are things that he can never really have and the scene turns darker when those present begin to attack one another for no reason while Cap watches, and Peggy disappears, leaving him, once again, alone. Shortly afterwards Scarlett Witch uses her mind-control powers on Bruce Banner too, turning him into a red-eyed, enraged and uncontrolled Hulk. We never learn what Banner's visions are comprised of, but the implication is that the scenes of mass destruction and devastation in Johannesburg, South Africa, which follow, where the Hulk goes on a full rampage, might be his worst fear literalised.

The Hulk scene in Johannesburg is the first time the destructive potential of the Hulk has been seen throughout the movie and is an exact dramatisation of what General Ross had stated the Hulk was capable of back in *The Incredible Hulk* in 2008. Stark and Banner had planned for this contingency in their co-creation of the Veronica programme, a satellite able to deploy Stark's Mark XLIV armour, known as the Hulkbuster suit, built in an effort to match the Hulk's prodigious strength. Stark initially attempts to pacify his friend by reminding him, '*You're* Bruce Banner!' but this only makes the Hulk angrier and later Bruce himself says, returning to a theme expressed earlier in this book: 'The world just saw the Hulk, the *real* Hulk for the first time.' Hulk's rampage is spectacularly destructive and

Whedon even gives him a Snorricam shot (sometimes referred to as a reverse-point-of-view shot) used extensively by filmmakers like Martin Scorsese and Spike Lee to represent extreme states of disorientation and disassociativeness. The sequence is undoubtedly an example of what Richard Corliss called 'disaster porn' and many of the images seem to self-consciously evoke 9/11 and what Karen Randell described as the 'lexicon of 9/11'. On the director's commentary for *Age of Ultron*, Whedon commented that it was imperative that the film portray 'real damage and that we say, "You don't just bust up a city and nobody pays for it"'. However, the price that Whedon mentions here seems to be largely absent as throughout the sequence not a single person is shown to be killed, seriously injured or even hurt, and the same is true for the even larger Battle of Sokovia which concludes the film. As if reacting, in some way, to criticisms levelled at *Man of Steel*, released in the previous year, which seemed to *never* pause for even a moment to consider the impact of its scenes of destruction on the civilians of Metropolis, Stark is shown to be very aware of innocent bystanders throughout, as he has been since the Stark Expo in *Iron Man 2*, and as he and the Hulk are about to crash into one huge building, the film shows him use J.A.R.V.I.S. to scan it quickly to make sure no one is inside. Agent Hill, watching the global news reporting the incident, says, 'There's been no official call for Banner's arrest, but it's in the air', an issue concerning the accountability of superheroes which will become the central narrative event of *Captain America: Civil War*.

In the aftermath, the Avengers flee to a safe house which is revealed to contain Hawkeye's secret family: his pregnant wife, Laura (Linda Cardellini) and two children. This idyllic scene with its bucolic rural homestead, replete with American flag waving conspicuously on the porch and an *actual* white picket fence, acts as a reminder to the Avengers of what they are fighting for, but also what some of them have lost, or what they might never be able to have. Cap is shown standing uncomfortably in the threshold of the doorway in a pose very similar to that of Ethan Edward's (John Wayne) at the dénouement of John Ford's *The Searchers*, as Peggy's 'we can go home...' echoes over the diegetic sound of Barton's children playing. Cap finds that he cannot go back inside and he turns with his iconic shield prominently placed on his back, walking away while still framed by the doorway. Like Wayne's Ethan, a similarly iconic figure of American masculinity, Cap is trapped between two worlds as *Age of Ultron* subtly evokes the mythological demands the American Monomyth still places on its heroes in 2015, as it did in both 1868, the year in which *The Searchers* is set, and in 1956, the year of its release.[3]

It might be regarded as somewhat problematic that what is to be found at Barton's homestead is implied to be such an aspirational pinnacle for those onscreen and beyond, as its vision of normalcy is a dated concept for twenty-first-

Fig. 22: Captain America feels ill at ease in Barton's idyllic homestead in *Avengers: Age of Ultron* (2015) as Joss Whedon recreates the final iconic image of John Ford's *The Searchers* (1956)

century American (and global) culture. Unfortunately the characterisation of Laura adds little to the MCU's limited depiction of women, as even though Whedon has been frequently praised for the strength of the female roles he has created in the past, which has seen him described as having an 'ongoing feminist project – a dialogue about gender politics, sexuality, and control of the body', especially those in *Buffy the Vampire Slayer* (Various, 1997–2003) and *Firefly*, arguably, there is little of distinction in his two Avengers outings to support this (see Schultz 2014: 357). Laura is relegated to looking after (and bearing) children, staring out the window waiting for her husband to return, both figuratively and literally keeping the home fires burning, and the interaction between Black Widow and Banner which take place at the homestead, in which they have an intimate discussion about the future of their relationship, proved to be one of the most widely discussed moments in the film on its release. Banner expresses the idea that because of his condition it would be impossible for them to have what Barton has, and that he is indeed the 'monster' he has been accused of being since *The Incredible Hulk*. Natasha empathises and reveals to him the details of her forced hysterectomy in the Red Room, which was alluded to in her earlier Scarlett Witch-induced vision, ending her account with the question, 'Still think you're the only monster on the team?' It was this conversation and indeed this question which caused something of a furore among fans and became so heavily criticised that it seemed to be instrumental in Joss Whedon's decision to leave social media. In an open letter to Whedon, Sara Stewart at *Indiewire* asked, 'Did we really need Natasha to have a mini-breakdown over the fact that she can't have children?' (2015). She also asked, 'Haven't we gotten to a point where the one lonely female superhero in our current landscape can just pursue the business of avenging without having to bemoan not being a mother?' (ibid.). These negative reactions coincided with anger at Jeremy Renner and Chris Evans jokingly referring to Black Widow as a 'slut' during a video interview and Mark Ruffalo's Facebook post complaining about the lack of availability of Black Widow toys for him to purchase for female members of his family (see Towers 2015; Ungerman 2015). Meredith Woerner and Katharine Trendacosta, writing for io9, asked a similar question:

> How is it okay to say this about Black Widow – someone who, to be very clear, has not hooked up on screen in any of the movies – but no one's going 'Tony Stark? Yeah, he's a total slut.' We actually have seen that on screen. As a thing that actually happened. He may have reformed and found his one and only – but Tony's badass boast in the first *Avengers* movie is 'Billionaire playboy philanthropist.' He gets 'playboy' as an accolade, but the Black Widow is somehow a slut. (2015)

As briefly explored previously, Black Widow does offer partial challenges to some of the most regressive aspects of the MCU's depiction of women, but has never been given anything approximating equal narrative agency (a fact emphasised by the lack of her own solo movie in Phases One through Three) and has repeatedly been defined by her emotions in ways that characters like Tony Stark, Steve Rogers, Bruce Banner and Thor have not. Whedon's *The Avengers* offered tantalising hints at the 'red' in her 'ledger': allusions to Dreykov's daughter, Sao Paulo and the hospital fire, but *Age of Ultron* chooses to manifest her greatest anxiety as her forced sterilisation and despair about not being able to be a mother. This is further problematised by the awkwardness of the maternal role she is forced to play in the film, in particular with the Hulk lullaby sequences and humorous lines like, 'I'm always picking up after you boys!' which, of course, are tongue in cheek, but perhaps have not been appropriately earned through the depth of her characterisation. It is also revealing that later *she* is the only Avenger to be captured by Ultron on Sokovia and even though she is widely acknowledged as a super spy and master assassin, it is Bruce Banner who rescues her. Not his alter ego the Hulk, but the meek, mild-mannered and personable scientist Bruce Banner who tells her, 'I'm here to get you to safety'.

In an effort to defeat the Avengers, Ultron attempts to create an improved version of himself in Seoul, South Korea, utilising the Mind Gem found in Loki's sceptre and Klaue's vibranium, but he is prevented in scenes which also show Scarlett Witch and Quicksilver turning against him when they finally become aware of his real plan to destroy humanity. Stark is then faced with another dilemma; should he complete the creation of the being Ultron started, which will be named Vision, who could possibly help them defeat the murderous robot, or would he be repeating the same mistake as he made before? Banner even suggests: 'I'm in a loop, I'm caught in a time loop, this is exactly where it went wrong!' Captain America orders him to 'Shut it down! You don't know what you're doing', but once again Stark refuses to listen to anyone and goes ahead with the process. Despite their fears, it is quickly clear that Stark was indeed right, as Vision emerges as one of the most virtuous of all the superheroes, even later shown to be able to lift Thor's hammer, a true sign of worthiness. In doing so, as much of the MCU has done, *Age of Ultron* legitimises and endorses Stark's impulsive actions and in Vision's integrity even his decision to make Ultron, even though the robot was evil, is also retroactively endorsed.

III.

The film's climax, the Battle of Sokovia, is certainly the largest-scale action sequence of the MCU films throughout Phases One and Two. Its expansive and largely CGI-driven nature is perhaps one of the main reasons (alongside Downey Jr.'s reputed $40 million salary) why the film was said to have cost $250–$300 million, with some estimates as high as $330 million (see Sylt 2014). It definitely would not have been possible without the advances in computer-generated imagery which have been instrumental in the emergence of the genre to prominence in recent years and if the Marvel Cinematic Universe has a single sequence which could be called 'disaster porn' then the Battle for Sokovia is it. To emphasise the raised stakes of the extinction level event they are facing Tony Stark informs the team, 'No way we all get through this ... there's gonna be blood on the floor'. Earlier Captain America had remarked 'Every time someone tries to win a war before it starts, innocent people die. *Every time*', but the film will show not a single innocent civilian injured, harmed or killed onscreen, nor will any be mentioned, even though in the following year *Captain America: Civil War* revealed that the financial cost of the Battle of Sokovia was $477 billion dollars and one hundred and seventy-seven people died. From the very start an emphasis is placed on the rescue of civilians and Captain America reminds everyone, 'Our priority is getting them out ... all they want is to live their lives in peace'. John C. McDowall, writing about *The Avengers*, but in an idea equally as applicable to *Age of Ultron*, suggested, 'Its violence is not portrayed in terms either of complex causalities or of bloody, unpredictable and harrowing loss and tragic catastrophism – it is the clear cut war of good against evil, and therefore, in a sense, "the good war" in which everything works out and the good wins in an anaemic happy ending' (2014: 65). Thus, as we have seen throughout the MCU, American interventions abroad are driven by altruism and remain casualty free, even in apocalyptic situations. It is also quite clear that the majority of those the film shows as being in peril are women and children, who require rescuing by heroic males in ways which Susan Faludi asserted had defined American popular culture responses to 9/11 in which 'the most showcased victims bore female faces' (2007: 5). These images were deliberately structured to feature women adopting more traditional roles which ignored the female first responders, fire-fighters and police officers in an act she described as a concerted attempt to restore 'the illusion of a mythic America where women needed men's protection and men succeeded in providing it' which 'belongs to a longstanding American pattern of response to threat, a response that we've been perfecting since our original wilderness experience' (2007: 151, 13). Arguably we have seen the MCU since *Iron Man* perpetuate many of these same stereotypes and *Age of Ultron* offers one of its most vivid examples.

The Avengers keep telling each other about how dangerous what they are doing is, and even Ultron tells them, 'You can't save them all!', but they do ... until it is revealed in *Captain America: Civil War* that *actually* they did not. As the situation becomes insurmountable, Black Widow informs Cap that it is impossible for them to save all the civilians, just as Rhodes had once informed Stark in *Iron Man 3*, but it is an idea he refuses to acknowledge regardless of the seemingly futile nature of their predicament. Cap's intransigence might be seen here as pronounced as Tony Stark's, and Black Widow's assertion that 'there's no math here' is a plea for pragmatism which goes ignored in favour of his refusal to accept any scenario that does not involve a complete win. When it becomes apparent the only thing they can do is blow up the huge rock the city is on in the sky which would kill *all* those on it including the superheroes, but save the *whole* world, Cap refuses. Fortunately, Nick Fury arrives with a giant helicarrier and loads the Sokovian civilians on it one by one, saving them all, meaning that Cap is not forced to deal with the consequences of his obstinacy. Fury's heroic entrance leads Quicksilver to ask, 'This is S.H.I.E.L.D.?' to which Cap replies, 'This is what

Fig. 23: The majority of those who need to be rescued throughout the MCU are women and children. Here in *Avengers: Age of Ultron*, civilians on the streets of Sokovia wait to be saved by noble and altruistic American superheroes

S.H.I.E.L.D. is *supposed to be'*, marking the transition that the Sokovian twins have made from despising Tony Stark (and by extension America) to joining the Avengers, conveniently forgetting that it was Stark who created Ultron, just as the film has already forgotten that Scarlett Witch had directly caused the Hulk to rampage in Johannesburg, which will not be mentioned again in *Age of Ultron*, nor will it be in *Captain America: Civil War*. Scarlett Witch, unlike Stark, at least expresses remorse at her actions, telling Hawkeye *'We* did this'. It is revealing that, out of all the superheroes, it is Scarlett Witch who suffers some sort of psychological breakdown during the Battle of Sokovia, starting a process of her infantilisation which will become even more conspicuous in *Captain America: Civil War*, yet another example of how female characters, even when they possess great powers, prove unable to cope with them and are both burdened and marginalised. When she retreats to a small house during the battle, unable to continue the fight, she reveals her frailties to Hawkeye (the man who has recently been revealed as a father) and it is hard to imagine his remark, 'I can't do my job *and* babysit' being directed to her brother Quicksilver, who is not coded as a child even though he is her twin *and* despite the fact Scarlett Witch is arguably *the most powerful* of all the superheroes. In *Civil War* this process continues when Steve Rogers and Tony Stark argue over what is best for her, leading to her complaining to the latter: 'You locked me in my room!'

What are we to make of the absolute refusal to portray or acknowledge the deaths or even injuries of civilians across the first two Phases of the MCU? It is not as if the superhero genre is unable to do this: witness the deaths of the innocent Belgian civilians in Veld in *Wonder Woman*, killed by poison gas; or the hospitable Munson family who invite Wolverine, Professor X and Laura (X-23) into their farmhouse in *Logan*, only to be all killed; or the many innocents attending the American football game in *The Dark Knight Rises* who are killed when Bane detonates a bomb under Gotham City Stadium. But *Age of Ultron*, like all MCU films before it, refuses to harm civilians onscreen. Might this be seen as a literalisation of what has been described as the 'Zero Factor' (sometimes referred to as a 'no body bags policy')? The idea that US military interventions abroad must result in as close to zero American casualties as possible, with indigenous civilians coming a distant second, something which has characterised America's pursuit of asymmetrical warfare in the twenty-first century (see Rogers 2000). It also might be considered as a manifestation of the 'victory culture' described by Tom Engelhardt in his volume *The End of Victory Culture: Cold War America and the Disillusioning of a Nation* (1997) which had defined America's participation in World War II but had been challenged by the vagaries of the Cold War, in particular the moral uncertainties of the conflicts in Vietnam and Southeast Asia. Engelhart was one of many to see its return in the aftermath of 9/11 and the early years of the 'War on Terror', as once again large portions of America felt convinced in their moral superiority and the righteousness of their cause. Yet, as Engelhardt observes, this certitude was unable to be sustained as the reality of the conflict became apparent:

> The question of whether a revivified war story could reanchor victory culture in American consciousness seems settled, not because its elements, which run deep in our history, have ceased to exist, but because it has proved impossible to force out of consciousness the quarter-century of that story's dissolution. Its boundaried and triumphant 'innocence' cannot be 'recalled' in the same way that the knowledge of the making of atomic weapons cannot be forgotten. (2007: 300–1)

One might argue that this moral certainty lost in the real world was able to be maintained in many American popular films in this era, films which view the world from an exclusively American perspective and refuse to consider the lives of others in their narratives. The MCU reaffirms and reconsolidates the sancity of the US mission abroad in its committed portrayal of both this 'Zero Factor', 'Victory Culture' and in the representation of its heroes' virtuous and altruistic extrajudicial conflicts around the globe which always result in total victory. In *Age of Ultron*, when it appears that an innocent life will be lost, the film quickly assures us that no such thing will happen, as in when Cap is shown to make a rare mistake and accidentally drops a car with an attractive young female Sokovian in it, only for Thor to catch it from below as a moment of fallibility and vulnerability is disavowed. Instead of throwing debris at the Avengers, as they had done at the Iron Legion at the start of the film, the Sokovians now welcome them, grateful for their heroic intervention, but perhaps unaware it was Tony Stark who has directly caused this chaos and *everything* they endure.

Age of Ultron perpetuates some of the most enduring myths of American heroes and American interventions around the globe as much of the MCU has done since 2008. Ultron earlier remarked that the Avengers were 'tangled in strings' and they are, but in a very different way to how the malevolent robot had suggested. The Avengers embody a vision of how America has come to see itself in a similar way to how Ty Solomon, in *The Politics of Subjectivity in American Foreign Policy Discourses*, asserted that 'the meaning of "America" and the "United States" is a tangle of meanings that brings together the various significations and investments in "democracy," the "free world," "leading a free-world," "freedom," "defender," and so on … [and it is] those strings of signifiers that construct the American subject' (2015: 151). The very American superheroes of the MCU are strictly defined and contained by the ideology and beliefs of the culture which created them. It is this which determines that the film rewards Cap for his intransigence, just as categorically as it endorses Stark's irresponsible individualism, or that it portrays women, even if they are superheroes, as overly emotional and require saving (both physically and emotionally) by their male counterparts. *Age of Ultron* shows that American power is as beneficent as it is virtuous, and that violence is redemptive *and* righteous. In this way, the film has demonstrated how it and the MCU films at large function as modern-day incarnations of mythic narratives which resolve complicated problems for their audiences just as the western genre was often able to before it. As we have seen, *Age of Ultron* offers a deliberate reference to *The Searchers*, but Whedon's film cannot attempt even the partial criticisms of American mythology that Ford's film did in 1956, where it's hero, John Wayne's Ethan Edwards, is certainly mythologised but also challenged in the portrayal of his relentless and obsessive drive to find his kidnapped niece Debbie. Douglas Pye contended that *The Searchers* 'detaches us from Ethan so that we are required to perceive the neurotic and irrational nature of his attitudes and actions' (1996: 229), and, one might ask, are there any such moments in *Age of Ultron* or other films in the MCU? A point at which we might be asked to doubt the sanctity of the superheroes and their mission? In Whedon's film, might this be Stark's creation of Ultron? Or Cap's refusal to consider a more pragmatic plan during the apocalyptic Battle of Sokovia? But, of course, both moments of ethical ambiguity are disavowed by later events which prove its heroes were right after all in a way that *all* similar moments are abrogated throughout the MCU.

Karen Randell is quite correct to write that *Age of Ultron* does not reward the Avengers with a 'collective victory moment' (2016: 138) within its diegesis, but it provides them, and audiences, with something even more substantial in its final images, a two-minute-long credit sequence comprised of twenty-seven separate shots of a sculpture of the Avengers immortalised and memorialised in marble, showing their victory over Ultron, reminiscent of the statue of the first responder heroes of the Battle of New York near the foot of the Avengers Tower and a callback to that extreme slow motion shot in Sokovia at the start of the film. However, the Avengers statue is, quite fittingly, given their transcendence to mythological status, very much in the Graeco-Roman Neoclassical mode and one designed to look, as visual effects creative director Jeremy Lasky stated, like 'something larger than life that you might see in a European plaza' (qtd. in Failes 2015). More specifically, Laskey and his team suggested that they 'were inspired by the 9/11 imagery of first responders and the Iwo Jima sculpture' (see experience-perception.com), amalgamating 11 September 2001 *and* World War II into a single image, something the Marvel Cinematic Universe has done with its triumphalist narratives since 2008, which have never failed to consolidate and reify very American views of the world in each and every instalment.[4]

Fig. 24: The consecration of the mythic status of the Avengers in the form of a marble statue 'inspired by the 9/11 imagery of first responders and the Iwo Jima sculpture' after the Battle of Sokovia in *Avengers: Age of Ultron*

Notes

1   Strucker is also mentioned in *Marvel's Agents of S.H.I.E.L.D.* in Season Two episodes like 'The Writing on the Wall' (2.07), 'Aftershocks' (2.11) and 'The Frenemy of My Enemy' (2.18).

2   The character of Quicksilver appeared simultaneously in two superhero franchises: here played by Aaron Taylor-Johnson and in *X-Men Days of Future Past* (2014) and *X-Men: Apocalypse* (2016) by Evan Peters as an American teen who discovers Magneto is his father.

3   It might be considered significant that the door does not close on Cap as it does on John Wayne's Ethan, as Cap's journey is not yet over. In *Captain America: Civil War* he develops a romantic relationship with Sharon Carter (Emily VanCamp), Peggy's niece.

4   Igor Holmogorov, writing in the Russian daily newspaper *Izvestia*, described the film as an 'American national epic. The Greeks had the Iliad, the French have The Song of Roland, we [Russia] have the epics, the Americans have Marvel comics about the superhero team, led by Captain America, which embodies the ideal American values. Despite the seeming European non-seriousness of the genre, we have the quintessence of American national self-consciousness... The Americans created a really strong national myth in which the global domination of the US is justified by the fact that American superheroes protect the world from monstrous global threats' (2015).

THE MARVEL CINEMATIC
UNIVERSE ON TELEVISION

CHAPTER NINE

'What does S.H.I.E.L.D. stand for?': The MCU on the Small Screen in *Marvel's Agents of S.H.I.E.L.D.* and *Marvel's Agent Carter*

The principle S.H.I.E.L.D. was founded upon was pure… Protection. One word. Sometimes to protect one man against himself, other times to protect the planet against an alien invasion from another universe … but the belief that drives us all is the same, whether it's one man, or all mankind…

– Nick Fury, *Marvel's Agents of S.H.I.E.L.D.* 'The Beginning of the End' (1.22)

I.

After the financial and critical success of the Phase One Marvel Cinematic Universe films and the purchase of Marvel Entertainment by the Walt Disney Company in 2009, Marvel Studios began exploring the possibility of expanding the MCU onto the small screen. With such a diverse cast of characters and a decade's worth of plots to explore already told in the comics, the possibilities seemed to be almost endless. The densely populated Marvel canon would allow a television show to draw from, complement and expand the mythology of the film series which had reached seven releases by the time of the broadcast of the first episode of *Marvel's Agents of S.H.I.E.L.D.* on 24 September 2013. What Marvel and ABC attempted was something that had never been done on such a scale in television history: the creation of a weekly programme which both existed in its own right, but at the same time was closely interwoven with a film franchise, with both properties running concurrently. As Jeph Loeb, then Head of Television for Marvel Studios, suggested, 'We love to tie into the films, and we're creating a sort of living jigsaw puzzle that we can add pieces to as we go' (qtd. in Benjamin 2015: 209).

This 'living jigsaw puzzle' that Loeb described has taken many forms since 2013. Almost every episode of *Marvel's Agents of S.H.I.E.L.D.* features references to the events and characters within the film franchise, as in when agent Grant Ward (Brett Dalton) is said to have scored the 'highest marks since Romanov' on a S.H.I.E.L.D. weapon range in 'Pilot' (1.01), or when the psychologist Andrew Garner (Blair Underwood) is shown to be working at Culver University where Bruce Banner once conducted research and was confronted by General Ross during *The Incredible Hulk* in 'One of Us' (2.13); or Mike Peterson (aka Deathlok) asks 'Did I beat Captain America's time?' in one S.H.I.E.L.D. training challenge in 'The Bridge' (1.10). One of the central narrative elements of the first season, the centipede serum, which is said to be a 'cocktail of the Erskine formula and gamma rays' in 'Pilot' (1.01) but also to contain the Extremis virus from *Iron Man 3*. At other times characters from the films themselves are featured, like Nick Fury in '0-8-4' (1.02) and the Season One finale 'Beginning of the End' (1.22), and Maria Hill, Lady Sif and President Matthew Ellis, who have each appeared multiple times throughout the television series. In one memorable episode at the start of Season Three, 'Laws of Nature' (3.01), President Ellis manages to refer to the dramatic events of *The Avengers*, *Avengers: Age of Ultron*, *Thor: The Dark World* and *Captain America: The Winter Soldier* all in one televised address, as he informs the world, 'I don't need to remind people of the recent catastrophes in New York, London and most recently Sokovia, tragedies that seem to be growing in number and scale and the organisations we had in place to protect us, S.H.I.E.L.D., brought airships raining down in our nation's capital…'. Events in the films are not only referenced but integrated into episodes like 'The Well' (1.08), which was broadcast the week after the cinematic release of *Thor: The Dark World* and dealt with the aftermath of Thor and Malekith's battle in Greenwich. The later episodes of the Season Two were shown to build up to the events of *Age of Ultron* with mentions of Strucker's experiments on humans in 'The Frenemy of My Enemy' (2.18) and Coulson's retrieval of a memory stick in 'The Dirty Half Dozen' (2.19) being key to finding Loki's sceptre which opens *Age of Ultron*.

Yet, as previously mentioned, there is a hierarchy across the MCU with the cinematic branch firmly established as the most important texts and events which happen within them flowing down towards the television shows, web series, video games and graphic novels, but very rarely the other way around.[1] The most obvious example of this is the fact that none of the film's major characters, the Avengers themselves, appear in anything other than news footage, images from the films or photographs outside of the cinematic releases. Several high-profile creative figures in the MCU have praised the television show, but at the same time been slightly dismissive of it, including Joss Whedon himself, who directed the pilot episode, but suggested that it was sometimes stuck with 'left-overs' (qtd. in Fitzpatrick 2016).[2] It is true that the show focuses primarily on 'the peripheral people … the people on the edges of the grand adventures' (Whedon qtd. in Wigler 2013), but *Marvel's Agents of S.H.I.E.L.D.*, *Marvel's Agent Carter* and the Netflix television shows *Daredevil, Jessica Jones, Luke Cage* and *Iron Fist* (explored in chapter ten) are able to forge a distinct identity of their own, at the same time as contributing to what we might refer to as the 'Marvel Cinematic Universe experience' in a range of palpable and compelling ways: whether in their ability to expand the mythology of the MCU with their extended and ex-pansive long form storylines, or in the case of the Netflix versions, exploring more adult-oriented themes. *Marvel's Agents of S.H.I.E.L.D.*, with its twenty-two episodes per season, is able to delve further into the world of the Marvel universe, linking the film series together in a way it would never be able to achieve given the inherent time constraints on the cinematic medium compared to its televi-sion counterpart. It is able to move around the globe on a weekly basis and even venture to other planets, dimensions and realities, it can go backwards and for-wards in time in episodes like 'Purpose in the Machine' (3.02), which dramatises early meetings of the HYDRA society in the nineteenth century, or return to World War II in episodes like 'Shadows' (2.01) which brings back characters like Peggy Carter, 'Dum Dum' Dugan and Jim Morita.[3]

Marvel's Agents of S.H.I.E.L.D. also adopts many of the narrative devices of the film series, with its own televisual version of the stingers or post-credits teas-ers which come after the final act break and before the end credits of the show, the most striking of which is perhaps the surprise Nick Fury cameo in 'Beginning of the End' (1.22), or the reveal of Skye's (also known by then as Quake) vigilante status in 'Ascension' (3.22), or the final episode of Season Four, 'World's End' (4.22), which shows Coulson waking up on a giant space station. With its glossy televisual aesthetic, extensive action scenes and comparatively large budget, *Marvel's Agents of S.H.I.E.L.D.* is certainly an example of what many have now come to refer to as 'Cinematic TV' (see Nelson 2007: 11). The superhero renais-sance, as the two following chapters explore, was not just a cinematic one, but a televisual one too. While during the 1990s superhero-themed TV shows were extremely rare – *Lois and Clark: The New Adventures of Superman* (ABC, 1993–97), being one of the very few to achieve success – the first decades of the new millennium saw a proliferation of them from *Heroes* (NBC, 2006–10), *Smallville* (Various, 2001–11), and *Arrow* (The CW, 2012–), to *The Flash* (The CW, 2014–),

Supergirl (CBS, 2015–), *Gotham* (Fox, 2014–) and many others. Unlike their DC counterparts, which were disconnected from the film versions and not part of the DCEU, *Marvel's Agents of S.H.I.E.L.D.*, *Marvel's Agent Carter* and the likes of *Daredevil*, *Jessica Jones*, *Luke Cage* and *Iron Fist* are an integral part of the expansive MCU project.

II.

As the title of the show suggests, *Marvel's Agents of S.H.I.E.L.D.* is set around the fictional organisation of S.H.I.E.L.D. which initially stood for Supreme Headquarters, International Espionage, Law-Enforcement Division when the agency first appeared in *Strange Tales #135* in August 1965. This original comic book incarnation drew inspiration from the popularity of fictional spy films and television shows in the 1960s, in particular organisations like U.N.C.L.E. in *The Man from U.N.C.L.E.* (NBC, 1964–68) with its antagonists T.H.R.US.H.[4] In the 1990s, the acronym remained but instead stood for Strategic Hazard Intervention Espionage Logistics Directorate, before becoming the much more post-9/11-sounding Strategic Homeland Intervention, Enforcement and Logistics Division, which is used throughout the MCU. Even though it is a fictional organisation it is clearly inspired by real-word agencies like the CIA, the FBI, the NSA and the National Security Council, for both its construction and its worldview. In the di-egetic world of the MCU, S.H.I.E.L.D. emerged from the SSR (Strategic Scientific Reserve) which was formed in 1940s to battle the Nazis and HYDRA, just as the CIA has its roots in the OSS (Office of Strategic Services), which was the US war-time intelligence agency created in 1942.

Marvel's Agents of S.H.I.E.L.D. is produced and very obviously set in the tu-multuous new millennial decades, and the series portrays a variety of threats to both American and global safety which come in many forms: from terrorism, organised violence and vigilantism, to supernatural enemies, enhanced beings and even those from other planets. Despite the often intergalactic nature of these fears, many of them are decidedly of our modern era, an age in which, as Coulson observes in 'Eye Spy' (1.04), 'between Facebook, Instagram and Flickr, people are surveiling themselves'. We are frequently informed that S.H.I.E.L.D. is a secu-rity agency with a global purview, but it is portrayed as a particularly American organisation in terms of the way it exercises its significant power and even the use of the word 'Homeland' in its title is suggestive of its American status. Just as the Avengers are American (or at the very least Americanised), so are the vast majority of S.H.I.E.L.D. agents: America is where its main bases seem to be lo-cated and while it is said to answer to the United Nations, it is President Ellis who is ultimately shown to be the figure the agency turns to most frequently for authorisation. Most importantly, the fears and anxieties which it dramatises mirror, through the prism of the superhero genre, those of the United States in the first decades of the twenty-first century. Thus, the subtitle of this chapter, 'What does S.H.I.E.L.D. stand for?', is a multi-layered one, referring both to the derivation of its acronym and also how the parastatal organisation functions both within and beyond the diegetic frames of the television show's narrative. It is a question which has been explicitly answered by various characters throughout the show's run: in the pilot episode Grant Ward suggested, 'It means we're the line between the world and the much weirder world. We protect people from news they aren't ready to hear. And when we can't do that we keep them safe' (1.01), but for Phil Coulson, who is at the centre of the show and an individual who had progressed from minor player in *Iron Man* to one of the central characters of *The Avengers*, the purpose of S.H.I.E.L.D. is 'to serve when everything else fails, to be humanity's last line of defence, to be the *shield...*' in 'Providence' (1.18).

Coulson, who according to Clark Gregg did not even have a name in the script for *Iron Man* he originally read (see Leane 2016), resonated to such an extent with fans of the Marvel Cinematic Universe that his death in *The Avengers* inspired a widespread demand that he be brought back into the MCU somehow, a movement which went by the name of 'Coulson lives/Fury lies' (see Asher-Perrin 2013). The first season of *Marvel's Agents of S.H.I.E.L.D.* uses Coulson's 'death' as its central narrative mystery and does not reveal how he was able to survive his own 'murder' at the hands of Loki until the final episode, 'Beginning of the End' (1.22), when audiences learn that he was revived using the dangerous drug GH25 made from alien DNA as a part of Project T.A.H.I.T.I. Coulson is understandably greatly traumatised by the process and criticises Fury's use of the unstable drug which 'was created to revive an Avenger in the event of being killed in battle' (Benjamin 2014: 3), to which Fury replies 'Exactly!', indicating the shift that Coulson has made from a small role in the MCU to being considered as an Avenger in his own right. On his return to active service Coulson is charged with putting together a new team of agents to respond to crises all over the globe in the aftermath of *The Avengers* and the wake of the realisation that enhanced individuals and supernatural beings are real. Prior to his appearances in the television show Coulson had received little screen time to explore his character, the sum of which was his love of vintage Captain America cards and the aside in *The Avengers* that revealed he had a girlfriend, the cellist in Portland. In the series, given his central role, Coulson's characterisation is expanded: we learn that he comes from a modest background, was recruited by S.H.I.E.L.D. after college and that he is an only child from Manitowac, Wisconsin, and once worked on classic cars with his father (just like Tony Stark did with his father Howard) who died when he was nine. Instead of the Stark family's red and gold 1932 Ford Flathead Roadster, the Coulsons worked on a cherry-red 1962 Corvette by the name of Lola, which Coulson uses the latest experimental technology on to enable it to fly.

The team that Coulson puts together become the co-protagonists of the show: the British scientists Leo Fitz (Ian De Caestecker) and Jemma Simmons (Elizabeth Henstridge), the hypermasculine field agent Grant Ward and the pilot/deputy commander, Melinda May, aka 'the Cavalry' (Ming-Na Wen). Coulson frequently functioned as the audience surrogate in the films, but given his leadership role and the secrets he has access to in the television series this position is instead given to the final member of the initial team line up, the only one to begin the narrative not as part of S.H.I.E.L.D. and our way into the world, Skye (Chloe Bennett), who has been described as 'the audience's point-of-view character' (Benjamin 2014: 25). Skye 'geeks out' around superheroes just as Coulson did and even admits to *once* being one of those 'sweaty cosplay girls crowding around Stark Tower' (1.01) in 'Pilot'. Skye begins the show as a civilian computer expert and member of the hacktivist group, the Rising Tide, who distrusts S.H.I.E.L.D., but before long comes to realise that they are actually a force for good in the world and becomes an agent herself. David Higgins classifies her as a character who 'quickly sacrifices her commitment to radical social and economic justice as she learns that S.H.I.E.L.D.'s totalitarian interventions are well-meaning and necessary in the face of the omnicrisis posed by alien and superhuman threats' (2015: 55), thereby mirroring the arcs of characters like Black Widow, Scarlett Witch and Quicksilver. If we as an audience are not convinced by the empathetic Skye's transition, the Rising Tide are thoroughly discredited in Season One before being erased from the show entirely after revealing that one of their best hackers, Skye's former boyfriend Miles Lydon, is both untrustworthy and unprincipled. He tells Skye, 'We can't let them get away with it. Manning, Snowden, Aaron Swartz. These are modern-day revolutionaries!' in 'The Girl in the Flower Dress' (1.05). But it is shown that he accepted money for information obtained from his hacking skills which leads to the death of the enhanced individual involved. Miles' perfidy is effectively contrasted with the honesty and integrity of people like Coulson, Fitz and Simmons who risk their lives on a daily basis to save innocents all over the world. By 'Providence' (1.18) Skye is able to tell Coulson, 'You were right all along. Having all this [secret information] out there in the world makes it too dangerous…'. Later, in Season Two, Skye is revealed to be an Inhuman herself and rejects her given name, adopting her birth name Daisy, but is often referred to by her superhero name, Quake, and is described as a 'walking weapon of mass destruction' by the duplicitous Senator Ellen Nadeer in 'Lockup' (4.05). Like the majority of women in the MCU, Skye is impossibly beautiful, as are *all* the other female co-protagonists in the television show, yet they are given much more time for character development and as a result often emerge as far more interesting characters than their female cinematic counterparts.

III.

The pilot episode of *Marvel's Agents of S.H.I.E.L.D.* quickly establishes that the series is set in a post-*The Avengers* world, where the public is now, after the devastation of the Battle of New York, very aware of the existence of superheroes, enhanced individuals, aliens and even gods. It is Skye's voice-over which opens the show and she informs the audience, 'The secret is out. For decades your organisation [S.H.I.E.L.D.] stayed in the shadows, hiding the truth. Now we know they are among us: heroes and monsters. The world is full of wonders.' Agent Maria Hill later confirms this view of the new world: 'Everything's changing. A little while ago people went to bed thinking the craziest thing in the world was a billionaire in a flying metal suit, then aliens invaded New York and were beaten back by, among others, a giant green monster, a costumed hero from the 1940s and a God' (1.01). Just as the Battle of New York was the central event of the cinematic MCU throughout Phase Two, it is pivotal for its televisual branch too and many of the episodes of the first season of *Marvel's Agents of S.H.I.E.L.D.* are linked to it: from the black-market sale of a Chitauri Neural Link found during the battle in 'Pilot' (1.01), to the mysterious powers given to a group of traumatised fire-fighters who were first responders in New York in 'FZZT' (1.06). This early episode is one of many which seek to distinguish Coulson's much more humanistic leadership style from the other authority figures in the MCU, notably the secretive Nick Fury, but later the authoritarian Agent Victoria Hand (Saffron Burrows) and Robert Gonzalez (Edward James Olmos). Coulson refuses to leave one of the fire-fighters alone even though the man is moments away from exploding, telling him, 'We [S.H.I.E.L.D.] were on the ground with you in New York'. It is in this episode that, for the first time, Coulson is able to admit to himself that he too had died during *The Avengers*, something he had until then been unable to process.

The first season came under criticism for its slow pace and failure to deliver on the promise of the initial Whedon-directed pilot. Willa Paskin at *Slate* called it 'too self-serious to be really goofy, and yet too fan-boyish to rescue even one hour of television from mediocrity' (2013) and Eric Goldman at *IGN* declared it 'a fun, light-hearted, but fairly disposable piece of entertainment' (2014). The episode 'End of the Beginning' (1.16), aired in the same week as the cinematic release of *Captain America: The Winter Soldier*, and saw the reveal of HYDRA's infiltration of S.H.I.E.L.D. spill over into *Marvel's Agents of S.H.I.E.L.D.* in an event which Colin Harvey described as having 'mammoth diegetic consequences' throughout the MCU (2015: 87). In the next episode, 'Turn, Turn, Turn' (1.17) Agent Grant Ward, who had been established as one of the focal points of the series and its handsome, rugged hero, is revealed to be a HYDRA agent having been recruited in his teens by the charismatic Garrett (Bill Paxton). As in the films, these events cause many to question S.H.I.E.L.D.'s global role and in the second and third seasons those agents that remain become fugitives, hunted by those who see little distinction between Coulson's S.H.I.E.L.D. and HYDRA. But, as Gail D. Rosen pointed out, we are never asked to question the commitment of the core group of agents and even though they might 'turn from loyal soldiers into outlaws, but they remain intact as a family devoted to protecting the world, even in secret' (2015: 216). Like their superhero counterparts the Avengers, the actions of Coulson's team and 'his' S.H.I.E.L.D. are unequivocally endorsed throughout the series and the show rarely pauses to reflect on the nature of such a powerful and clandestine organisation. In doing so it reifies the role of powerful and secretive government agencies in the real world that we are asked to trust unequivocally, secure in the knowledge that they are acting in our own interests. This is emphasised, as the films have been, by the frequent connections drawn between S.H.I.E.L.D.'s current role and World War II. These become literalised in the emergence of their enemy Daniel Whitehall, aka Werner Reinhardt, formerly a high-ranking Nazi official and HYDRA agent who uses Inhuman DNA to de-age himself, or when we are informed that modern agents had relations who fought in World War II. These include Antoine 'Trip' Triplett whose grandfather was one of the original Howling Commandoes, and Robert Gonzalez, the leader of the 'real S.H.I.E.L.D.', who is shown wielding his father's World War II-issue Colt M1911A1 and using it to kill members of HYDRA as his father had done decades before him.

The fact that S.H.I.E.L.D., despite the pretence of being a global agency, is unambiguously American in its formation, membership and construction is rarely commented on and neither are its frequent global interventions abroad, which are, for the most part, portrayed unproblematically. These journeys show them doing good in their role as international police officer in locations as diverse as Belarus (1.04), Hong Kong (1.05), South Ossetia (1.07), Cuba (1.18), Morocco (2.03), Puerto Rico (2.09), Bahrain (2.17), Colombia (3.11) and Russia (3.13), among others. When they are criticised for their actions, the audience knows that what they have done has always been for the greater good and, as in the film versions, those who tend to criticise them are shown to be compromised themselves. It is portrayed as entirely natural and logical that America would play this role and when, in episode '0-8-4' (1.02), Coulson's team visit Peru to retrieve a mysterious artefact they meet resistance from Camilla Reyes (Leonor Varela), a former associate of Coulson's, who tells him 'You stay in your borders, I'll stay

Figs 25–28: The global exculpatory tour of *Marvel's Agents of S.H.I.E.L.D.* might be regarded as an example of 'virtual terror tourism', featuring American superheroes thanklessly saving the world in places as diverse as Peru (1.02), Cuba (1.18) and Bahrain (2.17). The bottom image reads 'Caucasus Mountains' but the episode is primarily set in the disputed territory of South Ossetia (1.07)

in mine!' it is her who seems unreasonable. Reyes' perhaps understandable reluctance to cooperate with the categorically American S.H.I.E.L.D. is portrayed initially as intransigence and then duplicity, as it is revealed that her government wants to use the deadly alien weapon found on their soil against the rebels who oppose them. *Marvel's Agents of S.H.I.E.L.D.* informs us that it is better to leave these things to an altruistic and beneficent America and Coulson's assertion that 'An 0–8–4 supersedes all national claims' is meant to show that his agency is beyond these petty bureaucratic and nationalistic concerns. He suggests to her that 'borders are disappearing, aliens descended on New York remember?', revealing that the events in New York gave his agency the power to transgress international law in ways which offer parallels to the shifting ideological coordinates of America's global role after 9/11. As it was in the real world, the MCU's own 9/11 becomes 'the basis of a universal moral, ethical, and total-war response; all states must recognise, empathize, and interpret 9/11 as the United States posits' (Astrada 2010: 23). This global reach is emphasised in a number of ways and almost always disavowed or ignored as it is in 'T.R.A.C.K.S.' (1.13) when the Italian law enforcement officer Carlo Rota is shown as displeased with S.H..I.E.L.D.'s interference and tells Coulson, 'You're not asking me at all, Agent Coulson. You're telling me and my team to step aside!', but it is later revealed that he is working for the HYDRA-affiliated Cybertek.

This continues in the very next episode, 'The Asset' (1.03), where one of the antagonists of the first season is introduced, the billionaire inventor and industrialist Ian Quinn (David Conrad). He is shown to have become a naturalised citizen and resident of Malta to escape the clutches of the United States. It is a country, which he adds later, 'Where we are allowed to pursue progress and profit without the strangulation of regulations that are now choking our world'. Quinn is a 'bad' scientist, one of those who pursue technological advances for selfish reasons, the likes of which populate the MCU and are distinguished from the 'good' scientists like Banner and Stark, Fitz and Simmons. When S.H.I.E.L.D. are not allowed to mount an operation in Malta because of international law, or what Skye refers to as 'stupid rules', *they do so anyway*. Quinn questions Skye's motivations for joining S.H.I.E.L.D. given her hacktivist background: 'Don't you get it? SHIELD's against everything you stand for. They're Big Brother!' To which she answers, with a familiar image of how America sees itself: 'Maybe, but they're the nice big brother who stands up for his helpless little brother when he's getting beat up.' While Skye makes the transition to trusting S.H.I.E.L.D., Coulson's arc takes him, to a certain extent, the other way, from explicit faith in everything that the organisation represents to (selectively) questioning it. In 'The Hub' (1.07) he tells Skye how important it is to 'trust the system' but by the time of 'The Magical Place' (1.11) he acknowledges that, 'We need to root out all the secrets' and by 'Yes Men' (1.15) is able to suggest, 'To hell with any protocols or any code I used to be bound by!' It is important to acknowledge that Coulson *always* goes against protocol whenever he needs to and is *always* shown as being correct to do so, because of the positive results he is able to achieve, as in when he defies S.H.I.E.L.D. bosses in 'FZZT' (1.06) to save Gemma's life by putting the rest of the team in great danger, or in 'The Hub' (1.07) when he rescues Ward and Fitz from a suicide mission. He was not able to do this in the films as this maverick role was occupied by Tony Stark, but in the television series when *he* is the heroic lead, it is vital that he question authority as this is *simply what American heroes do*. The most interesting and ethically suspect example of this is in 'T.A.H.I.T.I.' (1.14) after Skye has been shot and left for dead by Quinn. Seemingly, the only way to save her is to get the same GH25 drug which revived him from a secret facility where it may or may not be kept and which may or may not work on her. The facility is protected by two S.H.I.E.L.D. guards who refuse to provide Coulson and his team with access, suspecting subterfuge. When they are unable to inform the guards of the correct password, Coulson and his team break in and *kill both* in order to *perhaps* find the material to save Skye. It is an action which is never questioned or mentioned again, and one which is endorsed when Skye is indeed cured by the drug. This pattern of S.H.I.E.L.D.'s extrajudicial intervention around the globe carries on through all of the seasons and has been persuasively connected to the post-9/11 environment by Samira Nadkarni who argues: 'The viewer is assured that eventually these [the weapons S.H.I.E.L.D. uses after New York] will no longer be required, and this echoes the rhetoric of American foreign policy with regard to wars waged after 9/11 regarding the withdrawal of troops after the purported end of terrorism' (2015: 2). This is how the MCU views the world: with the United States as a reluctant operator in global events, but one that is necessary and entirely moral in its actions, which I have elsewhere characterised as the 'necessary intervention' narrative paradigm (see McSweeney 2014: 87–97), in which films and television shows present a firmly Western-centric approach to complex geopolitical affairs. S.H.I.E.L.D.'s role and what it is representative of evoke what Andrew Bacevich suggests is the ultimate American objective for the twenty-first century: 'the creation of an open and integrated international order based on the principles of democratic capitalism, with the United States as the ultimate guarantor of order and enforcer of norms' (2002: 3).[5]

IV.

This very American view of the world is portrayed just as emphatically in *Marvel's Agent Carter*, the short-lived ABC series revolving around the character played by Hayley Atwell originally in *Captain America: The First Avenger*, who had, by the end of Phase Two featured in four films and episodes of *Marvel's Agents of S.H.I.E.L.D.* Even though it only ran for eighteen episodes, *Marvel's Agent Carter* remains an important addition to the MCU, being the first MCU project to have a female lead with her name in the title. Shortly after the release of the 'One Shot' called *Agent Carter* (2013) a full series was ordered by ABC which was first broadcast in the mid-season break in Season Two of *Marvel's Agents of S.H.I.E.L.D.* Peggy Carter's entrance to the MCU had been a memorable one back in *The First Avenger* when she punched the sexist recruit Gilmore Hodge in the face, knocking him to the floor. Hodge had asked her, 'Are we dancing? Cause I got a few moves I *know* you'd like', and later Peggy had informed Steve Rogers, 'I know what that's like, to have every door shut in your face'. The television series takes these two moments as the starting point for its narrative which explores Peggy's life in the male-dominated post-war world, where things are shown to have changed quite considerably for her and many millions of American women. Despite having proved herself as a formidable and resourceful operational agent during World War II she finds herself relegated to menial tasks like answering the phones and preparing lunch orders for her far less able male colleagues. While few women experienced the war like the fictional Peggy Carter, many did experience a similar change in status and opportunities afforded to them in the workplace. Peggy's flatmate, Colleen, talks of ten girls getting the sack in her factory and being replaced by returning G.I.s. World War II resulted in more than two million women in the workplace and 400,000 in the services which 'prompted popular consideration of gender equality, compelled unionists and employers to confront their commitments to gender hierarchy, and offered at least some working women the novel experience of equality' (Gabin 1995: 108). Not only is Peggy relegated to the duties of a secretary, but the men belittle her war-time achievements. Her well-meaning but chauvinist boss Chief Dooley says, 'Being Captain America's liaison brought you into contact with all sorts of people, *but the war's over*', and another male colleague suggests, 'I bet Carter *knew* a lot of guys during the war'. Peggy is understandably frustrated and explains: 'During the war I had a sense of purpose, responsibility, but now I connect the calls and never get a chance to make them.' Her colleague, Jack Thompson, explains that it is 'the natural order of the universe. You're a woman. No man will ever consider you an equal. It's sad but that doesn't make it any less true.' It takes Peggy the whole of the first season to convince those around her of her abilities in a way that few real women of the era had the opportunity to do.

Like many characters within the MCU, those in *Marvel's Agent Carter* are shown to be traumatised by their past experiences, in this case through World War II: Peggy is suffering from grief over the loss of Steve Rogers, Daniel DeSousa lost his leg and struggles to be recognised beyond his disability, Chief Dooley

Fig. 29: Peggy Carter (Hayley Atwell) from *Marvel's Agent Carter* dramatises her attempt to come to terms with life after World War II in late 1940s New York and Los Angeles

returned from service only to find that his wife had an affair and his commitment to his job has led to them becoming estranged, and Jack Thompson is feted as a war hero after having won the Navy Cross for bravery at Okinawa, but we later learn it is an honour he did not deserve. When Peggy saves Jack's life, she learns of his secret, but she does not judge him, even when at the end of the season he takes credit for the hard work she did in solving their most difficult case. It is these elements which make Peggy Carter one of the most human of 'superheroes' throughout the MCU, not just because she does not possess any powers, but because of the way her empathy and vulnerability is often shown to be her greatest strength, a fact that makes her a vivid protagonist. One of the writers of the series, Tara Butters, suggested that 'her superpower is the fact that other people underestimate her. And she often uses that to her advantage, because she doesn't have superstrength' (qtd. in Abrams 2015). *Agent Carter* is a rare entrant into the MCU which raises and addresses this issue explicitly within the context of its narrative, although its extended criticisms of post-war patriarchy are framed from the comforting perspective of being set in the distant past, allowing the writers to feel secure in their understanding of how very different things supposedly are now, refusing to acknowledge the precarious nature of the representations of women in the twenty-first-century MCU. So when Carter says to her chauvinist male colleagues, 'You think you know me. But I've never been more than what each of you has created. To you, I'm a stray kitten, left on your doorstep to be protected. The secretary turned damsel in distress. The girl on the pedestal, transformed into some daft whore' in 'Snafu' (1.07), the sentiments she articulates could very well be applied to all the MCU women, whether they have powers (Scarlett Witch) or do not (Pepper Potts, Jane Foster and Betty Ross).

The series draws almost as heavily on the MCU films as *Marvel's Agents of S.H.I.E.L.D.* and it is the figure of Captain America, as one might expect, who is a looming presence over Peggy's experiences. The pilot episode even begins with shots taken directly from the end of *Captain America: The First Avenger* and he is mentioned frequently not just by Peggy but other characters, with a radio show called 'The Captain America Adventure Programme' playing an exaggerated version of some of his adventures. Peggy shows her disdain for the serial, which features whimpering damsels in distress for Cap to save and in one artful scene she beats up a henchman while listening to one such damsel being saved on the radio show. Peggy reunites the Howling Commandoes in a mission in Russia which allows the show to explore the Red Room orphanage in more detail than it ever was in the film series and even gives the show a Soviet assassin called Dottie whose abilities parallel Peggy's own. Christopher Markus attempted to suggest that there was some sort of parity between Dottie and Peggy, stating that 'Peggy should consider that it wouldn't take her all the make to make *her* Dottie' (qtd. in Rodriguez 2015: 60). But the show, as its cinematic equivalent has always done, could never recognise these connections in anything other than a superficial fashion. It also gives a central role to a young Howard Stark (Dominic Cooper) and his butler Edwin Jarvis (who will inspire Tony Stark to create the AI which will be known as J.A.R.V.I.S.) and the overarching plot of the first season concerns itself with accusations directed at Howard Stark that he sold weapons technology to enemies of the United States, i.e. the Soviet Union. In scenes reminiscent of *Iron Man 2* where Tony Stark is brought before a similar committee, Howard is asked: 'Did you knowingly sell military grade technology to enemies of the United States?' When it looks like he will be found guilty, even though he is not, he goes on the run and only Peggy is able to help him clear his name. Stark is shown to have his flaws (like his son), but he is firmly identified as a patriotic capitalist and entrepreneur the likes of which have been said to have 'built America'.

Despite being well reviewed, the show was cancelled due to dwindling audience figures at the end of its second season: after having premiered with 6.91 million viewers for the pilot episode 'Now is Not the End' (1.01) on 6 January 2015, the ironically titled second season finale 'Hollywood Ending' (2.10) had a series low of 2.35 million, which was felt too small by ABC to justify the commission of a third season. Season Two had relocated to Los Angeles in 1947, but failed to develop the characters as well as it might have done. Having seemingly solved Peggy's second-class status by the end of the first season, the second flirts with McCarthyism, the Blacklist and racism, but only ever in a very superficial form.

Peggy has a chaste relationship with Jason Wilkes, an African-American scientist, but the show does little by way of exploring post-war racism than have him called 'boy' in a store in the episode 'Better Angels' (2.03) and have Stark observe that he was 'already a target because of the colour of his skin'. Like how it treated sexism, *Agent Carter* is able to frame post-war racism through the comforting prism of its present to audiences who are apparently secure in the knowledge that no such disparity exists in the modern world – conveniently ignoring the fact that in Phases One and Two black superheroes and even black characters were few and far between.

Notes

1 A rare example of this is the explanation of the mysterious appearance of a helicarrier at the climax of *Age of Ultron* which, for those who have not seen the television show, is just a fortuitous deus ex machina. But for those who have, it is explained how and why Fury came to have a helicarrier when they all seemed to have been destroyed at the end of *Captain America: The Winter Soldier*.

2 This was satirised in the webseries produced by *Screen Junkies* called *Interns of F.I.E.L.D* (2016–) which followed the interns of a secret agency which stood for Field; Intervention; Espionage; and Logistics Department. In 'Villians' (1.01) after the superhero named Staff Sergeant America has defeated his nemesis the Black Skull the interns are told, 'The cool part is over with. So, clean up all this crap...' in a series which very obviously makes fun of the often peripheral nature of the characters of *Marvel's Agents of S.H.I.E.L.D.*

3 It also has the webseries *Marvel's Agents of S.H.I.E.L.D. Slingshot* (2016) which featured S.H.I.E.L.D. Agent Elena 'Yo Yo' Rodriguez (Natalia Cordova-Buckley) set between Season Three and Season Four in six episodes of between three and six minutes long and all made available online on 13 December 2016. A slightly stranger title was *Marvel's Agents of S.H.I.E.L.D.: Double Agent* (2015) which featured someone employed in the 'real world' to retrieve secrets about upcoming episodes of the show with the cast playing versions of their real selves.

4 Stan Lee confirmed this in interviews (see Goldman 2014). These acronyms stand for, in order, United Network Command for Law and Enforcement; Technological Hierarchy for the Removal of Undesirables and the Subjugation of Humanity.

5 One of the best examples of this is S.H.I.E.L.D.'s incursion to Bahrain portrayed in 'Melinda' (2.17) where we learn how Melinda May was given the nickname 'The Cavalry'. Coulson initially refuses to allow May to enter a building where many agents have been kidnapped and taken hostage by the Inhuman Eva Belyakov, telling her 'S.H.I.E.L.D. is not authorised for any action'. However, when it is clear that there is no hope for those inside he tells her 'Go!' and May rescues the men, but is forced to

kill Eva and her daughter Katya. Such is the importance of this moment for the series that the show returns to it as the basis of the alternate reality narrative in Season Four. In this alternate reality May does not kill Katya and this leads directly to the Cambridge Incident where she is said to have murdered two hundred and seventy-nine innocents, a tragedy which sparks the resurgence of HYDRA in that reality.

CHAPTER TEN

The Necessary Vigilantism of the Defenders: *Daredevil, Jessica Jones, Luke Cage* and *Iron Fist*

> People needed someone that didn't require a warrant or a shield to get things done. Call it a vigilante or a superhero, call it what you will, but like it or not I finally accepted that that someone had to be me...
>
> – Luke Cage, in *Luke Cage*, 'You Know My Steez' (1.13)

Both *Marvel's Agents of S.H.I.E.L.D.* and *Marvel's Agent Carter* were produced and exhibited by terrestrial television companies and aside from their unique intertextual links between the ongoing films of the MCU, they are, in some ways, not too different from how episodic television had been produced and broadcast since the second half of the twentieth century. The four television shows discussed in this chapter – *Daredevil, Jessica Jones, Luke Cage* and *Iron Fist* – depart from this formula in a variety of significant ways due to being financed, exhibited and distributed by the media-streaming-service-turned-television-and-film production-company, Netflix. In the case of *Daredevil*, the first full season of thirteen episodes was placed online for those with a Netflix account to access all at the same time on 10 April 2015, as was *Jessica Jones* on 20 November 2015, *Luke Cage* on 30 September 2016 and *Iron Fist* on 17 March 2017. The impact of Netflix on contemporary television audiences and production practices is hard to overestimate. Veronique Dupont has suggested that the company 'has revolutionized the US television industry several times over [and] totally revamped the relationship Americans have with both TV shows and films' (2014). Dupont and many others have argued that this process has fundamentally changed not only the way television programmes are watched, but even how they are made. This places the four Netflix/Marvel collaborations alongside other high profile and award-winning productions like *House of Cards* (Netflix, 2013–), *Orange is the New Black* (Netflix, 2013–) and *Transparent* (Amazon Studios, 2014–) and in the middle of what has been described both as a 'binge watch' (Graves 2015: 227) or 'on-demand' culture by Chuck Tyron in *On-Demand Culture: Digital Delivery and the Future of Movies* (2013). Joe Quesada, then Chief Creative Officer of Marvel Entertainment, suggested that 'the Netflix model offers us the advantage of being able to construct the show in a manner that is very different than a weekly network TV show'. The advantages he saw were that 'we can sit there and look at 13 episodes and plan it out as a very large movie. It makes seeing the bigger picture a little bit easier' (qtd. in Dyce 2014).

Quesada's assertion is that the 'Netflix process', as opposed to more traditional television production, impacts on both *what* is able to be shown and *how* it is shown. As a result of this, the four television texts discussed in this chapter use the changing format allowed by Netflix to expand the parameters of the Marvel Cinematic Universe, in particular using the comparative freedoms afforded to explore more mature and complicated story arcs than would be possible in the films and also in the Marvel network television shows. Thus, *Daredevil* is by far the most explicitly violent entrant in the entirety of the MCU, featuring storylines which focus on drug-trafficking and prostitution and includes scenes of graphic beatings, beheadings and immolations; and the first season of *Jessica Jones* centres around a superhero-inflected domestic abuse drama with explicit mentions of rape and a sex scene between two superheroes, yet they are set in the same world of the family-friendly adventures embarked on by Tony Stark, Steve Rogers and even Rocket Raccoon and Groot. This sense of freedom was commented on by the showrunner of the first season of *Daredevil*, Drew Goddard:

> It felt that we'd have more freedom to make it on the small screen and make it more adult. Look, if we took the Netflix [show] and put it in theaters, it's rated R. And they're not doing R-rated movies. And we also really got to explore the character. I feel like Netflix was the best possible home for that, otherwise you'd end up with a watered-down version. (Qtd. in Singer 2015)

Like many of the Marvel films in Phase Two and beyond, the four Netflix television shows offer variations on the superhero genre by adopting distinctly hybridised narratives. So *Daredevil* is about a costumed hero cleaning up the streets of Hell's Kitchen at night, but at the same time it is also about his alter ego, Matt Murdock (Charlie Cox), a blind lawyer who tries to do the same thing by legal means during the day; Danny Rand (Finn Jones) aka the Iron Fist, is the billionaire heir to the Rand fortune, but also one of the world's most gifted martial artists; Luke Cage (Mike Colter) has superhuman strength and virtually impenetrable skin, the result of unethical prison experiments conducted on him after being convicted of a crime he did not commit, but he is also at the centre of a gritty crime drama with storylines seemingly ripped from very contemporary headlines which feature references to the likes of Trayvon Martin, Jordan Davies, Eric Garner and the Black Lives Matter movement. Luke, a hoodie-wearing African-American, who is framed and persecuted after footage of him seemingly attacking a police officer goes viral, resonated both inside and outside of the MCU on its release in 2016. As one character remarks in the episode entitled 'You Know My Steez' (1.13): 'Most of these guys [superheroes] wear spandex, who would have thought a black man in a hoodie would be a hero?' Luke Cage's roots in Blaxploitation films of the 1970s make for a very distinctive new millennial superhero, especially given the MCU's reluctance to centralise the experiences of African-American heroes. As Roz Kaveney has articulated, 'Luke is not just any African-American character; he was one of the more durable products of Marvel's attempt in the 1970s to open out the traditionally whitebread superhero. He was, specifically, Marvel's take on the trash-talking, no compromises hero of the Blaxploitation films' (2007: 82).

This is not to suggest that the Netflix shows do not perpetuate the dominant ideological values we have already observed, but rather they are able to offer some challenges to these paradigms much more frequently than the cinematic branch of the MCU. This complexity primarily (although not always) emerges in the characterisations of their protagonists. *Jessica Jones* follows the adventures of its eponymous super-powered heroine, who is also a private detective, in a New York-set narrative heavily influenced by the moral ambiguity and visual aesthetic of film noir, a duality which was acknowledged in the series winning a Peabody Award which described the show as, 'one part superhero saga, one part neo-noir program [which] asks unpopular questions about power and consent, while constructing vivid and compelling characters' (qtd. in Anon. 2015). As Paul Schrader famously asserted, film noir is not 'defined, as are the western and gangster genres, by conventions of setting and conflict, but rather by the subtler qualities of tone and mood' (1972: 8). One might argue that 'tone and mood' are as important to *Jessica Jones* as narrative and plot, and that it is because of this that Jessica Jones emerges, alongside Peggy Carter, as one of the most human of the superheroes in all of the MCU. She is truculent, manipulative, traumatised and memorably described by Luke Cage, who makes his first appearance in

Figs. 30–33: The evocative opening credits of the four Netflix Marvel series make their genre influences very clear: the legal/crime drama of *Daredevil*, the film noir stylings of *Jessica Jones,* the Blaxploitation roots of *Luke Cage,* and the martial arts of *Iron Fist*

Jessica Jones before having his own show later, as a 'hard drinking, short-fused mess of a woman' in 'AKA You're a Winner' (1.06). Issues of accountability and culpability which the films had been reluctant to engage with in Phases One and Two are placed at the foreground of *Jessica Jones* as she is often unable to help many of those around her and her actions sometimes result in the deaths of innocents. In the pilot episode, 'AKA Ladies Night' (1.01), she proves powerless to save the parents of Hope Schlottman (Erin Moriarty) from being murdered and later watches as Hope commits suicide in front of her in 'AKA 1,000 Cuts' (1.10), providing rare examples of Stephen Faller's 'false dichotomy choice' in which the superhero is not able to save all parties and redeem theirself in the process. In the Iron Man trilogy and his two appearances in *The Avengers* and *Avengers: Age of Ultron*, Tony Stark is shown onscreen saving *every single person* he is asked to (perhaps with the exception of Pepper Potts who refuses to take his hand in *Iron Man 3*, but who does not die) and the only person Steve Rogers is unable to save in *The First Avenger, The Winter Soldier, Civil War* and his two appearances in *The Avengers* and *Avengers: Age of Ultron*, is Bucky Barnes (who later returns), and even this is not entirely his fault. The comic book version of Jessica Jones was originally created for the more adult-oriented Max Marvel comic line, which meant she was 'at liberty to be foul-mouthed and drunken, and to sleep around' (Kaveney 2007: 68). Indeed, as something of a statement of intent, the first line in the first edition of her comic is 'Fuck!' in *Alias #1* November 2001. In this respect, Jessica is certainly a noteworthy addition to the female characters in the MCU, which we have seen as being very limited in terms of the complexity of their characterisation: her abilities are not at all connected to her gender (see Black Widow, Scarlett Witch, Lorelei), she does not wear sexually provocative clothing (Black Widow, Lady Sif), she is not infantilised (Scarlett Witch, Jane Foster), she is not pushed to the margins of the narrative (Gamora, Hope Van Dyne), nor is her fighting style sexualised (Black Widow), and furthermore she does not need a man to save her (Pepper Potts, Betty Ross, Gamora, Scarlet Witch), nor one to define her (Jane Foster). She *is* flawed and vulnerable, but these traits make her more human and a richer character as a result. Whether it is entirely true that *Jessica Jones* 'is a rare show that can truly be said to have a female gaze' (Seitz 2015) is a matter for audiences to decide, but her rejection of both a traditional superhero costume and, for much of Season One, even the mantle of being a superhero, marks her as not just a progressive female superhero, but one of Marvel's most complex characters regardless of her gender.

This complexity also frequently appears in the characterisations of the antagonists of the Netflix shows who often emerge as just as interesting as the superheroes who give their name to the programmes themselves. Unlike the one-dimensional histrionics of the likes of the Red Skull, Darren Cross or Malekith,

Jessica Jones is pitted against the charismatic Kilgrave (David Tennant) who possesses the power to physically compel people to do exactly what he wants merely by telling them to do it. This might take the form of something simple like insisting everyone in a crowded restaurant be silent, but more often in sadistic ways when he forces one victim to give up two kidneys for him after he is injured, or tells the innocent Ruben to cut his own throat. Much of Jessica's psychological trauma and her pronounced feelings of guilt derives from the fact that, before the start of Season One, she was once Kilgrave's victim and he had ordered her to be his sexual partner and then criminal accomplice. While Kilgrave is gleefully malevolent, he is decidedly human and the show encourages audiences to both *despise* and at times *understand* him in ways that the film series has found difficult outside of the characterisations of the beguiling Loki and the empathetic Winter Soldier. *Daredevil* has an even more interesting antagonist in the entrepreneur and gang boss Wilson Fiske (Vincent D'Onfrio), who is not a megalomaniacal pantomime villain, but rather a businessman with extensive resources and sociopathic tendencies. Much of Fiske's behaviour is monstrous, but he is also somehow sympathetic, and flashbacks to his childhood depict abuse by his father, who, the series later reveals, he murdered in order to save his mother. The antagonists in Season One of *Luke Cage* are also striking: the criminal cousins, gangster Cornell 'Cottonmouth' Stokes (Mahershala Ali) and the more superficially legitimate, but equally corrupt, politician Mariah Dillard (Alfre Woodward), who are bound together by their shared criminal upbringing. Both are shown in flashback to have wanted to leave the life of crime they were born into, as Cornell dreamed of being a musician and Mariah of pursuing an education, but found it impossible to break away from their grandmother's influence, even after her death. When Mariah kills Cornell in the episode called 'Manifest' (1.07) after he teases her about her childhood abuse at the hands of their uncle, it is one of the most shocking moments across the MCU, primarily because of the time and care invested into their characterisations.[1]

As with *Marvel's Agents of S.H.I.E.L.D.* and *Marvel's Agent Carter*, the Netflix shows also exist very tangibly within the Marvel Cinematic Universe, but events within them also do not impact on the film series. Therefore, in Season One of *Luke Cage* there is a teenager selling bootleg DVDs of the New York 'incident' on the street corner in 'Moment of Truth' (1.01) while telling everyone that they feature 'Tony Stark, the big blonde dude with the hammer, the old dude with the shield, the green monster!' Later in the season the weapons sold by Cornell and Willis Stryker are shown to be made from Chitauri metal and manufactured by Hammer Industries. Flashbacks return to Luke Cage's time in Seagate prison, which we have been told earlier is also where Justin Hammer and Trevor 'the Mandarin' Slattery are serving their sentences. In *Iron Fist*, Danny's apology to a mother whose son may have contracted a terminal illness from the pollutants discharged from a Rand-owned factory is recorded on camera and uploaded to the internet where it is said to have 'more YouTube views than that incredible green guy' in 'Immortal Emerges from the Cave' (1.06). It is perhaps *Daredevil* that is the most immersed in tapestry of the MCU: in small details like the front pages of newspapers which line the walls of journalist Ben Urich's office which read 'Harlem terror: Hulk emerges victorious in destructive uptown battle' referring to *The Incredible Hulk* and 'Buildings levelled hundreds killed in midtown battles' referring to the events of *The Avengers* in 'In the Blood' (1.04) or when characters ask how Daredevil is able to overcome so many henchmen: 'If he had an iron suit or a magic hammer maybe that would explain why you keep getting your asses handed to you!' In one of its most subtle allusions *Daredevil* informs audiences that Matt Murdock once lived in St. Agnes Orphanage as a child after the murder of his father, the same place Skye was said to be raised in *Marvel's Agents of S.H.I.E.L.D.*[2]

Aside from their connections to the broader MCU, the four Netflix shows are even more closely bonded to each other: from things like the radio show 'Trish Talk' starring Jessica Jones' friend Trish Walker (Rachel Taylor) being featured in both *Jessica Jones* and *Luke Cage*, and the lawyer Jeri Hogarth featuring in *Jessica Jones*, *Daredevil* and *Iron Fist*. The nurse Claire Temple (Rosario Dawson) is the only character to appear in all four separate series: in *Daredevil* she finds Matt Murdock seriously injured in a dumpster and rescues him; later she saves a dying Luke Cage in *Jessica Jones*; and in *Luke Cage* she leaves her job and begins to help the eponymous superhero in his mission to clean up the streets of Harlem, before embarking on a tentative relationship with him which is interrupted by his arrest and incarceration at the end of the season. In *Iron Fist* she befriends Danny Rand and Colleen Wing (Jessica Henwick) in their battle to reclaim the Rand name from first the deceitful Wendell family and then the villainous crime cartel, the Hand. She does enter into a relationship with both Murdock and Cage, but she is much more than one of the stereotypical girlfriend roles that the MCU has routinely offered women and is an intelligent, resourceful and multi-layered character.

While it might be something of a cliché to suggest that the city in which these four narratives are set becomes a character in and of itself, New York is even more vital to each of the four Netflix shows than it is to the cinematic branch of the MCU. It is where Matt Murdock and Wilson Fisk are shown to be have been raised in flashbacks in *Daredevil*, and later where they fight for control of the streets of Hell's Kitchen; in *Iron Fist* it is where Danny Rand lives as a child and then returns after fifteen years, first forced to sleep homeless in the park, before then once again living and working in opulent skyscrapers like the Stark

Tower-esque Rand Building. New York is where Jessica Jones prowls the streets at night as a detective and then on her hunt for Kilgrave. Similarly, in *Luke Cage* it is Harlem which becomes a battleground for Luke, Cornell 'Cottonmouth' Stokes and Mariah Dillard. It is more than just a *place* for them and its primarily African-American residents, as Mariah insists that 'Harlem is my birth right. *It's mine*' in 'Take it Personal' (1.10), but for Luke Cage Harlem 'is supposed to represent our hopes and dreams. It's the pinnacle of black art, politics, innovation. It's supposed to be a shining light to the world. It's our responsibility to push forward, so that the next generation will be further along than us', in 'You Know My Steez' (1.13). It is important to note that the New York portrayed in the Netflix television shows is not the sanitised version of the city which we have seen in the film series, but a much more visceral one where crime is rampant and injustice is endemic, reminiscent, in some ways of the 1970s New York brought to life in American films of the era like *Taxi Driver* and *Death Wish* (1974). It is this lawlessness which necessitates and legitimises the emergence of the Daredevil, Jessica Jones, Luke Cage and the Iron Fist in the way that Gotham City seemed to *need* Batman in Christopher Nolan's *Batman Begins* and *The Dark Knight*.

Of all the four Netflix shows *Luke Cage* is the most ardently connected to real-world fears and anxieties. Given the paucity of African-American superheroes in the history of the genre, with only *Blade* (1998), *Catwoman* and *Hancock* (2008) offering leading roles for black performers in the decade prior to the MCU, the significance of having the title character of a superhero-themed television show as a hoodie-wearing African-American male is quite profound and led to Joshua Ostroff describing *Luke Cage* as 'the most timely TV series since the *Battlestar Galactica* reboot took on the war on terror in the wake of 9/11' (2016). The star of *Luke Cage*, Mike Colter suggested, 'I can't imagine anything a black man would want to be more right now than bulletproof' (ibid.). Outside of Cage himself, the show offers a wide range of African-American characters, male and female, in its narrative and also in its evocation of figures from the past and present as a tapestry on which the drama takes place: from American Revolutionary icon Crispus Attucks to Walter Mosely and Ralph Ellison, Malcolm X and James Baldwin, to the prominent use of a portrait of Notorious B.I.G. and Method Man as himself, to the fact that all episode titles for the first season are taken from the titles of songs by the Brooklyn-based hip hop duo Gang Starr. In the process the show updates Cage from his 1970s Blaxploitation roots to the very contemporary concerns of the African-American community, or as Adilifu Nama, author of *Super Black: American Pop Culture and Black Superheroes* (2011), suggests, 'Thus there is a direct racial relationship between the meaning of Luke Cage and the history of black racial formation in America, no matter how many versions are created of the muscle-bound, skin-as-tough-as-steel 'Hero for Hire"

(2011: 66). The programme's showrunner, Cheo Hodari Coker, stated: 'When the bullets bounce off Superman there is no social context because the Kryptonian alien is bulletproof. But when you have a black person with impenetrable skin and have a bullet bounce off, whether that's a criminal bullet or a police bullet, it adds a whole other swath of political overtures to that interaction' (qtd. in Ostroff 2016).

Iron Fist faced something of a critical backlash on its release in March 2017 with critics seemingly falling over themselves to give it the most scathing review. Liz Shannon Miller at *Indiewire* said, 'Ultimately, Marvel's *Iron Fist* feels incredibly inessential, even boring at times. It's a show that doesn't push for bigger themes, doesn't seek to have its own voice beyond the Buddhist philosophy spouted by a white guy' (2017), and Danette Chavez at the *A.V. Club* said, 'The first half of the season is just a checked box. Filler episodes are one thing, but right now *Iron Fist* looks like a filler season' (2017). *Iron Fist* is not as bad as this veritable avalanche of negative reviews suggest, but it does suffer from numerous problems of narrative, tone and characterisation, plus the misfortune of coming after the popular and critically acclaimed *Daredevil*, *Jessica Jones* and *Luke Cage*. Danny Rand's quest to prove himself as the Iron Fist emerges as more insubstantial than it should be and his antagonists are the theatrical Meachums, father Harold (David Wenham), and son Ward (Tom Pelphrey). Criticisms were directed at the centralisation of an affluent white male in a show about martial arts and even though the character was originally conceived this way when created in 1974, it is the quality of the show's writing which makes these sustained examples of cultural appropriation even more problematic: scenes in which Danny lectures the Asian-American Colleen, who was raised in Japan and owns her own dojo, about martial arts, Chi and Asian philosophy, prove both ill-advised and misjudged in the episode 'Rolling Thunder Cannon Punch' (1.03). Similar concerns were raised about *Doctor Strange* and its narrative featuring a white Westerner venturing east for enlightenment: in both texts Asian cultures are seen exclusively through the eyes of a privileged Western male, who proves himself superior physically, intellectually and morally to his Asian counterparts without exception.

Like all the Netflix shows, and indeed the majority of the MCU narratives in general, *Iron Fist* is immersed in trauma. Danny's derives from the plane crash fifteen years before in which he saw his parents die, which he experiences throughout the series in clumsily-framed flashbacks. Finn Jones suggested: 'He has this eternal hope and drive that he's doing the right thing, but at the same time he's essentially suffering from PTSD' (Anon. 2017a: 116). It might be suggested that PTSD and trauma became one of the defining characteristics of the new millennial superhero. Of course, trauma has always been a part of superhero narratives but never to such an extent as it has been in the last two decades. In the case of Rand its presentation is not entirely convincing: on his return to New York his bed is too soft for him (as Steve Rogers and Sam Wilson also discuss in *The Winter Soldier*) and he obsessively plays the same hip hop music on the same iPod he had when he crashed (like Peter Quill and his mother's mix-tape in *Guardians of the Galaxy*). More credible is the portrayal of trauma in *Jessica Jones* and *Daredevil*: Jessica's is also the result of the childhood accident which led to the death of her mother, father and brother (which she is shown to be actually partially responsible for) and her persecution by Kilgrave, and Matt Murdock's from the loss of his father at the hands of mobsters when he was a child.

Given their street-level existence, as opposed to the more national and global impact of the characters from the Avengers, and the close relationships the Netflix superheroes have with their respective communities, vigilantism and its ramifications becomes a more central aspect of their narratives than it does in the film versions. Foggy Nelson criticises his friend Matt Murdock when he finally discovers that he is the Daredevil in 'Nelson v Murdock' (1.10) and he asks him, 'What are you doing Matt? You are a lawyer. You are supposed to be helping people!' Foggy's most persistent strain of criticism thereafter is to compare Matt to the criminal Fisk in a trope we have seen returned to frequently in the MCU, the dark mirror or shadow version of the hero. However, unlike the films this is given some substance as it is articulated not by a villain, but by one of the show's more sympathetic and likable characters. Both Fisk and Daredevil express the same desire to clean up Hell's Kitchen and both are willing to transgress the law to do so. Foggy asks of Matt's violent methods, 'How is that any different to the way *he* solves problems?', and when he hears that Matt wants to make New York a better place says, 'A better place? That kind of sounds like what Fisk keeps saying'. The connections between Murdock and Fisk, while ultimately disavowed, are presented in a more sustained fashion than any protagonist/antagonist relationship throughout the MCU. With their shared vigilante brands of justice and their dark pasts, each are undoubtedly formed by and revel in violence. Matt's masochistic tendencies also seem to strikingly complement Fisk's brutal sadism. However, these criticisms are negated, perhaps due to the demands of the genre, and towards the end of Season One Foggy comes to realise that what Matt does is necessary after all: that Daredevil is the only one able to stand up for the people of Hell's Kitchen when the law fails them, which the series presents ample examples of, from Matt beating up a father who sexually abuses his daughter, preventing a big business like Roxxon from mistreating its workers, or in the case of Fisk's ability to avoid punishment for his long list of crimes. By the beginning of Season Two all ethical doubts concerning what Daredevil does seem to have been erased: the police are grateful for his help, Foggy assists him with his 'work', and even the Catholic priest, Lantom, tells him 'I don't know what you didn't do or what you should have done, but the guilt means your work is not yet finished' in 'Penny and Dime' (2.04).

Having seemingly resolved for itself the issue of the morality of Daredevil's vigilantism in Season One, Season Two turned its attention to an even more complicated character, Frank Castle aka the Punisher, who originally had been a Vietnam veteran in his first Marvel comic appearance in *The Amazing Spider-Man #129* (February 1974), and had already featured in three poorly received films outside of the Marvel Cinematic Universe played by three different actors. The Netflix MCU incarnation of the character, this time played by the broodingly intense Jon Bernthal, would have such an impact on audiences that he was later given his own Netflix series, *The Punisher*, broadcast in 2017. Just as the first season of *Daredevil* ran parallel to Christopher Nolan's *Batman Begins*, and might well have been called *Daredevil Begins*, the second season explores similar territory to that of Nolan's *The Dark Knight*, revolving around the central theme of escalation. It becomes apparent that in the absence of the powerful Fisk (who was imprisoned at the end of the first season) a variety of criminal figures have emerged, each vying for power, and the actions of Daredevil have inspired a range of copycats which leads to escalating levels of violence and vigilantism throughout the city. As if in response to this, a mysterious costumed vigilante known as the Punisher appears, who, rather than handing criminals over to the police after apprehending them as Daredevil does, executes them. Murdock and Foggy's secretary and legal advocate, Karen Page (Deborah Ann Woll), wonder if Daredevil's actions might have been responsible for the emergence of the Punisher and asks 'Maybe we created him?' in 'Dogs to a Catfight' (2.02), but Matt Murdock refuses to believe there is a connection and expresses profound disapproval of the Punisher's extreme methods. Initially the Punisher is represented almost entirely negatively and he is criticised by not just Murdock, but also the public, the press and the law, but he becomes progressively more and more humanised as we learn of his background as the season progresses. It is revealed that he is a decorated veteran of the war in Afghanistan who might be suffering from PTSD, and that his family were killed by a drug boss who was never prosecuted for his crimes. When he comes face to face with Daredevil in 'New York's Finest' (2.03), Punisher insists 'I'm not a bad guy, Red' and that 'the people I kill *need* killing!' He even criticises Daredevil's code of ethics which prevents him from what needs to be done, calling him an 'altar boy' and telling him that New York 'stinks and it smells like shit and I can't get the stink out of my nose. I think that this world, it *needs* men who are willing to make the hard call' (in 'New York's Finest' [2.03]).[3] After he is finally captured by the police and placed on trial comments from jurors show the variety of responses to him: some call him 'an animal' or 'a fascist', but others refer to him as a 'hero, doing things the cops won't do' in 'Semper Fidelis' (2.04). The trial acts as a turning point in how the diegetic world sees Castle and how audiences are asked to view him too. Karen Page is the first to make this transition and she ponders, 'I keep asking myself if there's really a difference between someone who saves lives and some-one who prevents lives from needing to be saved at all?' and even Matt changes his mind due to the extent of the evil that is shown to sweep across the city. He even remarks, 'New York *needs* these people [like the Punisher], we *need* heroes'. Later he remarks to Frank, 'Maybe just this once your way is what its gonna take' before making the sign of the cross and embarking on a mission together.

Just as MCU films set up their characters in individual films and then brought them together at the end of Phase One in *The Avengers*, the same process was adopted for the four Netflix superheroes, with each given their own season (two in the case *Daredevil*) before being brought together in the eight episode mini-series *The Defenders* (2017–) broadcast on 18 August 2017. Show runner Marco Ramirez experienced the same issues Joss Whedon had in bringing very different characters, visual styles and genre influences together. He remarked, 'One of the things early on that I found helpful was not to think about how many differences [the other series] have but to go the opposite way and think about how much they have in common' (qtd. in Li 2017). *The Defenders*, set in New York, featured

Fig. 34: *The Defenders* brings together the four Netflix Marvel television shows as *The Avengers* once did with their cinematic superheroes: from right to left Luke Cage, Stick (Matt Murdock's trainer), Danny Rand, Jessica Jones and Matt Murdock

supporting characters from across all four shows, including Foggy Nelson and Karen Page from *Daredevil*, Misty Knight from *Luke Cage*, Colleen Wing from *Iron Fist*, and, of course, the ex-nurse Claire Temple, in a narrative designed to be a continuation of all the narrative arcs of the previous shows and a self-contained event in and of itself.

Notes

1   However, at the same time as this *Luke Cage* features the disappointingly simplistic and pantomime-like villain Willis 'Diamondback' Stryker and *Iron Fist* the unshaded Meachums, father and son.

2   Each has the prerequisite Stan Lee cameo too: in *Luke Cage* on a police poster which says 'See a crime? Report it!', in *Daredevil* (1.13), *Jessica Jones* and *Iron Fist* in the same photo in the police precinct as a decorated police officer.

3   In *Taxi Driver* Travis Bickle suggests something very similar: 'All the animals come out at night – whores, skunk pussies, buggers, queens, fairies, dopers, junkies, sick, venal. Someday a real rain will come and wash all this scum off the streets.'

'Whose side are you on?': Superheroes Through the Prism of the 'War on Terror' in *Captain America: Civil War*

The most interesting version of the story from the beginning, for us, was not giving an easy answer. We like complicated storytelling with movies that you can watch and rewatch, and take different things away from each viewing, so it was very important for us to craft a narrative where both Tony [Stark] and Steve [Rogers] were a little bit right and a little bit wrong. Our hope was that you get to the end of the film and are very torn over which side you're on. Or if you did choose a side, maybe someone close to you chose the opposite one.

— Joe and Anthony Russo (qtd. in Hunt 2016)

Who's in the right – Captain America, the self-sacrificing hero, or Iron Man, the war profiteer? They're both right. I think it's possible to be all kinds of different people with different personalities and you can all be right. The point is, both of them do good things. Both of them are good to other people and they make the world a better place in their own way. Which one I root for depends how you position them in the story...

— Stan Lee (2016: xv)

I.

This book concludes with an exploration of the thirteenth film in the Marvel Cinematic Universe and one of its most important texts. Several films have been especially significant in the evolution of the MCU: undoubtedly *Iron Man*, which started it all in 2008 and established both the stylistic and ideological parameters of the series; *The Avengers*, as the ambitious culmination of Phase One and its ground-breaking unification of diverse identities; *Captain America: The Winter Soldier*, as a widely regarded benchmark of quality for the Phase Two films, but also an affirmation of the series' continuing commitment to immersing itself in fractious real-world events; and *Guardians of the Galaxy* as an indication of the malleability of the Marvel brand moving forward. *Captain America: Civil War*, the topic of this closing chapter, is, as we will see, as important as these films for a variety of reasons and is, arguably, the defining film in the MCU to date.

Despite the huge financial success of *Avengers: Age of Ultron* there was something of a critical backlash directed towards the film which had been building throughout Phase Two. While it was well received in general, several reviewers and sections of the fan community had taken issue with what was perceived as it's reversion to formula, its tangible lack of peril and its status as 'disaster porn'. These criticisms had periodically echoed throughout Phase Two, directed towards bland antagonists like Aldrich Killian, Malekith and Darren Cross, the MCU's refusal to kill off any of its major characters, the seeming lack of interest in pursuing the ramifications of the numerous extra-judicial incursions of the Avengers around the globe and the resultant destruction which often followed in their wake. As if in part as a reaction to these critiques, for the opening film of Phase Three Marvel turned to one of the most widely read and important comic book events of the last few decades, Mark Millar's *Civil War*, which had originally been a seven-issue limited edition story published between July 2006 and January 2007. The comic had its detractors (see Trabold 2006), but was certainly one of, if not the most, impactful comic releases in recent memory. Robert Weiner in the foreword to a scholarly study of the series entitled *Marvel Comics' Civil War and the Age of Terror: Critical Essays on the Comic Saga* wrote that, 'There are those events in the history of comics that are significant and then there are those comic events that are *really important*' (2015: 1). In the same volume, its editor, Kevin Michael Scott, described the full extent of the allegorisation attempted by the comic's ambitious narrative which, he asserted, contained references to 'Guantanamo Bay, the fearfulness of American citizenry, the use of bad criminals to catch worse criminals, the creation of a new national police force with undefined powers, the redefinition of citizenship, trials without juries [and] incarceration without charges' (2015: 4). Not all of these elements mentioned by Scott are central to the film version released in the summer of 2016 directed by Joe and Anthony Russo, the brothers who had been responsible for the hugely successful *Captain America: The Winter Soldier*, as the coordinates of American film and culture had shifted somewhat almost exactly ten years later, but many of them are still compellingly realised within the frames of the film.

In both the comic and the film version, instead of supervillains as the antagonists, it is the superheroes themselves led by Captain America on one side and Iron Man on the other, who participate in an argument about the parameters of security and freedom, regulation and accountability, which undoubtedly are both a reflection of and an engagement with some of the defining issues of the post-9/11 era. On the initial release of the comic and in the years since many have drawn parallels between its storyline and the tumultuous events of the new millennial decade: Matthew Costello described *Civil War* as an explicit 'allegory of the War on Terror' (2009: 229) and Mark D. White in *A Philosopher Reads … Marvel Comics' Civil War: Exploring the Moral Judgment of Captain America, Iron Man, and Spider-Man* called it 'a self-conscious allegory to the events of September 11 and its aftermath' (2016: 1). In fact, it is hard to find a critically reflective piece on the comic series which does *not* connect it to the post-9/11 climate in which it was conceived and written.[1] Both the comic and the subsequent film used the evocative question 'Whose side are you on?' in their marketing, asking audiences to pick sides in the debate at the centre of their narratives, and for many it proved difficult to choose between Tony Stark's embrace of the Superhero Registration Act, which in the film is called the Sokovia Accords, and Steve Rogers' equally unequivocal rejection of it.[2] Even academics interpreted the political perspective of the series profoundly differently as the conflict moved outside of the panels of the comic into its real-world reception (see Bouie 2014).[3] Did the comic's allegorisation of the divisive post-9/11 era offer a criticism of Bush-era policies like the USA PATRIOT Act, or an endorsement of them? Francisco Veloso and John Bateman insisted that the comic should be understood as a reactionary treatise in which

> The entire story arc thus manages to convey that, when Iron Man wins, despite all the resistance (which ultimately surrenders as a gesture of patriotism, of considering things from a collective perspective, for the good of society), the necessary role of the Government has been reaffirmed. There might be problems, but there are still the means to solve them – that is, they have the cure for the anomalies. The Government remains the antidote and the cure for all illnesses, and should be trusted on all counts. In this manner, the Government is saved and emerges from the whole situation stronger as a reliable institution. (2013: 14)

Yet in a similarly categorical argument, Benton Bond comes to very different conclusion, suggesting that the series is 'grounded in the rhetorical space of anti-war patriotism that was palpable during the Iraq war' (2013: 80) and Max Erdemandi stated that it 'critiqued the American hyper-nationalism of the time by portraying Captain America's alienation from American patriotic ideology, which had previously been his character's foundation' (2013: 214). A decade later critics also connected *Captain America: Civil War* to the prevailing cultural climate in which it was made: so Alex Abad-Santos expressed that is was a 'cautionary tale about American retaliation and vengeance. It's a progression about what happens to American responsibility and policy in the wake of 9/11' (2016) and Justin Chang, writing in *Variety*, suggested that the film 'feels sincerely invested in the questions it raises about freedom vs. responsibility, heroism vs. vigilantism, and what those distinctions say about the heroes making them' (2016). While the film version has several differences to the comic narrative, which we will consider in more detail later, their premises remain fundamentally similar. Both feature a superhero mission which goes terribly wrong in their opening scenes, causing the loss of many innocent lives and in the aftermath of the tragedy governmental representatives come to the conclusion that superheroes have been left unregulated for too long and need to be brought under some sort of legislative control. Tony Stark agrees to support the idea, but Steve Rogers considers it both counter-productive and an infringement on the civil liberties of the superheroes who have done so much to protect those in need.

II.

After a brief prologue set very specifically on 16 December 1991 in which the Winter Soldier, formerly Captain America's friend Bucky Barnes, is shown undergoing brain conditioning treatment by his Russian-speaking HYDRA guards, then completing a mysterious mission which involves the assassination of unknown individuals and the retrieval of what appears to be the Super Soldier Serum in their possession, the film moves to the present day with an intrusively large onscreen caption, as if to categorically demarcate between the past and the present. However, the subsequent narrative, which is deeply rooted in trauma and loss, will make it very clear that no such easy juxtaposition is possible as the past bleeds into the present for multiple characters in the film. The incident which initialises the path to what will become known as the Sokovia Accords begins with a regular Avengers mission in Lagos, the likes of which have populated the MCU since *Iron Man*. Captain America, Falcon, Black Widow and Scarlett Witch are in Nigeria in order to prevent the former S.H.I.E.L.D./HYDRA agent

Brock Rumlow (now known as Crossbones) from securing a biological weapon from the Lagosian Institute for Infectious Diseases and selling it 'to terrorists' according to the Nigerian newspapers *The Daily* and *The Spot* shown onscreen. In locating the scene in Lagos, the MCU continues the practice of what we have described as 'virtual terror tourism' as the superheroes have been shown to inter- ject themselves around the globe with seemingly no consideration of the wishes of foreign governments and only limited awareness of the impact on those who live in the region at the same time as demonstrating their altruism and spectacu- lar abilities. The choice of Lagos, as that of other places like Afghanistan in *Iron Man*, Puerto Rico and Bahrain in *Marvel's Agents of S.H.I.E.L.D.,* Pakistan in *Iron Man 3* and the *favelas* of Brazil in *The Incredible Hulk*, is not a random one. The year before the film's release the Global Peace Index had placed Nigeria 151st out of 162 countries analysed, one of only twelve countries around the world to have been assigned the RED rating of 'Very low' and stories about Boko Haram, one of the world's deadliest terror groups, were regularly reported by the news media.

After Rumlow and his team of mercenaries steal the biological weapon they deliberately flee through the crowded Lekki market, which is full of people going about their daily business. In always presenting their narratives from the point of view of their American superheroes, the MCU has shown the distinct challenges they face in their confrontations against antagonists who have little regard for civilian casualties and even actively seek to cause them. One of Rumlow's hench- men threatens to release the virus into the crowd but Black Widow and Falcon are able to stop him, saving hundreds if not thousands of lives. Confronting Crossbones, Captain America engages him in hand-to-hand combat and when the villain attaches a sticky grenade onto Captain America's shield, the superhe- ro throws it high above the innocent people who have gathered to watch before it detonates, again saving many. When Cap finally subdues Rumlow he is momen- tarily distracted by the mercenary's talk of Bucky Barnes: 'He *remembered* you. I was there, he got all weepy about it… 'Til they put his brain back in a blender.' While Cap is preoccupied, Rumlow discharges an explosive suicide device hid- den under his armour which is only prevented from killing Cap and many in the crowd by Scarlett Witch who, using her telekinetic powers, contains the blast and propels it (and Rumlow) into the air. Unfortunately, she is unable to direct it away from a nearby office building where, we learn later, it kills numerous civilians including eleven citizens from Wakanda, who had been visiting Nigeria on an outreach mission. Scarlett Witch holds a hand up to her face, devastated at what she has done and Captain America looks to the building with an exclamation of 'Oh my God!' His first thought, as always, is of rescuing civilians. The moment is a shocking one as the MCU has refused to acknowledge the deaths of civilians in its narratives *while* the traumatic events unfold in the films: no innocents were shown or said to have been killed *during* the Battle of New York in *The Avengers*, nor in the destruction of the Helicarriers in Washington DC at the end of *The Winter Soldier*, not even during the extinction level event at the conclusion of *Avengers: Age of Ultron*.

Even though no one is physically shown onscreen to be killed in Lagos, the impact of these deaths is considerable. Back at the Avengers Compound, both Captain America and Scarlett Witch are deeply moved by what has transpired, and importantly they both claim responsibility for it. Scarlett Witch says, 'People died ... it's on me' and Cap tells her, 'This job... We try to save as many people we can, sometimes that doesn't mean everybody, but if we can't find a way to live with that, next time maybe nobody gets saved.' It is the traumatic event in Lagos, described by Kevin Feige as 'the straw that breaks the camel's back' (qtd. in Johnston 2016: 65), that acts as a catalyst for the narrative of the film which follows.[4] In the aftermath of Lagos, an international outcry leads to the demand that superheroes become regulated by an external governmental group for the first time in the MCU. On the news we hear a newsreader ask the question, 'What legal authority does an enhanced individual like Wanda Maximoff have to operate in Nigeria?', raising an issue which has been something of a taboo within the MCU films until then, and T'Chaka (John Kani), king of the small but wealthy reclusive African country of Wakanda and father of T'Challa aka Black Panther (Chadwick Boseman) states, 'Our people's blood is spilled in foreign soil, not only because of the actions of criminals but the indifference of those pledged to stop them. Victory at the expense of the innocent is no victory at all.' Yet the audience, having witnessed the scene in Lagos in its entirety, knows that this is not true. The Avengers, as they have always done, put themselves in harm's way to save innocents and even though some civilians were tragically killed, many more were saved by their actions.

The impetus for the comic book equivalent of the Sokovia Accords, the Super-human Registration Act, is very different although it is similarly impactful and even more catastrophic. In a seven-page prologue in *Civil War #1* a team of small-time superheroes called the New Warriors, who are the stars of a reality television show, try to catch a group of dangerous super-powered villains live on air in an attempt to boost their falling ratings. Confronted on the streets of Stamford in Connecticut, the most powerful of the villains, Nitro, triggers his explosive superpower which incinerates the surrounding buildings and a bright yellow school bus, killing, as we later learn, more than eight hundred people. It is the death of civilians in both the comic and cinematic versions of the narrative that triggers the furore which leads to the SHRA/Sokovia Accords, but unlike the irresponsible and reckless New Warriors, in the film Captain America, Falcon,

Black Widow and Scarlett Witch are shown to have done all they could to protect the innocent residents of Lagos.

In *Captain America: Civil War* the Avengers are called to a meeting by Thaddeus Ross, last seen trying to apprehend Bruce Banner in *The Incredible Hulk* eight years before. He has now left the military and become Secretary of Defense, claiming to have found 'perspective' after a heart attack. Bringing Ross back into the MCU is one of a myriad of ways the film is able to draw on the tapestry of events in the previous twelve films discussed in this monograph: returning to plotlines, characters and thematic motifs without the burden of having to introduce time-consuming back story for the majority of its key players, considering audiences have already, by the time of *Captain America: Civil War*, spent so much time with them. Yet their perspective on the events portrayed in these twelve films is altered somewhat. On a large screen the superheroes are confronted with footage of the collateral damage caused by many of the incidents they have participated in from the past few years, which until then the MCU had portrayed rather unproblematically. As well as the events in Lagos the screens show both the casualties and the financial costs from the Battle of New York at the climax of *The Avengers* (with onscreen figures stating that there were seventy-four dead and a financial cost of $18.8 billion), the destruction of the Helicarriers at the end of *Captain America: The Winter Soldier* in Washington, DC (twenty-three dead/ $28 billion) and most recently the incident in Sokovia from *Avengers: Age of Ultron*, which is shown to have been the most destructive of all (one hundred and seventy-seven dead/$474 billion).[5] The screened images of the events shown are themselves striking and not taken from the original films; instead it is comprised of hand-held footage seemingly from the perspectives of civilians caught up in the turmoil. Perhaps for dramatic expediency not all incidents the Avengers have participated in are featured: there is no mention of the battle between Hulk and the Abomination in Harlem in *The Incredible Hulk*, the destruction of Greenwich in *Thor: The Dark World*, or Hulk's Johannesburg rampage in *Avengers: Age of Ultron*, in which, as in all of those included in Ross's presentation, not a single civilian was shown being killed or seriously injured onscreen at the time.[6] Yet by consciously showing these events the MCU acknowledges, for the first time, both the diegetic ramifications of their actions and non-diegetic criticisms of the genre which arguably intensified with the release of *Man of Steel*, a film which seemed to show such a blatant disregard for civilians that it could no longer be ignored within the frames of either the MCU or the DCEU. What this shift from revelling in the 'disaster porn' elements of the superhero film to an explicit acknowledgement of it (while at the same time largely continuing to practice it) might tell us about the genre and the cultural moment in which they are being produced is uncertain. However, accountability, in some form or another was at the centre of the two highest profile superhero films released in the summer of 2016: *Captain America: Civil War* and *Batman v Superman: Dawn of Justice*.[7] Of course, the issue of accountability had been raised by Tony Stark back in 2008 in *Iron Man*, although his observation that 'I saw young Americans killed by the very weapons I created to defend and protect them' proved to be a questionable one. The perspective of innocent civilians has rarely been portrayed (or considered) in the MCU and it is they who might be regarded as the most prominent Other of the genre: for the most part only present to be saved by the superheroes or bear witness to the spectacular heroics. A true reverse focalisation in the genre would be to see the events from the perspective of the civilians which *Captain America: Civil War* very briefly offers, and the deaths of innocents provide the impetus for the Sokovia Accords, but after this very little consideration is given to them.

The concerns that Ross articulates are both relevant and timely, and he begins by thanking the Avengers for their service – 'The world owes the Avengers an unpayable debt. You have fought for us, protected us, risked your lives...' – before he comes to the central thrust of his argument – '...but while a great many people see you as *heroes*, there are some who would prefer the word *vigilantes*.' This has been left largely unspoken in the MCU and if expressed quickly disavowed by focusing on the humanitarian and often self-sacrificing actions of the superheroes. But here Ross explicitly confronts the idea that the Avengers (and by implication all of the superheroes throughout the MCU) have operated with no oversight, jurisprudence or even legality, enabling them to do, in effect, anything they want, as they have been largely portrayed as quite literally beyond the law. With the question, 'What would you call a group of US-based enhanced individuals who routinely ignore sovereign borders and inflict their will wherever they choose

Fig. 35: *Captain America: Civil War* confronts some of the unspoken taboos of the superhero genre: their endorsement of vigilantism, the America-centric nature of their heroes and the collateral damage their activities often result in

and who frankly seem unconcerned about what they leave behind?', Ross challenges two of the essential tenets of the superhero genre in a single sentence: by his categorisation of the Avengers as American (although using the words 'US-based') and the fact that they have routinely ignored sovereign borders since 2008. As Ross elaborates,

> For the past four years you have operated with unlimited power and no supervision. That's an arrangement the governments of the world can no longer tolerate... It [the Sokovia Accords] states that the Avengers shall no longer be a private organisation instead they'll operate under the supervision of a United Nations panel. Only when, and if, that panel deems it necessary.[8]

The individual Avengers are faced with a simple choice, to agree to abide by the Sokovia Accords (which is signed by one hundred and seventeen countries including the United States, the United Kingdom, Russia, France, Germany and Sokovia) or they will be forced to retire, and if they do not do so they will be regarded as criminals.

While many of Ross's points are certainly valid it is perhaps unfortunate that they are expressed by a character so compromised by his previous actions within the MCU. As most who have written about the comic book and the film have suggested, it is not inherently unreasonable that there should be some form of oversight concerning superheroes and their relationship to society, but the *way* it is framed in both versions and *who* it is framed by, proves significant. Just as criticisms of the behaviour of the Avengers by the likes of Senator Stern in *Iron Man 2* and the US government committee at the conclusion of *Captain America: The Winter Soldier* are rendered unconvincing by who they come from, the formation of this debate by Ross (and the later reveal that it was all part of an anti-superhero power play) skews the balance of objectivity concerning the Sokovia Accords immediately against it. Furthermore, Ross's assertion that the superheroes 'seem unconcerned about what they leave behind' contradicts what we have already seen just moments before as both Captain America and Scarlett Witch were shown to be intensely distraught by the events in Lagos and accepted responsibility for their actions. The film does not acknowledge, but we as an audience know, that despite the deaths and destruction featured in all the events Ross shows on his screen, without the presence of the superheroes the losses in every single one of them would have been much greater.

The prospect of the Sokovia Accords immediately polarises the superhero community, or rather the slightly restricted part of it we see in the film, and an impassioned debate then emerges between the two sides, which is the eponymous civil war of the film's title. Somewhat ironically the pro-Accords argument is led by Tony Stark who, given his previous rejection of government intervention into his affairs, at first seems an unlikely figure to welcome such an intrusion. Equally ironically perhaps, considering his military background and the fact that he was created by a government programme, it is Steve Rogers who stands in opposition to them. This then is the ideological fracture at the centre of the film: one side led by the man from the past and the other led by the self-proclaimed futurist. Both Stark and Rogers are patriarchal figures within the Avengers who have clashed over their methodologies and ethics before, but who had seemed to have resolved their differences and recognised the worth of each other's contribution to the team by the end of *Age of Ultron*. Rogers is very clear as to why the Sokovia Accords will prevent the Avengers from doing good around the world and his rationale – 'If we sign this, we surrender our right to choose. What if this panel sends us somewhere we don't think we should go? What if there is somewhere we *need* to go and they don't let us?' – does not sound too far removed from the claims of those like John Bolton, former US ambassador to the United Nations, who commented after 9/11 that, 'It's a big mistake for us to grant any validity to international law, even when it may seem in our short-term interest to do so – because, over the long term, the goal of those who think that international law really means anything are those who want to constrict the United States' (qtd. in Power 2005). The MCU has repeatedly shown politicians to be inherently untrustworthy and Cap questions the ability and motives of those who would decide *for them* what they should and should not do, like Alexander Peirce from *The Winter Soldier*, Senator Stern from *Iron Man 2*, Vice President Rodriguez from *Iron Man 3* and even the World Security Council, who targeted a nuclear weapon at New York at the climax of *The Avengers* just four years earlier. If the World Security Council functioned as a proxy for familiar American suspicions of the United Nations, *Captain America: Civil War* offers the intrusion of the UN directly in the form of a panel which will decide when, where and how the Avengers are permitted to act, and this is something Captain America cannot countenance.

Yet Cap's decision in the film, while sincere and passionately articulated, is ethically ambiguous for a variety of reasons: he might be right to suggest that 'governments have agendas' but it is equally fair to make the case that superheroes have agendas too. His rejection of the Sokovia Accords is based on his belief that 'We may not be perfect, but the safest hands are still our own', and the films prior to this one have proven that *his* hands are the safest, but there are many other superheroes out there who are considerably less reliable than him both in the film versions (for example Tony Stark) and the broader world of the MCU television narratives. One might suggest that the rigidity of his beliefs, which seemed unproblematic in the mythopoetic recreation of World War II in *The*

First Avenger and in the symbolic recreation of that same conflict against Loki and the Chitauri in *The Avengers*, might not be as easily compatible with the complexities of the post-9/11 world, even in its diluted sense in the arguments created by *Captain America: Civil War*. Karl E. Martin stated, 'As a consequence of his origins, Captain America does not deal with the moral ambiguity faced by many of his fellow superheroes' (2015: 100). The potential problems of this inflexibility and his unshakeable moral compass were briefly hinted at in *Age of Ultron* with his refusal to accept compromise in the later stages of the Battle of Sokovia, but quickly erased by the film's denial of the vulnerability of Sokovian civilians and thus resulting in his unwavering determination being ardently endorsed rather than questioned. Whether Steve's certainty and intransigency (which is accurately replicated from the comic) is supposed to be regarded critically by audiences is ambiguous, but Mark Veloso and John Bateman's assertions that, 'The values embodied by Captain America are therefore progressively discursively constructed as obsolete and no longer applying to the problems heroes need to deal with in the twenty-first century: the new threats demand new combative strategies and, consequently, new laws' (2013: 12) are too boldly stated when applied to both the comic (which they are originally directed at) and the film.

Those who favour the Sokovia Accords are just as convinced of the legitimacy of their positions and each seems to have a logical reason for their support of it. James Rhodes aka War Machine (after having his name changed back from Iron Patriot in *Iron Man 3*) even challenges Steve on his dismissive reaction to the prospect of being overseen by a United Nations panel, suggesting that his stance is 'dangerously arrogant, this is the United Nations we are talking about here, it's not S.H.I.E.L.D., it's not HYDRA!' He also praises Secretary of Defense Ross, talking about how many medals the former general has won, but whether he would say the same if he were party to the knowledge we audiences have of him after having seen his actions in *The Incredible Hulk* is perhaps doubtful. It is understandable that a military man like Rhodes would be more likely to follow orders proposed by a former general and the government he represents, but the fact that Black Widow joins the pro-Registration side is surprising. At the end of *The Winter Soldier* we had seen her perform the Snowden-like act of uploading S.H.I.E.L.D. and HYDRA secrets onto the internet, including everything about herself, an action that saw her threatened with imprisonment. Yet her reasons seem more pragmatic than Rhodes' sense of duty as she suggests: 'We have made some very public mistakes, we *need* to win their trust back … maybe if we have one hand on the wheel we can still steer…'

It is the principled android Vision, who we had seen worthy enough to wield Thor's hammer in *Age of Ultron*, that formulates the most persuasive argument for the regulation of their superheroic activities. He suggests:

In the eight years since Mr Stark announced himself as Iron Man, the number of known enhanced persons has grown exponentially and during the same period the number of potentially world-ending events has risen at a commensurate rate... I'm saying there may be a causality, our very existence invites challenge, challenge insights conflict and conflict breeds catastrophe...

Whether this is true or not is debatable: Steve Rogers refuses to acknowledge the possibility of anything other than the fact that 'we've done good' and the Avengers have undoubtedly saved hundreds and thousands, if not millions of lives, but many of the incidents in which they have participated have arguably been *directly caused* if not by their actions then by their presence. It is relevant that it is Tony Stark who has, more frequently than not, played the primary role in this: without the Iron Man suit in *Iron Man* there would have been no Iron Monger; it is hatred for Stark that motivates Ivan Vanko, Justin Hammer and Aldrich Killian in *Iron Man 2* and *Iron Man 3*; and the Sokovia disaster would never have happened if he had not conducted experiments on Loki's sceptre and created Ultron. Vision's words bleed beyond the frames of the screen and also address both the escalating levels of destruction seemingly necessitated by the superhero genre as film after film attempts to show more spectacular and excessive sights of destruction onscreen *and* America's foreign policy decisions before and after 9/11 which have been said by some to have contributed to global instability rather than prevented it (see Bacevich 2002; Butler 2006; Kinzer 2006; Chomsky 2007).

It is Tony Stark who leads the pro-Accords side of the argument and emerges as its strongest proponent. One might ask, how did the Randian figure of *Iron Man 2* who told the government 'I have successfully privatised world peace!' become a signatory of the Sokovia Accords, which would effectively tell him when and where he was *allowed* to be Iron Man? From the very beginning of the MCU Stark has rejected all forms of outside interference, be it the requests of the Senate Armed Forces Committee or even refusing to listen to other members of the Avengers in what he characterised as their 'don't meddle medley', an act which culminated in the creation of Ultron, something he pointedly *refused* to apologise for during the films. However, as we have seen, each of Stark's ethically dubious choices have been ultimately overturned by the films' narratives, which, after cursory levels of criticism, embraced Stark's lone wolf vigilantism and even rewarded him for it by the time of their end credits. Yet the Stark of *Civil War*, to the credit of the Russo brothers, the screenwriters and the performance of Robert Downey Jr. believably changes his mind, as he once had about being a weapons contractor after his moral epiphany in the caves of Kunar Province in Afghanistan. The primary reasons for this are his pronounced feelings of guilt and his psychological state in the aftermath of the events of *Age of Ultron*. Towards the beginning of the film he had presented a generous gift of funding to students from his alma mater, MIT (Massachusetts Institute of Technology), after which he was confronted by Miriam (Alfre Woodward), the parent of a young American killed during the Battle of Sokovia.[9] She poignantly tells Stark that her son had graduated from university and decided to spend some time doing charitable work in Eastern Europe. Handing him a photo she adds, 'His name was Charlie Spencer. You murdered him … in Sokovia. Not that that matters in the least to you. You think you fight for us? You just fight for yourself. Who's going to avenge my son Stark? He's dead and I blame *you*.' Her blame of Stark is itself ambiguously presented as she never clearly expresses what she blames him *for*: is it for the fact that he could have saved Charlie but did not? Or because, as Vision suggested, the very existence of superheroes has escalated the occurrences of catastrophic events? Or is it because of the fact that Stark created Ultron, which is not mentioned, nor is it entirely certain whether this is public knowledge in the film's diegetic world. The comic offers a variation of this scene as Stark is confronted by the same Miriam (who is white rather than African-American in this version) at the funeral of the victims of the Stamford Incident, of which her son Damien was one. Unlike the private moment in the film, it is a very public display in front of the press who record her condemnation of Stark and her spitting in his face while yelling 'Who's been telling kids for years that they can live outside the law as long as they are wearing tights?' (*Civil War #1*). In the film version Miriam never reappears, but in the comic she becomes one of the figureheads of the SHRA and later hands Stark a toy Iron Man figure which used to belong to Damien in order to 'remind you why you are doing this' (*Civil War #4*).

In the meeting with the rest of the Avengers Stark tells the team: 'He [Charlie Spencer] wanted to make a difference, I suppose, but we won't know since we dropped a building on him while we were *kicking ass*.' He also acknowledges that, 'There's no decision-making process here, we need to put in check. Whatever form that takes, I'm game. If we can't except limitations we're boundaryless, we are no better than the bad guys.' Yet of course he has spent most of his time in his three standalone *Iron Man* films and two Avengers outings refusing to accept or place limitations on himself and on a few occasions skated perilously close to being 'the bad guy' before being redeemed by the results of his violent actions. Like Black Widow he is also pragmatic about the reality of their situation and has realised that the Sokovia Accords are inevitable no matter how they feel about them, so it is better to participate and have some sort of control than exclude themselves from the process. He states, 'If we don't do this now it is going to be done to us later. That's the fact.'[10] It is clear that both sides have legitimate, if exaggerated, claims and also that their dispute is intrinsically connected to real-world debates in the first decades of the new millennium, echoing the policy decisions which were undertaken during the Bush era, but continued throughout the Obama administration and, after the release of the film, that of Donald Trump.

It is relevant to observe that both Captain America and Tony Stark's decisions are being made not just for ethical and political reasons, but also for very private ones too. Arguably it is this dimension, largely absent from the comic version, which gives the film greater resonance and, interestingly, raises the stakes in a way that few MCU films have been able to achieve. This is not done by increasing the levels of destruction on display but by making the drama more personal, similar to what the Russo brothers were able to achieve with *Captain America: The Winter Soldier*. Stark admits to Rogers that Pepper Potts has left him: 'A few years ago I almost lost her so I trashed all my suits [at the end of *Iron Man 3*], then we had to mop up HYDRA, and then Ultron, *my fault*, and then and then … and then I never stopped, because the truth is I don't wanna stop. I don't want to lose her and I thought maybe the Accords could split the difference.' This is the first time Stark has acknowledged his responsibility for the creation of Ultron and also the first time he has verbalised how important *being* Iron Man is to him. Captain America is also personally involved, as the signing of the Sokovia Accords in Vienna had been interrupted by a bombing which injured seventy people and killed thirteen, including King T'Chaka of Wakanda, which the press reports was perpetrated by none other than Captain America's childhood friend, Bucky Barnes, the Winter Soldier. When the authorities are sent to apprehend Bucky in Bucharest and are given a shoot-to-kill order, Cap is compelled to intervene, not just to save his friend, but also to save the lives of the police officers tasked with the mission. Coming face to face for the first time since Bucky saved his life by pulling him from the Potomac at the conclusion of *The Winter Soldier*, Steve realises his old friend is no longer the Winter Soldier and did not commit the terrorist act that he is accused of. Over the course of the film Bucky is revealed to be a much more reflective character, in many ways, than either Steve or Tony. Unlike Tony, Bucky is filled with remorse for his actions, even though his brainwashing and torture by HYDRA means he cannot be held directly responsible for them. He tells his friend, 'I don't know if I am worth all this' but Cap reminds him, 'What you did all those years. It wasn't you, you didn't have a choice.' Bucky says 'I know … but I did it' and when Steve implores him to stop fighting, he answers: 'It *always* ends in a fight.' It is the introduction of Bucky to the narrative of *Captain America: Civil War* which, more than anything else, marks the film as the conclusion of the Captain America trilogy rather than *Avengers 2.5* as many referred to the film (see Mendelson 2016; Romano 2016). In the comic book Bucky is not featured, but given his centrality to the MCU Captain

America narrative arc it is fitting that he becomes an integral part of the film. In Bucharest, aside from the police officers, Bucky is also targeted by Black Panther (Chadwick Boseman) in his sleek vibranium-weave suit, desirous of revenge on the man who he believes killed his father. Because of his failure to submit to the Sokovia Accords, Captain America's actions in Romania are deemed illegal and when War Machine arrives, now as a fully-signed Accord member and an official representative of the United Nations, he states 'Congratulations Cap, you're a criminal' and arrests him.[11]

III.

The next time Iron Man and Captain America come face to face, those who make up what is referred to as Team Cap are fugitives and are now regarded as out-laws by the international community. For the confrontation that takes place at Berlin Airport, which, it should be added, is conveniently entirely free of civil-ians, both Cap and Stark have recruited additional superheroes to join them. Hawkeye has renounced his retirement, giving no ethical reasons for leaving his idyllic homestead and joining the conflict other than the words 'Cap needs us' and the declaration that he owes 'a debt' to Scarlett Witch, in an allusion to her brother, Quicksilver, who saved his life in *Age of Ultron*. Cap also enlists the help of Scott Lang, aka Ant-Man, who brings some levity to the proceedings with his unabashed admiration of the iconic hero. Cap explains to him, 'We're outside of the law on this one so if you come with us you're a wanted man' to which Scott replies, referring to his criminal past, 'Yeah well, what else is new?' However, it is Tony Stark who introduces the most significant new superhero into Team Stark, Peter Parker, aka Spider-Man, and Tom Holland's portrayal of the character as a fifteen-year-old science prodigy is the first time as a minor in his cinematic histo-ry. Marvel had leased the cinematic rights to the character to Sony in 1999 which resulted in five films (where he was played by two different actors), but came to an agreement which resulted in the character's appearance in *Captain America: Civil War* and then *Spider-Man: Homecoming* in 2017. Peter Parker gives a speech on why heroes have a moral responsibility to intervene, 'If you can do the things I do and you don't, and then the bad things happen – then it's because of you', which is perhaps not as memorable as the Raimi era's 'With great power comes great responsibility', six words which arguably framed the role of the superhero throughout the decade. However, Peter Parker's reasons for joining a potentially deadly conflict seem as ambiguous as the ethics of Stark's recruitment of a child (even if he does possess super powers) and lying to his legal guardian, Aunt May (Marisa Tomei), especially in the light of the film's earlier focus on the death of Charlie Spencer as a motivation for Stark's pro-Registration beliefs.[12]

In the *Civil War* comic, Spider-Man also joined Team Stark and even agreed to remove his mask live on television to prove his commitment to the cause, before later becoming disillusioned with Stark's extreme actions and siding with Team Cap. In fact, the teams in the comic version are considerably different (and much more populous) compared to their cinematic counterparts given the fact that Marvel has a more extensive use of its characters in print than in the cinematic medium, as many of them have been licensed out to other studios. The pro-Registration side in the comic not only features the Fantastic Four, with Reed Richards, aka Mr. Fantastic, being one of the architects of the SHRA, but also characters like Stature (Cassie Lang, Scott Lang's daughter), Blade and even Deadpool. The comic's anti-Registration forces include Hercules, a still living Quicksilver and, in a reversal of the film, Black Panther. No one in *Captain America: Civil War* is portrayed as remaining neutral, but in the comic the X-Men refuse to join either side and Dr Stephen Strange, who would get his own cinematic origin story a few months later in October 2016, does the same with the declaration, 'There is no right or wrong in this debate. It is simply a matter of perspective' (*Civil War #6*).[13]

The absence of two of the Avengers Prime, Thor and Hulk, does not go uncommented on within the film's diegesis and once again this is a rarity in the genre where questions like 'Where was the Hulk during the events of *Winter Soldier*?', 'Wouldn't Stark have called on Captain America to help him fight the Mandarin in *Iron Man 3*?', or 'Why does Thor not ask another Avenger for help in his battle against Malekith in Greenwich?' instead of relying on Erik Selvig, Jane Foster and Darcy, have to be ignored. This was addressed briefly in *Ant-Man*, with a rather startled Scott Lang telling Hank Pym, 'The first thing we should do is call the Avengers!', but Hank's mistrust of the Stark family made his rejection

Fig. 36: Whose side are you on? Team Iron Man: those that chose to sign the Sokovia Accords and be supervised by a United Nations panel

of this idea somewhat plausible. However, in *Civil War*, Ross puts the absence of Bruce Banner and Thor into his argument in favour of the Sokovia Accords and even suggests: 'If I misplaced a couple of thirty megaton nukes, you bet there'd be consequences.' This is later followed by Stark asking Black Widow if she knows the whereabouts of Hulk and whether she might be able to persuade him to join their side. She answers with her own question: 'You really think he'd be on *our side*?' Banner has understandably not trusted the government or the military since the events of *The Incredible Hulk* and might be especially reluctant to work with Ross given their troubled history; however, his guilt and trauma as a result of his Hulk rampages, which caused him to leave the Avengers at the end of *Age of Ultron*, might lead him to be more open to some sort of oversight. In the case of the Norse God Thor, given his literal otherworldly status and his affection for Captain America, it might be seen as unlikely that he would be in agreement with the Accords.[14]

The ensuing clash at Berlin airport is the central narrative set piece of the film and certainly the most important single action sequence in the MCU until that point. It is one which resonates not just because of its spectacle and physicality, but the fact that the reasons that the individuals are fighting have been so firmly established and that we have spent so much time with the characters in the build up to it. As a result of this, the battle between Cap and Stark is imbued with their personal rivalry, and the fight between Black Widow and Hawkeye with the history of their friendship. When Captain America comes to blows with Spider-Man, once one moves past the fact that Captain America is fighting a child, Spider-Man's glee at meeting and then fighting his hero is the kind of interaction between beloved and iconic characters that film audiences have been waiting for decades to see onscreen. Some reviewers criticised the Berlin airport

Fig.37: Whose side are you on? Team Cap: those who choose to reject the Sokovia Accords and thus become regarded as outlaws by the international community

scene for having the superheroes quite obviously holding back from really hurting one another, which is true, but this reluctance is entirely appropriate due to the motivations of both sides, who are not there to kill or even to harm one another, but to achieve their desired goal: in the case of Team Iron Man, to apprehend those they regard as outlaws and in the case of Team Cap, to escape Berlin and undertake what Falcon calls 'the real fight', that is the pursuit of the architect of many of their problems, the 'Sokovian terrorist' (O'Sullivan 2017: 1) Helmut Zemo (Daniel Bruhl), in Siberia.[15] While this might somewhat mediate the sense of threat, it is not ignored but rather integrated into the dynamic of the scene: so War Machine brandishes a non-lethal stun baton and informs Captain America, 'Sorry Cap, this won't kill you, but it ain't gonna tickle either', and when both Black Widow and Hawkeye seem to be holding back, Scarlett Witch intervenes using her powers to propel Black Widow across the tarmac, scolding Hawkeye: 'You were pulling your punches!' This is rather different to the much more brutal scenes of violence in the comic where it seems that many of the superheroes are out to do serious harm to one another and the pro-Registration superhero Goliath is killed at the hands of the clone of Thor. The film's only casualty is the accidental shooting of War Machine by Vision, who does not die but is paralysed, Vision having been momentarily distracted in a very human way by his affection for Scarlett Witch. This human cost of the conflict is in some ways more impactful given how deaths in the MCU are almost always impermanent (for example Loki in *Thor: The Dark World*, Nick Fury in *Captain America: The Winter Soldier*, Pepper Potts in *Iron Man 3* and Coulson in *The Avengers*).

Despite having offered a reasonably balanced argument thus far in the film and allowed both Captain America and Iron Man the opportunity to present their perspective and the audience to choose between two empathetic heroes who they have followed across several previous adventures, it is in the Berlin Airport scene that it arguably becomes apparent that the film itself has sided with Rogers. Captain America had revealed himself open to a revised version of the Sokovia Accords, but after witnessing Bucky's mistreatment (not only in the form of the shoot on sight order, but also the refusal to allow him legal representation) and Scarlett Witch's involuntary incarceration, which he describes with the loaded term 'internment', it became untenable for him. At this point in the narrative both Captain America and the audience know that much of the conflict has been engineered by a Sokovian intelligence operative by the name of Helmut Zemo who had orchestrated the Vienna bombings to make them look like they were committed by Bucky. Zemo now seems to be in possession of an army of Winter Soldiers (about which Bucky informs us that they 'can take a whole country down in one night') which he intends to unleash on the world. Cap tries to tell Stark about this plot at the airport, but he refuses to listen, instead telling his former friend, 'Your judgement is askew. Your war buddy killed innocent people yesterday!', but the audience know this is not true and it appears that if Cap acquiesces to Stark's demands hundreds, if not thousands, might be killed.[16] Cap's position has been further validated by the fact that two members of the pro-Accords side have assisted him instead of Stark in defiance of the law, Agent 13 (Emily Van Camp) who gives him information and weapons (including his shield) and Black Widow who switches to his side in the middle of the Berlin airport scene allowing him and Bucky to escape. Furthermore, after those on Cap's side are apprehended (Falcon, Scarlett Witch and Ant-Man) they are imprisoned in an undersea prison seemingly far from the jurisdiction of any government, known as the Raft, and Ross's 'perspective' is shown to have been a cynical power play rather than a true embrace of accountability. Despite his undeniable intransigence, Captain America's refusal to sign the Accords in the manner in which they were presented to him has been shown to be correct and shortly after, when Stark learns that Bucky was not responsible for the Vienna bombing after all, he not only admits his culpability for the second time in the film – 'Clearly I made a mistake, Sam [Wilson], I was wrong' – but he too chooses to disobey the Sokovia Accords just a matter of days after signing them by lying to Ross, disobeying the government and flying to Siberia to join Captain America. This event is presented in a rather offhand fashion but it is significant in a variety of ways; Stark agreed to abide by international law as long as it suited him, and the very moment it did not he opted out, entirely fitting for the way the character has been portrayed since *Iron Man*.

The film's climax is quite fittingly set in an abandoned Soviet nuclear missile silo in Siberia and both the characters within the diegesis and the audience have been led to believe it will involve Captain America, Bucky Barnes and Iron Man putting aside their differences to unify against a much greater threat, in this case, an army of Winter Soldiers. This is very similar to what happened at the conclusion of *Batman v Superman: Dawn of Justice* released in the same year, as the eponymous battling heroes realised they had been manipulated by Lex Luthor and combined forces to fight the powerful Doomsday. *Captain America: Civil War* subverts these diegetic and non-diegetic expectations with the reveal of Zemo's motivation and plan. Like Miriam, he too had lost loved ones in the Battle of Sokovia and as a result has sought revenge on the Avengers. He explains that,

> My father lived outside the city, I thought we would be safe there. My son was excited he could see the Iron Man from the car window. I told my wife don't worry they're fighting in the city, we are miles from harm. When the dust cleared and the screaming stopped. It took me two days until I found their bodies. My father

still holding my wife and son in his arms. And the Avengers? They went home…
I knew I couldn't kill them, more powerful men than me have tried, but if I could
get them to kill each other…

Zemo, for a brief moment, personifies the role of the ignored civilian in the film's narrative, and it is easy to understand his pain, especially given Bruhl's understated performance, but his killing of innocents makes it hard to empathise with him and he joins the long line of critics of the superheroes whose accusations are largely invalidated by their actions. Instead of unleashing the Winter Soldiers, quite unexpectedly, Zemo has killed them all and instead directs Stark's attention to an old-fashioned video monitor as a grainy CCTV tape begins to play. The footage returns the film to its ambiguous prologue set very specifically in 1991 that had earlier seemed to be a routine Winter Soldier mission, which, in a startling act of narrative *legerdemain*, is now revealed to have been the assassination of Tony Stark's parents, Howard and Maria. The film had effectively foreshadowed this moment on a number of occasions, chiefly with Stark's presentation to MIT showcasing his $611 million technology, Binarily Augmented Retro Framing (BARF), which had enabled him to relive his last moments with his family and tell his father 'I love you Dad, and I know you did the best you could' in an attempt to mediate his trauma at their loss.[17] The scene's reveal of the nature of the murder of Stark's parents is an intimate moment from more than twenty years ago and an emotionally potent one for those who have become invested in Robert Downey Jr.'s characterisation of Tony Stark, who had by then appeared in six separate films, especially for a genre about which director Alejandro González Iñárritu remarked, 'They have been poison, this cultural genocide, because the audience is so overexposed to plot and explosions and shit that doesn't say anything about the experience of being human' (qtd. in Fleming Jr. 2014).

Earlier Zemo had suggested that, 'An empire toppled by its enemies can rise again but one which crumbles from within … that's dead, forever', and this emerges as the reason why he had deliberately orchestrated the conflict between the superheroes. Stark is understandably grief-stricken and enraged with the person he sees as responsible standing in front of him. Even though Rogers protests that Bucky cannot be held accountable for his actions considering he was brainwashed by HYDRA at the time, Stark is unable to see the distinction. This is made worse by the further revelation that Captain America had known about it and chosen not to tell Tony. So, the film's final battle is not between the superheroes and an army of Winter Soldiers, but two friends, each with very human reasons for their actions. As opposed to the battle at Berlin airport it seems as if they are not holding back at all and for the first time since Gulmira in *Iron Man* there are no quips or witty one-liners from Stark. Barnes, once again, emerges as more emotionally reflective than those around him; when asked by Stark, 'Do you even remember them?' he answers, 'I remember *all* of them', referring to all of those who were victims of his life as the assassin Winter Soldier and accepting the responsibility for his actions in ways more sustained than Stark has ever done.[18]

The entire narrative of *Civil War* has been shown to be immersed in trauma: from Zemo's tragic loss of his family during the Battle of Sokovia, Barnes' post-traumatic stress disorder after freeing himself from his identity as the Winter Soldier, to Miriam's loss of her son Charlie and Tony Stark's loss of his parents. Black Panther, who had attempted to kill Bucky Barnes in the streets of Bucharest, believing he was responsible for the murder of his father, is able to do what Stark cannot, and work through his trauma. Instead of killing Zemo, who *was* the one responsible for his father's death, he prevents the Sokovian from committing suicide and tells him, 'Vengeance has *consumed* you, it is *consuming* them. I am done letting it *consume* me...'. In a film with such a large cast, Joe and Anthony Russo are still able to give the Black Panther, a character who many in the audience would not have heard of before, a genuine character arc even with his limited screen time, due in large part to Chadwick Bosman's sympathetic performance, which primed audiences for his solo adventure released two years later, *Black Panther*.

As their battle comes to a conclusion Cap explains to Stark that he cannot turn his back on Bucky, because 'He's my friend'; to which Stark answers, 'So was I' with a different inflection to that used in the trailer which, after its release on 10 March 2016, was the second-most viewed online video of all time, securing almost one hundred million views in the first twenty-four hours (then second only to *Star Wars: The Force Awakens* which achieved a staggering 128 million views). Stark's repulsor beam blasts off Bucky's metal arm and he seems to have overpowered them both, but as we have seen before Cap never gives up and in a call back to *The First Avenger*, tells Stark, 'I could do this all day' before finally defeating him. It is strange to see Stark, who over the course of his film appearances has never lost a fight, finally be defeated, and when Cap turns away to leave, Stark cries out to him, 'That shield doesn't belong to you, you don't deserve it! My father made that shield!' Captain America – although whether he still goes by that name after refusing to sign the Sokovia Accords is unclear – drops it to the floor as Marshal Will Kane once did with his badge in *High Noon*, similarly disillusioned with those he had been charged with representing. It is left ambiguous as to whether Zemo's plan actually worked, as the Avengers end the film still divided, but Captain America sends Stark a conciliatory letter in which he assures Stark if he is ever needed he will return.[19]

The ending of the comic version of *Civil War* is very different to that of the film given that the Bucky character is not involved with the narrative. The murder of Goliath at the hands of the Thor clone and the use of supervillains on the pro-Registration team led many superheroes to lose faith in the cause championed so vociferously by Tony Stark and Reed Richards: including Spider-Man and Mr Fantastic's wife, Sue 'Invisible Girl' Reed, who both switch sides to join Captain America's anti-Registration forces. The final confrontation between the two sides is on the streets of New York and, as in the film, it appears that Cap has got the better of Stark before, out of nowhere, a group of civilians try to restrain him. At first it is unclear what they are doing and when Cap tells them he is not trying to hurt them one of them answers, 'It's a little late for that, man!' (*Civil War #7*). It is then Captain America who realises that even though he feels he was right to stand by his convictions, he had lost sight of *who* and *what* the superheroes ultimately fight for, as the panels around him show the destruction that the events of *Civil War* have caused. He drops his shield, as he does in the film, and gives himself up to the authorities who lead him away in handcuffs.

Captain America: Civil War is further evidence of Marvel Studios' acknowledgement that the MCU needs to adapt to continue to resonate and an attempt to, in some ways, deconstruct some of the essential tenets of the genre, at the same time as continuing to provide the prerequisite spectacle demanded by audiences. It is a film which interweaves the events of twelve previous films in the franchise in the last eight years together in a way which no series has ever done on such a scale. While it is true of the film, as Veloso and Bateman suggest of the comic, 'Its splitting into two sides is presented as essentially Manichean, almost a constitutive feature of superhero mainstream comics, and so appears to overlook the complexity of reality placing things on a two-sided coin, where one automatically excludes the other' (2013: 5), much is done within these parameters and for the first time, for much of the film at least, there is no right or wrong answer to the ethical dilemma at its centre, and for many members of the audience, the possibility was there for them to choose to side with Tony Stark or Steve Rogers. One might suggest that if Stark and Rogers had been less obdurate and extreme in their positions the conflict could have been resolved without the need for the 'civil war' of the film's title, but, of course, this is not allowed within the paradigm of the genre. As Bucky Barnes said, 'It *always* ends in a fight' because the genre and perhaps even the culture which it services, demands it. Zemo, and the Russo brothers themselves, exploit the refusal of the superheroes to negotiate, their disdain for diplomacy and the belief that the only solution for problems is violence. In this way the genre is grounded in reactionary conservative fantasies, elements that it may very well always struggle to transcend. The differences between the comic and the film are revealing and represent more than the transition from one medium to another, as they also reflect the shifting coordinates of the cultural climate in the ten years between 2006 and 2016. Even though recreations of the contentious issues at the heart of the narrative were not as heated as they were in 2006, the film's debates, coming as they did during the run up to the 2016 presidential elections, were again on the cultural landscape as both Team Clinton and Team Trump articulated the direction America needed to take in the future on matters of security and freedom, which are at the centre of the film.

Notes

1 The Stamford Incident is also described by Kevin Michael Scott as a '9/11-like tragedy' (2015: 6) and the *Civil War* comic was called 'a fairly transparent effort to parallel the debates over the Iraq War, the PATRIOT Act, the Bush domestic surveillance programme' by Benton Bond (2013: 75–6).

2 For a more detailed legal analysis of the Superhero Registration Act in the comics see *The Law of Superheroes* (2013) by James Daily and Ryan Davidson.

3 Mark Millar himself asserted that the series was designed to be even handed, but suggests that, in his opinion, it leaned more towards Iron Man's position (see Millar and McNiven 2007: 169).

4 Kevin Feige here echoes the description of the Stamford Incident by the superhero Daredevil, who does not feature in *Captain America: Civil War*, when he remarks 'Stamford's just the straw that broke the camel's back' (*Civil War #1*).

5 In the directors' commentary, the Russo brothers made it clear that these figures only included civilian casualties and not police officers, soldiers or other governmental workers. The comics had their own similarly tragic but different events which lead up to the Stamford incident: the bombing of Philadelphia by the Winter Soldier (*Captain America #6*), and a destructive Hulk rampage in Las Vegas (*Fantastic Four #533–535*).

6 It is the exclusion of this last event which is perhaps the most significant for the narrative of *Captain America: Civil War* in many ways, but it is one that is entirely ignored. Hulk's rampage in *Age of Ultron* was directly caused by Scarlett Witch's decision to use her powers on him and she is more responsible for these deaths (which are not named or numbered) than she is for those in Lagos. However, a return to this act would certainly have had an impact on audience sympathy for the character and thus is erased from the narrative.

7 There are considerable similarities between the two films. Both concern superheroes clashing with one another on a matter of principle who are being manipulated behind the scenes by someone else who does not engage with them physically. Additionally, both films rely on the past trauma of their superheroes to motivate their actions in the present.

8 This is not the first time heroes have been regulated in comics or in films: it was a central element of the Keene Act in *Watchmen* (2009) which made costumed vigilantism

illegal, the forced retirement and relocation programmes for superheroes featured in *The Incredibles* (2004), but perhaps most often in the *X-Men* franchise and the Mutant Registration Act which involves the enforced registration of every mutant.

9   Alfre Woodard is one of the few performers who have played more than one role in the MCU: she plays Miriam here in *Civil War* and in the same year the duplicitous politician Mariah Dillard in *Luke Cage*.

10 The film's representation of the debate, arguably, has more nuance than aspects of the comic book. The Sokovia Accords are a measure of oversight and if the super-heroes choose not to sign they are allowed to retire (even though none of them do). In the comic, anyone who does not sign is immediately arrested and imprisoned. Furthermore, Stark's actions in the comic book are even more extreme than those in the film: he secretly clones Thor, who murders one of the anti-Registration side, par-ticipates in the construction of the Negative Zone (a Guantanemo Bay-esque prison facility in another dimension) and also hires super villians to apprehend those who do not sign.

11 None of the superheroes are physically shown signing the Sokovia Accords. The first to do so was Agent Elena 'Yo Yo' Rodriguez in the web series *Marvel's Agents of S.H.I.E.L.D. Slingshot* (2016) during the episode 'John Hancock' (1.02).

12 This was made even more interesting by the four-minute-long video diary recorded by Peter Parker included in *Spider-Man: Homecoming*. Peter tells the camera: 'No one has actually told me why I'm in Berlin or what I'm doing. Something about Captain America going crazy...'

13 Interestingly Daredevil, the Punisher and Luke Cage, who have each appeared in the Netflix shows discussed in the previous chapter, all join the anti-Registration side.

14 During the course of the filming of *Thor: Ragnarok*, the director Taika Waititi and star Chris Hemsworth released a three-minute-long humorous paratextual video for fans called *What Thor was doing during Captain America: Civil War* (2016) to inform Marvel where Thor was at this time. The answer was that apparently he was living in Australia with his new flatmate Daryl anxiously waiting for either Captain America or Iron Man to contact him; or, as it is revealed in *Thor: Ragnarok* he was on the planet Sakaar fighting alongside (and against) the Hulk.

15 In an excellent example of how every succeeding MCU film comments on those which preceded it, in *Spider-Man: Homecoming* Tony Stark informs Peter, 'Trust me kid, if Cap had wanted to lay you out, he would have', adding a layer of complexity to Stark's decision to bring along Peter.

16 Of course, for those that have already seen the film and know the twist, they are aware that Zemo has no such army and that if Rogers and Stark had stopped fighting they might have been able to resolve things by having a conversation.

17 These final words to his father are different to those presented in the MCU comic book *Iron Man 2: Public Identity* (2010) which were 'I know what I am doing old man'.

18 It might be regarded as ironic that the death of the mother of a superhero plays such an important role in both *Civil War* and *Batman v Superman* (as it also does in *Thor: The Dark World* and *Guardians of the Galaxy*), but while in the MCU film it acts as a catalyst for violence, in the DCEU the widely derided revelation of the shared names of Batman and Superman's mother leads Batman to recognise the humanity of the man he had thought of as his enemy.

19 In *Spider-Man: Homecoming* Coach Wilson (Hannibal Buress) suggests: 'The guy is a war criminal I guess, but whatever.'

The Superhero as Transnational Icon

We do not copy the Hollywood production [sic], we create our own mythology, based on our own historical cultural code. In our case it is a common Soviet past of tens of millions of people. That's why we have several characters that represent different republics of the former Soviet Union… In order to [ask the] question: 'Who of the superheroes do you like most?' The answer of our child, for example, was 'Russian Arsus' rather than Superman or Batman.

> – Sarik Andreasyan (qtd. in Sahay 2017)

What bothers me most, is that it's always here to show the supremacy of America, and how they are great. I mean, which country in the world would have the guts to call a film, 'Captain Brazil' or 'Captain France?' I mean, no one. We would be so ashamed and say, 'No, no, c'mon, we can't do that.' They can call it 'Captain America' and everybody thinks it's normal. I'm not here for propaganda, I'm here to tell a story.

> – Luc Besson (qtd. in Gunderman 2017)

Writing a monograph about something as expansive and as contemporary as the superhero films and television shows created by Marvel Studios, as one might expect, presents a variety of challenges, chief of which might be an acknowledgement of the remarkable pace with which new texts are added to the MCU. In 2008, Marvel released only two films, their first as a fully-fledged and independent studio, *Iron Man* and *The Incredible Hulk*, but by 2017 the frequency of additions had become almost overwhelming, with a major new release in nearly every month of the year. Between January and May of 2017 audiences were able to watch the twenty-two episodes of Season Four of *Marvel's Agents of S.H.I.E.L.D.*, which were divided into three distinct but overlapping 'pods'; then in March the much criticised *Iron Fist*, the fourth and arguably least successful of Marvel's Netflix collaborations; in May James Gunn's *Guardians of the Galaxy: Vol. 2* which was even more financially successful than the original and made close to a billion dollars world-wide; in July *Spider-Man: Homecoming* brought the iconic web-slinger firmly into the world of the MCU and also featured Robert Downey Jr. playing Tony Stark/Iron Man for the seventh time (eighth if one counts his cameo in *The Incredible Hulk*) in ten years and in a major film for the third straight summer in succession; in August Netflix's *The Defenders*, featuring the stars of *all* of its four previous shows onscreen together; in September *The Inhumans* (ABC, 2017–), which, even though it was a television show, debuted its first two episodes in IMAX cinemas all over the globe; in October *Thor: Ragnarok*, the conclusion of the Thor trilogy which had started in 2011, bringing back Loki but also integrating the Hulk into its narrative in ways which would have considerable ramifications for *Avengers: Infinity War* to be released the following year in 2018; and in November the Netflix series *The Punisher*, in which the brooding antihero originally introduced in Season Two of *Daredevil* returned to the television screens in his own series. All of these films and television programmes, more than fifty hours of screen time, are set in the same diegetic world, one which was established by Jon Favreau's *Iron Man* back in 2008.

It is Marvel, more than any other production company, that has fuelled what we have seen described both as a 'resurgence' (Chermak *et al.* 2003: 11) and a 'renaissance' (Green and Roddy 2015: 2), but also a 'cultural catastrophe' (Alan Moore qtd. in Flood 2014) and a 'cultural genocide' (Iñárritu qtd. in Fleming Jr. 2014). In 2011 Richard J. Gray II and Betty Kaklamanidou called the phenomenon a superhero decade (2011: 1), but given its longevity we need to acknowledge the necessity of turning their use of the singular 'decade' into the plural 'decades'. This volume has attempted to outline and interrogate the ideological parameters of the MCU, but also provide a critical framework designed to transcend the films and television shows contained within it, with much of its analysis just as applicable to future Marvel productions and to other entrants to the superhero genre, whether it is the films of the DCEU (2013–), the X-Men series (2000–), or even those made in other countries, many of which engage with the motifs explored in this book in compelling ways. While we have correctly categorised the superhero renaissance as being a primarily American one, its audience has been extraordinarily global and only the first three MCU films made more money in the US than in international markets, something that is highly unlikely to ever happen again. As a result of the genre's tremendous financial success and cultural impact it comes as no surprise that other national film industries have sough to create their own superhero films in an attempt to return domestic audiences to indigenously produced narratives. Japan's *Ultraman: The Next* (2004), *Casshern* (2004) and *Gatchaman* (2013), Finland's *Rendel* (2017), Malaysia's *Cicak-man* (2006), Denmark's *Antboy* (2013), Thailand's *Mercury Man* (2006), Italy's *They Call Me Jeeg* (2015), and Britain's *SuperBob* (2015) and *iBoy* (2017), to name just a few, are superheroes as intrinsically connected to their own cultures as the MCU is to the turbulent new millennial decades of the United States. They are texts which should be understood as manifestations of their own unique national identities and monomyths, but impacted upon and influenced in complicated ways by the domination of the superhero form by the American cultural industries which undoubtedly stands at the very apex of the genre. In this understanding the relationship between, for example, a Russian and an American superhero film, or an Indian and an American superhero film, is a distinctly transnational one that should be considered, as Anurima Chanda commented, not as an example of 'marginal cultural production' based on 'mimicking' (2015: 70), but rather as a process of transcreation or cross pollination understood as 'a transnational and translational instantiation of the superhero embedded in familial and vernacular conventions' (Kaur 2013: 293) of their own cultures.

Thus, the Russian superhero film released internationally with the English title of *Guardians* (2017) is quite palpably a response to the deluge of American superhero films which have flooded Russian multiplexes in recent years and was billed as 'Russia's answer to Marvel's superhero adventures' (qtd. in Ryan 2017). Made on a budget of just $5 million dollars, not much more than the cost of a single episode of *Daredevil*, *Guardians* features a team of disparate superheroes as co-protagonists created by a secret Soviet organisation called 'Patriot' during the Cold War, but, as one might imagine, its enemies and the fears and anxieties it dramatises are quite different to those found in films like *Iron Man* and *The Avengers*. The four superheroes at its centre are self-consciously designed as representative of the different nationalities which comprised the former Soviet Union and are shown to embody what is commonly regarded as the qualities and traditions (and even the natural resources) of the region where they are from. Therefore, the Armenian Ler (whose name means mountain in Armenian) has the ability to manipulate stone and soil and is first seen meditating at Khor Virap at the foot of Mount Ararat; Khan is the proud and mysterious Kazakh who is said to have killed his brother in a blood feud, but can command the wind, teleport and is a master with all forms of blades; Ksenia, the only female on the team, has the power to become invisible and mould her form to any substance that she touches (she even jokes that her extra superpower is 'I make an excellent borscht!'); finally, Ursus, the Bruce Banner-like genius Russian scientist, is able to transform into a huge bear, the most potent Russian symbol of all. The film embraces the thematic tropes of the superhero film but offers its own variations on them and is inextricably connected to Russian culture and ideology with its evocations of World War II, the Cold War and its Moscow-set climax, a city with perhaps an even more vivid and traumatic history for Russian audiences than New York has for Americans. It is not a coincidence that the film was released on 23 February, the Russian public holiday known as 'День защитника Отечества' ('Defender of the Fatherland Day'), and the film's title could just as accurately have been translated as *Defenders*. The film opened at number one at the Russian box office with respectable earnings of $3.7 million in its first weekend, but was quickly eclipsed by a wave of American superhero films released in the weeks after, starting with *Logan* which earned $7.7 million across the same time period and those other guardians in *Guardians of the Galaxy: Vol. 2*, which opened to $12 million in their opening weekend. These cases are examples of the issues facing many national film industries and markets all around the world, where audiences overwhelmingly tend to prefer American films to those produced in their own country. In 2016, Russian films occupied just 17.8% of the national market share (up from 15% in the previous year) and only a single Russian film appeared in the Russian top twenty-five box office in 2016 (see Holdsworth and

Fig. 38: *Guardians* (2017) offers Russian variations on the superhero narrative with its band of disparate heroes from all corners of the former Soviet Union united against an apocalyptic threat

Kozlov 2015; Barraclough 2017). In the UK, the situation is even worse, despite annual assurances by the British Film Institute that the British film industry is booming, as independently produced British films were only able to secure 7.4% of the total box office in 2016, down from 10.5% in 2015 (see Anon. 2017b).

In the last decade it is the Indian film industry which has, outside of the United States, produced the most superhero films and for Indian audiences the genre has been largely defined by the phenomenal success of *Koi... Mil Gaya* (2003), *Krrish* (2006) and *Krrish 3* (2013). The films, directed by Rakesh Roshan and starring his son, Hrithik Roshan, have become one of the biggest franchises in Indian film history, expanding beyond the cinema to television, comics and video games. As we have habitually seen with the American film industry, the films have become bigger as the series progresses: with larger budgets, more characters, increasing amounts of special effects and more and more elaborate action sequences. The trilogy draws extensively and fairly explicitly on American superheroes like Spider-Man, Superman and Batman, but also on American films as diverse as *First Blood* (1982), *E.T. The Extra-Terrestrial* and *The Matrix*, with even their soundtracks leaning rather heavily on Alan Silvestri's score for *The Avengers* and Hans Zimmer's for *Pirates of the Caribbean: The Curse of the Black Pearl* (2003) for inspiration. *Krrish* and *Krrish 3* follow the adventures of the pure-of-heart Krishna, who inherits superpowers from his father (who had been gifted them by an alien), as he moves from a rural Indian countryside idyll to embrace his destiny as a superhero in the modern metropolitan of Mumbai. However, its depiction of India is very different to that of *The Avengers* with Banner's sojourn to the slums of Kolkota. Krishna becomes the masked superhero known as Krrish, who is constructed as a particularly Indian superhero who embodies and articulates Indian religious beliefs in ways very far removed from the secular humanism of the MCU superheroes. Hinduism not only informs Krishna's name, but also his values and what he comes to represent to the local community who he serves and who come to revere him. He tells those he saves, who are most often women and children, that *they too* are Krrish and that 'Anyone who takes away tears and spreads happiness *is* Krrish', which culminates in a remarkable scene in *Krrish 3* when a statue is erected in his honour with the inscription 'Superhero of India' at its base in English. While offering some similarities to the statue of the Avengers at the end of *Age of Ultron*, the film shows a large crowd assembling around the figure breaking into the song and dance number, 'God, Allah, Aur Bhagwan', with the three gods in its title embodying the extent of the film's immersion in religion. The lyrics of the song suggest, 'He's in me too. He's in you too. Somewhere or the other, he's there in all of us', but whether they refer to Krrish himself or broader Hindu deities, remains ambiguous, as even though Krrish is portrayed as godlike throughout the series (his appearance is often prefaced with lines like,

Fig. 39: "Anyone who takes away tears and spreads happiness is Krrish": The Hindu "Superhero of India" in *Krrish 3* (2013)

'God, please help us!') the implication that *Krrish* and *Krrish 3* offers is not that Krrish is a deity, but rather he is an instrument of god and a living embodiment of the religious faith of the Indian people.

Krrish 3 mounts an impressive spectacle on its, by Hollywood standards, very limited budget of $15 million dollars, about the same as the pilot episode of *Marvel's Agents of S.H.I.E.L.D.* released in the same year. But unlike the case of films like *Guardians* or *SuperBob* mentioned above, which were unable to compete financially with American superhero films, *Krrish 3* was embraced by Indian audiences to the tune of around $45–50 million at the Indian box office in the same year as *Iron Man 3* made only $11.1 million and *Man of Steel* $6 million in the same region. India is a rare market where, unlike Russia, the UK and most other countries, Hollywood films receive a minority share of the box office revenue of only around 10% per year (see Bhushan 2014).

Krrish 3 and Indian superhero films are certainly more melodramatic and light-hearted than their American counterparts. With their outlandish plots and extravagant dance numbers they eschew the veristic turn embraced by most American films of the genre and are not mired in trauma, even though India has had more than its own share of tragedies in the last few decades. But unlike the MCU superheroes, Krrish does experience the deaths of civilians first-hand; in one sequence he carries a dying, plague-infected girl in his arms as he runs through the contaminated streets of Mumbai, a city where people are shown to be hurt and even die onscreen, leading the hero to admit to his father: 'I can hear their screams and *I am helpless…*' David Chute at *Variety* wrote that *Krrish 3* was not 'an audience-pummeling industrial product like most of Hollywood's superhero films. It has the off-hand, anything-is-possible spirit of a children's book or fairy tale' (2013), and his description of the film as a fairy tale is a relevant one not just for Indian superhero films, but those of the MCU which we have

Fig. 40: Moving into its second decade, the MCU released *Black Panther* (2018), ten years after *Iron Man* (2008)

explored throughout the course of this book. Thomas Elsaesser has described the contemporary blockbuster film, of which the superhero genre is without a doubt the superlative example, as 'the natural, that is, technologically more evolved, extension of fairy tales' (2001: 17) and Stan Lee himself, the creator of many of the characters discussed in this book, saw the allure of the superhero narrative in similar terms: 'One reason people like these superhero stories so much is just about everybody reads fairytales when they're young. Well, when you become older, you don't read fairytales anymore, but I think you never outgrow your love for stories of people who are bigger than life and can do things that normal people can't do' (2016a: 96). It is important to note that the adoption of the term 'fairy tale' by both Elssaesser and Lee here is not employed in the casual and pejorative sense it is used by many. We can choose to see fairy tales or their modern incarnations, the blockbuster, as stories only suitable for children, or we can see them as a richly-textured tapestry of cultural mythology and ask what they are able to reveal about the societies which form them and very often seem to *need* them. As Jack Zipes offered in his remarkable study of the form, *Fairy Tales and the Art of Subversion*, 'The fairytales we have come to revere as classical are not ageless, universal and beautiful in and of themselves, and they are not the best therapy in the world for children. They are historical prescriptions, internalized, potent, explosive, and we acknowledge the power they hold over our lives by mystifying them' (2006: 11). Similarly, superhero films are historical prescriptions formed by the ideologies of the times in which they are made and should be considered as resonant cultural artefacts rather than disregarded as 'just a movie'. If the superhero genre revealed anything at all to new millennial audiences, it was that we in the real world need fictional superheroes just as much as the diegetic populations of the films they feature in.

FILMOGRAPHY

12 Years a Slave (Steve McQueen, 2013)
2012 (Roland Emmerich, 2012)
2001: A Space Odyssey (Stanley Kubrick, 1968)

Act of Valor (Mike McCoy and Scott Waugh, 2012)
A Good Day to Die Hard (John Moore, 2013)
Alexander (Oliver Stone, 2004)
The All-Star Bond Rally (Michael Audley, 1945)
The Amazing Spider-Man (Marc Webb, 2012)
The Amazing Spider-Man 2 (Marc Webb, 2014)
AmericanEast (Hesham Issawi, 2008)
American Graffiti (George Lucas, 1973)
American Sniper (Clint Eastwood, 2014)
Antboy (Ask Hasselbalch, 2013)
Ant-Man (Peyton Reed, 2015)
Ant-Man and the Wasp (Peyton Reed, 2018)
Armageddon (Michael Bay, 1998)
Apocalypse Now (Francis Ford Coppola, 1979)
Arrow (The CW, 2012–)
Avatar (James Cameron, 2009)
Avengers: Age of Ultron (Joss Whedon, 2015)

The Avengers (Joss Whedon, 2012) [in the U.K *Avengers Assemble*]
The Avengers (Jeremiah S. Chechik, 1998)

Barbarella (Roger Vadim, 1968)
Batman (Tim Burton, 1989)
Batman & Robin (Joel Schumacher, 1997)
Batman Begins (Christopher Nolan, 2005)
Batman Returns (Tim Burton, 1992)
Batman v Superman: Dawn of Justice (Zack Snyder, 2016)
Beasts of the Southern Wild (Benh Zeitlin, 2012)
Behind Enemy Lines (John Moore, 2001)
Beowulf (Robert Zemeckis, 2007)
The Big Short (Adam McKay, 2016)
The Birth of a Nation (Nate Parker, 2016)
Black Hawk Down (Ridley Scott, 2001)
Black Panther (Ryan Coogler, 2018)
The Boss Baby (Tom McGrath, 2017)
The Bourne Ultimatum (Paul Greengrass, 2007)

Captain America: The First Avenger (Joe Johnston, 2011)

Captain America: The Winter Soldier (Russo Brothers, 2014)

Captain America: Civil War (Russo Brothers, 2016)

Captain Marvel (Anna Boden and Ryan Fleck, 2019)

Casshern (Kazuaki Kiriya, 2004)

Chaplin (Richard Attenborough, 1993)

Charade (Stanley Donen, 1963)

Chinatown (Roman Polanski, 1974)

Chronicle (Josh Trank, 2012)

Cicak-man (Yusry Abd Halim, 2006)

Cloverfield (Matt Reeves, 2008)

Close Encounters of the Third Kind (Steven Spielberg, 1977)

Crazy Heart (Scott Cooper, 2009)

Daredevil (Netflix, 2015–)

The Dark Knight (Christopher Nolan, 2008)

The Dark Knight Rises (Christopher Nolan, 2012)

Dawn of the Dead (George Romero, 1978)

Dawn of the Planet of the Apes (Matt Reeves, 2014)

The Day After Tomorrow (Roland Emmerich, 2004)

Deadpool (Tim Miller, 2016)

Deep Impact (Mimi Leder, 1998)

The Deer Hunter (Michael Cimino, 1978)

Defendor (Peter Stebbings, 2009)

Dick Tracy (Warren Beatty, 1990)

Die Hard (John McTiernan, 1988)

Dirty Harry (Don Siegel, 1971)

The Dirty Dozen (Robert Aldrich, 1967)

Doctor Strange (Scott Derrickson, 2016)

Dracula Untold (Gary Shore, 2014)

Elf (Jon Favreau, 2003)

Entrapment (John Amiel, 1999)

The Empire Strikes Back (Irving Kershner, 1980)

E.T. The Extra-Terrestrial (Steven Spielberg, 1982)

Ex Machina (Alex Garland, 2015)

Fantastic Four (Tim Story, 2005)

Fantastic Voyage (Richard Fleischer, 1966)

Fatal Attraction (Adrian Lynne, 1987)

Fight Club (David Fincher, 1999)

Firefly (Fox, 2002–3)

First Blood (Ted Kotcheff, 1982)

The Flash (CW, 2014–)

Flash Gordon (Frederick Stephani, 1936)

Fruitvale Station (Ryan Coogler, 2013)

Fury (David Ayer, 2014)

Full House (ABC, 1987–95)

Footloose (Herbert Ross, 1984)

Futurama (FOX, 1999–2003, Comedy Central, 2008–13)

Gatchaman (Toya Sato, 2013)

Get Out (Jordan Peele, 2017)

The Goldbergs (ABC, 2013–)

The Goonies (Richard Donner, 1985)

Gotham (Fox, 2014–)

Grace is Gone (James C. Strouse, 2007)

The Green Hornet (Michel Gondry, 2010)

The Great Wall (Zhang Yimou, 2016)

Green Lantern (Martin Campbell, 2011)

Guardians (Sarik Andreasyan, 2017)

Guardians of the Galaxy (James Gunn, 2014)

Guardians of the Galaxy: Vol. 2 (James Gunn, 2017)

Hancock (Peter Berg, 2008)

Harsh Times (David Ayer, 2005)

Heat (Michael Mann, 1995)

Hellboy (Guillermo Del Toro, 2004)

Hellboy II: The Golden Army (Guillermo Del Toro, 2008)

High Noon (Fred Zinneman, 1952)

A History of Violence (David Cronenberg, 2007)

House of Cards (Netflix, 2013–)

Hulk (Ang Lee, 2003)

The Hurt Locker (Kathryn Bigelow, 2008)

I am Legend (Francis Lawrence, 2007)

iBoy (Adam Randall, 2017)

The Incredible Hulk (Louis Leterrier, 2008)

The Incredibles (Brad Bird, 2004)

Independence Day (Roland Emmerich, 1996)
In the Valley of Elah (Paul Haggis, 2007)
Invasion of the Body Snatchers (Philip Kaufman, 1978)
I, Robot (Francis Lawrence, 2004)
Iron Fist (Netflix, 2016–)
Iron Man (Jon Favreau, 2008)
Iron Man 2 (Jon Favreau, 2010)
Iron Man 3 (Shane Black, 2013)
It (Andrés Muschietti, 2017)

Jack Ryan: Shadow Recruit (Kenneth Branagh, 2014)
Jaws (Steven Spielberg, 1975)
Jessica Jones (Netflix, 2016–)
Jewel of the Nile (Lewis Teague, 1985)
Jericho (CBS, 2006–8)

Kick Ass (Matthew Vaughn, 2010)
King Kong (John Guillermin, 1976)
Kiss Kiss Bang Bang (Shane Black, 2005)
Koi... Mil Gaya (Rakesh Roshan, 2003)
Korengal (Sebastian Junger, 2014)
Knowing (Alex Proyas, 2009)
Kong: Skull Island (Jordan Vogt-Roberts, 2017)
Krrish (Rakesh Roshan, 2006)
Krrish 3 (Rakesh Roshan, 2013)

The LEGO Batman Movie (Chris McKay, 2017)
The LEGO Movie (Phil Lord and Christopher Miler, 2014)
Lethal Weapon (Richard Donner, 1987)
The Last Boy Scout (Tony Scot, 1991)
Leaves of Grass (Tim Blake Nelson, 2009)
Little Big Man (Arthur Penn, 1970)
Logan (James Mangold, 2017)
Lois and Clark: The New Adventures of Superman (ABC, 1993–97)
Lone Survivor (Peter Berg, 2013)
Luke Cage (Netflix, 2016–)

Made (Jon Favreau, 2001)
Mad Men (AMC, 2007–15)
The Maltese Falcon (John Huston, 1941)
Man of Steel (Zack Snyder, 2013)
The Manchurian Candidate (John Frankenheimer, 1962)

The Man Who Shot Liberty Valence (John Ford, 1962)
The Marathon Man (John Schlesinger, 1972)
Margin Call (J.C. Chandor, 2011)
Marvel's Agents of S.H.I.E.L.D. (ABC, 2013–)
Marvel's Agent Carter (ABC, 2015–16)
Mercury Man (Bhandit Thongdee, 2006)
Melinda and Melinda (Woody Allen, 2005)
Metropolis (Fritz Lang, 1927)
Moscow Doesn't Believe in Tears (Vladimir Menshov, 1980)
The Mummy (Alex Kurtzman, 2017)

O.J.: Made in America (Ezra Edelman, 2016)
Oldboy (Chan-wook Park, 2004)
Orange is the New Black (Netflix, 2013–)

The Parallax View (Alan J. Pakula, 1974)
Pearl Harbour (Michael Bay, 2001)
Pinocchio (Ben Sharpsteen and Hamilton Luske, 1940)
Pirates of the Caribbean: The Curse of the Black Pearl (Gore Verbinski, 2003)
Platoon (Oliver Stone, 1986)
Predator (John McTiernan, 1987)
Primal Fear (Gregory Hoblitt, 1996)
The Punisher (Jonathon Hensleigh, 2004)
The Punisher: War Zone (Lexi Alexander, 2008)
The Punisher (Mark Goldblatt, 1989)
Push (Paul McGuigan, 2009)

Raiders of the Lost Ark (Steven Spielberg, 1981)
Rambo: First Blood Part Two (George P. Cosmatos, 1985)
Redacted (Brian De Palma, 2007)
Rendel (Jesse Haaja, 2017)
Rendition (Gavin Hood, 2007)
The Right Stuff (Philip Kaufman, 1983)
Restrepo (Tim Hetherington & Sebastian Junger, 2010)
Rocky IV (Sylvester Stallone, 1985)
Rogue One: A Star Wars Story (Gareth Edwards, 2016)
Romancing the Stone (Robert Zemeckis, 1984)

Salt (Philip Noyce, 2010)

Sands of Iwo Jima (Allan Dwan, 1949)

Saving Private Ryan (Steven Spielberg, 1998)

The Searchers (John Ford, 1956)

Serenity (Joss Whedon, 2005)

Sesame Street (Various, 1969–)

Shakespeare in Love (John Madden, 1998)

Six Days and Seven Nights (Ivan Reitman, 1998)

Sky High (Mike Mitchell, 2005)

Slither (James Gunn, 2006)

Smallville (The WB, 2001–6, The CW, 2006–11)

The Singing Detective (Keith Gordon, 2003)

Soldier Blue (Ralph Nelson, 1970)

Sons of Anarchy (FX, 2008–14)

Special (Hal Haberman and Jeremy Passmore, 2006)

Spider-Man (Sam Raimi, 2002)

Spider-Man 3 (Sam Raimi, 2007)

Spider-Man: Homecoming (Jon Watts, 2017)

Split (M. Night Shyamalan, 2017)

Star Wars: A New Hope (George Lucas, 1977)

The Sum of All Fears (Phil Alden Robinson, 2002)

Star Trek: Into Darkness (J.J. Abrams, 2013)

Star Wars: The Force Awakens (J.J. Abrams, 2015)

Stranger Things (Netflix, 2016–)

Stop-Loss (Kimberly Peirce, 2008)

Suicide Squad (David Ayer, 2016)

Super 8 (J.J. Abrams, 2011)

SuperBob (Jon Drever, 2015)

Supergirl (CBS, 2015–)

Superman (Richard Donner, 1978)

Superman II (Richard Donner and Richard Lester)

Superman III (Richard Lester, 1983)

Superman IV: The Quest for Peace (Sidney J. Furie, 1987)

Superman Returns (Bryan Singer, 2006)

Taxi Driver (Martin Scorsese, 1976)

Taxi to the Dark Side (Alex Gibney, 2008)

The Texas Chainsaw Massacre (Tobe Hooper, 1974)

There Will be Blood (Paul Thomas Anderson, 2007)

They Call Me Jeeg (Gabriele Mainetti, 2015)

Three Days of the Condor (Sydney Pollack, 1975)

Thor (Kenneth Branagh, 2011)

Thor: The Dark World (Alan Foster, 2014)

Thor: Ragnarok (Taika Waititi, 2017)

Titanic (James Cameron, 1997)

Top Gun (Tony Scott, 1986)

Transformers: Age of Extinction (Michael Bay, 2014)

Transformers (Michael Bay, 2007)

The Transporter (Louis Leterrier, 2002)

Transparent (Amazon Studios, 2014–)

Tropic Thunder (Ben Stiller, 2009)

U-571 (Johnathan Mostow, 2000)

Ultraman: The Next (Kazuya Konaka, 2004)

United 93 (Paul Greengrass, 2006)

Unleashed (Louis Leterrier, 2005)

Up in the Air (Jason Reitman, 2009)

Veronica Mars (UPN, 2004–6, the CW 2006–7)

W. (Oliver Stone, 2008)

Wanted (Timur Bekmambetov, 2008)

Wall Street (Oliver Stone, 1987)

The Wars of the Roses (Danny DeVito, 1989)

War of the Worlds (Steven Spielberg, 2005)

Watchmen (Zack Snyder, 2009)

Wonder Woman (Patty Jenkins, 2017)

The Wolf of Wall Street (Martin Scorsese, 2013)

World War Z (Marc Forster, 2015)

X-Men (Bryan Singer, 2000)

X-Men: Days of Future Past (Bryan Singer, 2014)

X-Men Origins: Wolverine (Gavin Hood, 2009)

Yankee Doodle Dandy (Michael Curtiz, 1942)

Zathura (Jon Favreau, 2005)

Zero Dark Thirty (Kathryn Bigelow, 2012)

BIBLIOGRAPHY

Abad-Santos, Alex (2016) 'The Avengers was an authoritarian fantasy. Captain America: Civil War challenges it', Vox.com 17 May 2016. Online. Available: http://www.vox.com/2016/5/17/11663484/captain-america-civil-war-authoritarian (accessed 20 January 2017).

Abramowitz, Rachel (2005) 'Scared Silly', Los Angeles Times. 8 May. E26.

Abrams, Natalie (2015) 'Agent Carter Crashes the Boys Club', Entertainment Weekly. 8 January. Online. Available: http://ew.com/article/2015/01/08/agent-carter-crashes-boys-club/ (accessed 7 February 2017).

Ackerman, Spencer (2012) 'Pentagon Quit The Avengers Because of Its "Unreality"', Wired. 7 May. Online. Available: https://www.wired.com/2012/05/avengers-military/ (accessed 21 January 2017).

Acuna, Kirsten (2014) 'Tom Hiddleston Sent an Amazing Email to Director Joss Whedon After Reading The Avengers Script For The First Time', Business Insider. 25 July. Online. Available: http://www.businessinsider.com/tom-hiddlestons-avengers-email-to-joss-whedon-2014–7?IR=T (accessed 20 January 2017).

Alford Matthew and Tom Secker (2017) National Security Cinema: The Shocking New Evidence of Government Control in Hollywood. Self-Published: Drum Roll Books.

Amarillo, Ignacio Andrés (2014) 'De la II Guerra a la era Snowden', El Litoral. 3 April. Online. Available: http://www.ellitoral.com/index.php/diarios/2014/04/03/escenariosysociedad/SOCI-05.html (accessed 20 June 2017).

Anderson, Benedict (1983) Imagined Communities: Reflections on the Origins and Spread of Nationalism. London: Verso.

Anon. (2005) 'Robert Downey Jr. I'm absolutely normal really', The Independent. 8 March. Online. Available: http://www.independent.co.uk/news/people/profiles/robert-downey-jr-im-absolutely-normal-really-6150848.html. (accessed 17 February 2015).

____ (2012) 'ScarJo, Ruffalo shot in India?', The Times of India. 25 April. Online. Available: http://timesofindia.indiatimes.com/entertainment/english/hollywood/news/ScarJo-Ruffalo-shot-in-India/articleshow/12851450.cms (accessed 22 April 2016).

____ (2015) *Peabody Awards* '75th Annual Entertainment & Children's Programming Winners'. Online. Available: http://www.peabodyawards.com/stories/story/75th-annual-entertainment-childrens-programming-winners (accessed 9 June 2017).

____ (2017a) 'Street Fighter', *Total Film*, 257, 116–17.

____ (2017b) 'New BFI statistics show robust year for film in the UK in 2016', *British Film Institute*. 26 January. Online. Available: http://www.bfi.org.uk/news-opinion/news-bfi/announcements/highest-grossing-films-uk-box-office-2016 (accessed 11 June 2017).

Arnold, Martin (2011a) *Thor: Myth to Marvel*. New York: Continuum.

____ (2011b) 'Thor the Movie: Politics with a Hammer – A guest post by Martin Arnold, author of *Thor: Myth to Marvel*', *Bloomsbury History*. 23 May. Online. Available: http://bloomsburyhistory.typepad.com/bloomsbury-history/2011/05/thor-the-movie-politics-with-a-hammer-a-guest-post-by-martin-arnold-author-of-thor-myth-to-marvel.html (accessed 22 November 2016).

Asher-Perrin, Emily (2012) '"Agent Coulson Lives": A New Movement Springs Up in Avengers Fandom', *TOR*. 12 October. Online. Available: http://www.tor.com/2012/10/12/qagent-coulson-livesq-a-new-movement-springs-up-in-avengers-fandom/ (accessed 10 January 2017).

Astrada, Marvin (2010) *American Power After 9/11*. London: Palgrave.

Auster, Albert (2005) 'Saving Private Ryan and American Triumphalism', in Robert T. Eberwein (ed.) *The War Film*. New Brunswick, NJ: Rutgers University Press, 205–13.

Axe, David (2011) 'Buyer's Remorse: How much has the F22 really cost?' *Wired*. 14 December. Online. Available: http://www.wired.com/2011/12/f-22-real-cost/ (accessed 15 May 2016).

Bacevich, Andrew (2002) *American Empire: The Realities and Consequences of U.S. Diplomacy*. Washington, DC: Harvard University Press.

____ (2003) *The Imperial Tense: Prospects and Problems of American Empire*. Lanham, MD: Ivan R. Dee.

Bailey, George (2004) 'Why We (Should Not) Fight: Colonel Frank Capra Interviewed', in Leland Poague (ed.) *Frank Capra Interviews*. Jackson, MS: University of Mississippi Press, 124–31.

Baker-Whitelaw, Gavia (2016) 'Where's Gamora in the new "Guardians of the Galaxy, Vol. 2" trailer?', *The Daily Dot*. 5 December. Online. Available: https://www.dailydot.com/parsec/gamora-guardians-galaxy-2-trailer-sexism/?fb=dd (accessed 14 June 2017).

Baron, Cynthia (2009) '*Doctor No*: Bonding Britishness to racial sovereignty', in Christoph Lindner (ed.) *The James Bond Phenomenon: A Critical Reader*. Manchester: Manchester University Press, 153–68.

Baron, Cynthia, Diane Carson and Mark Bernard (2013) *Appetites and Anxieties: Food, Film and the Politics of Representation*. Detroit, MI: Wayne State University Press.

Barraclough, Leo (2017) 'Russian Box Office Grows 9.5% to $727 Million in 2016', *Variety*. 16 January. Online. Available: http://variety.com/2017/film/global/russian-box-office-2016-1201961000/ (accessed 11 June 2017).

Bazin, André (1968) 'La Politique Des Auteurs', in Peter Graham (ed.) *The New Wave*. London: Secker and Warburg, 143–4.

Bearman, Jonathan (1986) *Qadhafi's Libya*. London: Zed Books.

Beck, Glenn (2014) 'Captain America directors admit the film is a critique of Obama's drone policy and NSA', *GlennBeck.com*. 7 April. Web. Online. Available: http://www.glennbeck.com/2014/04/07/captain-america-directors-admit-the-film-is-a-critique-of-obamas-drone-policy-and-nsa/?utm_source=glennbeck&utm_medium=contentcopy_link?utm_source=glennbeck&utm_medium=contentcopy_link (accessed 10 May 2016).

Bell, J. Bowyer (1999) *Dragonwars: Armed Struggle and the Conventions of Modern War*. London: Transaction.

Benjamin, Troy (2014) *Marvel's Agents of S.H.I.E.L.D: Season One Declassified*. New York: Marvel Worldwide.

____ (2015) *Marvel's Agents of S.H.I.E.L.D: Season Two Declassified*. New York: Marvel Worldwide.

Bennett, William J. (2002) *Why We Fight: Moral Clarity and the War on Terrorism*. New York: Doubleday.

Berger, Arthur Asa (1972) 'Comics and American Culture', in George Lewis (ed.) *Side-Saddle on the Golden Calf: Social Structure and Popular Culture in America*. Pacific Palisades: Goodyear.

Berger, James (1999) *After the End: Representations of Post-apocalypse*. Minneapolis, MN: University of Minnesota Press.

Bernstein, Carl and Bob Woodward (1974) *All the President's Men*. New York: Simon and Schuster.

Bhushan, Nyay (2014) 'India Box Office Grows 10 Percent in 2013', *Hollywood Reporter*. 12 March. http://www.hollywoodreporter.com/news/india-box-office-grows-10-687933 (accessed 12 October 2017).

Blow, Charles M. (2011) 'My Very Own Captain America', *The New York Times*. 29 July. Online. Available: http://www.nytimes.com/2011/07/30/opinion/blow-my-very-own-captain-america.html (15 June 2016).

Bodnar, John (2010) *The 'Good War' in American Memory*. Baltimore, MD: Johns Hopkins University Press.

Bond, Benton (2013) 'Redemptive anti-Americanism and the death of Captain America', *Studies in Communication Sciences*. 13, 1, 75–83.

Booker, M. Keith (2007) *Postmodern Hollywood: What's New in Film and Why It Makes Us Feel So Strange Hardcover*. Westport CT: Praeger.

Boot, John (2010) '*Iron Man 2*: A Love Letter to Ronald Reagan?', *Pjmedia*. 7 May. Online. Available: https://pjmedia.com/blog/iron-man-2-a-love-letter-to-ronald-reagan/ (accessed 12 July 2015).

Boot, Max (2017) 'Donald Trump: A Modern Manchurian Candidate?', *The New York Times*. 11 January. Online. Available: https://www.nytimes.com/2017/01/11/opinion/donald-trump-a-modern-manchurian-candidate.html (accessed 22 May 2017).

Borrelli, Christopher (2009) 'Talking to the Chicago college student who may be behind Obama-as-Joker poster', *Chicago Tribune*. 19 August. Online. Available: http://articles.chicagotribune.com/2009–08-19/entertainment/0908180509_1_posters-joker-adobe-photoshop (accessed 9 March 2017).

Boucher, Geoff (2006) 'Ka-pow, Spidey!', *Los Angeles Times*. 22 July. Online. Available: http://articles.latimes.com/2006/jul/22/entertainment/et-comic22 (accessed 6 June 2015).

Bouie, Jamelle (2014) 'Marvel's Civil War is a Far-Right Paranoid Fantasy – and a Mess. Can the Movies Fix It?' *Slate*. 20 October. Online. Available: http://www.slate.com/blogs/browbeat/2014/10/20/marvel_s_civil_war_storyline_is_a_far_right_paranoid_fantasy_and_a_mess.html (accessed 12 June 2016).

Bowles, Scott (2008) 'First look: Downey forges a bond with *Iron Man* role', *USA Today*. 27 April. Online. Available: http://usatoday30.usatoday.com/life/movies/news/2007–04-26-iron-man_N.htm (accessed 3 January 2016).

Boykin, William G. (2008) *Never Surrender: A Soldier's Journey to the Crossroads of Faith and Freedom*. New York: Hachette.

Bradley, William (2010) 'Iron Man's Post-Modern Howard Hughes is Back and Confused', *The Huffington Post*. 13 May. Online. Available: http://www.huffingtonpost.com/william-bradley/iiron-manis-post-modern-h_b_575392.html. (2 February 2016).

Braudy, Leo (2002) *The World in a Frame: What We See in Films*. Chicago: University of Chicago Press.

Brew, Simon (2011) 'Mickey Rourke on where *Iron Man 2* went wrong', *Den of Geek*. 31 October. Online. Available: http://www.denofgeek.com/movies/18260/mickey-rourke-on-where-iron-man-2-went-wrong (accessed 17 March 2016).

Brewer, Michael (2004) *Who Needs a Superhero? Finding Virtue, Vice and What's Holy in Comics*. Ada, MI: Baker Publishing.

Breznican, Anthony (2012) '*The Avengers*: Hero worship', *Entertainment Weekly*. 27 April. Online. Available: http://ew.com/article/2012/04/27/avengers-hero-worship/ (accessed Web. 22 August 2015).

Brittan, Arthur (1989) *Masculinity and Power*. Oxford: Blackwell.

Brody, Richard (2012) '*The Avengers*: Not Unlike An F-16 Stunt Run', *The New Yorker*. 4 May. Online. Available: http://www.newyorker.com/online/blogs/movies/2012/05/the-avengers-review.html (accessed 22 March 2015).

Brown, Jeffrey (2016) *The Modern Superhero in Film and Television: Popular Genre and American Culture*. New York and London: Routledge.

Buchanan, Kyle (2013) 'Is It Possible to Make a Hollywood Blockbuster Without Evoking 9/11?', *The Vulture*. 13 June. Online. Available: http://www.vulture.com/2013/06/hollywood-blockbusters-cant-stop-evoking-911.html (accessed 2 June 2017).

Buckley, Roger (2002) *The United States in the Asia-Pacific Since 1945*. Cambridge: Cambridge University Press.

Bumiller, Elizabeth (2002) 'THREATS AND RESPONSES: THE ALLIES; Bush, at NATO Meeting, Firms Up His "Posse"', *The New York Times*. 22 November. Online. Available: http://www.nytimes.com/2002/11/22/world/threats-and-responses-the-allies-bush-at-nato-meeting-firms-up-his-posse.html (accessed 11 June 2017).

Burch Jr., Barry (n.d.) 'Barry Burch: The Hulk is a Metaphor for Rage in the Black Man Created by White Supremacy', *Black/Blue Dog*. Online. Available: http://blackbluedog.com/2013/07/news/barry-burch-the-hulk-is-a-metaphor-for-rage-in-the-black-man-created-by-white-supremacy/ (accessed 22 January 2017).

Burke, Jason (2012) *9/11 Wars*. New York and London: Penguin.

Burlingame, Russ (2012) 'Robert Downey Jr. Says Shane Black Did Uncredited Work on the First Iron Man', *Comicbook.com*. 16 December. Online. Available: http://comicbook.com/blog/2012/12/16/robert-downey-jr-says-shane-black-did-uncredited-work-on-the-first-iron-man/ (accessed 7 June 2017).

Burr, Ty (2014) 'Things get darker for Captain America', *The Boston Globe*. 3 April. Online. Available: https://www.bostonglobe.com/arts/movies/2014/04/03/movie-review-things-get-darker-for-captain-america/wGmB3MyFS3gxsnOZo6L5SK/story.html (accessed 12 January 2017).

Burroughs, John (1913) *Writings* (Volume 17). Boston: Houghton Mifflin.

Bush, George H. W. (1992) 'Convention of the National Guard Association', Salt Lake City, 15 September.

Bush, George W. (2001a) 'Inauguration Speech', 20 January.

____(2001b) 'Address to Joint Session of Congress on Administration Goals', Washington, 27 February.

____(2001c) 'Bush Addresses Nation After 9/11', 12 September.

____(2001d) 'Bush Addresses the Nation', 20 September.

____(2001e) 'Georgia World Congress Center speech' Georgia, 9 November.

____(2001f) 'Address before UN General Assembly', New York, 10 November.

____(2002) 'Ellis Island speech', New York, 12 September.

____(2004) 'President Bush's Acceptance Speech to the Republican National Convention', New York, 2 September.

Butler, Judith (2006) *Precarious Life: The Powers of Mourning and Violence*. London: Verso.

____(2010) *Frames of War: When is Life Grievable?* London: Verso.

Calhoun, Bob (2011) 'The politics of Captain America', *Salon*. 19 July. Online. Available: http://www.salon.com/2011/07/19/captain_america_politics/ (accessed 22 September 2016).

Campbell, Joseph (1949) *The Hero with a Thousand Faces*. Pantheon: New York.

Carnevale, Rob (n.d.) 'Iron Man – Jon Favreau Interview. *indie London*. Online. Available: http://www.indielondon.co.uk/Film-Review/iron-man-jon-favreau-interview (accessed 22 June 2015).

Carroll, Larry (2010) 'Exclusive: Anthony Hopkins talks *Thor*, says thou shalt not hear Shakespearean talk', *MTV*. 9 February. Online. Available: http://www.mtv.com/news/2596022/exclusive-anthony-hopkins-talks-thor-says-thou-shalt-not-hear-shakespearean-talk/ (accessed 22 June 2016).

Carroll, Sean (2010) *From Eternity to Here*. London: Oneworld.

Carter, Sean and Klaus Dodds (2014) *International Politics and Film: Space, Vision and Power*. London: Wallflower Press.

Catalan, Cristobal Giraldez (2008) '"Heckuva Job, Tony!": Racism and Hegemony Rage in *Iron Man*', *Bright Lights Film Journal*, 61. 31 July. Online. Available: http://brightlightsfilm.com/heckuva-job-tony-racism-and-hegemony-rage-in-ironman/#.WGzrmpLiLIU (accessed 12 June 2015).

Chambliss, Julian (2012) 'A Terrible Privilege: The Invincible Iron Man and the Burden of Hegemonic Power', A paper delivered at The Popular Culture Association / American Culture Association in the South Annual Conference. 27 September.

Chanda, Anurima (2015) 'Postcolonial Responses to the Western Superhero: A Study though Indian Nonsense Literature', *Lapis Lazuli: An International Literary Journal*, 5, 1, 68–89.

Chang, Justin (2016) 'Review', *Variety*, 13 April. Online. Available: http://variety.com/2016/film/reviews/captain-america-civil-war-review-1201752643/ (accessed 22 April 2016).

Chapman, James (2007) *Licence to Thrill: A Cultural History of the James Bond Films*. London: IB Tauris.

Chaudhuri, Shohini (2014) *Cinema of the Dark Side: Atrocity and the Ethics of Film Spectatorship*. Edinburgh: Edinburgh University Press.

Chavez, Danette (2017) 'Blandness is *Iron Fist*'s greatest enemy', *AV Club*. 13 March. Online. Available: http://www.avclub.com/review/blandness-iron-fists-greatest-enemy-251943 (accessed 9 June 2017).

Cherkowski, Robert (n.d.) 'Review', *Filmstarts*. Online. Available: http://www.filmstarts.de/kritiken/136557/kritik.html (accessed 9 June 2017).

Chermak, Steven, Frankie Y. Baily and Michelle Brown (2003) 'Introduction', in Steven Chermak, Frankie Y. Baily and Michelle Brown (eds) *Media Representations of September 11*. Westport, CT: Praeger, 1–14.

Chomsky, Noam (2001) *9–11*. New York: Seven Stories Press.

___(2007) *Failed States. The Abuse of Power and the Assault on Democracy*. New York: Penguin.

Chute, David (2013) 'Review', *Variety*. 1 November. Online. Available: http://variety.com/2013/film/reviews/krrish-3-review-1200786415/ (accessed 11 June 2017).

Clarke, Arthur Charles (1973) *Profiles of the Future: An Inquiry into the Limits of the Possible*. New York: Harper & Row.

'CNN Poll: Afghan War arguably most unpopular in US History', 30 December 2013. Online. Available: http://politicalticker.blogs.cnn.com/2013/12/30/cnn-poll-afghanistan-war-most-unpopular-in-u-s-history/ (accessed 22 January 2017).

Coleman, Loren (2017) 'Mangold Corn: Logan, Shane, Perdition', *Twilight Language*. 20 March. Online. Available: http://copycateffect.blogspot.co.uk/2017/03/MangoldCorn.html (accessed 11 June 2017).

Collinson, Gary (2015) 'Robert Downey Jr. talks *Avengers: Age of Ultron* and Tony Stark's relationship with Steve Rogers', *Flickering Myth*. 27 March. Online. Available: http://www.flickeringmyth.com/2015/03/robert-downey-jr-talks-avengers-age-of-ultron-and-tony-starks-relationship-with-steve-rogers/ (accessed 22 December 2015).

Colucci, Lamont (2008) *Crusading Realism: The Bush Doctrine and American Core Values After 9/11*. Lanham, MD: University Press of America.

Comolli, Jean-Louis, and Jean Narboni (1977 [1969]) 'Cinema/Ideology/Criticism', in Bill Nichols (ed.) *Movies and Methods* (volume 1). Berkeley, CA: University of California Press, 22–30.

Comtois, Pierre (2009) *Marvel Comics in the 1960s: An Issue-By-Issue Field Guide to a Pop Culture Phenomenon*. Raleigh, NC: TwoMorrows.

Controvich, James T. (2015) *African-Americans in Defense of the Nation: A Bibliography*. Lanham, MD: Scarecrow Press.

Coogan, Peter (2006) *Superhero: The Secret Origin of a Genre*. Austin, TX: Monkeybrain.

Corliss, Richard (2009) '*2012* End of the World Disaster Porn', *Time*. 12 November. Online. Available: http://www.time.com/time/arts/article/0,8599,1938799,00.html (accessed 27 May 2010).

___(2010) 'Hero Worship: *Iron Man 2*'s Troubled Heart', *Time*. 17 May. Online. Available: http://content.time.com/time/magazine/article/0,9171,1987584,00.html (accessed 22 May 2016).

Costa, Jordi (2015) 'El gestor de mitologías', *El Pais*. 30 April. Online. Available: http://cultura.elpais.com/cultura/2015/04/30/actualidad/1430398196_289707.html (accessed 12 May 2017).

Costello, Matthew (2009) *Secret Identity Crisis: Comic Books and the Unmasking of Cold War America*. New York: Continuum.

Coventry, Tyler (2015) 'Masculinity, fatherhood in superhero films', *The Buchtelite*. 18 March. Online. Available: https://buchtelite.com/26463/arts_and_life/movies-arts_and_life/masculinity-fatherhood-in-superhero-films/ (accessed 12 March 2016).

Cowden, Caterina (2015) 'Movie attendance has been on a dismal decline since 1940s', *Business Insider UK*, 6 January. Online. Available: http://uk.businessinsider.com/movie-attendance-over-the-years-2015–1 (accessed 22 May 2016).

Cross, David (n.d.) 'Iron Man-sion: Tony Stark's House Listed for $117.2 million', *Movoto*. Online. Available: http://www.movoto.com/blog/novelty-real-estate/iron-man/ (accessed 22 March 2016).

Crossley-Holland, Kevin (1980) *The Penguin Book of Norse Myths: Gods of the Vikings*. New York. Penguin.

Cullen, Jim (2017) *Democratic Empire: The United States Since 1945*. 2017. Chichester: Wiley Blackwell.

Curtis, Neal (2016) *Sovereignty and Superheroes*. Manchester: Manchester University Press.

Daily, James and Ryan Davidson (2013) *The Law of Superheroes*. New York: Gotham Books.

Dargis, Manohla (2012) 'A Rejected Superhero ends up at Ground Zero', *The New York Times*. 18 July. Online. Available: http://movies.nytimes.com/2012/07/20/movies/the-dark-knight-rises-with-christian-bale.html?pagewanted=all (accessed 7 July 2015).

____ (2013) 'Bang, Boom: Terrorism as a Game', *The New York Times*. 2 May. Online. Available: http://movies.nytimes.com/2013/05/03/movies/iron-man-3-with-robert-downey-jr.html?pagewanted=all&_r=0 (accessed 9 November 2013).

Darowski, Joseph J. and John Darowski (2015) 'Smashing Cold War Consensus Culture: Hulk's Journey from Monster to Hero', in Joseph Darowski (ed.) *The Ages of the Incredible Hulk: Essays on the Green Goliath in Changing Times*. Jefferson, NC: McFarland, 7–23.

Daughtry, J. Martin (2015) *Listening to War: Sound, Music, Trauma and Survival in Wartime Iraq*. Oxford: Oxford University Press.

David, Peter (2008a) *Iron Man*. London: Titan Books.

____ (2008b) *The Incredible Hulk*. New York: Ballantine Books.

David, Brandon (2017) 'Spider-Man's Peter Parker Confirmed to Have Appeared in *Iron Man 2*', *Comicbook.com*, June 26. Online. Available: http://comicbook.com/marvel/2017/06/26/spider-man-peter-parker-iron-man-2-cameo-/ (accessed 7 July 2017).

Dayal, Samir (2015) *Dream Machine: Realism and Fantasy in Hindi Cinema*. Philadelphia: Temple University Press.

DeFalco, Tom (2003). *The Hulk: The Incredible Guide*. London: Dorling Kindersley.

Delaney, Sam (2009) 'Crash, bang, wallop what a picture', *The Guardian*. 22 May. Online. Available: https://www.theguardian.com/film/2009/may/22/shane-black-12-rounds (accessed 21 May 2015).

Delcroix, Oliver (2012) '*The Avengers*: le film étendard des années Obama', *Le Figero*. 20 April. Online. Available: http://www.lefigaro.fr/cinema/2012/04/19/03002-20120419ARTFIG00783--the-avengers-le-film-etendard-des-annees-obama.php (accessed 13 February 2017).

Denison, Rayna and Rachel Mizsei-Ward (eds) (2016) *Superheroes on World Screens*. Jackson, MS: University Press of Mississippi.

Dershowitz, Alan (2008) *Why Terrorism Works: Understanding the Threat, Responding to the Challenge*. New Haven, CT: Yale University Press.

De Semlyen, Nick (2008) 'Fight Club', *Empire*. June, 64–72.

Dillon, Sarah (2007) *The Palimpsest: Literature, Criticism, and Theory*. London: Continuum.

DiPaolo, Marc (2011) *War, Politics and Superheroes: Ethics and propaganda in Comics and Film*. Jefferson, NC: McFarland and Company.

Dittmer, Jason (2005) 'Captain America's Empire: Reflections on Identity, Popular Culture, and Post-9/11 Geopolitics', *Annals of the Association of American Geographers*, 95, 3, 626–43.

____ (2010) 'American Exceptionalism, Visual Effects, and the Post-9/11 Cinematic Superhero Boom', *Environment and Planning D: Society and Space*, 29, 114–30.

____ (2012) *Captain America and the Nationalist Superhero: Metaphors, Narratives, and Geopolitics*. Philadelphia, PA: Temple University Press.

Donovan, Barna William (2011) *Conspiracy Films: A Tour of Dark Places in the American Conscious*. Jefferson, NC: McFarland.

Douglas, Edward (2008) 'Exclusive: An In-Depth *Iron Man* Talk with Jon Favreau', *Superherohype*. 29 April. Online. Available: http://www.superherohype.com/features/96427-exclusive-an-in-depth-iron-man-talk-with-jon-favreau#mdJrXzj105J4olDF.99 (accessed 3 March 2015).

Duncan, Randy and Matthew Smith (eds) (2013) *Icons of the American Comic Book: From Captain America to Wonder Woman*. Santa Barbara, CA: Greenwood.

Dupont, Veronique (2014) 'Netflix Has Revolutionized the TV Industry Several Times in Just 17 Years', *Business Insider*. 12 September. Online. Available: http://www.businessinsider.com/afp-netflix-the-revolution-that-changed-the-us-tv-landscape-2014–9?IR=T (accessed 22 July 2015).

Durham, Robert (2015) *Supplying the Enemy: The Modern Arms Industry & the Military–Industrial Complex*. Lulu.com.

DuToit, Kim (n.d.) 'The Pussification of the Western Male', *Tall Town*. Online. Available: http://talltown.us/guns/nancyboys.htm (accessed 6 June 2015).

Dyce, Andrew (2012) 'David S. Goyer Says *Man of Steel* Will Be "Realistic" Like Nolan's Batman', *Screenrant*. 10 January. Online. Available: http://screenrant.com/superman-man-of-steel-realistic-david-goyer-christopher-nolan-batman/ (accessed 3 March 2015).

____ (2014) 'Marvel Says Netflix's *Daredevil* Planned as "One Large Movie"', *Screenrant*. 11 May. Online. Available: http://screenrant.com/daredevil-netflix-series-movie-story/ (accessed 12 June 2016).

Easthope, Anthony (1992) *What a Man's Gotta Do: The Masculine Myth in Popular Culture*. New York: Routledge.

Eaton, Lance (2013) 'The Hulking Hyde: How the Incredible Hulk Reinvented the Modern Jekyll and Hyde Monster', in Aalya Ahmad and Sean Moreland (eds) *Fear and Learning: Essays on the Pedagogy of Horror*. Jefferson, NC: McFarland, 138–55.

Eaton, Mick (1978/79) 'Television Situation Comedy', *Screen*, 19, 4, 61–89.

Eddy, Max (2014) 'Is *Captain America: The Winter Soldier* a Post-Snowden Superhero Movie? Not Quite', *PC Magazine*. 29 April. Online. Available: http://uk.pcmag.com/opinion/9881/is-captain-america-the-winter-soldier-a-post-snowden-superhe (accessed 22 April 2015).

Edelstein, David (2014) 'Edelstein on *Captain America: The Winter Soldier*: Beneath the CGI, an Old-School Conspiracy Thriller', *New York Magazine*. 4 April. Online. Available: http://www.vulture.com/2014/04/review-captain-america-the-winter-soldier.html (accessed 10 May 2016).

Elsaesser, Thomas (2001) 'The Blockbuster: Everything connects, but not everything goes', in Jon Lewis (ed.) *The End of Cinema as We Know It: American Film in the Nineties*. New York: New York University Press, 11–22.

Engelhardt, Tom (2007 [1995]) *The End of Victory Culture: Cold War America and the Disillusioning of a Generation*. Amherst, MA: University of Massachusetts Press.

Erdemandi, Max (2013) 'Marvel Comics' *Civil War*: An Allegory of September 11 in an American Civil War Framework', *Traces: The UNC-Chapel Hill Journal of History*, 2, 213–23.

Everheart, Bill (2009) 'Summer comes earlier to movie season', *The Berkshire Eagle*. 1 May. Online. Available: http://www.berkshireeagle.com/stories/summer-comes-earlier-to-movie-season,216397 (accessed 7 June 2017).

Experience Perception (n.d.s) 'THE AVENGERSAGE OF ULTRON MAIN ON END TITLE SEQUENCE', Online. Available: http://experienceperception.com/avengers-age-of-ultron. html (accessed 11 June 2017).

Failes, Ian (2015) 'Casting the vendors on Avengers', *FX Guide*. 4 May. Online. Available: https:// www.fxguide.com/featured/casting-the-vendors-on-avengers/ (accessed 3 June 2017).

Faller, Stephen (2010) 'Iron Man's Transcendent Challenges' in Mark D. White (ed.) *Iron Man and Philosophy*. Hoboken, NJ: John Wiley, 256–64.

Faludi, Susan (2007) *The Terror Dream: Fear and Fantasy in Post-9/11 America*. Melbourne: Scribe.

Faraci, Devan (2014) 'The Badass Interview: James Gunn On *Guardians of the Galaxy*', *Birth. Movies. Death*. July 29. Online. Available: http://birthmoviesdeath.com/2014/07/29/the-badass-interview-james-gunn-on-guardians-of-the-galaxy (accessed 12 July 2015).

Favara, Jeremiah (2016) 'Gods and Freaks, Soldiers and Men: Gender, Technologies and Marvel's Avengers', in Matthew J. McEniry, Robert Moses and Robert G. Weiner (eds) *Marvel Comics into Film: Essays on Adaptations Since the 1940s*. Jefferson, NC: McFarland, 177–88.

Favreau, John (2010) 'Elon Musk', *Time*. 29 April. Online, Available: http://content.time.com/time/ specials/packages/article/0,28804,1984685_1984745_1985495,00.html (accessed 7 July 2015).

Fernandez, Charmaine (2013) 'Déjà New in Joss Whedon's Marvel's *The Avengers*', *Limina: A Journal of Historical and Cultural Studies*, 18, 2, 1–15.

Fernholz, Tim and Tankersley, Jim (2011) 'The Cost of Bin Laden: $3 Trillion Over 15 Years', *The Atlantic*, 7 May. Online. Available: https://www.theatlantic.com/business/archive/2011/05/ the-cost-of-bin-laden-3-trillion-over-15-years/238517/ (accessed 18 July 2017).

Feulner, Edwin J. and Brian Tracey (2012) *The American Spirit: Celebrating the Virtues and Values That Make Us Great*. Nashville, TN: Thomas Nelson.

Fingeroth, Danny (2004) *Superman on the Couch*. New York: Continuum.

Finke, Nikki (2012) 'Marvel's *The Avengers*: Records & Factoids', *Deadline*. 6 May. Online. Available: http://deadline.com/2012/05/marvels-the-avengers-records-factoids-267389/ (accessed 7 June 2017).

Finkelstein, Norman (1995) *The Way Things Never Were: The Truth about the 'Good Old Days'*. Lincoln, BE: Authors Guild.

Fiske, John (2010) *Television Culture*, second edition. Abingdon: Routledge.

Fitzpatrick, Kevin (2016) 'Joss Whedon defends *Agents of Shield* comments, Says Marvel TV gets "leftovers"', *Screencrush*. 3 January. Online. Available: http://screencrush.com/joss-whedon-agents-of-shield-coulson-marvel-tv/ (accessed 8 January 2017).

Flanagan, Martin, Andrew Livingstone and Mike McKenny (2016) *The Marvel Studios Phenomenon: Inside a Transmedia Universe*. New York and London: Bloomsbury Academic.

Fleming Jr., Mike (2014) 'Alejandro G. Iñárritu and "Birdman" Scribes on Hollywood's Superhero Fixation: 'Poison, Cultural Genocide' – Q&A', *Deadline*. 15 October. Online. Accessed: http://deadline.com/2014/10/birdman-director-alejandro-gonzalez-inarritu-writers-interview-852206/ (accessed 2 March 2016).

Flood, Alison (2014) 'Superheroes a "cultural catastrophe", says comics guru Alan Moore', *The Guardian*. 21 January. Online. Available: https://www.theguardian.com/books/2014/jan/21/ superheroes-cultural-catastrophe-alan-moore-comics-watchmen (accessed 9 June 2017).

Foster, Thomas (2005) 'Cynical Nationalism', in Dana Heller (ed.) *The Selling of 9/11: How a National Tragedy Became a Commodity*. New York: Palgrave MacMillan, 254–87.

Franich, Darren (2013) '17 Signs It's a Marvel Studios Movie', *Entertainment Weekly*. 8 November. Online. Available: http://ew.com/gallery/17-signs-its-marvel-studios-movie/ (accessed 13 December 2015).

____ (2014) 'The real, subversive politics of "Captain America: The Winter Soldier", *Entertainment Weekly*. 6 April. Online. Available: http://ew.com/article/2014/04/06/captain-america-the-winter-soldier-hydra-shield-paranoia/ (accessed 16 December 2015).

Frankel, Valerie Estelle (2017) *Superheroines and the Epic Journey: Mythic Themes in Comics, Film and Television*. Jefferson, NC: McFarland.

Fraser, Jody Duncan (2012) 'The Avengers', *Cinefex*, 130, 64–93.

Freeman, Hadley (2017) 'Kirk Douglas: "I never thought I'd live to 100. That's shocked me"', *The Guardian*. 12 February. Online. Available: https://www.theguardian.com/film/2017/feb/12/kirk-douglas-i-never-thought-id-live-to-100-thats-shocked-me (accessed 3 March 2017).

French, Phillip (2012) 'Review', *The Observer*. 29 April, 22.

Friedman, Thomas (2014) 'Ready, Aim, Fire. Not Fire, Ready, Aim', *New York Times*, 2 September. Online. Available: https://www.nytimes.com/2014/09/03/opinion/thomas-friedman-what-are-we-really-dealing-with-in-isis.html?_r=0 (accessed 28 April 2015).

Füchtjohann, Jan (2011) 'Superheld für Nerds', *Süddeutsche Zeitung*, 17 August. Online. Available: http://www.sueddeutsche.de/kultur/captain-america-the-first-avenger-im-kino-superheld-fuer-nerds-1.1131805 (accessed 25 June 2017).

Gabin, Nancy Felice (1995) 'Women Defense Workers in World War II: Views on Gender Equality in Indiana', in Kenneth Paul O'Brien and Lynn H. Parsons (eds) *The Home-front War: World War II and American Society*. Westport, CT: Greenwood Press, 107–18.

Gaine, Vincent M. (2016) 'Thor God of Borders: Transnationalism and celestial connections in the superhero film', in Rayna Denison and Rachel Mizsei-Ward (eds) *Superheroes on World Screens*. Jackson, MS: University Press of Mississippi, 36–52.

Gallaway, Lauren (2016) 'Jon Favreau: Superhero Movies are Going to be Around for a Long Time', *CBR*. 20 April. Online. Available: http://www.cbr.com/jon-favreau-superhero-movies-are-going-to-be-around-for-a-long-time/ (accessed 16 February 2017).

Gallup Poll, (N.D.S) 'Afghanistan', *Gallup Poll*. Online. Available: http://www.gallup.com/poll/116233/afghanistan.aspx (accessed 22 February 2017).

Gamesradar (2008) 'Edward Norton talks Incredible Hulk', 7 March. Online. Available: http://www.gamesradar.com/edward-norton-talks-incredible-hulk/ (accessed 9 February 2015).

Gans, Herbert (1999) *Popular Culture and High Culture: An Analysis and Evaluation of Taste*. New York: Basic Books.

Gilmore, James N. and Matthias Stork (2014) 'Introduction: Heroes Converge!', in James N. Gilmore and Matthias Stork (eds) *Superhero Synergies: Comic Book Characters Go Digital*. Lanham, MD: Rowman & Littlefield, 1–10.

Ginn, Sherry (2017) 'Introduction: Black Widow's Place in Marvel's Universes and Our Own', in Sherry Ginn (ed.) *Black Widow from Spy to Superhero: Essays on an Avenger with a Very Specific Skill Set*. Jefferson, NC: McFarland, 1–10.

Gladstone, Brooke and Bob Garfield (2008) 'Reign of Terror', *BBC World Service*. WNYC. 10 October. Online. Available: http://www.onthemedia.org/story/131169-reign-of-terror/transcript/ (accessed 16 February 2017).

Go Compare (2016) 'Director's Cut', Online. Available: http://www.gocompare.com/life-insurance/directors-cut (accessed 9 June 2017).

Gopolam, Nisha (2008) 'The Many Superhero Faces of Barack Obama' *io9*, 23 October. Online. Available: http://io9.gizmodo.com/5067987/the-many-superhero-faces-of-barack-obama (accessed 12 February 2017).

Goldman, Erik (2014) 'Marvel's Agents of SHIELD: Season 1 Review', *IGN*. 24 May. Online. Available: http://uk.ign.com/articles/2014/05/22/marvels-agents-of-shield-season-1-review (accessed 16 February 2017).

Goulart, Ron (1993) *The Comic Book Reader's Companion*. New York: HarperCollins.

Graham, David, A. (2015) 'The Wrong Side of "the Right Side of History"', *The Atlantic*. 21 December. Online. Available: https://www.theatlantic.com/politics/archive/2015/12/obama-right-side-of-history/420462/ (accessed 7 June 2017).

Graham, Mark (2010) *Afghanistan in the Cinema*. Chicago: University of Illinois Press.

Grant, Barry Keith (2012) *The Hollywood Film Musical*. Malden, MA: Wiley Blackwell.

Graser, Marc (2015) 'Marvel's Merchandise Plan for "Avengers: Age of Ultron": Make the Big Bigger', *Variety*, 11 March. Online. Available: http://variety.com/2015/film/news/marvels-merchandise-plan-for-avengers-age-of-ultron-make-the-big-bigger-1201449832/ (accessed 25 June 2017).

Graves, Michael (2011) '"Chalk one up for the Internet: It has killed Arrested Development": The Series' Revival, Binge Watching and Fan/Critic Antagonism', in Kristin Barton (ed.) *A State of Arrested Development: Critical Essays on the Innovative Television Comedy*. Jefferson, NC: McFarland, 224–36.

Gray II, Richard J. and Betty Kaklamanidou (2011) 'Introduction', in Richard J. Gray II and Betty Kaklamanidou (eds) *The 21st Century Superhero: Essays on Gender, Genre and Globalization in Film*. Jefferson, NC: MacFarland, 1–14.

Green, Darragh and Kate Roddy (2015) 'Introduction', in Darragh Green and Kate Roddy (eds) *Grant Morrison and the Superhero Renaissance: Critical Essays*. Jefferson, NC: McFarland, 1–16.

Greenwald, Glen (2013) 'The NSA's mass and indiscriminate spying on Brazilians', *The Guardian*. 7 July. Online. Available: https://www.theguardian.com/commentisfree/2013/jul/07/nsa-brazilians-globo-spying (accessed 22 June 2016).

Grieder, William (2009) *Come Home, America: The Rise and Fall (and Redeeming Promise) of Our Country*. Emmaus: Rodale Press.

Grow, Kory (2014) 'Hooked on a Feeling: Inside the Hit "Guardians of the Galaxy" Soundtrack', *Rolling Stone*. 3 September. Online. Available: http://www.rollingstone.com/music/features/inside-guardians-of-the-galaxy-soundtrack-20140903 (accessed 8 June 2015).

Gunning, Tom (1986) 'The Cinema of Attractions: Early Film, Its Spectator and the Avant-Garde', *Wide Angle*, 8, 3/4, 63–70.

____(1990 [1986]) 'The Cinema of Attractions: Early Film, Its Spectator and the Avant-Garde', in Thomas Elsaesser (ed.) *Early Cinema: Space, Frame, Narrative*. London: British Film Institute, 56–62.

Guffey, Ensley F. (2014) 'Joss Whedon Throws His Mighty Shield: Marvel's The Avengers as War Movie', in Rhonda Wilcox, Tanya R. Cochran, Cynthea Masson and David Lavery (eds) *Reading Joss Whedon*. New York: Syracuse University Press, 280–96.

Gunderman, Dan (2017) 'Director Luc Besson labels Captain America U.S. "propaganda"', *New York Daily News*. 14 August. Online. Available: http://www.nydailynews.com/entertainment/movies/director-luc-besson-blasts-captain-america-propaganda-article-1.3410398 (accessed 2 September 2017).

Gwaambuka, Tatenda (2016) 'Nelson Mandela's Friendship with Gadaffi Irritated the West', *African Exponent*. 5 December. Online. Available: https://www.africanexponent.com/post/8136-nelson-mandelas-friendship-with-gaddafi-that-irritated-the-west (accessed 22 April 2017).

Hack, Brian. E (2009) '"*Weakness is a Crime*": Captain American and the Eugenic Ideal in Early Twentieth Century America', in Robert Weiner (ed.) *Captain America and the Struggle of the Superhero: Critical Essays*. Jefferson, NC: McFarland, 79–89.

Hagley, Annika (2016) 'America's need for superheroes has led to the rise of Donald Trump', *The Guardian*. 28 March. Online. Available: https://www.theguardian.com/commentisfree/2016/mar/28/america-superheroes-donald-trump-brutal-comic-book-ideal (accessed 22 May 2017).

Hagley, Annika & Harrison, Michael (2014) 'The resurgent superhero genre in film gives insights into the American psyche and political identities post-September 11', *LSE US Centre Blog*. 20 January. Online. Available: http://blogs.lse.ac.uk/usappblog/2014/01/20/avengers-politics/ (accessed 11 June 2016).

Hall, Eleanor (2010) 'UN rapporteur says Assange shouldn't be prosecuted', *ABC*. 9 December. Online. Available: http://www.abc.net.au/worldtoday/content/2010/s3089025.htm (accessed 22 March 2017).

Hamad, Hannah (2013) *Postfemininism and Paternity in Contemporary US Film: Framing Fatherhood*. New York: Routledge.

Han, Angie (2016) 'Natalie Portman Is "Done" With the Marvel Cinematic Universe', *Slash Film*. 17 August. Online. Available: http://www.slashfilm.com/natalie-portman-marvel/ (accessed 11 February 2017).

Harnden, Toby (2001) 'Bin Laden is wanted: dead or alive, says Bush', *The Telegraph*. 18 September. Online. Available: http://www.telegraph.co.uk/news/worldnews/asia/afghanistan/1340895/Bin-Laden-is-wanted-dead-or-alive-says-Bush.html (accessed 18 January 2015).

Harrickton, Patrick (2008) 'Patrick Harrington interviews, Jacks Shaheen, author of *Reel Bad Arabs*', *Thirdway*. 30 January. Online. Available: http://thirdway.eu/2008/01/30/reel-bad-arabs/ (accessed 22 April 2015).

Harris, Lance (n.d.) '*Winter Soldier*: Snowden superheroics', *Tech Central*. Online. Available: https://www.techcentral.co.za/winter-soldier-snowden-superheroics/47258/ (accessed 12 February 2017).

Hart, Tom (2015) 'The politics of *Iron Man*: how Marvel sold an arms dealing billionaire to liberal America', *New Statesman*. 22 April. Online. Available: http://www.newstatesman.com/culture/2015/04/politics-iron-man-how-marvel-sold-arms-dealing-billionaire-liberal-america (accessed 11 February 2017).

Harvey, Colin (2015) *Fantastic Transmedia: Narrative, Play and Memory Across Science Fiction and Fantasy Storyworlds*. Basingstoke: Palgrave Macmillan.

Hassler-Forest, Dan (2012) *Capitalist Superheroes: Caped Crusaders in the Neoliberal Age*. Alresford: Zero Books.

Hawks, Rebecca (2016) '"F___ Marvel!": *Suicide Squad* director David Ayer apologises for insulting DC's rivals at premiere', *The Telegraph*. 2 August. Online. Available: http://www.telegraph.co.uk/films/2016/08/02/suicide-squad-director-david-ayer-apologises-for-marvel-insult/ (accessed 22 February 2017).

Heise, Tatiana (2012) *Remaking Brazil: Contested National Identities in Contemporary Brazilian Cinema*. Cardiff: University of Wales Press.

Heller, Dana (2005) 'Introduction', in Dana Heller (ed.) *The Selling of 9/11: How a National Tragedy Became a Commodity*. New York: Palgrave MacMillan, 1–26.

Herman, Barbara and Hannah Sender (2015) 'Hollywood Couples: Age Difference in Movies, Visualized', *The IB Times*. 26 May. Online. Available: http://www.ibtimes.com/hollywood-couples-age-difference-movies-visualized-1935671 (accessed 29 September 2016).

Herr, Michael (1977) *Dispatches*. New York: Alfred A. Knopf.

Hiatt, Brian (2017) 'Inside the *Guardians of the Galaxy Vol. 2* Soundtrack', *Rolling Stone*. 19 April. Online. Available: http://www.rollingstone.com/music/features/inside-the-guardians-of-the-galaxy-vol-2-soundtrack-w477515 (accessed 8 June 2017).

Hiddlestone, Tom (2012) 'Superheroes movies like *Avengers Assemble* should not be scorned', *The Guardian*. 19 April. Online. Available: https://www.theguardian.com/film/filmblog/2012/apr/19/avengers-assemble-tom-hiddleston-superhero (accessed 10 June 2017).

Higgins, David (2015) 'American science fiction after 9/11', in Gerry Canavan and Eric Link (ed.) *The Cambridge Companion to American Science Fiction*. Cambridge: Cambridge University Press, 44–57.

Hill, Kyle (2013) 'Getting the God of Thunder's Science Straight', *Scientific American*. 8 November. Online. Available: https://blogs.scientificamerican.com/but-not-simpler/getting-the-god-of-thundere28099s-science-straight/ (accessed 12 June 2016).

Hoberman, J. (2012) '*The Avengers*: Why Hollywood is no longer afraid to tackle 9/11', *The Guardian*. 11 May. Online. Available: http://www.guardian.co.uk/film/2012/may/11/avengers-hollywood-afraid-tackle-9–11 (accessed 11 January 2017).

Hodgeson, Godrey (2009) *The Myth of American Exceptionalism*. New Haven, CT: Yale University Press.

Hoffman, Jordan (2014) 'Marvel Movies Are Bringing 9/11 Back to Pop Culture, and It's Still Too Soon', *Vanity Fair*. 4 April. Online. Available: http://www.vanityfair.com/hollywood/2014/04/marvel-movies-9–11-pop-culture (accessed 10 August 2015).

Holdsworth, Nick and Vladimir Kozlov (2015) 'Russia Box Office 2015: Mixed Fortunes as Holly-wood Gains Share, But Ruble Falls', *The Hollywood Reporter*. 30 December. Online. Available: http://www.hollywoodreporter.com/news/russia-box-office-2015-mixed-851470 (accessed 22 May 2017).

Holloway, David (2008) *9/11 and the War on Terror*. Edinburgh: Edinburgh University Press.

Holmogorov, Igor (2015) 'Гудбай, Капитан Америка!', Известия. 29 April. Online. Available: http://iz.ru/news/585932 (accessed 20 June 2017).

Honeycutt, Kirk (2010) 'Review', *The Hollywood Reporter*. 14 October. Online. Available: http://www.hollywoodreporter.com/review/iron-man-2-film-review-29527 (accessed 12 February 2017).

Hoogland-Noon, David (2004) 'Operation Enduring Analogy: World War II, the War on Terror, and the Uses of Historical Memory', *Rhetoric & Public Affairs*, 7, 3, 339–364.

Hundley, Jessica (n.d.) 'Joss Whedon Interview', *Time Out London*. Online. Available: http://www.timeout.com/london/film/joss-whedon-interview (accessed 15 December 2016).

Hunt, Elle (2017) 'Elon Musk: I can fix South Australia power network in 100 days or it's free', *The Guardian*. 10 March 2017. https://www.theguardian.com/technology/2017/mar/10/elon-musk-i-can-fix-south-australia-power-network-in-100-days-or-its-free (accessed 12 March 2017).

Hunt, James (2014) 'James Gunn interview: Guardians, music, Marvel and more', *Den of Geek*. 31 July. Online. Available: http://www.denofgeek.com/us/movies/guardians-of-the-galaxy/237876/james-gunn-interview-guardians-music-marvel-and-more (accessed 27 June 2016).

____ (2016) 'Joe and Anthony Russo interview: Captain America: Civil War' *Den of Geek*. April 28. Online. Available: http://www.denofgeek.com/movies/captain-america-civil-war/40265/joe-and-anthony-russo-interview-captain-america-civil-war (accessed 16 June 2016).

Huntington, Samuel P. (1999) 'The Lonely Superpower', *Foreign Affairs*. 78, 2, 43.

Institute for Economics and Peace. 'Global Peace index 2015', Online. Available: http://economicsandpeace.org/wp-content/uploads/2015/06/Global-Peace-Index-Report-2015_0.pdf (accessed 22 December 2016).

International Court of Justice (1986) 'Military and Paramilitary Activities in and against Nicaragua (Nicaragua v. United States of America)', *ICJ*, 27 June. Online. Available: http://www.icj-cij.org/docket/index.php?sum=367&code=nus&p1=3&p2=3&case=70&k=66&p3=5 (accessed 8 January 2017).

Inuhiko, Yomota (2007) 'The Menace from the south seas: Hondo Ishirō's *Godzilla*', in Alastair Phillips and Julian Stringer (eds) *Japanese Cinema: Texts and Contexts*. Routledge: New York, 102–11.

Irvine, Alexander (2010) *Iron Man 2*. New York: Grand Central.

Izo, David Garret (ed.) (2014) *Movies in the Age of Obama*. Lanham, MD: Rowman & Littlefield.

Jacobsen, Annie (2014) *Operation Paperclip: The Secret Intelligence Program that Brought Nazi Scientists to America*. New York: Little, Brown.

Jameson, Frederic (1981) *The Political Unconscious: Narrative as a Socially Symbolic Act*. Ithaca, NY: Cornell University Press.

____ (1984) 'Postmodernism, or The Cultural Logic of Late Capitalism', *New Left Review,* 146, 53–92.

Jeffords, Susan (1994) *Hard Bodies: Hollywood Masculinity in the Reagan Era*. New Brunswick, NJ: Rutgers University Press.

Jenkins, Henry (2006) *Convergence Culture: Where Old and New Media Collide*. New York: New York University Press.

____ (2009) '"Just Men in Tights": Rewriting Silver Age Comics in an Era of Multiplicity', in Angela Ndalianis (ed.) *The Contemporary Comic Book Superhero*. New York: Routledge, 16–43.

Jenkins, Thomas E. (2015) *Antiquity Now: The Classical World in the Contemporary American Imagination*. Cambridge: Cambridge University Press.

Jenkins, Tricia (2012) *The CIA in Hollywood: How the Agency Shapes Film and Television*. Austin, TX: University of Texas Press.

Jensen, Jeff (2012) 'Avengers': New Hulk Mark Ruffalo on replacing Edward Norton, plus Oscar buzz for *The Kids Are All Right*', *Entertainment Weekly*. 29 July. Online. Available: http://ew.com/article/2010/07/29/avengers-new-hulk-mark-ruffalo/ (accessed 17 January 2017).

Johnson, Andrew (2013) 'Tony Stark is a Villain: How the "Iron Man" Films Subvert Traditional Views of the War on Terror', *Movie Mezzanine*. 18 May. Online. Available: http://movie-mezzanine.com/tony-stark-is-a-villain-how-the-iron-man-films-subvert-traditional-views-of-the-war-on-terror/ (accessed 27 May 2015).

Johnson, Chalmers (2002) *Blowback: The Costs and Consequences of Empire*. London: Time Warner.

____ (2004) *The Sorrows of Empire: Militarism, Secrecy, and the End of the Republic*. New York: Metropolitan Books.

Johnston, Jacob (2015) *The Art of Marvel: Avenger's Age of Ultron*. New York: Marvel.

____ (2016) *Marvel's Captain America: Civil War: The Art of the Movie*. New York: Marvel.

Jolin, Dan (2012) 'Infographic: Movie Franchise Lexicon', *Empire*, 9 January. Online. Available: http://www.empireonline.com/movies/features/movie-franchise-lexicon-infographic/ (accessed 12 January 2017).

Jones, Nick (2015) *Hollywood Action Films and Spatial Theory*. New York: Routledge.

Kaes, Anton (2011) *Shell Shock Cinema: Weimar Culture and the Wounds of War*. Princeton, NJ: Princeton University Press.

Kakalios, James (2010) *The Physics of Superheroes*. New York: Penguin.

Kaller, Brian (2016) 'Why We Need Superheroes', *The American Conservative*. 27 May. Online. Available: http://www.theamericanconservative.com/articles/why-we-need-superheroes/ (accessed on 7 June 2017).

Kaplan, E. Anne (1997) *Looking for the Other: Feminism, Film, and the Imperial Gaze: Nation, Woman and Desire in Film*. New York: Routledge.

____ (2005) *Trauma Culture: The Politics of Terror and Loss in Media and Literature*. New Brunswick, NJ: Rutgers University Press.

Kaur, Raminder (2013) 'The fictions of science and cinema in India', in K. Moti Gokulsing, Wimal Dissanayake (eds) *Routledge Handbook of Indian Cinemas*. Abingdon: Routledge, 282–96.

Kaur, Raminder and Ajay Sinha (eds) (2005) *Bollyworld: Popular Indian Cinema Through a Transnational Lens*. New Delhi: Sage.

Kaveney, Roz (2007) *Superheroes!: Capes and Crusaders in Comics and Films*. London: IB Tauris.

Kaveney, Roz and Jennifer Stoy (eds) (2010) *Battlestar Galactica: Investigating Flesh, Spirit, and Steel*. London: IB Tauris.

Kellner, Douglas (1995) *Media Culture: Cultural Studies, Identity and Politics Between the Modern and the Postmodern*. New York: Routledge.

____ (2003) *From 9/11 to Terror War: The Dangers of the Bush Legacy*. Lanham, MD: Rowman & Littlefield.

____ (2004) '9/11, Spectacles of Terror, and Media Manipulation', *Critical Discourse Studies*, 1, 1, 41–64.

____ (2009) *Cinema Wars: Hollywood Film and Politics in the Bush-Cheney Era*. Chichester: Wiley Blackwell.

Khatchatourian, Maana (2015) 'Zack Snyder Says Batman and Superman Are Not Like "Flavor of the Week Ant-Man"', *Variety*. 10 September. Online. Available: http://variety.com/2015/film/news/zack-snyder-batman-superman-not-flavor-of-week-ant-man-1201589800/ (accessed 11 June 2016).

Kimble, James (2006) *Mobilising the Home Front: War Bonds and Domestic Propaganda*. College Station, TX: Texas A and M University Press.

King, Claire Sisco (2012) *Washed in Blood: Male Sacrifice, Trauma, and the Cinema*. New Brunswick, NJ: Rutgers University Press.

King, Geoff (2000) *Spectacular Narratives: Hollywood in the Age of the Blockbuster*. London: IB Tauris.

____ (2005) '"Just Like a Movie"?: 9/11 and Hollywood Spectacle', in Geoff King (ed.) *The Spectacle of the Real: From Hollywood to Reality TV and Beyond*. Bristol: Intellect, 47–58.

____ (2016) 'Responding to Realities or Telling the Same Old Story? Mixing Real-world and Mythic Resonances in *The Kingdom* (2007) and *Zero Dark Thirty* (2012)', in Terence McSweeney (ed.). *American Cinema in the Shadow of 9/11*. Edinburgh: Edinburgh University Press, 49–66.

King, John (2002) 'Bush calls Saddam "the guy who tried to kill my dad"', *CNN*. 27 September. Online. Available: http://edition.cnn.com/2002/ALLPOLITICS/09/27/bush.war.talk/ (accessed 27 January 2017).

Kinzer, Stephen (2006) *Overthrow: America's Century of Regime Change from Hawaii to Iraq*. New York: Henry Holt.

Kleefeld, Sean (2014) 'On -isms: The Hulk Metaphor', *Kleefeld On Comics*. 27 November. Online. Available: 11 2014. http://www.kleefeldoncomics.com/2014/11/on-isms-hulk-metaphor.html (accessed 11 June 2016).

Klein, Naomi (2008) *The Shock Doctrine: The Rise of Disaster Capitalism*. New York: Penguin.

Kluger, Jeffrey (2010) 'Charting the Emotions of 9/11 – Minute by Minute', *Time*. 3 September. Online. Available: http://content.time.com/time/health/article/0,8599,2015528,00.html (accessed 3 May 2017).

Knowlton, Brian (2001) 'Terror in America / "We're Going to Smoke Them Out": President Airs His Anger', *New York Times*. 19 September. Online. Available: http://www.nytimes.com/2001/09/19/news/19iht-t4_30.html (accessed 9 January 2014).

Kord, Susanne and Elisabeth Krimmer (2011) *Contemporary Hollywood Masculinities: Gender, Genre, and Politics*. New York: Palgrave Macmillan.

Kracauer, Siegfried (1947) *From Caligari to Hitler: A Psychological Profile of the German Film*. Princeton, NJ: Princeton University Press.

Kurutz, Steven (2014) 'Russians: Still the Go-To Bad Guys', *The New York Times*. 17 January. Online. Available: https://www.nytimes.com/2014/01/19/opinion/sunday/why-are-russians-still-the-go-to-bad-guys.html?_r=0 (accessed 12 June 2015).

Kyriazis, Stefan (2016) 'Guess Steven Spielberg's favourite superhero film? He leaves its director "in tears"', *Express*. 18 May. Online. Available: http://www.express.co.uk/entertainment/films/671438/Steven-Spielberg-BFG-guardians-of-the-galaxy-best-superhero-film (accessed 3 January 2017).

Labuza, Peter (2011) 'Thor: The God Who Fell to Earth', *Labuza Movies*. 23 May. Online. Available: http://labuzamovies.blogspot.co.uk/2011/05/thor-god-who-fell-to-earth.html (accessed 20 June 2017).

____ (2014) *Approaching the End: Imagining Apocalype in American Film*. Jenkintown, PA: Critical Press.

Lambie, Ryan (2014) 'Captain America 2: 2014's most subversive superhero film?', *Den of Geek*. 1 August. Online. Available: http://www.denofgeek.com/movies/captain-america-the-winter-soldier/31534/captain-america-2-2014s-most-subversive-superhero-film#ixzz4UhAqS9de (accessed 17 August 2015).

Lang, Jeffrey S. and Patrick Trimble (1988) 'Whatever Happened to the Man of Tomorrow?: An Examination of the American Monomyth and the Comic Book Superhero', *Journal of Popular Culture*, 22, 157–73.

Langley, Travis (2016) *Captain America vs. Iron Man: Freedom, Security, Psychology*. New York: Sterling Publishing.

LaSalle, Mick (2013) 'Nordic downhill: Ponderous "Dark World" lacks charm of 1st "Thor"', *San Francisco Chronicle*. 7 November. Online. Available: http://www.sfgate.com/movies/article/Thor-The-Dark-World-review-A-ho-hum-exercise-4965629.php (accessed 25 February 2017).

Lauzen, Martha M. (2016) 'It's a Man's (Celluloid) World: Portrayals of Female Characters in the Top 100 Films of 2015', Center for the Study of Women in Television & Film. Online.

Available: http://womenintvfilm.sdsu.edu/files/2015_Its_a_Mans_Celluloid_World_Report. pdf (accessed 14 June 2017).

Lawrence, John Shelton and Robert Jewett (1977) *The American Monomyth*. New York: Anchor Press/Doubleday.

____(2002) *The Myth of the American Superhero*. Grand Rapids, MI: Wm. B. Eerdmans.

____(2003) *Captain America Complex: The Dilemma of Zealous Nationalism*. Grand Rapids, MI: Wm. B. Eerdmans.

Lax, Eric (2009) *Conversations with Woody Allen: His Films, the Movies, and Moviemaking*. New York: Alfred A. Knopf.

Leane, Rob (2016) 'Clark Gregg interview: Marvel, S.H.I.E.L.D., Civil War', *Den of Geek*. 11 January. Online. Available: http://www.denofgeek.com/tv/clark-gregg/35927/clark-gregg-interview-marvel-shield-civil-war#ixzz4ZrcTWI2l (accessed 5 March 2017).

Lee, Stan (2016a) 'Interview', *Total Film*, July, 248, 92–9.

____(2016b) 'Foreword', in Travis Langley (ed.) *Captain America vs. Iron Man: Freedom, Security, Psychology*. New York: Sterling Publishing, xiii–xv.

Lee, Stan and George Mair (2002) *Excelsior!: The Amazing Life of Stan Lee*. New York: Simon & Schuster.

Lefler, Rachel (2015) 'Why a feminist takeover of Hollywood is a problem and why it's happening', *A Voice for Men*. 27 May. Online. Available: https://www.avoiceformen.com/featured/why-a-feminist-takeover-of-hollywood-is-a-problem-and-why-its-happening/ (accessed 11 June 2017).

Lev, Peter (2000) *American Films of the 1970s: Conflicting Visions*. Austin, TX: University of Texas Press.

Li, Shirley (2017) 'The Defenders EP talks juggling four heroes – and the "crisis" that unites them', *Entertainment Weekly*. 13 January. Online. Available: http://ew.com/tv/2017/01/13/defenders-marco-ramirez-interview/2/ (accessed 7 June 2017).

Lindow, John (2002) *Mythology: A Guide to Gods, Heroes, Rituals, and Beliefs*. Oxford: Oxford University Press.

LoCicero, Don (2007) *Superheroes and Gods: A Comparative Study from Babylonia to Batman*. Jefferson, MC: McFarland.

Loughlin, Sean (2003) 'Bush warns militants who attack U.S. troops in Iraq', *CNN*, 3 July. Online. Available: http://edition.cnn.com/2003/ALLPOLITICS/07/02/sprj.nitop.bush/ (accessed 5 July 2017).

Lovece, Frank (2014) 'Soldier showdown: Joe and Anthony Russo take the helm of "Captain America" franchise', *Film Journal*. 25 March. Online. Available: http://www.filmjournal.com/node/9232 (accessed Web 16 January 2016).

Luceri, Marco (2012) 'Una grande, furbissima, operazione di marketing? Non solo. Ecco il nuovo film targato Marvel', *Corriere Fiorentino*. 5 May. Online. Available: http://corrierefiorentino. corriere.it/firenze/notizie/spettacoli/2012/5-maggio-2012/the-avengers-20148646638. shtml?refresh_ce-cp (accessed 12 March 2017).

Luttwak, Edward N. (1993) *The Endangered American Dream*. New York: Touchstone.

Mangels, Andy (2008) *Iron Man: Beneath the Armor*. New York: Del Rey.

Maraniss, David (2012) *Barack Obama: The Making of the Man*. London: Atlantic Books.

Markus, Christopher and Stephen McFeely (2014) *Captain America: The First Avenger – the Screenplay*. New York: Marvel.

Martin, Karl. E. (2015) 'Competing Authorities in the Nation State of Marvel', in Kevin Michael Scott (ed.) *Marvel Comics' Civil War and the Age of Terror: Critical Essays on the Comic Saga*. Jefferson, NC: McFarland, 98–107.

Martínez, Luis (2013) 'Obama, contado por Hollywood', *El Mundo*. 22 January. Online. Available: http://www.elmundo.es/elmundo/2013/01/22/cultura/1358843834.html (accessed 7 May 2017).

Masters, Kim (2011) '"Thor 2" Star Natalie Portman Furious Over Director Patty Jenkins' Departure', *The Hollywood Reporter*. 14 December. Online. Available: http://www.hollywood-reporter.com/news/thor-2-natalie-portman-marvel-patty-jenkins-272978 (accessed 15 January 2017).

Mathews, Jessica (2015) 'The Road from Westphalia', *The New York Review of Books*, March. Online. Available: http://www.nybooks.com/articles/2015/03/19/road-from-westphalia/ (accessed 2 June 2016).

Matthews, Peter (2001) 'Aftermath', *Sight and Sound*, 11, 11, 20–2.

Maxwell, Jared (2013) *Unsung: Memoirs of an Infantryman*. Pittsburgh, PA: Dorrance.

McAteer, John (2016) 'The Gospel According to Marvel', *Christian Research Journal*, 38, 3. Online. Available http://www.equip.org/PDF/JAF1383.pdf (accessed 25 June 2017).

McCullagh, Declan (2010) 'Congressman wants WikiLeaks listed as terrorist group', *CNET*. 28 November. Online. Available: https://www.cnet.com/news/congressman-wants-wikileaks-listed-as-terrorist-group/#ixzz16keYyAPb (accessed 9 April 2017).

McDowall, John C. (2013) 'National Treasures: Joss Whedon's Assembling of Exceptional Avengers', in Anthony R. Mills, John W. Morehead and J. Ryan Parker (eds) *Joss Whedon and Religion: Essays on an Angry Atheist's Explorations of the Sacred*. Jefferson, NC: McFarland, 183–95.

____(2014) *The Politics of Big Fantasy: The Ideologies of Star Wars, the Matrix and the Avengers*. Jefferson, NC: McFarland.

McGrath, Derek (2016) 'Some Assembly Required: Joss Whedon's Bridging of Masculinities in Marvel Films', in Elizabeth Abele and John A. Gronbeck-Tedesco (eds) *Screening Images of American Masculinity in the Age of Postfeminism*. Lanham, MD: Lexington, 135–54.

McMillan, Graeme (2014) 'Why *Guardians of the Galaxy* is the riskiest Marvel Film Since *Iron Man*', *Hollywood Reporter*. 19 February. Online. Available: http://www.hollywoodreporter.com/heat-vision/why-guardians-galaxy-is-riskiest-681656 (accessed 23 February 2017).

____(2015) 'Steven Spielberg Says Superhero Movies Will Go "the Way of the Western"', *The Hollywood Reporter*. 2 September. Online. Available: http://www.hollywoodreporter.com/heat-vision/steven-spielberg-predicts-superhero-movies-819768 (accessed 9 June 2017).

____(2017) '*Guardians of the Galaxy 2*: It's Time to Rethink All of Stan Lee's Marvel Cameos', *Variety*. April 28. Online. Available: http://www.hollywoodreporter.com/heat-vision/guardians-galaxy-2-time-rethink-all-stan-lees-marvel-cameos-998558 (Accessed 12 May 2017).

McSweeney, Terence (2010) '*Land of The Dead*: George Romero's Vision of a Post 9/11 America', in Jeff Birkenstein, Karen Randell and Anna Froula (eds) *Reframing 9/11: Film, Popular Culture and the War on Terror*. New York: Continuum, 172–89.

____(2014) *The 'War on Terror' and American Film: 9/11 Frames Per Second*. Edinburgh: Edinburgh University Press.

Melamid, Alex (2017) 'Blame Donald Trump's Rise on the Avant-Garde Movement', *Time*. 12 May. Online. Available: http://time.com/4777118/avant-garde-koons-trump/ (accessed 22 May 2017).

Mellor, Louisa (2013) 'Joss Whedon on Marvel's Agents of S.H.I.E.L.D. and Buffy's The Zeppo', *Den of Geek*. 22 August. Online. Available: http://www.denofgeek.com/tv/marvels-agents-of-shield/26995/joss-whedon-on-marvels-agents-of-shield-and-buffys-the-zeppo (accessed Web. 22 October 2015).

Melnick, Jeffrey P. (2009) *9/11 Culture: America Under Construction*. Oxford: Wiley Blackwell.

Mendelson, Scott (2016) '"Captain America: Civil War" Box Office: Was It "Captain America 3" Or "Avengers 3"?' May 9. *Forbes*. Online. Available: http://www.forbes.com/sites/scottmendelson/2016/05/09/captain-america-civil-war-box-office-was-it-captain-america-3-or-avengers-3/#6230c06a2e4a (accessed 11 May 2016).

Milbank, Dana and Jim VandeHei (2003) 'Washington Post Poll May 1, 2003 Gallup Poll'.

Miles, Donna (2007) 'Movie makers team with military to create realism', *AF.MIL*. 21 June. Online. Available: http://www.af.mil/News/Features/Display/Article/143457/movie-makers-team-with-military-to-create-realism/ (accessed 7 June 2017).

Millar, Mark (2006–7) *Civil War*. New York: Marvel Comics.

Millar, Mark and Steve McNiven (2007) *Civil War Script Book*. New York: Marvel Comics.

Miller, Liz Shannon (2017) '"Marvel's Iron Fist" Review: Season 1 Lacks Punch, Proves Incredibly Skippable', *IndieWire*. 17 March. Online. Available: http://www.indiewire.com/2017/03/marvels-iron-fist-review-season-1-skippable-defenders-1201794442/ (accessed 9 June 2017).

Mills, Anthony R. (2013) *American Theology, Superhero Comics, and Cinema: The Marvel of Stan Lee and the Revolution of a Genre*. Abingdon: Routledge.

Mirrlees, Tanner (2014) 'How to Read *Iron Man*: The Economics, Politics and Ideology of an Imperial Film Commodity', *Cineaction: Canada's Leading Film Studies Journal*, 92, 1, 4–11.

Mitra, Ananda (2016) *India on the Western Screen: Imaging a Country in Film, TV, and Digital Media*. New Delhi: Sage.

Moore, Stuart and Marie Javins (2013) *Marvel's Thor: The Dark World – The Art of the Movie*. New York: Marvel.

Morrison, Grant (2012) *SuperGods: Our World in the Age of the Superhero*. London: Random House.

Nadkarni, Samira (2015) '"I Believe in Something Greater than Myself": What Authority, Terror-ism, and Resistance Have Come to Mean in the Whedonverses', *Slayage: The Journal of Whedon Studies*, 13, 2, 42, 1–26. Online. Available: http://www.whedonstudies.tv/uploads/2/6/2/8/26288593/nadkarni.pdf (accessed 22 May 2016).

Nama, Adilifu (2011) *Super Black: American Pop Culture and Black Superheroes*. Austin, TX: University of Texas Press.

Nashawaty, Chris (2015) 'Review', *Entertainment Weekly*. 23 April. Online. Available: http://ew.com/article/2015/04/23/avengers-ag e-ultron-ew-review/ (accessed 25 January 2015).

Nelson, Robin (2007) *State of Play: Contemporary High-End TV Drama*. Manchester: Manchester University Press.

Newman, Michael Z. Elana and Levine (2011) *Legitimating Television: Media Convergence and Cultural Status*. New York: Routledge.

Nicholson, Amy (2013) 'Thor Returns, Diminished', *The Village Voice*. 5 November. Online. Available: http://www.villagevoice.com/film/thor-returns-diminished-6439975 (accessed 25 June 2015).

Niemi, Robert (2006) *History in the Media: Film and Television*. Santa Barbara, CA: ABC CLIO.

Noonan, Peggy (2001) 'Welcome Back, Duke: From the ashes of Sept. 11 arise the manly virtues', *Wall Street Journal*. 12 Oct. Online. Available: http://online.wsj.com/article/SB122451174798650085.html (accessed 12 June 2015).

___(2003) 'The Right Man', *The Washington Post*. 30 January. Online. Available: http://online.wsj.com/article/SB1043895876926710064.html (accessed 3 June 2017).

Norton, Edward (2007) 'The Incredible Hulk Screenplay', *PDF Scripts*. 13 May. Online. Available: http://pdfscripts.weebly.com/uploads/9/1/6/8/916864/incredible20hulk2c20the.pdf (accessed 9 June 2017).

Obama, Barack (2009) 'Address to Joint Session of Congress' Washington, 24 February.

___(2010) 'Remarks at American University', Washington, 1 July.

___(2015) 'Address to Nation', Washington, 16 December.

O'Mara, Sean (2015) *Why Torture Doesn't Work: The Neuroscience of Interrogation*. Cambridge, MA: Harvard University Press.

Ostroff, Joshua (2016) 'Marvel's Luke Cage is the Bulletproof Black Superhero We Need Right Now', *Huffington Post*. 30 September. Online. Available: http://www.huffingtonpost.ca/2016/09/29/marvel-luke-cage_n_12202516.html?ncid=fcbklnkushpmg00000047 (accessed 9 June 2017).

O'Sullivan, Michael (2015a) *Guidebook to the Marvel Cinematic Universe: Marvel's Iron Man*. New York: Marvel.

___(2015b) *Guidebook to the Marvel Cinematic Universe: Iron Man 2*. New York: Marvel.

___(2016) *Guidebook to the Marvel Cinematic Universe: Marvel's Avengers: Age of Ultron*. New York: Marvel.

___(2017) *Guidebook to the Marvel Cinematic Universe: Marvel's Captain America: Civil War*. New York: Marvel.

Palmeri, Christopher (2012) 'Disney assembles a cast of "Avengers" merchandise', *Bend Bulletin*. 5 May. Online. Available: http://www.bendbulletin.com/news/1370642–151/disney-assembles-a-cast-of-avengers-merchandise (accessed 13 May 2017).

Parry, Robert (2008) '4,000 dead, zero accountability', *Baltimore Chronicle*, March 25. Online. Available: http://baltimorechronicle.com/2008/032508Parry.html (accessed 8 June 2017).

Paskin, Willa (2013) 'With Great Power Comes … Nothing New', *Slate*. 24 September. Online. Available: http://www.slate.com/articles/arts/television/2013/09/marvel_s_agents_of_shield_reviewed.html (accessed 11 January 2015).

Patterson, John (2017) '*Get Out*: The First Great Paranoia Movie of the Trump Era', *The Guardian*. 6 March. Online. Available: https://www.theguardian.com/film/2017/mar/06/get-out-movie-jordan-peele-trump (accessed 22 March 2017).

Patrick, Christopher and Sarah Patrick (2008) 'The Incredible Hulk', in Robin Rosenburg and Jennifer Canzoneri (eds) *The Psychology of Superheroes: An Unauthorized Exploration*. Dallas, TX: Benbella Books, 213–28.

Pease, Donald (2009) *The New American Exceptionalism*. Minneapolis, MN: University of Minnesota Press.

Peberdy, Donna (2011) *Masculinity and Film Performance*. New York: Palgrave Macmillan.

Peltonen, Hannes (2013) *International Responsibility and Grave Humanitarian Crises: Collective Provision for Human Security*. London and New York: Routledge.

Peters, Megan (2016) 'Could the Final Guardians of the Galaxy Easter Egg Be Hidden in the Sky?', *Comicbook.com*. 27 November. Online. Available: http://comicbook.com/marvel/2016/11/27/could-the-final-guardians-of-the-galaxy-easter-egg-be-hidden-in-/ (accessed 8 January 2017).

Peyser, Andrea (2012) 'Extremely, Incredibly Exploitive', *New York Post*. 19 January. Online. Available: http://nypost.com/2012/01/19/extremely-incredibly-exploitive/ (accessed 5 July 2017).

Pheasant-Kelly, Francis (2013) *Fantasy Film Post 9/11*. New York: Palgrave MacMillan.

Pinkerton, Nick (2010) '*Iron Man 2* Will Lead to 3 and Probably 4', *The Village Voice*. 4 May. Online. Available: http://www.villagevoice.com/film/iron-man-2-will-lead-to-3-and-probably-4-6393455> (accessed 25 April 2015).

Political Ticker, (2013) 'CNN Poll: Afghan War arguably most unpopular in US History', 30 December. Online. Available: http://politicalticker.blogs.cnn.com/2013/12/30/cnn-poll-afghanistan-war-most-unpopular-in-u-s-history/ (accessed 8 June 2017).

Pollard, Tom (2011) *Hollywood 9/11 Superheroes, Supervillains and Super Disasters*. Boulder, CO: Paradigm.

Power, Mick and Tim Dalgleish (2016) *Cognition and Emotion: From Order to Disorder*. Hove: Psychology Press.

Power, Samantha (2005) 'Boltonism', *The New Yorker*. March 21. Online. Available: http://www.newyorker.com/magazine/2005/03/21/boltonism (accessed 22 February 2017).

Prince, Stephen (2009) *Firestorm: American Film in the Age of Terrorism*. New York: Columbia University Press.

Pulver, Andrew (2012) 'Avengers' slum scenes trigger anger in India', *The Guardian*. 8 May. Online. Available: https://www.theguardian.com/film/2012/may/08/avengers-slum-scenes-anger-india (accessed 12 August 2015).

Purse, Lisa (2011a) *Contemporary Action Cinema*. Edinburgh: Edinburgh University Press.

____ (2011b) 'Return of the "Angry Woman": Authenticating Female Physical Action in Contemporary Cinema', in Melanie Waters (ed.) *Women on Screen: Feminism and Femininity in Visual Culture*. London: Palgrave Macmillan, 185–98.

Pye, Douglas (1996) 'Double Vision: Miscegenation and Point of View in *The Searchers*', in Ian Cameron and Doug Pye (eds) *The Movie Book of the Western*. New York: Continuum, 229–35.

Ramsay, Debra (2015) *American Media and the Memory of World War II*. New York: Routledge.

Randell, Karen (2016) '"It Was Like a Movie," Take 2: Age of Ultron and a 9/11 Aesthetic', *Cinema Journal*, 56, 1, 137–41.

Reagan, Ronald (1981) 'Inaugural address', Washington, 20 January.

Reef, Catherine (2001) *Sigmund Freud: Pioneer of the Mind*. New York: Clarion.

Rehling, Nicola (2009) *Extra-Ordinary Men: White Heterosexual Masculinity in Contemporary Popular Cinema*. Plymouth: Lexington Books.

Reinhartz, Adele (2003) 'Jesus on the Silver Screen', in Nissan N. Perez (ed.) *Revelation: Representations of Christ in Photography*. London: Merrell/The Israel Museum, Jerusalem, 186–9.

Reynolds, Richard (1992) *Superheroes: A Modern Mythology*. Jackson, MS: University Press of Mississippi.

Robb, David L. (2004) *Operation Hollywood: How the Pentagon Shapes and Censors the Movies*. New York: Prometheus Books.

Robehmed, Natalie (2014) 'The World's Highest-Paid Actors 2015: Robert Downey Jr. Leads With $80 Million Haul', *Forbes*. 4 August. Online. Available: http://www.forbes.com/sites/natalierobehmed/2015/08/04/the-worlds-highest-paid-actors-2015-robert-downey-jr-leads-with-80-million-haul/#6e4b34fa2298 (accessed 11 March 2015).

Roberts, Garyn (2004) 'Understanding the Sequential Art of Comic Strips and Comic Books and Their Descendants in the Early Years of the New Millennium', *The Journal of American Culture*, 27, 2, 210–17.

Robinson, Joanna (2016) 'Iron Man 3's Director Says Marvel Canceled Its First Female Villain Because of Toy Sales', *Variety*. 16 May. Online. Available: http://www.vanityfair.com/hollywood/2016/05/iron-man-3-villain-rebecca-hall (accessed 10 May 2016).

Rodriguez, Sarah (2015) *Marvel's Agent Carter: Season One Declassified*. New York: Marvel Worldwide.

Rogers, A.P.V. (2000) 'Zero Casualty Warfare', *IRRC*, 82, 177–8.

Rojek, Chris (2001) *Celebrity*. London: Reaktion.

Romano, Nick (2016) 'How Captain America: Civil War Will Avoid Becoming Avengers 2.5', *Cinemablend*. Online. Available: http://www.cinemablend.com/new/How-Captain-America-Civil-War-Avoid-Becoming-Avengers-2-5-85477.html (accessed 10 February 2017).

Rommel-Ruiz, W. Bryan (2011) *American History Goes to the Movies. Hollywood and the American Experience*. New York: Routledge.

Rose, Brian A. (1996) *Jekyll and Hyde Adapted: Dramatizations of Cultural Anxiety*. Westport, CT: Greenwood Press.

Rosen, Gail D. (2015) 'Whedon's Women and the Law: Parallels from Slayers to S.H.I.E.L.D.', in Valerie Estelle Frankel (ed.) *The Comics of Joss Whedon: Critical Essays*. Jefferson, NC: McFarland, 209–18.

Rosenberg, Alyssa (2012) 'The Avengers and The Dictator Take On 9/11', *ThinkProgress*. 10 May. Online. Available: https://thinkprogress.org/the-avengers-and-the-dictator-take-on-9–11-82899ec1e57#.hn14phfmc (accessed 22 February 2016).

Rosenzweig, Roy and David Thelen (1998) *The Presence of the Past*. New York: Columbia University Press.

Rossen, Jake (2008) *Superman vs. Hollywood: How Fiendish Producers, Devious Directors, and Warring Writers Grounded an American Icon*. Chicago: Chicago Review Press.

Rothe, Anne (2011) *Popular Trauma Culture: Selling the Pain of Others in the Mass Media*. New Brunswick, NJ: Rutgers University Press.

Roublou, Yann (2012) 'Complex Masculinities: The Superhero in Modern American Movies', *Culture, Society 7 Masculinities*. 4, 1, 76–91.

Ryan, Fergus (2017) 'China, Russia Team up to Take on "The Avengers" with Communist Superheroes', *China Film Insider*. 16 January. Online. Available: http://chinafilminsider.com/china-russia-team-take-avengers-communist-superheroes/ (accessed 11 June 2017).

Ryan, Michael and Kellner Douglas (1990) *Camera Politica: The Politics and Ideology of Contemporary Hollywood Film*. Bloomington, IN: Indiana University Press.

Ryan, Tom (2005) 'In defence of big, expensive films', *The Age*. 14 July. Online. Available: http://www.theage.com.au/news/film/defending-the-blockbuster/2005/07/14/1120934352863.html (accessed 9 June 2017).

Sahay, Nilesh (2017) 'Interview with Sarik Andreasyan', *AMDB*. 26 February. Online. Available: http://amdb.in/interview-with-sarik-andreasyan/ (accessed 22 May 2017).

Salvá, Nando (2014) 'De turisteo por el "zeitgeist" Capitán América: el soldado de invierno', *El Periódico*. 28 March. Online. Available: http://www.elperiodico.com/es/noticias/ocio-y-cultura/turisteo-por-zeitgeist-capitan-america-soldado-invierno-3225203 (accessed on 20 June 2017).

Sanderson, Peter (2007) *The Marvel Comics Guide to New York City*. New York: Simon & Schuster.

Sandhu, Sukhdev (2011) 'Review', *The Daily Telegraph*. 28 July. Online. Available: http://www. telegraph.co.uk/culture/film/filmreviews/8668935/Captain-America-The-First-Avenger-review.html (accessed 29 June 2015).

Savage, Charlie (2015) *Power Wars: Inside Obama's Post-9/11 Presidency*. Boston, MA: Little, Brown.

Saunders, Ben (2012) *Do Gods Wear Capes?: Spirituality, Fantasy, and Superheroes*. London and New York: Bloomsbury.

Saunders, Martin (2016) 'Doctor Strange: The Most Theological Marvel Movie So Far', *Christian Today*. 26 October. Online. Available: https://www.christiantoday.com/article/doctor.strange. the.most.theological.marvel.movie.so.far/98950.htm (accessed 25 June 2017).

Schiemann, John W. (2015) *Does Torture Work?* Oxford: Oxford University Press.

Schjeldahl, Peter (2009) 'Hope and Glory', *The New Yorker*. 23 February. Online. Available: http:// www.newyorker.com/magazine/2009/02/23/hope-and-glory (accessed 11 June 2015).

Schlegel, Johannes and Frank Haberman (2011) '"You Took My Advice About Theatricality a Bit ... Literally": Theatricality and Cybernetics of Good and Evil in *Batman Begins*, *The Dark Knight*, *Spider-Man*, and *X- Men*', in Richard J. Gray II and Betty Kaklamanidou (eds) *The 21st Century Superhero: Essays on Gender, Genre and Globalization in Film*. Jefferson, NC: MacFarland, 29–48.

Schlüter, Christian (2014) 'Kinostart "The Return Of The First Avenger" Das bessere Amerika', *Berliner Zeitung*. 25 March. Online. Available: http://www.berliner-zeitung.de/kultur/film/ kinostart--the-return-of-the-first-avenger--das-bessere-amerika-1158504 (accessed 20 June 2017).

Schmidt, Hugo (2010) 'A Capitalist Superhero?', *The Atlas Society*. 16 June. Online. Available: http://atlassociety.org/commentary/commentary-blog/3680-a-capitalist-superhero (accessed 12 January 2015).

Schrader, Paul (1972) 'Notes on Film Noir', *Film Comment*, 8, 1, 8–13.

Schultz, Lauren (2014) '"Hot Chicks with Superpowers": The Contexted Feminism of Joss Whedon', in Rhonda Wilcox, Tanya R. Cochran, Cynthea Masson and David Lavery (eds) *Reading Joss Whedon*. New York: Syracuse University Press, 356–70.

Schwartzel, Erich (2016) 'A Look at the Five Fastest-Growing Markets for Movies', *The Wall Street Journal*, 18 September. Online. Available: https://www.wsj.com/articles/a-look-at-the-five-fastest-growing-markets-for-movies-1474250942 (accessed 25 June 2017).

Sciretta, Peter (2010) 'Interview: *Iron Man 2* Screenwriter Justin Theroux', *Slash Film*. 10 May. http://www.slashfilm.com/interview-iron-man-2-screenwriter-justin-theroux/ (accessed 22 July 2015).

____(2014a) 'On Set Interview: "Captain America 2" Screenwriters Stephen McFeely & Christopher Markus', *Slash Film*. 6 March. Online. Available: http://www.slashfilm.com/ interview-stephen-mcfeely-christopher-markus-captain-america-winter-soldier/ (accessed 16 June 2015).

____(2014b) 'James Gunn Interview: How making guardians of the galaxy is like a nirvana song', *Slash Film*. 8 July. http://www.slashfilm.com/james-gunn-interview-guardians-of-the-galaxy/ (accessed 1 July 2015).

Scott, A.O. and Manohla Dargis (2013) 'Movies in the Age of Obama', *The New York Times*. 16 January. Online. Available: http://www.nytimes.com/2013/01/20/movies/lincoln-django-unchained-and-an-obama-inflected-cinema.html (accessed 12 August 2015).

____(2014) 'Sugar, Spice and Guts: Representation of Female Characters in Movies is Improving', *The New York Times*. 3 September. Online. Available: https://www.nytimes.com/2014/09/07/movies/fall-arts-preview-representation-of-female-characters-in-movies-is-improving.html?_r=0 (accessed 16 June 2017).

Scott, Kevin Michael (2015) 'Introduction', in Kevin Michael Scott (ed.) *Marvel Comics' Civil War and the Age of Terror: Critical Essays on the Comic Saga*. Jefferson, NC: McFarland, 3–10.

Scott, Shirley, V. (2012) *International Law, US Power: The United States' Quest for Legal Security*. Cambridge: Cambridge University Press.

Segal, Lynne (2001) 'Back to the boys?: Temptations of the good gender theorist', *Textual Practice*, 15, 2, 231–50.

Seitz, Matt Zoller (2015) 'Jessica Jones Is a Stylish, Striking Neo-Noir Drama for Adults', *Vulture*. 20 November. Online. Available: http://www.vulture.com/2015/11/jessica-jones-is-as-good-as-youve-heard.html (accessed 9 June 2017).

Seroword (2015) '*Die Another Day: Skyfall* and the Nolanization of James Bond', *Seroword*. 5 September. Online. Available: http://seroword.com/film/die-another-day-skyfall-and-the-nolanization-of-james-bond/ (accessed 8 December 2016).

Shaheen, Jack (1994) 'Arab images in American comic books', *Journal of Popular Culture*, 28, 1, 123–33.

____(2009) *Reel Bad Arabs: How Hollywood Vilifies a People*. Olive Branch Press: New York.

Shambaugh, David (ed.) (2016) *The China Reader: Rising Power*. Oxford: Oxford University Press.

Shapiro, T. Rees (2011) 'Joe Simon, co-creator of the Captain America comics, dies at 98', *The Washington Post*. 15 December. Online. Available: https://www.washingtonpost.com/local/obituaries/joe-simon-co-creator-of-the-captain-america-comics-dies-at-98/2011/12/15/gIQADjarwO_story.html?utm_term=.5b7c32c0c035 (accessed 1 March 2015).

Shelley, Mary (1818) *Frankenstein*. London: Lackington, Hughes, Harding, Mavor & Jones.

Sims, David (2014) 'Edgar Wright Departs Marvel's "Ant-Man" Over "Differences in Vision"', *The Atlantic*. 23 May. Online. Available: https://www.theatlantic.com/entertainment/archive/2014/05/edgar-wright-departs-marvels-ant-man-over-differences-in-vision/371546/ (accessed 3 February 2016).

Singer, Leah (2015) 'Drew Goddard on How He Would've Made the Sinister Six Movie and Comparisons to Suicide Squad', *IGN*. 28 September. Online. Available: http://uk.ign.com/articles/2015/09/29/drew-goddard-on-how-he-wouldve-made-the-sinister-six-movie-and-comparisons-to-suicide-squad (accessed 19 February 2017).

Singer, Matt (2011) 'The Summer's New Hero: Thor-Ge W. Bush', *The Atlantic*. 9 May. Online. Available: http://www.theatlantic.com/entertainment/archive/2014/05/edgar-wright-departs-marvels-ant-man-over-differences-in-vision/371546/ (accessed 12 June 2015).

Slattery, Dennis (2017) 'Trump speculates on Fox News if ABC anchor David Muir would support torture if his kid was kidnapped', *The New York Daily News*. 26 January. Online. Available: http://www.nydailynews.com/news/politics/trump-david-muir-support-torture-kid-abducted-article-1.2956961 (accessed 27 January 2017).

Slotkin, Richard (1973) *Regeneration Through Violence*. Norman, OK: University of Oklahoma Press.

____(1998) *Gunfighter Nation: The Myth of the Frontier in Twentieth-Century America*. Norman, Oklahoma: University of Oklahoma Press.

Smelser, Neil (2004) 'Epilogue: September 11, 2001, as cultural trauma', in Jeffrey C. Alexander, Ron

Eyerman, Bernhard Giesen, Neil J. Smelser, and Piotr Sztompka (eds) *Cultural Trauma and Collective Identity*. Berkeley, California and London: University of California Press, 264–282.

Smith, Kyle (2010) 'Iron Man, Capitalist Hero', *New York Post*. 9 May. Online. Available: http://nypost.com/2010/05/09/iron-man-capitalist-hero/ (accessed 12 March 2015).

Smith, Stacy L., Katherine Pieper and Marc Choueiti (2017) 'Inclusion in the Director's Chair?: Gender, Race, & Age of Film Directors Across 1,000 Films 2007–2016'. Online. Available: http://annenberg.usc.edu/pages/~/media/MDSCI/Inclusion%20in%20the%20Directors%20Chair%202117%20Final.ashxhttp://annenberg.usc.edu/pages/~/media/MDSCI/Inclusion%20in%20the%20Directors%20Chair%202117%20Final.ashx (accessed 11 June 2017).

Smith, Stacy L., Katherine Pieper, Marc Choueiti, Traci Gillig, Carmen Lee and Dylan DeLuca (2015a) 'Inequality in 700 Popular Films: Examining Portrayals of Gender, Race, & LGBT Status from 2007 to 2014'. Online, Available: http://annenberg.usc.edu/pages/~/media/MDSCI/Inequality%20in%20700%20Popular%20Films%208215%20Final%20for%20Posting.ashx (accessed 11 June 2017).

_____ (2015b) 'Inequality in 800 Popular Films: Examining Portrayals of Gender, Race, & LGBT Status from 2007 to 2015'. Online, Available: http://annenberg.usc.edu/pages/~/media/MDSCI/Dr%20Stacy%20L%20Smith%20Inequality%20in%20800%20Films%20FINAL.ashx (accessed 11 June 2017).

Sontag, Susan (2011) 'The Talk of the Town', *The New Yorker*. 24 September. Online. Available: http://www.newyorker.com/archive/2001/09/24/010924ta_talk_wtc (accessed 10 December 2015).

Solomon, Ty (2015) *The Politics of Subjectivity in American Foreign Policy Discourses*. Ann Arbour: University of Michigan Press.

Sotinel, Thomas (2012) '"Avengers": concile oecuménique pour superhéros', *Le Monde*. 24 April. Online. Available: http://www.lemonde.fr/cinema/article/2012/04/24/concile-oecumenique-pour-superheros_1690490_3476.html (accessed 27 May 2017).

Spanakos, Antony Peter (2011) 'Exception Recognition. The US global dilemma in *The Incredible Hulk, Iron Man*, and *Avatar*', in Richard J. Gray II and Betty Kaklamanidou (eds) *The 21st Century Superhero: Essays on Gender, Genre and Globalization in Film*. Jefferson, NC: MacFarland, 15–28.

Starck, Kathryn (ed.) (2010) *Between Fear and Freedom: Cultural Representations of the Cold War*. Cambridge: Cambridge Scholars Publishing.

Stewart, Andrew (2012) 'Avengers breaks all-time B.O. record with $200 mil', *Variety*. 6 May. Online. Available: http://variety.com/2012/film/box-office/avengers-breaks-all-time-b-o-record-with-200-mil-1118053576/ (accessed 15 May 2017).

_____ (2013) 'Post-"Avengers" Effect: How "Thor: The Dark World" Leveraged Marvel Heritage', *Variety*. 10 November. Online. Available: http://variety.com/2013/film/box-office/post-avengers-effect-how-thor-the-dark-world-leveraged-marvel-heritage-1200816515/ (accessed 10 December 2016).

Stewart, Henry (2011) 'Blockbuster: Bush v. Thor', *The L Magazine*. 5 June. Online. Available: http://www.thelmagazine.com/2011/05/blockbuster-bush-v-thor/ (accessed 22 June 2015).

Stewart, Sara (2015) 'An Open Letter to Joss Whedon from a Disappointed Feminist Fan After Watching "Age of Ultron"', *Indiewire*. 30 April. Online. Available: http://www.indiewire.com/2015/04/an-open-letter-to-joss-whedon-from-a-disappointed-feminist-fan-after-watching-age-of-ultron-203833/ (accessed 22 July 2015).

Stevenson, Robert Louis (1886) *Strange Case of Jekyll and Hyde*. London: Longman, Green.

Stolworthy, Jacob (2015) 'Michael Douglas: "CGI could lead to a second act in my career"', *Esquire*. 15 July. Online. Available: http://www.esquire.co.uk/culture/film/news/a8552/michael-douglas-ant-man-interview/ (accessed 12 January 2017).

Strauven, Wanda. *The Cinema of Attractions Reloaded*. Amsterdam: Amsterdam University Press, 2006.

Stork, Matthias (2014) 'Assembling the Avengers: Reframing the Superhero movie through Marvels' Cinematic Universe', in James N. Gilmore and Matthias Stork (eds) *Superhero Synergies*. Lanham, MD: Rowman & Littlefield, 77–95.

Suid, Lawrence H. (2002) *Guts & Glory: The Making of the American Military Image in Film*. Lexington, KY: The University Press of Kentucky.

Surrell, Jason (2012) *Avengers: The Art of Marvel's The Avengers*. New York: Marvel.

Sutliff, Jackson (2009) 'The Ultimate American?', in Robert Weiner (ed.) *Captain America and the Struggle of the Superhero: Critical Essays*. Jefferson, NC: McFarland, 121–4.

Sweney, Mark (2016) 'Disney breaks $7bn global box office record for 2016', *The Guardian*. 20 December. Online. Available: https://www.theguardian.com/film/2016/dec/20/walt-disney-sets-7bn-box-office-record-2016-star-wars-rogue-one (accessed 4 July 2017).

Sylt, Christian (2014) 'Disney Spends Record $580 Million Making Movies in Britain', *Forbes*. 13 November. Online. Available: http://www.forbes.com/sites/csylt/2014/11/13/disney-spends-record-580-million-making-movies-in-britain/#27fe55d536fa (accessed 11 December 2015).

Tasker, Yvonne (1993) *Spectacular Bodies: Gender, Genre and the Action Cinema*. London and New York: Routledge.

____ (2015) *The Hollywood Action Adventure Film*. New York: Wiley Blackwell.

Toh, Justine (2010) 'The Tools and Toys of (the) War (on Terror): Consumer Desire, Military Fetish, and Regime Change in *Batman Begins*', in Jeff Birkenstein, Karen Randell and Anna Froula (eds) *Reframing 9/11: Film, Popular Culture and the War on Terror*. New York: Continuum, 127–39.

Tompkins, Jane (1992) *West of Everything: The Inner Life of Westerns*. Oxford: Oxford University Press.

Towers, Andrea (2015) 'Mark Ruffalo: Black Widow toys needed', *Entertainment Weekly*, 3 March. Online. Available: http://ew.com/article/2015/03/03/mark-ruffalo-black-widow-toys/ (accessed 21 June 2017).

Trabold, Jim (2006) 'Ultimate Marvel Handbook #184', *Comics Nexus*. Inside Pulse. 7 October.

Travers, Peter (2015) 'Review', *Rolling Stone*. 21 April. http://www.rollingstone.com/movies/reviews/avengers-age-of-ultron-20150421 (accessed 3 August 2016).

Trump, Donald J. (2016) 'Election night victory speech', New York, 9 November.

____ (2017) 'Inauguration speech', Washington, 20 January.

Tumarkin, Maria (2005) *Traumascapes: The Power and Fate of Places Transformed by Tragedy*. Melbourne: Melbourne University Publishing.

Tyron, Chuck (2013) *On-Demand Culture: Digital Delivery and the Future of Movies*. New Brunswick, NJ: Rutgers University Press.

Tyson, Neil Degrasse (2013) Twitter feed. 5 February. Online. Available: https://twitter.com/neiltyson/status/298856970180505600 (accessed 25 January 2015).

Ungerman, Alex (2015) 'Chris Evans and Jeremy Renner Call Black Widow a Slut, Endure the Wrath of Marvel Fans', *Entertainment Tonight*. 23 April. Online. Available: http://www.

etonline.com/news/163350_chris_evans_and_jeremy_renner_call_black_widow_a_slut_ and_anger_marvel_fans_then_apologize/ (accessed 21 June 2017).

Upton, Bryn (2014) *Hollywood and the End of the Cold War: Signs of Cinematic Change.* Lanham, MD: Rowman & Littlefield.

Valenti, Jack (2001) 'Hollywood, and our nation, will meet this test', *Variety.* 27 September. Online. Available: http://variety.com/2001/voices/columns/hollywood-and-our-nation-will-meet-this-test-1117853266/ (accessed 10 February 2015).

Van Der Werff, Todd (2016) 'Superhero movies have become an endless attempt to rewrite 9/11', *Vox.* 11 September. Online. Available: https://www.vox.com/2015/5/19/8577803/avengers-age-of-ultron-review-politics (accessed 9 April 2017).

Van Syckle, Katie (2016) 'Joss Whedon Was "Beaten Down" by "Avengers: Age of Ultron"', *Variety.* 18 April. Online. Available: http://variety.com/2016/film/news/joss-whedon-avengers-age-of-ultron-tribeca-1201756155/ (accessed 22 July 2016).

Vary, Adam B. (2014) 'Evangeline Lilly Tried to Quit Acting, But Acting Would Not Quit Her', *Buzzfeed.* 2 December. https://www.buzzfeed.com/adambvary/evangeline-lilly-ant-man-the-hobbit-squickerwonkers?utm_term=.rkVPmvZgN#.og8QvyVEO (accessed 11 January 2015).

Veloso, Mark and John Bateman (2013) 'The multimodal construction of acceptability: Marvel's Civil War comic books and the PATRIOT Act', *Critical Discourse Studies*, 10, 4, 1–17.

Vignold, Peter (2017) *Das Marvel Cinematic Universe Anatomie einer Hyperserie.* Marburg: Schüren.

Walderman, Simon A. and Emre Caliskan (2017) *The New Turkey and its Discontents.* Oxford: Oxford University Press.

Walderzak, Joseph (2016) 'Damsels in Transgress: The Empowerment of the Damsel in the Marvel Cinematic Universe', in Matthew J. McEniry, Robert M.Peaslee and Robert G. Weiner (eds) *Marvel Comics into Film: Essays on Adaptations Since the 1940s.* Jefferson, NC: McFarland, 150–64.

Walser, Robert (2014) *Running with the Devil: Power, Gender, and Madness in Heavy Metal.* Middletown, CT: Wesleyan Press.

Walters, Ben (2010) 'Iron Man 2: the first superhero film of the Obama era?', *The Guardian.* 28 April. Online. Available: https://www.theguardian.com/film/filmblog/2010/apr/28/iron-man-2-superhero-barack-obama (accessed 22 July 2016).

Warmoth, Brian (2009) 'Iron Man 2 research puts Mickey Rourke in a Russian Prison. *MTV.* 17 March. Online. Available: http://www.mtv.com/news/2593811/iron-man-2-research-puts-mickey-rourke-in-a-moscow-prison/ (accessed 1 July 2015).

Watercutter, Angela (2016) 'The "Jane Test," a New Way to Tell if Your Scripts Are Sexist', *Wired.* 12 February. Online. Available: https://www.wired.com/2016/02/jane-test-movie-gender-roles/ (accessed on 28 June 2017).

Watkins, Tom (2013) 'U.S. reaction to Chavez's death: from mourning to celebration', *CNN.* 6 March. Online. Available: http://edition.cnn.com/2013/03/05/us/venezuela-us-react/ (accessed 22 April 2017).

Webber, Cynthia (2006) *Imagining America at War: Morality, Politics and Film.* Abingdon: Routledge.

Weiner, Robert (2009) 'Introduction', in Robert Weiner (ed.) *Captain America and the Struggle of the Superhero: Critical Essays.* Jefferson, NC: McFarland, 9–14.

____(2015) 'Foreword', in Kevin Michael Scott (ed.) *Marvel Comics' Civil War and the Age of Terror: Critical Essays on the Comic Saga.* Jefferson, NC: McFarland, 1–2.

Weintraub, Steve (2008a) 'Gale Anne Hurd Interview – THE INCREDIBLE HULK', *Collider*. 16 June. Online. Available: http://collider.com/gale-anne-hurd-interview-the-incredible-hulk/ (accessed 11 June 2016).

____ (2008b) 'Director Louis Leterrier Interview – THE INCREDIBLE HULK', *Collider*. 16 June. Online. Available: http://collider.com/director-louis-leterrier-interview-the-incredible-hulk/ (accessed 11 June 2016).

____ (2009) 'Director Jon Favreau Comic-con interview *Iron Man 2* – He talks War Machine and Whiplash', *Collider*. 27 July. Online. Available: http://collider.com/director-jon-favreau-comic-con-interview-iron-man-2-he-talks-writing-war-machine-and-whiplash/ (accessed 11 February 2016).

____ (2010) 'Exclusive: Screenwriter Justin Theroux Talks IRON MAN 2, ZOOLANDER 2, YOUR HIGHNESS, Easter Eggs, IRON MAN 3, and More', *Collider*. 4 May. Online. Available: http://collider.com/justin-theroux-interview-iron-man-2-zoolander-2-your-highness-iron-man-3-space-invaders-iron-man-3/ (accessed 1 January 2016).

Weisberg, Jacob (2008) *The Bush Tragedy*. London: Bloomsbury.

Weisman, Aly (2014) 'One Man in the Department of Defense Controls All of Hollywood's Access to the Military', *Business Insider*. 5 March. Online. Available: http://www.businessinsider.com/phil-strub-controls-hollywoods-military-access-2014–3?IR=T (accessed 15 May 2015).

____ (2016) *A Philosopher Reads... Marvel Comics' Civil War: Exploring the Moral Judgment of Captain America, Iron Man, and Spider-Man*. Aberdeen: Ockham Publishing.

Wertham, Frederic (1954) *Seduction of the Innocent*. New York: Rinehart & Co.

West, Amy (2016) '"Captain America and other comic book films are made by fascists" claims Die Hard director', *The IB Times*. 13 July. Online. Available: http://www.ibtimes.co.uk/captain-america-other-comic-book-films-are-made-by-fascists-claims-die-hard-director-1570371 (accessed 9 June 2017).

Westfahl, Gary (2003) 'Space Opera', in Edward James and Farah Mendlesohn (eds) *The Cambridge Companion to Science Fiction*. Cambridge: Cambridge University Press, 197–208.

Westwell, Guy (2014) *Parallel Lines: Post-9/11 American Cinema*. London: Wallflower Press.

White, Hayden (1980) 'The Value of Narrativity in the Representation of Reality', *Critical Inquiry*, 7, 1, 5–27.

Wigler, Josh (2013) 'Joss Whedon's "S.H.I.E.L.D." Is About "Powers," "Spectacle" And "Little Things" That Matter', *MTV News*. 11 January. Online. Available: http://www.mtv.com/news/2601839/joss-whedon-shield-details/ (accessed 14 May 2015).

Willmore, Alison (2014) 'Captain America and the age of Snowden', *Buzz Feed*. 8 April. Online. Available: https://www.buzzfeed.com/alisonwillmore/captain-america-and-the-age-of-snowden?utm_term=.oxvqv6arR#.pl4PWpJy2 (accessed 22 August 2015).

Wills, Gary (1997) *John Wayne's America: The Politics of Celebrity*. London: Faber and Faber.

____ (1999) 'Bully of the free world', *Foreign Affairs*. 1 March. Online. Available: https://www.foreignaffairs.com/articles/1999–03-01/bully-free-world (accessed 23 August 2015).

Woerner, Meredith and Katharine Trendacosta (2015) 'Black Widow: This Is Why We Can't Have Nice Things', *Io9*. 5 May. Online. Available: http://io9.gizmodo.com/black-widow-this-is-why-we-can-t-have-nice-things-1702333037 (accessed 25 October 2016).

Wood, Michael (1975) *America in the Movies, Or, 'Santa Maria, it Had Slipped My Mind'*. New York: Basic Books.

Wood, Robin (1986) *Hollywood from Vietnam to Reagan*. New York: Columbia University Press.

——(1998) *Sexual Politics and Narrative Film, Hollywood and Beyond*. New York: Columbia University Press.

Woolf, Daniel (2011) *A Global History of History*. Cambridge: Cambridge University Press.

Wooton, Tom (2012) 'The Avengers – Dr. Banner's Wisdom About Bipolar', *Psychology Today*, 10 May. Online. Available: https://www.psychologytoday.com/blog/bipolar-advantage/201205/the-avengers-dr-banners-wisdom-about-bipolar (accessed 10 October 2015).

Wright, Bradford (2003) *Comic Book Nation: The Transformation of Youth Culture in America*. Baltimore, MD: Johns Hopkins University Press.

Wynn, Neil (2010) *The African American Experience during World War II*. Lanham, MD: Rowman & Littlefield.

Yanes, Nicholas (2009) 'Graphic Imagery: Jewish American Comic Book Creators' Depictions of Class, Race, Patriotism and the Birth of the Good Captain', in Robert Weiner (ed.) *Captain America and the Struggle of the Superhero: Critical Essays*. Jefferson, NC: McFarland, 53–65.

Young, Marilyn (2005) 'Permanent War Positions', *East Asia Cultures Critique*, 13, 1, 177–93.

Zacharek, Stephanie (2017) '*Shane*, with claws and bloodlust to spare', *Time*. 13 March. 50.

Zakarin, Jordan (2012a) '"Avengers" Damage to Manhattan Would Cost $160 Billion, Disaster Expert Estimates (Exclusive)', *The Hollywood Reporter*. 9 May. Online. Available: http://www.hollywoodreporter.com/news/avengers-damage-manhattan-would-cost-160-billion-322486 (accessed 11 March 2015).

——(2012b) 'David Cronenberg Slams Superhero Films, Calls "Dark Knight Rises" Boring', *The Hollywood Reporter*. 15 August. Online. Available: http://www.hollywoodreporter.com/heat-vision/david-cronenberg-slams-superhero-films-batman-boring-362780 (accessed 5 July 2015).

Zeldin-O'Neill, Sophie and Jonross Swaby (2017) '"There are gay characters in the Marvel Universe": *Guardians of the Galaxy Vol 2* cast and crew interviewed – video', *The Guardian*. 1 May. Online. Available: https://www.theguardian.com/film/video/2017/may/01/gay-characters-marvel-guardians-of-the-galaxy-vol-2-chris-pratt-karen-gillan (accessed 3 May 2017).

Zipes, Jack (2006) *Fairy Tales and the Art of Subversion. The Classical Genre for Children and the Process of Civilisation* (Second Edition). New York and London: Routledge.

Žižek, Slavoj (2013) *Welcome to the Desert of the Real*. London: Verso.

INDEX

9/11 17, 23, 36, 129, 203
  films, 8, 19, 41, 85, 94, 99, 107, 111, 119,
    121–4
  post-9/11 period, 8, 9, 11, 12, 16–18,
    23–32, 57, 239

AC/DC (band) 43, 58
Affleck, Ben 83
Afghanistan 17, 18, 86, 233
  Avengers 78, 80
  Iron Man 18, 37n5, 43, 44, *45 fig. 5*, 81,
    102, 131, 189, 190, 241
  Kunar Province 17, 43, 44, 46, 47, 51, 193,
    248
  Stark 27, 28, 31, 46–60, 87, 88, 90, 113,
    133, 151, 192, 248
  veterans 153, 233
  War on Terror 17
Alford, Matthew 22
Alkhateeb, Firas 10
Al Qaeda 48
Althusser, Louis 16, 35
Amanpour, Christine 64
American exceptionalism 16, 23–4, *25 fig.
  3*, 57, 60, 124, 151
Anderson, Benedict 16
Ant-Man (film) 167–85
Ant-Man and the Wasp (film) 35, 183–4

Argentina 2
Arnold, Martin 72, 73, 76, 81
Asano, Tadanobu 75
Astrada, Marvin 54, 216
Auster, Albert 49
Avengers, The (film) 3, 5, 78, 80, 109–25,
  143, 146, 151, 192, 246, 249
Avengers: Age of Ultron (film) 3, 5, 6–7, 11,
  25 fig. 3, 27, 28, 32, 34, 63, 82, 94, 98, 119,
  130, 133, 138–42, 167, 180, 186–204, 208,
  227, 238, 242, 243, 246–53, 266

Bacon, Kevin 175
Badreya, Sayed 52–3
Baldwin, James 230
Bale, Christian 83
Batman (film) 2
Batman & Robin (film) 83
Batman Begins (film) 1, 12, 29, 78, 83, 90,
  230, 233
Batman Forever (film) 2
Batman Returns (film) 2
Batman v Superman: Dawn of Justice (film)
  2, *8 fig. 1*, 32, 83, 168, 169, 244, 255
Bazin, André 20, 106
Berger, James 101
Bin Laden, Osama 9–10, 19, 30, 37n5, 111,
  135, 146

Bixby, Bill 84, 96n10
Black Panther (film) 5, 35, 257, *268 fig. 40*
Blake-Nelson, Tim 84
Boden, Anna 35
Boseman, Chadwick 35, 140, 242, 251
Bowyer Bell, J. 24
Branagh, Kenneth 24, 74, 75, 95, 143, 145
Braudy, Leo 32
Brazil 88–90, 155, 241
Brewer, Michael 93
Bridges, Jeff 44, 50, 141
Britain 19, 159, 244, 264, 265, 267
    London 27, 144, 147, 208
Buchanan, Kyle 19, 112
Burke, Jason 17
Burrell, Ty 91
Burton, Tim 2, 32, 45
Bush, George H. W. 24, 30
Bush, George W. *See* Bush administration
Bush administration 9, 20, 22
    9/11 10, 21, 24, 111, 164
    Bush Doctrine 61, 76
    films, reflected in 18, 24, 51, 54, 77, 78,
        122, 160
    Iraq 77, 134
    policies 156, 239, 250
    Powell, Colin 61
    rogue states 61
    Rumsfeld 55
    War on Terror 47
Butler, Judith 49, 66

California 22, 44, 134
Campbell, Joseph 84, 188
Canada 94
Captain America: Civil War (film) 2, 5, 26,
    27, 28, 36, 60, 62, 64, 83, 94, 98, 162,
    187, 189, 194, 196, 199, 200–1, 237–61
Captain America: The First Avenger (film)
    9, 18, 27, 28, 30, 50, 97–108, 109, 112,
    138–40, 142, 218, 220
Captain America: The Winter Soldier (film)
    19, 27, 62, 67, 106, 111, 130, 150–66, 168,
    179, 189, 208, 213, 227–8, 232, 238–57
Captain Marvel (film) 35,141
Carter, Sean 27, 49, 56

Catalan, Cristobal Giraldez 51, 55, 56–7
CGI (computer-generated imagery) 5, 56,
    65, 93, 94, 199,
Cheadle, Don 61, 65, 140
Chechnya 78
China 6–7, 63, 90
Chomsky, Noam 165n5
Clinton, Bill 30
Cold War 15, 16, 30, 42, 62, 158, 163, 201,
    265
    Ant-Man 179
    Guardians of the Galaxy 264
    Incredible Hulk 18, 82, 89
    Thor 73
    Top Gun 21
    Winter Soldier 159
Colucci, Lamont 54, 81
Comolli, Jean-Louis 35
Congress. *See* US Congress
Coogan, Peter 7, 82
Coogler, Ryan 35
Corliss, Richard 58, 111, 196
Costello, Matthew 8, 24, 29, 42, 53–4, 239
Croce, Benedetto 31
Cronenberg, David 3, 4
Cruise, Tom 23, 42, 140, 171, 181
Cuba 158, 214, *215 fig. 26*
Cuban Missile Crisis 42, 158, 159
Cullen, Jim 23, 100, 101
Curtis, Neal 22

Damon, Matt 49
Dargis, Manohla 21, 119, 135
Dark Knight trilogy 56, 83, 164
Dark Knight, The (film) 2, 12, 29, 57, 119,
    201, 230, 233
Dark Knight Rises, The (film) 3, 83
Daughtry, J. Martin 43
David, Peter 68n3, 94
DC Extended Universe (DCEU) 8, 29, 56,
    142, 210, 243
Deadpool (film) 2, 9, 252
Defenders (series) 35, 223–35, 263, 265
Defense Department. *See* US Department of
    Defense
Delcroix, Oliver 21

Deleuze, Gilles 87
Dennings, Kat 75
Depp, Johnny 80
D'Esposito, Louis 95
Disney 3, 4, 158, 207
Dittmer, Jason 20, 60, 97, 99, 151
Doctor Strange (film) 2, 5, 20, 67, 148, 231
DOD. *See* US Department of Defense
Dodds, Klaus 27, 49, 56
Donner, Richard 5, 32, 66
Douglas, Edward 66
Douglas, Michael 5, 141, 179, *181 fig. 21*
Downey Jr., Robert 5, 17, *29 fig. 4*, 42, 44,
    50, 56, 57, 65, 80, 110, 130–1, 140, 192,
    193, 199, 248, 256, 263
Doyle, Patrick 78
Durkheim, Émile 35
DuToit, Kim 80, 98

Eastwood, Clint 9
Eaton, Mick 60
Eisenhower, Dwight D. 42, 68n9
Elba, Idris 75
Ellison, Larry 43
Ellison, Ralph 230
El Mundo (newspaper) 21
Elsaesser, Thomas 4, 267–8
Engelhardt, Tom 30, 201, 202
Escape From New York (film) 5
Evans, Chris 80, 101, *104 fig. 10*, 140, 198

Fairey, Shepard 20
Faludi, Susan 3, 4, 24, 199
Favreau, Jon 41, 42, 43, 44, 46, 47, 57, 62,
    66, 73, 131, 179, 263
Feige, Kevin 84, 92, 94, 143, 179, 242
Fernandez, Charmaine 8
Feulner, Edwin J. 75
Fingeroth, Danny 7, 81, 84
Finke, Nikki 3, 164
Fiske, John 33
Fleck, Ryan 35
Flynn, Errol 43
Ford, John 53, 196, *197 fig. 22*
FOX News 64
Franich, Darren 78, 151, 158, 164

French, Philip 18
Füchtjohann, Jan 4

Gaine, Vincent M. 75
Garfield, Andrew 83
Germany 27, 100, 115, 189, 244
    Nazis 31, 73
    Weimar 15
Gilmore, James N. 85
Godzilla 82
Goldblum, Jeff 67
Goyer, David 32, 124n2
Graham, Mark 53
Grant, Barry Keith 9
Gregg, Clark 56, 114, 211
Guardians of the Galaxy (film) 5, 31, 35, 67,
    75, 130, 139–42, 167–85, 232, 238
Guardians of the Galaxy: Vol. 2 (film) 5, 21,
    34, 67, 178, 263, 265
Guatemala 90, 158
Gulf War 55
Gunn, James 34, 170, 171, 172, 175, 176–7,
    263
Gunning, Tom 5–6

Haberman, Frank 1
Hagley, Annika 75
Hancock (film) 2, 230
Hanks, Tom 49, 101
Harrison, Michael 75
Hart, Tom 46
Hassler-Forest, Dan 55, 56, 151
Hellboy (film) 2
Hellboy II: The Golden Army (film) 9
Hemsworth, Chris 80, 140, 147
Hercules 7, 122, 252
Hitler, Adolf 30, 98, 102, 103, 192
Hodgeson, Geoffrey 23
Holland, Tom 83, 251
Hollis, Dave 3
Holloway, David 15, 85
Holocaust 31, 108n2, 115
Honeycutt, Kirk 58
Hopkins, Anthony 74, 141
Howard, Terrence 44, 45, 51
Hughes, Howard 43, 70n29

Hulk (film) 32, 82, 86
Hurd, Gale 83
Hurt, William 85, 141
Hussein, Saddam 30, 86

IMAX 59, 263
Incredible Hulk, The (film) 2, 32, 57, 81–95,
    112, 182, 195, 208, 243, 263
    Abomination 26
    actors 140, 141, 191
    Avengers 110
    Banner 78
    Brazil 241
    Bush administration 20
    Cold War 18
    India 113
    military 36, 247, 253
    Rio 113
    Stark 67
    violence 151, 188, 229
    War on Terror 111
    women 138, 142, 144, 178, 197
    World War Two 7
Incredible Hulk, The (television) 82
India 6, 112–13, 266, 267
Invincible Iron Man, The (comic) 64
Iran 17, 61, 63, 135, 158
Iraq 37n5, 75
    Bagram Air Base 47
    Bush 17, 134
    deaths 51, 57
    displacement 51, 52
    invasion of 61
    veterans 153
    war 43, 46, 53, 69n18, 77–8, 86, 152, 158,
        240, 259n1
Iron Fist (series) 35, 90, 209, 210, 223, 225,
    226 fig. 33, 228–31, 235, 263
Iron Man 5, 7, 8, 10, 17, 18, 20, 24, 55, 89,
    92
    Avengers, 249
    Captain America 116, 123, 237, 239, 251
    CGI 93–4
    Cold War 82
    creation of 98
    masculinity 107

Iron Man *cont.*
    military 111
    patriotism 59
    Stark 193, 244, 263
    suit 34, 49, 52, 54, 59–61, 63, 65, 116, 147,
        189, 248
    Winter Soldiers 255
    wit 143
Iron Man (film) 2, 6, 11, 14, 17, 18, 20–2,
    41–71, 73, 82, 110, 112, 130, 179, 182,
    238, 263
    actors 140–1
    Afghanistan 53, *54 fig. 6*, 81, 87, 102, 113,
        189–90, 241
    Captain America 97, 254
    Cold War 264
    Coulson 211
    dialogue 156
    father 115
    Iraq 75
    military 36, 37n5, 43, 50, 55, 89
    Nigeria 240
    PTSD 31, 132
    science 90
    Stark 78, 192, 194, 248, 250, 255, 256
    stereotypes 200
    Team Iron Man *252 fig. 36*, 254
    villain 135
    War on Terror 136, 239
    women 138, 142, 178
Iron Man 2 (film) 20, 28, 41–71, 76, 78, 95,
    103, 112, 114, 130, 180, 182
    actors 140
    Black Widow 110
    Captain America 97
    father 115
    military 36, 89
    science 90
    society 245, 246
    Stark 134, 196, 220, 248
    women 138–9, 178
Iron Man 3 (film) 6, 7, 19, 28, 48, 67, 110,
    119, 129–49, 227, 267
    Afghanistan 131
    Captain America 252
    military 37n5, 247

Iron Man 3 (film) *cont.*
  Pakistan 241
  PTSD 26, 31, 153
  society, 246
  Stark, 191, 192, 200, 248
  women 33–4, 38n17, 145, 147, 250, 254
Italy 100, 104, 105, 121

Jackman, Hugh *11 fig. 2*
Jackson, Samuel L. 62, 141, *157 fig. 19,*
James Bond franchise 1, 19, 188
Jameson, Fredric 16, 173–4
Jeffords, Susan 24, 25, 74, 80, 169, 176
Jenkins, Henry 84–5, 155, 167
Jenkins, Patty 142, 187
Jenkins, Tricia 22
Jessica Jones (series) 34, 35, 209, 210,
  223–35
Jewett, Robert 8, 10, 15, 19, 55, 99, 186–8
Johnson, Andrew 133
Johnson, Chalmers 46, 77, 132

Kaes, Anton 15, 16
Kaller, Brian 3
Kaplan, E. Anne 55, 109, 121
Keaton, Michael 28
Kellner, Douglas 15, 22, 129, 163
Kennedy, John F. 42, 129
Killian, Aldrich 26, 28, 37n5, 63, 132–7,
  238, 248
King, Geoff 10–11, 17, 53, 119
Kirby, Jack 82, 98
Klein, Naomi 51
Kord, Susanne 47, 169
Korea
  Japan 108n1
  North Korea 17, 61, 63
  South Korea 103, 155, 198
Kosovo 27, 189
Krimmer, Elisabeth 47, 169

Labuza, Peter 76
Lacan, Jacques 48–9
Lawrence, John Shelton 8, 10, 15, 19, 55, 99,
  186–8
Lee, Ang 32, 82, 86

Lee, Stan 29, 43, 82, 92, 159, 191, 237, 268
Le Figero (newspaper) 21
Le Monde (newspaper) 19
Leone, Sergio 53
Leterrier, Louis 32, 82–8, 93–5, 113
Lev, Peter 15
LoCicero, Don 14, 72
Lucas, George 172
Lucasfilm 4

Maguire, Tobey 83
Maher, Bill 10
Man of Steel (film) 29, 32, 66, 119, 168, 169,
  196, 243, 267
Martínez, Luis 21
Marvel Entertainment 4, 207, 224
Marvel's Agent Carter (television) 31, 34,
  62, 63, 139, 195, 207–22, 223, 228,
Marvel Studios 14, 18, 43, 44, 46, 73, 94, 95,
  98, 110, 129, 130, 155, 179, 187, 207, 208,
  258, 262,
Marx, Karl 18
McDowall, John C. 31, 199
McQueen, Steve 101
Mexico 90
Middle East 32, 78, 86, 135, 162, 165
militainment 22
Military Industrial Complex 36, 42, 52, 56,
  86, 89, 92, 94, 111, 151
Mills, Anthony R. 76
Mirrlees, Tanner 21, 52, 55
Moore, Alan 2, 263
Morrison, Grant 32, 72
Motion Picture Association of America 12

Narboni, Jean 35
NATO 16
New Mexico 67
New York 29, 30, 63, 129–34, 208, 216, 217,
  219 fig. 29, 265
  Avengers 5, 111, 112, 117, 119, 122, 123,
    143, 146, 151, 192, 246
  Battle of New York 19, 73, 110, 114, 122,
    156, 191, 203, 213, 242–3
  Captain America 107, 258
  Defenders 225, 228, 229, 230, 232–4

New York *cont.*
  Ground Zero 10
  Incredible Hulk 93, 113
  Iron Man 59
  Iron Man 2 65
New York Post (newspaper) 62, 121
New York Times (newspaper) 105
Nigeria 6, 240–2
  Lagos 240–3, 246
Nixon administration 75
Nolan, Christopher 8, 12, 29, 32, 56, 83,
  164, 230, 233,
Noonan, Peggy 10, 25, 26, 80, 98
Norris, Chuck 25, 80
Norse mythology 24, 67, 73, 76, 78, 79, 112,
  115, 253
Norton, Edward 83–4, 87, *91 fig. 9*, 92–4,
  113, 140, 191

Obama administration 10, 14, 20, 21, 23,
  24, 163, 164, 250
  drones 150, 162
  security 156

Pakistan 62, 78, 134, 135, 160, 241
Paltrow, Gwyneth 44, 50, 140
PATRIOT Act. *See* USA PATRIOT Act
patriotism 32, 46, 56, 98, 99, 153, 161, 239,
  240
Pearl Harbor 22, 30, 98, 101
Pearlman, Nicole 35
Pease, Donald 23
Pentagon 65, 134
Peru 6, 171, 214, *215 fig. 25*
Pheasant-Kelly, Francis 17, 49, 56, 61, 94,
  121, 174
Pitt, Brad 80, 101
Pixar 4
Pollard, Tom 17, 49, 85
Portman, Natalie 74, 140, 142, *146 fig. 17*,
  147
Pratt, Chris 80, 140, 171, 180
Prince, Stephen 45
PTSD (post-traumatic stress disorder) 132,
  231, 233
    Stark, 19, 26, 31, 51, 111, 131, 132, 137, 190

Punisher (film) 233–4, 263
Punisher: War Zone and *Wanted* (film) 2
Purse, Lisa 25–6, 50
Pym, Hank 5, 90, 141, 179–80, *181 fig. 21*,
  182, 183, 252

Raimi, Sam 11, 251
Reagan administration 23, 74, 75, 105, 165,
  176, 192
Reeve, Christopher 45
Reeves, Keanu 80
Reilly, John C. 176
Reinhartz, Adele 79
Renner, Jeremy 78, 198
Robb, David L. 22
Rockwell, Sam 58
Rogue One: A Star Wars Story (film) 5, 6
Rojek, Chris 7
Romero, George 78
Rommel-Ruiz, W. Bryan 57
Roosevelt, Franklin Delano 116
Roosevelt, Theodore 46
Roth, Tim 89, 93
Roublou, Yann 26
Rourke, Mickey 28, 58, 62
Ruffalo, Mark 87, 93, 94, 110, 113, 140, 191,
  198
Russell, Kurt 5, 178
Russia 27, 62–3, 103, 112, 152, 155, 214, 220,
  244, 264, 265, 267
Ryan, Michael 15, 163

Sanderson, Peter 29
Saunders, Ben 72
Schjeldahl, Peter 20
Schlegel, Johannes 1
Schmidt, Hugo 62
Schumacher, Joel 2, 32, 45
Schwartzel, Eric 6
Schwarzenegger, Arnold 25, 80
Scott, A.O. 21
Secker, Tom 22
Shaheen, Jack 45, 133
Shandling, Gary 61
Shelley, Mary 82
Siegel, Jerry 7

Singer, Bryan 11, 66
Skarsgård, Stellan 73, 141
Slotkin, Richard 16, 26, 58, 170
Smith, Kyle 62
Snyder, Zack 66, 169
Solo: A Star Wars Story (film) 6
Sotinel, Thomas 19
Soviet Union 42–3, 48, 100, 159, 165, 220,
    262, 264, 265
Spanakos, Antony Peter 88, 94, 113
Spider-Man (film) 7, 11, 41, 42, 43, 82, 118,
    136, 239
Spider-Man 2 (film) 83
Spider-Man 3 (film) 83
Spider-Man: Homecoming (film) 28, *29 fig.
    4*, 251, 263
  Iron Man 5
Spider-Man, The Amazing (film) 83
Spider-Man, The Amazing (comic) 233, 252
Spielberg 12, 21, 49, 101, 119, 167–8, 169,
    170, 181
Stallone, Sylvester 24, 25, 26, 27, 80, 176
Star Wars franchise 1, 6, 155, 172, 173
Star Wars: A New Hope (film) 15, 173
Star Wars Missile Defence system 192
Star Wars: The Force Awakens (film) 6, 141,
    187, 257
Stevenson, Robert Louis 82, 92
Stone, Oliver 78
Stork, Matthias 67, 85, 122
Suicide Squad (film) 2, 177
Superman (film) 5, 7, 32, 45, 66
Superman II (film) 2
Superman IV: The Quest for Peace (film) 83
Superman Returns (film) 11, 83, 136
Switzerland 48, 131

Tasker, Yvonne 5, 24, 80
Theroux, Justin 58
Thing, The (film) 5
Thor (film) 5, 17–18, 24, 67, 72–81, 85, 91,
    93, 95, 103, 109–12, 140–4, 151, 168,
    176, 178, 263
Thor: Ragnarok (film) 5, 67, 195, 263
Thor: The Dark World (film) 27, 34, 67, 73,
    81, 129–49

Time (magazine) 58
Toh, Justine 78
Tompkins, Jane 9
Top Gun (film) 22–3
Tracey, Brian 75
Trump administration 10, 21, 75, 160–1,
    163, 250, 259
  Conway, Kelly, 21
Tucci, Stanley 102
Tyler, Live 86, 140

UK. *See* Britain
Ukraine 103
United Kingdom. *See* Britain
United Nations (UN) 16, 123, 210, 244,
    246–7, 251, *252 fig. 36*
  WMD 61–2
Upton, Bryn 24
US Air Force 23
USA PATRIOT Act 36, 61, 152, 156, 157,
    239
US Army 18, 85, 104, 105
US Congress 105
US Department of Defense (DOD) 21–2,
    22–3, 37n10, 45
US Department of Homeland Security 63
US Navy 22, 23, 44

Valenti, Jack 12
Variety (magazine) 6, 240, 267
Venezuela 6,
Vietnam War 16, 20, 42, 43, 48, 53, 158, 201
  Hulk 85
  images 129
  Punisher 233
  Stark 54
  Thor 73
Vignold, Peter 6

Walderzak, Joseph 33–4, 138, 147
Walters, Ben 20
War on Terror 7, 8, 16, 17, 19, 23, 28, 29, 30,
    32, 43, 47–9, 51, 53, 54, 56, 57, 62, 85,
    89, 111, 114, 123, 133, 135, *136 fig. 16*,
    151, 152, 153, *157 fig. 19*, 161, 202, 230,
    237–61

Wayne, John 9, 24–7, 38n14, 101, 196, 203
Weiner, Robert 30, 238,
Weisberg, Jacob 78
Wertham, Fredric 33
Westwell, Guy 66
Whedon, Joss 3, 21, 32, 42, 110, 112, 114,
    115, 119, 124, 187, 188, 193, 196, 198,
    203, 109, 213, 234
Wiseman, Len 42
WMD (weapons of mass destruction) 17,
    43, 48, 52, 62, 85, 86, 89, 94, 103, 114,
    115, 132
Wolverine 8, *11 fig. 2*, 20, 201
Wonder Woman 8, 9, 141, 142, 201
Wood, Michael 36
Wood, Robin 15, 147
World War I 101

World War II 7, 16, 18, 20, 23, 26, 27, 30–1,
    42, 48–50, 62, 86, 97–108, 111–16, 153,
    157–9, 161, 162, 191, 192, 193, 201, 203,
    209, 214, 218, *219 fig. 29*, 246, 265
Wright, Bradford 17
Wright, Edgar 179, 187

X-Men (film) 8, *11 fig. 2*, 263
X-Men (comic) 252
X-Men: Apocalypse (film) 2
X-Men Origins: Wolverine (film) 20

Zemeckis, Robert 17
Zimbabwe 2
Žižek, Slavoj 36, 48–9

CPSIA information can be obtained
at www.ICGtesting.com
Printed in the USA
LVOW13s0136040418
572193LV00001B/1/P